"Although the political and legal environments surrounding judicial elections have changed considerably in recent years, policy debates regarding judicial selection and retention institutions tend to remain stagnant in their reliance on rhetorical appeals rather than systematic evidence. In this volume, an all-star cast offers new insight into how contemporary judicial elections operate and impact American politics. With coverage spanning the judicial hierarchy and addressing fundamental issues such as voting, campaign finance, advertising, performance, legitimacy, and diversity, this comprehensive collection is a must have for anyone interested in contemporary judicial elections."

– ***Greg Goelzhauser***, *Utah State University*

"Bonneau and Hall have done it again! This time they have assembled an all-star line-up of scholars of state courts to give us their analyses of a variety of pressing issues surrounding the electing of judges. This collection of chapters is state-of-the-art, filled with unexpected findings and insights, and will be excellent for use in the classroom. I heartily recommend this book not only to judicial scholars but to non-judicial folks interested in larger issues of elections, campaign effects, and the like."

–***James Gibson***, *Washington University in St. Louis*

"Bonneau and Hall have assembled an incredibly insightful and thought-provoking set of essays by leading authorities on judicial elections. This book would be a fantastic choice for any professional or graduate class on the judiciary or elections as well as upper division undergraduate classes on the legal system."

–***Jeffrey Yates***, *Binghamton University*

# JUDICIAL ELECTIONS IN THE 21ST CENTURY

Leading authorities present the latest cutting-edge research on state judicial elections. Starting with recent transformations in the electoral landscape, including those brought about by U.S. Supreme Court rulings, this volume provides penetrating analyses of partisan, nonpartisan, and retention elections to state supreme courts, intermediate appellate courts, and trial courts. Topics include citizen participation, electoral competition, fundraising and spending, judicial performance evaluations, reform efforts, attack campaigns, and other organized efforts to oust judges. This volume also evaluates the impact of judicial elections on numerous aspects of American politics, including citizens' perceptions of judicial legitimacy, diversity on the bench, and the consequences of who wins on subsequent court decisions. Many of the chapters offer predictions about how judicial elections might look in the future. Overall, this collection provides a sharp evidence-based portrait of how modern judicial elections actually work and their consequences for state judiciaries and the American people.

**Chris W. Bonneau** is Associate Professor of Political Science at the University of Pittsburgh. His research focuses on judicial elections and state courts.

**Melinda Gann Hall** is Distinguished Professor of Political Science at Michigan State University. Her research concentrations are judicial politics and state courts.

# LAW, COURTS AND POLITICS

Edited by Robert M. Howard, Georgia State University

In *Democracy in America*, Alexis de Tocqueville famously noted that "scarcely any political question arises in the United States that is not resolved, sooner or later, into a judicial question." The importance of courts in settling political questions in areas ranging from health care to immigration shows the continuing astuteness of de Tocqueville's observation. To understand how courts resolve these important questions, empirical analyses of law, courts and judges, and the politics and policy influence of law and courts have never been more salient or more essential.

*Law, Courts and Politics* was developed to analyze these critically important questions. This series presents empirically driven manuscripts in the broad field of judicial politics and public law by scholars in law and social science. It uses the most up to date scholarship and seeks an audience of students, academics, upper division undergraduate and graduate courses in law, political science and sociology as well as anyone interested in learning more about law, courts and politics.

1. **The Dual System of Privacy Rights in the United States**
   *Mary McThomas*
2. **Making Law and Courts Research Relevant**
   *Brandon L. Bartels and Chris W. Bonneau*
3. **The Europeanization of Judicial Review**
   *Nicola Corkin*
4. **The New Myth of the Court**
   The Media, the Court, and the Misrepresentation
   *Rorie Spill Solberg and Eric N. Waltenburg*
5. **EU Treaties and the Judicial Politics of National Courts**
   A Law and Politics Approach
   *Pablo José Castillo Ortiz*
6. **Judicial Politics in Mexico**
   The Supreme Court and the Transition to Democracy
   *Edited by Andrea Castagnola and Saúl López Noriega*
7. **Judicial Elections in the 21st Century**
   *Edited by Chris W. Bonneau and Melinda Gann Hall*

# JUDICIAL ELECTIONS IN THE 21ST CENTURY

*Edited by Chris W. Bonneau and Melinda Gann Hall*

Routledge
Taylor & Francis Group
LONDON AND NEW YORK

First published 2017
by Routledge
711 Third Avenue, New York, NY 10017

and by Routledge
2 Park Square, Milton Park, Abingdon, Oxon, OX14 4RN

*Routledge is an imprint of the Taylor & Francis Group, an informa business*



*Library of Congress Cataloging in Publication Data*
Names: Bonneau, Chris W. | Hall, Melinda Gann.
Title: Judicial elections in the 21st century /
edited by Chris W. Bonneau and Melinda Gann Hall.
Description: New York : Routledge, [2017] |
Includes bibliographical references and index.
Identifiers: LCCN 2016026313 | ISBN 9781138185883 (hbk) |
ISBN 9781138185890 (pbk)
Subjects: LCSH: Judges–United States–Election. | Judges–United States–States–Election. | Courts of last resort–United States–States–Election. | Appellate courts–United States–States.
Classification: LCC KF8776 .J85 2017 | DDC 347.73/14–dc23
LC record available at https://lccn.loc.gov/2016026313

ISBN: 978-1-138-18588-3 (hbk)
ISBN: 978-1-138-18589-0 (pbk)
ISBN: 978-1-315-64417-2 (ebk)

Typeset in Bembo Std
by Out of House Publishing

To Heather and Robinson … who make my work better
by making my life better.
– Chris W. Bonneau

To Henry Joseph Price and Fiona Catherine Price … for the
infinite joy and laughter.
– Melinda Gann Hall

# TABLE OF CONTENTS

# LIST OF FIGURES

# LIST OF TABLES

# ABOUT THE CONTRIBUTORS

**Larry T. Aspin** is Professor Emeritus of Political Science at Bradley University. His scholarly research spans numerous fields within political science. In American politics, he has documented and analyzed judicial retention elections and cumulative voting for the last thirty years. The Judicial Retention Project continuously updates and expands a comprehensive database of judicial retention elections in the United States.

**Lawrence Baum** is Professor Emeritus of Political Science at the Ohio State University, where he received the Distinguished Scholar Award in 2009. He is author of five books, including the award-winning *Judges and Their Audiences* (2006), and over 50 articles in journals and law reviews. His research focuses on both the U.S. Supreme Court and state courts.

**Chris W. Bonneau** (co-editor) is Associate Professor of Political Science at the University of Pittsburgh. His work on judicial elections has been published in the *American Journal of Political Science*, *Journal of Politics*, and many other outlets. He is coauthor of *Strategic Behavior and Policy Choice on the U.S. Supreme Court* (2005), *In Defense of Judicial Elections* (2009), and the award-winning *Voters' Verdicts: Citizens, Campaigns, and Institutions in State Supreme Court Elections* (2015), as well as co-editor of *Making Law and Courts Research Relevant: The Normative Implications of Empirical Research* (2015). He is currently co-editor of *State Politics and Policy Quarterly*.

**Brian Frederick** is Associate Professor and Chair of the Political Science Department at Bridgewater State University. His research focuses on campaigns and elections, and women and politics. He is author of the book *Congressional Representation and Constituents: The Case for Increasing the House of Representatives*.

His research has appeared in *Political Research Quarterly*, *Public Opinion Quarterly*, *Political Behavior*, *American Politics Research*, *Social Science Quarterly and State Politics and Policy Quarterly*, among others.

**Charles Gardner Geyh** is the John F. Kimberling Professor at the Indiana University Maurer School of Law, and was a 2016 Andrew Carnegie Fellow. One of the foremost experts in judicial ethics and judicial selection, his most recent book is *Courting Peril: The Political Transformation of the American Judiciary* (2015). He is author of over 60 articles and chapters, and editor of *What's Law Got To Do With It? What Judges Do, Why They Do It, and What's At Stake* (2011).

**Rebecca D. Gill** is Associate Professor of Political Science at the University of Nevada-Las Vegas. Her research focuses on issues of gender bias in courts, as well as on decision making in a comparative context. She is the co-author of *Judicialization of Politics: The Interplay of Institutional Structure, Legal Doctrine, and Politics on the High Court of Australia* (2012). Her work has also appeared in *Law and Society Review*, the *Ohio State Law Journal*, *Catholic University Law Review*, *Justice System Journal*, and *Judicature*. She is the recipient of a multi-year National Science Foundation grant to study gender and race bias in performance evaluations of state judges.

**Thomas R. Gray** is a graduate student in the Department of Politics at the University of Virginia. His dissertation research is focused on the influence governors and legislatures exert over state courts' decision making when they have the power to reappoint justices.

**Melinda Gann Hall** (co-editor) is Professor of Political Science, faculty affiliate in the College of Law, and recipient of the Distinguished Faculty Award at Michigan State University. She specializes in judicial politics, especially state supreme court decision making and elections. She has published two books and over 50 articles, chapters, and essays, and has received numerous awards for research excellence. Her most recent book, *Attacking Judges: How Campaign Advertising Influences State Supreme Court Elections*, received the C. Herman Pritchett Award. Professor Hall is co-creator of the State Supreme Court Data Project, sponsored by the National Science Foundation. In 2016–2017, she will hold a Fulbright Distinguished Chair at the University of Edinburgh School of Law and will be launching a new line of research on subnational courts in the United Kingdom.

**Mark S. Hurwitz** is Professor of Political Science at Western Michigan University. He serves as Editor-in-Chief of *Justice System Journal*. He is Co-Principal Investigator of a grant from the Department of Justice (National Institute of Justice) to fund the WMU Cooley Law School Innocence Project, designed to exonerate wrongfully convicted individuals in Michigan. His research has appeared in several journals and law reviews, including the *American Political Science Review, Journal of Politics, Justice System Journal, Law and Policy, Political Research Quarterly, Review of Policy Research, State Politics and Policy Quarterly*, and others.

**Jenna Becker Kane** is Assistant Professor of Political Science at West Chester University. Her areas of research are judicial politics, American political institutions, and state politics. She received her Ph.D. from Temple University, where her dissertation examined the influence of interest groups participating as amicus curiae in state supreme courts.

**David E. Klein** is Professor and Department Head at Eastern Michigan University, as well as editor of the *Journal of Law and Courts*. He is the author of numerous works on judicial decision making and judicial elections, as well as *Making Law in the United States Courts of Appeals* (2002).

**Herbert M. Kritzer** is the Marvin J. Sonosky Chair of Law and Public Policy at the University of Minnesota Law School and an Affiliated Professor of Political Science. He is the author or coauthor of seven books and more than 100 articles or book chapters. His most recent books are *Justices on the Ballot: Continuity and Change in State Supreme Court Elections* (2015) and *Lawyers at Work* (2015). He is the editor of *Legal Systems of the World* (2002) and co-editor of the *Oxford Handbook of Empirical Legal Research* (2010).

**Casey LaFrance** is Associate Professor in the Department of Political Science at Western Illinois University and was named the 2014–2015 First Year Experience Professor of the Year. His work has appeared in the *International Journal of Police Science and Management*, the *Law Enforcement Executive Forum, Public Organization Review, Policing: A Journal of Policy and Practice*, the *National Civic Review, Politics and Policy, American Politics Research*, and *Judicature*, among others.

**Drew Noble Lanier** is Associate Professor of Political Science at the University of Central Florida. His work focuses on the intersection of courts and politics in the American political context. His work has appeared in such prominent journals as the *American Journal of Political Science, Political Research Quarterly, State Politics and Policy Quarterly*, and *Social Science Quarterly*, among other outlets. He is at work, with Mark Hurwitz (Western Michigan University), on a comprehensive account of diversity within the American judiciary.

**Mark Jonathan McKenzie** is Associate Professor of Political Science at Texas Tech University. His primary fields of research are judicial decision making and state judicial elections. He has published in a variety of journals, including *Political Research Quarterly, American Politics Research*, and *Justice System Journal*. He is currently working on a project examining decision making on the Danish Supreme Court.

**Michael J. Nelson** is Assistant Professor of Political Science and Affiliate Law Faculty at Pennsylvania State University. He studies judicial elections, state judicial politics, and public evaluations of judicial institutions. His research has been published in outlets including the *American Journal of Political Science*, *Political Research Quarterly*, *State Politics and Policy Quarterly*, and *Journal of Law and Courts*.

**Ryan J. Rebe** is Assistant Professor of Legal Studies at William Paterson University in New Jersey. A member of the State Bar of Texas since 2002 and formerly a private practitioner in criminal law at both trial and appellate levels, he has published several studies on state courts and judicial elections.

**Kimberly Rice** is assistant professor of political science at Western Illinois University, where she teaches courses on American government, the judiciary, and the Supreme Court. Her research interests include administrative law and inter-branch politics, judicial selection, and juvenile justice. She has published in the *Justice System Journal* and *Law Enforcement Executive Forum*.

**Matthew J. Streb** is Professor of Political Science at Northern Illinois University. He is the author of two books, *The New Electoral Politics of Race* (2002) and *Rethinking American Electoral Democracy* (2008, 2011, 2016), and the editor or co-editor of five others including *Running for Judge* (2007) and *Academic Freedom at the Dawn of a New Century* (2006). Streb has published numerous articles and book chapters, including pieces in *Political Research Quarterly*, *Public Opinion Quarterly*, *State Politics and Policy Quarterly*, *Political Behavior*, *Social Science Quarterly*, *Election Law Journal*, and *American Politics Research*.

**Katherine Thrapp** is a 2016 graduate of the Indiana University Maurer School of Law and an associate at Jones Day's Chicago office.

**Matthew J. Zalewski** is a Ph.D. candidate in political science at Michigan State University, where he studies American politics, public policy, and methodology. His research focuses on state supreme court campaigns and institutional influences on state legal actors, and he has published co-authored work in *Urban Affairs Review*. He also has a J.D. from Wayne State University Law School and is a member of the Bar of the State of Michigan, Eastern District of Michigan, and the U.S. Court of Appeals for the Sixth Circuit.

# ACKNOWLEDGEMENTS

This project started with considerable excitement at a professional conference about all of the excellent work on judicial elections being done by our colleagues and a lament that many scholars outside our field, as well as those in the legal community concerned with judicial reform, may be missing the extraordinarily rich theoretical and substantive insights being produced at a rapidly increasing pace. In our view, this was problematic given the importance and highly salient nature of judicial elections in recent years and the implications of empirical scholarship for public policy choices about the most effective ways to select and retain judges. Thus, our goal was to assemble the top scholars (both veterans and rising stars) working on various aspects of judicial elections and have them present original research in a single volume. This book represents that achievement, and we are thrilled to have had a chance to work with each of these authors in reaching this goal.

In editing this volume, we incurred the usual debts to others. First, we thank our talented contributors, who turned in superb chapters and were a pleasure to work with over the past months. Although we have been studying judicial elections for decades, we both learned a great deal while editing this volume, which is a strong testament to the quality and originality of the research here. Both of us also had worked with Routledge on previous projects (including our book *In Defense of Judicial Elections*), and based on our uniformly positive experiences we were eager to do so again. Routledge did not disappoint. Natalja Mortensen and Lillian Rand are models of support, flexibility, and good humor (which was needed on occasion, for sure).

Bonneau benefited greatly from the support and guidance of his colleagues Damon Cann, Kris Kanthak, and Jon Woon. As always, Heather Rice and Robinson Jeter Rice-Bonneau were very patient and supportive as deadlines approached (and passed). It is no surprise that my best work has been done with the love and support of Rice.

Hall acknowledges the College of Law at Michigan State University for hosting her as Scholar in Residence during the 2015–2016 year and for providing an outstanding professional and collegial environment within which to pursue this and other projects. She also appreciates the never-ending patience and love of Anthony R. Duce (Tony), who always is wonderfully supportive of every task undertaken, even when it means way more work than planned. Tony—the perfect partner in every way—remains the love of my life. I also am grateful for the frequent FaceTime chats and visits with my amazing grandchildren Henry Joseph Price (age 10) and Fiona Catherine Price (age 8), who manage to bring infinite joy and laughter to the day no matter what. Their parents, Amber Hall Price and Joseph Price, are pretty awesome, too. My work and life would be so much less without all of these remarkable people.

# SECTION 1

# Electing Judges in Contemporary American Politics

# 1

# JUDICIAL ELECTIONS IN THE 21ST CENTURY

*Chris W. Bonneau and Melinda Gann Hall*

One of the most heated debates in American politics today concerns the practice of electing judges to the state court bench, including vigorous disagreements about the various benefits and disadvantages of replacement schemes. In fact, according to the National Center for State Courts Gavel to Gavel website (www.ncsc.org/gaveltogavel), almost 1,300 bills were introduced in state legislatures from 2008 through 2014 that would affect judicial selection in the states and an additional 550 bills that would modify the requisite qualifications of judges and their terms of office. Thus, it certainly is not a stretch to assert that the politics of judicial selection is a hot topic currently occupying a significant amount of state policymakers' time and agenda space.

Driving much of this activity is strident advocacy from interest group organizations and the legal academy about how best to reform judicial selection methods.[1] Endemic in these discussions are highly negative evaluations of partisan and, to a much lesser extent, nonpartisan elections. In fact, public policy advocates based in the legal community (including prestigious groups such as the American Bar Association and the Quality Judges Initiative founded by former United States Supreme Court Justice Sandra Day O'Connor) increasingly are challenging the very efficacy of judicial elections, citing as the most pressing dangers various manifestations of vigorous electoral politics.

At the same time, political scientists in growing numbers are turning their attention toward understanding how judicial elections actually work and their consequences for state judiciaries and the American people. In recent years, for example, there have been numerous pathbreaking books (and a wide array of scholarly articles) on various aspects of state judicial selection. Among these are studies of the causes and consequences of judicial legitimacy (e.g., Cann and Yates 2016; Gibson 2012); the determinants of voter participation, candidate choice, and campaign spending in state supreme court elections (e.g., Bonneau and Cann 2015; Bonneau and M. Hall 2009; M. Hall 2015); long-term trends in contestation, competition, and other fundamental features of state supreme court races (M. Hall 2015; Kritzer 2015); historical factors promoting the emergence of judicial elections (Shugerman 2012); the longstanding tension between accountability and independence (Tarr 2012); the nature of campaign advertising, particularly the impact of attack advertising and other televised messages on the election returns and voter mobilization (M. Hall 2015); the consequences of the various selection systems on the quality of judges (Goelzhauser 2016); and even empirically based normative arguments about the benefits of electing judges, particularly in partisan elections (Bonneau and M. Hall 2009). This relatively recent burst of academic productivity on the issue of state judicial selection, including the various forms of elections, constitutes a sea change in the discipline of political science and unprecedented participation by political scientists in the judicial reform debate if only by contributing much-needed objective empirical evidence to the discussion.

Part of the urgency driving many policy advocates and political scientists in their pursuits is the rapid change in some aspects of judicial elections in recent years. Among other notable trends, the cost of seeking office has risen appreciably since the early 1990s. The speech rights of judicial candidates have been redefined in some states by the United States Supreme Court's decision in *Republican Party of Minnesota v. White* (2002) and subsequent revisions in state codes of judicial conduct implemented in response to this landmark decision. Numerous states have redesigned their selection and retention systems after being bombarded with claims and counterclaims about the benefits and disadvantages of the various options.[2] Television advertising has become the norm in many, but not all, types of contested races. Interest group involvement in the form of independent spending has increased, especially in connection with the sponsorship of harsh attacks in nonpartisan elections. Political activists are paying greater attention to these races. The U.S. Supreme Court has opened the door to unrestrained spending by interest groups and other moneyed players in political campaigns with their controversial decision in *Citizens United v. Federal Election Commission* (2010). Retention elections may also be heating up as evidenced by the defeats in 2010 of three justices on the Iowa Supreme Court for their decision supporting same-sex marriage.

## Our Goals for this Volume

Given these extraordinary transformations in the electoral context and the exciting new work that has been generated by political scientists in recent years, our primary goal with this project is to capture in a single volume the best of the latest cutting-edge research on state judicial elections in their current form. We believe that we have accomplished this task. The contributions composing the volume are (1) original in content, and (2) authored by many of the nation's leading authorities on judicial elections. Most of the contributions are empirical in nature but are written to be easily accessible to those without advanced statistical skills or knowledge of complex empirical methodologies.

Using the latest available data, one of our main emphases is on how present-day judicial elections operate in relation to the past. Many of the chapters also extrapolate outward to future elections, leaving readers with reasonable predictions, and in many cases testable hypotheses, about how things might continue to change, remain stable, or reverse course in the next few decades.

Importantly, our purpose in this volume is not to make normative or empirical arguments favoring or opposing the practice of electing judges. Instead, our goal is to report some of the latest scientific evidence to improve knowledge about how judicial elections across the nation actually function. In this way, we hope to shift the judicial selection debate away from anecdotal evidence, unsubstantiated claims, and projected fears to more systematic evidence drawn from across the American states. We leave any normative inferences to the readers and the discretion of our authors. Of course, from the perspective of political science, this research also helps to inform theories of elections, state politics, and judicial politics, as many of these works utilize the analytical advantages of systematic comparative research designs.

At the same time, we caution that empirical findings should not be construed as implicit normative statements for or against a particular selection scheme. For instance, that interest groups interject less campaign negativity into partisan elections than nonpartisan elections is not a tacit argument condemning nonpartisan elections, nor does this result seek to provide a definitive test of which judicial selection system is best. Instead, the finding is nothing more than a straightforward fact to be added to the body of evidence about how judicial selection and retention systems actually work and the advantages and disadvantages of each method for staffing the state court bench.

Another distinct advantage of this project is the breadth of coverage. This volume includes a great deal about state supreme courts—the most frequently studied state judicial institutions—but also evaluates elections to state intermediate courts and state trial courts. Although state supreme court elections are vital, judicial elections are far more diverse than the overall body of extant work reflects. We also provide fascinating details about retention elections at all levels of the state judiciary (major trial courts, intermediate appellate courts, and supreme courts). The several chapters about retention elections are particularly significant given that these races are often overlooked by political scientists and misunderstood by both practitioners and policymakers. Finally, this volume reports the latest evidence about the impact of judicial elections on some of the most important aspects of American politics, including citizens' perceptions of the legitimacy of courts, the diversity of the state court bench, and the consequences of membership change brought about by elections on the decisions of courts on some of the most divisive and significant issues of the day.

## Overview of the Chapters

The chapters in this volume strive to provide a comprehensive portrait of contemporary judicial elections. Charles Gardner Geyh and Katherine Thrapp begin this enterprise with a deft discussion of how the legal landscape of judicial elections has changed since 2000. Within a fairly short period of time, the U.S. Supreme Court has made a series of landmark decisions fundamentally reshaping what judicial candidates can say during their campaigns, when elected judges must recuse themselves if complex campaign financing issues are involved, and how these elections are financed. Although the empirical consequences of these changes are far from clear, Geyh and Thrapp describe how judicial elections in the 21st century are being conducted under different rules than previous elections and then contemplate some of the plausible implications of these changes.

Chapter 3 is the first of four chapters on state supreme court elections. Herbert M. Kritzer provides a valuable context for understanding contemporary judicial elections by offering a rare longitudinal perspective on contestation and competition (i.e., vote shares) from 1946 through 2015, including competition in retention elections. Building on his earlier epic work (Kritzer 2015), he focuses in this chapter on state-to-state differences, providing a detailed overview of just how some of the fundamental features of these elections have (and have not) changed in each state. Fundamentally, Kritzer shows us that claims of increasing electoral intensity are overstated while highlighting the partisan transformation of the South in the 1980s.

In Chapter 4, Melinda Gann Hall and Matthew J. Zalewski examine state supreme court campaigns from 2002 through 2013 within the context of theories of partisanship in United States elections. Overall, they describe the prevalence and sponsorship of the various types of televised messages in recent contested elections, focusing particularly on derisive messages targeting incumbents. Chapter 4 also documents major differences between partisan and nonpartisan elections when justices are seeking reelection and draws contrasts between open-seat races and those involving incumbents. In numerous ways, the evidence in Chapter 4 contradicts claims about a degenerating campaign climate for incumbents while challenging the effectiveness of nonpartisan elections for shielding incumbents from the gutter politics sponsored by interest groups.

Chris W. Bonneau examines trends in campaign fundraising and spending in Chapter 5. Whereas state supreme court races have become more expensive over the last fifteen years, fundraising and spending have not risen at any kind of alarming rate. Indeed, in many states, there has been less campaign spending in recent years compared to earlier in the decade. Moreover, the amounts raised and spent on these races pale in comparison to the amounts raised and spent in other statewide races (e.g., those for governor and U.S. Senate).

Larry T. Aspin closes our discussion of state supreme court elections with his detailed and meticulous examination of retention elections in Chapter 6. Actually, this chapter fits well within several sections of this volume because Aspin provides information about retention elections, mostly from 1984 through 2014, for the major trial courts, intermediate appellate courts, and supreme courts. He also assesses the 2010 through 2014 elections for the impact of various forms of opposition, including "Do Not Retain" recommendations from bar associations and Judicial Performance Review Commissions, a theme fitting well with Rebecca D. Gill's discussion in Chapter 9. Aspin's rare insights about the types of opposition in retention elections and their consequences, especially for courts other than supreme courts, provide an important foundation for discussions about the extent to which modern campaign politics are affecting retention elections and the lower state courts.

Chapter 7 shifts the focus to state lower courts, starting with intermediate appellate courts. Forty-one of fifty states now have intermediate appellate courts to handle appeals from the trial courts as a matter of right (much like the U.S. Courts of Appeals in the federal system).[3] In Chapter 7, Matthew J. Streb, Brian Frederick, Casey LaFrance, and Kimberly Rice provide a comprehensive description of the elections to these courts while comparing them to state supreme court races. Interestingly, some of the most powerful factors affecting the election results at the state supreme court level do not necessarily matter at the intermediate appellate court level.

In Chapter 8, Mark Jonathan McKenzie and Ryan J. Rebe consider campaigns for the state trial courts, perhaps the least understood of all major judicial institutions. Specifically, they investigate the extent to which issue-based and other polarizing rhetoric was utilized by major trial court candidates across the nation during the 2012–2013 election cycle. In this groundbreaking investigation, they assess whether the "new style" judicial campaigns at the state supreme court level have filtered down to trial courts, which are the courts most citizens experience in their dealings with the legal system. As with other reports in this volume, the news is good for those concerned about campaign negativity and other aspects of aggressive campaign politics.

In Chapter 9, Rebecca D. Gill expertly gauges the impact of judicial performance evaluations in retention elections at all levels of the state judiciary in a select set of states chosen to facilitate standardization of coding and thus robust measurement. Specifically, she examines whether these evaluations affect the percentage of the vote received by judges who have been evaluated. Gill finds that these recommendations matter, even outside the extreme "Do Not Retain" recommendation. Whereas a recommendation not to retain certainly makes it more difficult for a judge to keep her seat, critical comments have an effect on electoral performance even without this strongly negative signal. Given the demonstrated consequences of judicial performance evaluations in retention elections, these results suggest the need for scholars and practitioners to pay more attention to who is evaluating judges and the criteria being utilized.

In Chapter 10, Lawrence Baum, Thomas R. Gray, and David E. Klein present an analytical strategy for estimating the consequences of membership change brought about by judicial elections on the decisions subsequently made by courts. Developing and utilizing a novel method for examining how cases might have been decided differently if a particular judge had won an election as opposed to her opponent, they conclude that a significant number of decisions would have turned out differently if the election results were switched. Of course, these effects vary by state. In this fascinating analysis, the authors focus substantively on tort law and criminal law and procedure, two sets of issues frequently taking center stage in contested judicial races. This chapter represents a significant step forward in assessing the myriad consequences of elections on the decisions of state courts and subsequent public policy.

Chapter 11 turns to legitimacy, one of the most important assets of any institution. Michael J. Nelson uses rare individual-level data to study the effects of judicial elections on citizen perceptions of the legitimacy of courts while also discussing some of the latest research on this topic. Remarkably, Nelson shows that citizens living in states that elect judges report that their courts have more legitimacy than states using other selection methods, all other things considered. In other words, electing judges does not diminish judicial legitimacy but instead enhances it, a finding that stands in sharp contradistinction to the conventional wisdom on this issue but which fits well with other empirical work on the subject (Gibson 2012).

The issue of diversity, particularly gender, ethnic, and racial diversity, is another concern frequently raised in the debate about electing judges. One pejorative stereotype of judicial elections is that the electoral process inhibits diversity, whereas appointment systems enhance such representation. In Chapter 12, Drew Noble Lanier and Mark S. Hurwitz take on this topic by examining which methods of selection, if any, promote or inhibit diversity on the state supreme court bench. Overall, they discount the notion that judicial elections have negative effects on the recruitment and retention of women and other minorities to the states' highest courts.

In Chapter 13, Chris W. Bonneau and Jenna Becker Kane consider the judicial reform process itself by examining some of the most recent successful and failed attempts to change the method by which judges are selected and retained in the states. As noted at the beginning of this chapter, attempts by state legislatures to modify the way judges are chosen, retained, and serve are ever-present in state politics. Among other valuable contributions, Bonneau and Kane shed light on what make proposals more likely to succeed or fail in the political process.

Finally, Melinda Gann Hall and Chris W. Bonneau conclude by highlighting some of the principal findings of this volume. Chapter 14 also describes several of the most fruitful areas for future research on judicial elections and the other methods for selecting and retaining the state court bench.

## Methods of Judicial Selection: The Basics

In order to place in proper context the discussions in this volume, a brief description of the various ways the American states select and retain state court judges is useful. Overall, there are four basic methods: partisan elections, nonpartisan elections, the Missouri Plan (also known as the commission-retention plan), and appointment schemes.[4]

First, some states elect their judges in partisan elections. In these races, which resemble elections to the highest offices in politics such as presidential and gubernatorial contests, candidates run for their party's nomination in primaries (or conventions) and, once selected, compete against the nominees of the other party or parties in the general election. In partisan elections, political party affiliation is listed on the ballot next to each candidate's name, so that voters can acquire this information simply by reading the ballot.

Second, nonpartisan elections are used to select judges. In these races, political parties are neither officially responsible for nor involved in the nominations or campaigns of the candidates. Instead, candidates compete in primaries in which the partisan affiliations of the candidates are not listed and where all candidates seeking the office compete regardless of party. Thus, in any given nonpartisan primary race there could be several Democrats, numerous Republicans, or a mix of various partisan candidates vying for each seat. Generally, if no candidate receives a majority of the vote in the primary, the top two proceed to the general election, again with no party labels on the ballot to guide voters and where the candidates might be from the same political party.

An interesting variation of nonpartisan elections is typically referred to as a "hybrid" system.[5] This currently applies to two states: Michigan and Ohio. In hybrid systems, the political parties select their nominees either in primaries or conventions, but in the general election, partisan affiliations are not shown on the ballot. Thus, in this variant of nonpartisan elections, political parties are more directly and overtly involved in the nomination process than in the typical nonpartisan election, although it would be a mistake to assume that political parties, or partisan politics, are not involved in some form in all judicial selection systems, including appointment plans. The best evidence of this is the highly partisan process of federal court appointments, which have no direct electoral component.

Third is the Missouri Plan, or the commission-retention system. In this type of selection process, judges are nominated by a Judicial Nominating Commission (JNC), the composition of which varies widely across states (Fitzpatrick 2009) but typically consists of members appointed by the governor, legislature, and state bar association. The JNC presents a list of names (usually between three and five) to the governor for each vacancy, and the governor must appoint someone from this list to the bench.[6] After a period of time, usually the next general election, the judge must seek voter approval in a retention election, which is a simple referendum on whether the judge should keep his/her job. There are no opposing candidates in these elections but rather voters are asked whether a judge should or should not be retained. If the judge receives a majority of "yes" votes,[7] then he/she serves a full term of office before standing for retention again. If the judge does not receive a majority of "yes" votes, the judge is removed from office and the process begins anew. The two key components of the commission-retention system are (1) the power of the JNC to constrain the choices of the governor, and (2) the mandate that judges must seek additional terms in periodic retention elections.

Finally, judges may be appointed to the bench by either the governor or the state legislature. The distinguishing feature of these systems is that judges never have to face the electorate to obtain or retain their jobs; instead, judges in most of these states are appointed for fixed terms and must seek approval from the legislative or executive branch to continue in office. Only three states at the supreme court level (Massachusetts, New Hampshire, and Rhode Island) provide lifetime tenure.

There are lots of other variations among the states in how judges are selected and serve (such as the size of the electoral constituency, term of office, etc.), but the four systems just described are the basic methods currently operating in the American states. Also, it is important to note that there may be variations in how judges are selected even within a single state. For example, trial court judges, intermediate appellate court judges, and state supreme court justices may be chosen by different methods within the same state. Likewise, in Arizona and Kansas for example, there are differences from county to county in how trial court judges are selected, with some chosen in partisan elections and others through a commission-retention plan.

To illustrate some of these complex arrangements and to classify the states, we focus on supreme courts. Table 1.1 shows the various selection systems presently operating across the nation and the terms of office. As Table 1.1 indicates, the large majority of states have established a formal electoral connection between their citizens and their highest courts. Overall, thirty-eight states use partisan, nonpartisan, or retention elections to select or retain supreme court justices. Terms of office range in these election systems from six to twelve years. Thus, terms for high court justices tend to be considerably longer than terms for other important political offices in the United States.

Otherwise, twelve states utilize appointment plans to staff their highest courts. Governors make these nominations, except in South Carolina and Virginia, where state legislatures choose judges. In some, but not all, gubernatorial appointment plans, the governor's nominations are restricted to the list of candidates forwarded by a nominating commission. Similarly, appointments must be confirmed by one or both houses of the state legislature except in Massachusetts and New Hampshire, where appointments are approved by an elected Executive Council. As just mentioned, only Massachusetts, New Hampshire, and Rhode Island provide lifetime

**TABLE 1.1** Selection Systems and Terms of Office for State Supreme Courts, 2016

| *Partisan election* | *Term* | *Nonpartisan election* | *Term* | *Retention election (Missouri Plan)* | *Term* | *Appointment* | *Term* |
|---|---|---|---|---|---|---|---|
| Alabama | 6 | Arkansas | 8 | Alaska | 10 | Connecticut | 8 |
| Illinois[a] | 10 | Georgia | 6 | Arizona | 6 | Delaware | 12 |
| Louisiana | 10 | Idaho | 6 | California | 12 | Hawaii | 10 |
| New Mexico[a] | 8 | Kentucky | 8 | Colorado | 10 | Maine | 7 |
| Pennsylvania[a] | 10 | Michigan[b] | 8 | Florida | 6 | Massachusetts | Life |
| Texas | 6 | Minnesota | 6 | Indiana | 10 | New Hampshire | Life |
| | | Mississippi | 8 | Iowa | 8 | New Jersey | 7 |
| | | Montana[c] | 8 | Kansas | 6 | New York | 14 |
| | | Nevada | 6 | Maryland | 10 | Rhode Island | Life |
| | | North Carolina[d] | 8 | Missouri | 12 | South Carolina | 10 |
| | | North Dakota | 10 | Nebraska | 6 | Vermont | 6 |
| | | Ohio[b] | 6 | Oklahoma | 6 | Virginia | 12 |
| | | Oregon | 6 | South Dakota | 8 | | |
| | | Washington | 6 | Tennessee[e] | 8 | | |
| | | West Virginia | 12 | Utah | 10 | | |
| | | Wisconsin | 10 | Wyoming | 8 | | |

*Source*: American Judicature Society, *Judicial Selection in the States*, see www.judicialselection.us.

a. Justices initially are selected in partisan elections but run in retention elections for subsequent terms (but only for uncontested seats in New Mexico).

b. Partisan affiliations are not listed on general election ballots, but partisan methods (party conventions, partisan primaries) are used to nominate candidates.

c. Retention elections are used if the incumbent is unopposed.

d. Justices are allowed to seek reelection in retention elections if preferred (but litigation is pending on this issue).

e. Nominating commissions are not part of this plan. Justices are appointed by the governor and confirmed by the state legislature but then face retention elections for regular terms.

tenure (subject to any mandatory retirement age provisions). In the remaining nine states, justices are appointed for terms ranging from six years (Vermont) to fourteen years (New York), with any subsequent terms subject to the approval of a judicial commission (Hawaii), governor, and/or one or both houses of state legislature. This reliance on fixed terms in nine of the twelve appointment states is one of the primary differences between appointment plans for the state courts and the federal judiciary, where judges are appointed with lifetime tenure.

Overall, nonpartisan and retention elections (which are part of the Missouri Plan) tie as the most popular method for staffing state high courts. Appointment systems come in second, and partisan elections are last. This represents a dramatic change over the past few decades. Although the number of states electing judges has remained relatively constant since 1960 (M. Hall 2015), partisan elections have transitioned from being the most typical means for selecting state supreme court justices in the 1960s (in nineteen states in 1960) to the least common plan by 2016 (see, e.g., M. Hall 2015, 2016, 2017).

Table 1.1 highlights other significant variations within single systems. For example, although Tennessee best fits within the Missouri Plan category because of its use of retention elections, judicial nominating commissions have been abandoned. Instead, the governor nominates, and these nominees must be confirmed by the state legislature. Thereafter, state supreme court justices must seek voter approval for fixed terms in retention elections. Thus, the new Tennessee plan constitutes another hybrid form, differing at present from any other system currently operating in the nation.

Chapters 2 through 14 provide intriguing insights into the operations of the various state election systems in all of their diverse forms, as well as their some of their most notable consequences. These chapters also should help to stimulate and guide additional research for any scholars interested in the intriguing subject of judicial elections.

## Notes

1 The judicial reform community consists almost entirely of attorneys, legal academicians, and others in the legal profession. Overall, the legal profession has been the motivating force for each transformation in state judicial selection, including the movement to elect judges in the first place (e.g., K. Hall 1984, 2005; Hanssen 2004). Unfortunately, many of their recommendations have been based on assumptions derived from normative theories of judging, anecdotal observation, or self-interested advocacy from legal interest groups. Increasingly, many of the assertions offered in the discussion are proving to be overly broad or patently incorrect by more systematic analysis.

2 Some of the most recent states to make major changes to their selection systems are West Virginia, Tennessee, and North Carolina. First, for their courts at all levels, West Virginia replaced partisan elections with nonpartisan elections starting with the 2016 races. In Tennessee, a 2014 ballot measure eliminated judicial nominating commissions for all appellate judgeships, allowing instead for governors to make these choices subject to legislative confirmation and subsequent retention elections. Finally, North Carolina, which typically uses nonpartisan elections, passed legislation in 2015 allowing

supreme court justices to seek additional terms in retention elections. However, a state court recently ruled (in March 2016) that the statute violates the state constitution, and litigation continues on this issue.

3 Delaware, Maine, New Hampshire, North Dakota, Rhode Island, South Dakota, Vermont, West Virginia, and Wyoming do not have intermediate appellate courts. However, Montana appoints temporary appellate panels to review cases sent back down from the state supreme court, and Nevada has a new intermediate appellate court with three permanent judges but with the authority to hear only those cases sent down from the supreme court. Thus, the intermediate appellate courts in Montana and Nevada differ considerably from those in states having permanent judgeships and the ability to receive cases directly from the major trial courts.

4 It is important to note that scholars vary in how they categorize states according to judicial selection systems. Although we believe the most accurate way to group states is how we do so here in Chapter 1, other scholars may disagree (and have legitimate reasons for doing so) depending upon the purposes of their studies. For example, if the interest in a project is on the correlates of voter participation or vote choice, classifying Michigan and Ohio as nonpartisan rather than partisan is entirely appropriate given the crucial role played by ballot format and the stark differences between Michigan and Ohio and the other partisan election states (i.e., Michigan and Ohio do not list each candidate's partisanship on the general election ballot while partisan elections do provide this invaluable heuristic cue). Alternatively, scholars more focused on the nominations process or on the formal role played by political parties might make a different choice. Other scholars simply create an additional category "hybrid" in their projects. In this volume, we gave our contributors complete latitude on this issue; we asked only that they be explicit about their categorical schemes.

5 As indicated below in Table 1.1, there are three states (Illinois, New Mexico, and Pennsylvania) using partisan elections for judges' initial terms of office but retention elections for subsequent terms. Thus, these states constitute another hybrid form of judicial selection. As Table 1.1 suggests, there are other more detailed classification schemes possible based on "hybrid" features.

6 Some states permit the governor to reject the entire list, requiring the Judicial Nominating Commission to come up with a new set of candidates.

7 In New Mexico, 57 percent of the vote is required for retention; in Illinois, 60 percent of the vote is required.

## References

Bonneau, Chris W. and Damon M. Cann. 2015. *Voters' Verdicts: Citizens, Institutions, and Campaigns in State Supreme Court Elections*. Charlottesville: University of Virginia Press.

Bonneau, Chris W. and Melinda Gann Hall. 2009. *In Defense of Judicial Elections*. New York: Routledge.

Cann, Damon M. and Jeff Yates. 2016. *These Estimable Courts: Understanding Public Perceptions of State Judicial Institutions and Legal Policy-Making*. New York: Oxford University Press.

*Citizens United v. Federal Election Commission*. 2010. 558 U.S. 310.

Fitzpatrick, Brian T. 2009. "The Politics of Merit Selection." *Missouri Law Review* 74: 675–709.

Gibson, James L. 2012. *Electing Judges: The Surprising Effects of Campaigning on Judicial Legitimacy*. Chicago: University of Chicago Press.

Goelzhauser, Greg. 2016. *Choosing State Supreme Court Justices: Merit Selection and the Consequences of Institutional Reform*. Philadelphia: Temple University Press.

Hall, Kermit L. 1984. "Progressive Reform and the Decline of Democratic Accountability: The Popular Election of State Supreme Court Judges, 1850–1920." *American Bar Foundation Research Journal* 1984: 345–369.

Hall, Kermit L. 2005. " Judicial Independence and the Majoritarian Difficulty." In *Institutions of American Democracy: The Judicial Branch*, edited by Kermit L. Hall and Kevin T. McGuire. New York: Oxford University Press.

Hall, Melinda Gann. 2015. *Attacking Judges: How Campaign Advertising Influences State Supreme Court Elections*. Stanford: Stanford University Press.

Hall, Melinda Gann. 2016. "Partisanship, Interest Groups, and Attack Advertising in the Post-*White* Era, Or Why Nonpartisan Judicial Elections Really Do Stink." *Journal of Law and Politics* 31 (Spring): 429–456.

Hall, Melinda Gann. 2017. "State Courts: Politics and the Judicial Process." In *Politics in the American States: A Comparative Analysis* 11th edition, edited by Virginia Gray, Russell L. Hanson, and Thad Kousser. Washington, D.C: Congressional Quarterly Press.

Hanssen, F. Andrew. 2004. "Learning about Judicial Independence: Institutional Change in the State Courts." *Journal of Legal Studies* 33: 431–473.

Kritzer, Herbert M. 2015. *Justices on the Ballot: Continuity and Change in State Supreme Court Elections*. New York: Cambridge University Press.

*Republican Party v. White*. 2002. 536 U.S. 765.

Shugerman, Jed Handelsman. 2012. *The People's Courts: Pursuing Judicial Independence in America*. Cambridge: Harvard University Press.

Tarr, G. Alan. 2012. *Without Fear Or Favor: Judicial Independence and Judicial Accountability in the States*. Stanford: Stanford University Press.

# 2

# THE CHANGING LEGAL LANDSCAPE OF JUDICIAL ELECTIONS

*Charles Gardner Geyh and Katherine Thrapp*

The law governing judicial campaigns is in a state of flux. This changing legal landscape has not occurred in a vacuum but is reactive to the changing political landscape at issue in many of the remaining chapters of this volume. To contextualize the evolving law of judicial campaigns, we begin with a thumbnail sketch of the political developments that have catalyzed those changes. We then describe the law's response to those developments, before concluding with a discussion of the implications.

## The Changing Political Landscape

Controversy over judicial selection methods and concern over the impact of judicial elections on judicial independence and legitimacy are nothing new (Shugerman 2012). What *is* new is the changing nature of the judicial campaigns themselves.

A confluence of developments has contributed to the so-called "new politics" of judicial elections. In the 1970s, elections in southern and New England states—long Democratic strongholds—became more competitive affairs in the aftermath of the Johnson administration and reached their denouement with the 1980 election of President Ronald Reagan (Tarr 2003). The reemergence of two-party politics portended new conflict and competition in judicial elections (Tarr 2003), starting with Texas in the early 1980s, when trial lawyers and the defense bar grappled to control how their supreme court was constituted.

Other contemporaneous developments elevated the political profile of state supreme courts. In the late 1970s, Justice William Brennan and others began to encourage progressive-cause lawyers to move their highly visible and often controversial litigation campaigns from federal to state courts (Brennan 1977).

Beginning in the mid-twentieth century, most states established intermediate appellate courts and made their supreme court appellate jurisdiction discretionary, as a means to alleviate docket congestion (Carrington, Meador, and Rosenberg 1976). One unintended consequence of this development was to restrict state supreme courts' diet to fewer, often more divisive cases that called upon the high courts to make law rather than simply correct errors—cases that made state supreme court justices more visible political targets in judicial races (Cordray and Cordray 2001; Tarr 2003).

In the 1980s, President Reagan's popular campaign to "get tough" on crime and drugs became an issue in judicial races, and in 1986, California Chief Justice Rose Bird and two of her colleagues lost their retention elections for their perceived refusal to uphold the death penalty (Sample 2011a). In the 1990s, allegations that a supreme court candidate was "soft on crime" remained a potent issue (leading to the electoral defeat of incumbent justices on the Tennessee and Nebraska Supreme Courts), but campaigns over candidate ideology and decision making expanded to include issues ranging from abortion and same-sex marriage, to school funding, water rights, and, most importantly (for the future of campaign finance) tort reform (Geyh 2003). As judicial election campaigns transformed into referenda on ideologically charged issues, attack advertising underwritten by organizations with independent expenditures, and contributions to the candidates themselves escalated (Geyh 2008).

At the turn of the 21st century, the U.S. Chamber of Commerce, among others, began spending unprecedented sums in state supreme court races, in support of business-friendly judicial candidates sympathetic to tort reform (Heller and Ballard 2000). The trial bar (and some unions) responded in kind, throwing financial support behind pro-consumer plaintiff candidates (American Bar Association 2003, 20–22). Non-candidate spending in supreme court races (meaning spending by independent organizations and individuals) increased nine-fold between the 2001–2002 and 2011–2012 election cycles. A 2013 joint report of the Brennan Center for Justice, the National Institute for Money in State Politics, and the Justice at Stake Campaign found that non-candidate spending rose from $2.68 million during the 2001–2002 election cycle to over $24 million in 2011–2012 (Bannon et al. 2013).

## The Changing Legal Landscape

These developments invited a series of heretofore unresolved legal questions. Does the First Amendment freedom of speech entitle judicial candidates to announce their views, make campaign promises, solicit campaign contributions, and otherwise run their campaigns like any other candidate for elective office? Or does the state's interest in preserving the impartiality, integrity, and independence of its judiciary justify a greater degree of regulation? What about the First Amendment right of individuals and corporations to align themselves with their judicial candidates of choice through their financial support—should that right likewise yield to the needs of an impartial and independent judiciary? And regardless of whether a candidate has a right to speak and a person has right to contribute, do the due process rights of litigants impose on the judge a duty to disqualify herself from hearing specific cases in which the exercise of those rights casts doubt on the judge's impartiality?

The search for answers begins with recourse to applicable law. Judicial candidates, like candidates for public office generally, are subject to statutes governing campaign conduct—fundraising, reporting requirements, and so on. This general body of statutory law includes restrictions on the support candidates may receive, which implicates the rights of campaign supporters, addressed by the U.S. Supreme Court's decision in *Citizens United v. FEC* (2010), discussed below. The logical starting point in a discussion of the regulatory environment for judicial candidates per se, however, is with the Model Code of Judicial Conduct and its corollary for lawyers, the Model Rules of Professional Conduct.

With very few exceptions, judges (and hence judicial candidates generally) must be lawyers: Within state systems, constitutions, statutes, and administrative regulations generally demand that judges be licensed to practice or otherwise learned in the law (National Center for State Courts 2015). Insofar as judges are licensed practitioners, they are subject to states' rules of professional conduct for lawyers, virtually all of which are derived from the American Bar Association's Model Rules of Professional Conduct. Rule 8.2(b) of the ABA Model Rules subjects lawyers who become judicial candidates to applicable rules in their respective codes of judicial conduct.

The American Bar Association first promulgated hortatory canons of judicial ethics in 1924. In 1972, the ABA transformed the canons into an enforceable Model Code of Judicial Conduct, which it substantially revised in 1990 and again in 2007. The preamble to the Model Code describes its dual purpose as being to "provide guidance and assist judges in maintaining the highest standards of judicial and personal conduct" and also to "provide a basis for regulating their conduct through disciplinary agencies" (American Bar Association 2010). All fifty states now have judicial conduct organizations that enforce codes of judicial conduct based on the ABA Model.

The current Model Code is divided into four canons. The first three have occasional bearing on judicial candidates. For example, a candidate's speech or conduct may call her impartiality into question later as a judge when she is presiding over a case, thus triggering the need for judicial disqualification under Canon 2, as discussed later in relation to the U.S. Supreme Court's decision in *Caperton v. Massey Coal Company* (2009).

Canon 4, however, regulates campaign activity per se. Central to the structure of Canon 4 are rules 4.1 and 4.2. Rule 4.1 provides a laundry list of "don'ts." It directs that judges and judicial candidates shall not: (1) be leaders in political organizations; (2) make speeches for political organizations; (3) publicly endorse or oppose candidates for public office; (4) make contributions to candidates or political organizations; (5) attend events of candidates or political organizations; (6) publicly identify themselves as candidates of political organizations; (7) seek or accept endorsements of political organizations; (8) solicit contributions except through a campaign committee; (9) use campaign contributions for private benefit; (10) use court resources in judicial campaigns; (11) knowingly or recklessly make false or misleading statements; (12) make statements that could affect the fairness of pending or impending court proceedings; or (13) make pledges or promises regarding future cases.

Rule 4.2 then relaxes some of the directives of Rule 4.1 during delineated campaign seasons, when judges and judicial candidates (defined to include candidates for contested and retention elections) may: (1) publicly endorse or oppose candidates for the same judicial office for which they are running; (2) attend events of candidates or political organizations; (3) seek or accept endorsements from political organizations that are not avowedly partisan; and (4) contribute limited amounts to candidates and political organizations. The rule lifts two additional restrictions for candidates in partisan elections: They may identify themselves as candidates of political organizations, and they may seek and accept endorsements of partisan political organizations.

As the foregoing summary highlights, Canon 4 regulates the ethics of judicial candidates by restricting candidate speech and association, which raises questions concerning the First Amendment rights of judicial candidates and their limits, to which we now turn.

## *First Amendment Limits on Regulation of Judicial Candidate Speech*

It has long been assumed that when judges accept their positions, they surrender certain rights to speak and conduct themselves as other citizens in order to preserve their independence, impartiality, and integrity. Recent U.S. Supreme Court decisions, however, have called into question the extent to which that is so.

*Republican Party of Minnesota v. White* (2002) concerned the constitutionality of Minnesota's "announce clause," which was embedded in Minnesota's Code of Judicial Conduct, in its Canon 4 corollary. This clause provided that a candidate for judicial office could not "announce his or her views on disputed legal or political issues."[1] In 1996, Gregory Wersal ran for associate justice on the Minnesota Supreme Court. Candidate Wersal publicly criticized the Court's previous decisions on issues such as crime, welfare, and abortion. A disciplinary complaint, which alleged that Wersal's statements had violated Minnesota's announce clause, was filed with the Minnesota Lawyers Board. The Board dismissed the complaint against Wersal and questioned the constitutionality of the announce clause.

Two years later, Wersal decided to run again. This time, he—along with his campaign committee and the Republican Party of Minnesota—filed a lawsuit in federal court seeking an injunction against enforcement of the announce clause (along with several other code of conduct provisions), claiming it violated his right to free speech. In 2002, a closely divided United States Supreme Court sided with Wersal. In a 5–4 opinion, the majority held that Wersal had a First Amendment right to announce his views and invalidated Minnesota's announce clause. The Court interpreted the announce clause as a content-based restriction on speech and determined that as such it was subject to "strict scrutiny," which requires the regulation to be narrowly tailored to serve a compelling government interest. Minnesota argued that two state interests were sufficiently compelling to justify the announce clause: preserving judicial impartiality and the appearance of judicial impartiality. However, the Court decided that no matter how one defined the word "impartiality," the clause did not pass strict scrutiny. If impartiality meant a lack of bias for or against the parties, the clause was "barely tailored" to serve that interest because it prohibited speech about the issues, not the parties. If impartiality meant a lack of preconception against a particular legal view, then this was not a compelling interest because it is "neither possible nor desirable" to completely avoid these preconceptions. Finally, if impartiality meant open-mindedness and willingness to consider views that oppose one's preconceptions, then the announce clause was "woefully underinclusive" because it barred speech on legal and political issues during election campaigns, but neither before nor after.

The U.S. Supreme Court's conclusion in *White* that judicial candidates could not be prevented from "announcing" their views during election campaigns was not altogether surprising. Minnesota's announce clause was derived from a provision in the ABA's 1972 Model Code of Judicial Conduct,[2] which the ABA had removed from its 1990 Model Code out of concern that the clause unduly restricted judicial candidates' ability to express their views (Milord 1992). But the decision raised questions about how the Court would treat other rules that limited judicial speech and association (Hasen 2007). Legal scholars speculated on the scope of *White*, with some predicting it could dramatically change the face of judicial elections. Robert Hirshon, former president of the ABA, called *White* a "bad decision" and said it would "open a Pandora's box" (Greenhouse 2002). Georgetown Law Professor Roy A. Schotland agreed, explaining that "[t]he decision will change judicial election campaigns in such a way that the quality of the pool of candidates for the bench will likely diminish ... [and] good judges will be less willing to seek reelection" (Schotland 2002, 7–10). Others, like the U.S. Chamber of Commerce, praised the decision, because it would allow the public to learn more about the views of judicial candidates (Greenhouse 2002).

After *White*, lower courts divided over the validity of other code of conduct restrictions on judicial speech. Some courts read the decision broadly and used it to strike down rules barring judges from making pledges, promises, or commitments; prohibiting judges from personally soliciting campaign funds; and engaging in partisan activities of various kinds.[3] Others adopted a narrower reading of *White* and upheld similar restrictions on judicial conduct.[4]

In 2015, the Supreme Court revisited the issue of judicial campaign speech in *Williams-Yulee v. Florida Bar* (2015). This time the Court considered the validity of the "solicitation clause" in the Florida Code of Judicial Conduct. The solicitation clause, included in many codes across the states, as well as the 2007 ABA Model Code of Judicial Conduct, authorized judicial candidates to solicit funds only through their campaign committees and prohibited them from soliciting funds from prospective contributors directly.

Lanell Williams-Yulee was a Florida lawyer who decided to run for county court judge and wrote a letter announcing her candidacy and asking for contributions. She posted the letter online and distributed it via a mass mailing. After she lost the election, the Florida Bar filed a complaint against Williams-Yulee for violating the solicitation clause. Although Williams-Yulee admitted to signing and sending the letter that solicited financial support, she argued that she was not subject to discipline because the solicitation clause violated her First Amendment rights.

In another 5–4 decision, the U.S. Supreme Court disagreed. The Court held that the prohibition on personal solicitation of campaign funds did not violate the First Amendment because it was narrowly tailored to serve the compelling government interest of maintaining public confidence in the integrity of the judiciary. The Court also discussed the easy alternative afforded judicial candidates during elections: They could simply raise money through committees or third parties instead.

Whereas *Williams-Yulee* resolved the discrete issue at stake, it did little to resolve uncertainty post-*White*. The Court's decision in *Williams-Yulee* hinged on its conclusion that judicial elections are different from other elections: "Judges are not politicians, even when they come to the bench by way of the ballot. And a State's decision to elect its judiciary does not compel it to treat judicial candidates like campaigners for political office" (1662). In contrast, the Court in *White* rejected the "judges are different" rationale, on its way to concluding that judicial candidates, like candidates for public office generally, have a right to announce their views on issues they will later address as office-holders. The majority in *White* took issue with Justice Ginsburg's dissenting opinion (which turned on the differences between judicial and other candidates), asserting that it "greatly exaggerates the difference between judicial and legislative elections." The majority explained, in effect, that judges, like other elected officials, make policy too:

> Complete separation of the judiciary from the enterprise of "representative government" might have some truth in those countries where judges neither make law themselves nor set aside the laws enacted by the legislature. It is not a true picture of the American system. Not only do state-court judges possess the power to "make" common law, but they have the immense power to shape the States' constitutions as well (784).

*White*'s implications remain potentially broad, given the strict scrutiny the Court applied in both *White* and *Williams-Yulee* and the emphasis the Court placed in the latter case on how rarely strict scrutiny will be satisfied (even as the Court applied a seemingly softer form of strict scrutiny in its assessment of the solicitation clause). Questions concerning the validity of restrictions on judicial candidate pledges, promises, commitments, and political activities remain unanswered.

Uncertainty likewise remains concerning the applicability of *White* outside the context of judicial races. One can argue that judges (as distinguished from challengers) acquiesce to greater restrictions on their speech when they don the robe; however, if such restrictions are subject to bona fide strict scrutiny, their survival is uncertain. Consider, for example, the case of *Mississippi Commission on Judicial Performance v. Wilkerson* (2004). Connie Wilkerson, a Mississippi judge, wrote a letter to his local paper expressing his belief that "gays and lesbians should be put in some type of mental institute." The Mississippi Commission on Judicial Performance charged the judge with breaching a canon of the state code of judicial conduct (likewise embedded in the ABA Model Code and the codes of other states), which provided that "[a] judge should respect and comply with the law and should conduct himself at all times in a manner that promotes public confidence in the integrity and impartiality of the judiciary."[5] The Supreme Court of Mississippi applied strict scrutiny and held that Judge Wilkerson's derogatory comments were protected by the First Amendment and thus were not subject to sanction under the applicable canon.

## *Due Process Limits on the Risk of Judicial Bias Resulting From Campaign Support*

In addition to its ongoing interest in restrictions on judicial campaign speech, the U.S. Supreme Court has been concerned with constitutional questions raised by the financial support judicial candidates receive, and its impact on the due process rights of litigants to a fair hearing before an impartial judge. In 2009, the Supreme Court considered the due process implications of non-disqualification in *Caperton v. A.T. Massey Coal Company* (2009). There, Massey Coal Company had lost a $50 million verdict in West Virginia state court, and while its appeal was pending, Massey's CEO spent over $3 million in a West Virginia Supreme Court race to oust the incumbent and elect the challenger, Brent Benjamin. Those independent expenditures on Benjamin's behalf exceeded the total spent by all other Benjamin supporters and more than tripled the spending of Benjamin's own committee. After Benjamin won the election by a 53 to 47 percent margin, he declined to disqualify himself from the pending case and cast the deciding vote for Massey.

In another 5–4 decision, the Supreme Court found that the Due Process Clause required Justice Benjamin's disqualification due to a "probability of actual bias" (Caperton 2009, 887). The Court stressed the multiple factors at play and the fact that this was an "extraordinary situation" (Caperton 2009, 887):

> We conclude that there is a serious risk of actual bias—based on objective and reasonable perceptions—when a person with a personal stake in a particular case had a significant and disproportionate influence in placing the judge on the case by raising funds or directing the judge's election campaign when the case was pending or imminent. The inquiry centers on the contribution's relative size in comparison to the total amount of money contributed to the campaign, the total amount spent in the election, and the apparent effect such contribution had on the outcome of the election (884).

These factors have been read to create a constitutional floor that the Due Process Clause affords litigants (Sample 2011b)—a floor above which, the Court took pains to add, the states are free to adopt more rigorous disqualification rules.

State disqualification rules typically follow the ABA Model, which begins with the general rule that judges must withdraw from any case in which their "impartiality might reasonably be questioned"—meaning when an objective observer fully informed of the facts would doubt the judge's impartiality.[6] This general, observer-based perception of bias standard is patently more demanding than the due process threshold established in *Caperton*, insofar as a reasonable person might doubt a judge's impartiality under circumstances falling well short of those needed to establish a probability of actual bias. Hence, state rules more rigorous than those demanded by the Due Process Clause are already in place. The problem, however, is that this general rule may not be consistently applied in the specific context of campaign support. Indeed, the *Caperton* case became necessary because Justice Benjamin neither discussed nor applied his own state's general disqualification rule,[7] opining that an appearance of bias standard invited mischief and that he would apply an "actuality" of bias standard instead.[8]

Accordingly, after *Caperton*, the bench and bar turned their attention toward developing a disqualification rule specific to campaign finance (Gibeaut 2012). The ABA Model Code follows its general rule with a list of specific examples where a judge's impartiality is presumptively in doubt. A 1999 amendment added Rule 2.11(A)(4) to that list. The 1999 amendment does not address independent expenditures but requires disqualification when the party or party's attorney has provided the judge with direct campaign contributions in excess of an amount left open for individual states to specify.[9] The amended Rule was not widely adopted in the succeeding years. Post-*Caperton*, the ABA Standing Committee on Ethics and Professional Responsibility undertook a multi-year effort to amend 2.11(A)(4) to include independent expenditures but failed in large part due to objections from the ABA's Judicial Division that any such a rule should be a matter of procedure, not ethics (Geyh et al. 2015).

### *First Amendment Limits on Regulation of Campaign Finance*

*White* and *Williams-Yulee* addressed the rights of judicial candidates, and *Caperton* explored the rights of litigants. That leaves the rights of those who lend financial support to judicial campaigns. *Citizens United v. FEC* (2010) addressed the First Amendment rights of corporations and unions to spend money in support of candidates for legislative and executive branch races, which may or may not apply with equal force to judicial races.[10]

At the time of *Citizens United*, federal law prohibited "corporations and unions from using their general treasury funds to make direct contributions to candidates or independent expenditures that expressly advocate the election or defeat of a candidate, through any form of media, in connection with certain qualified federal elections."[11] The Bipartisan Campaign Reform Act (BCRA) extended this prohibition to "electioneering communications" that were publicly distributed, referred to a clearly identified candidate for federal office, and were made within thirty days of a primary or sixty days of a general election.[12]

Shortly before the 2008 Democratic primaries, *Citizens United*—a nonprofit corporation—released a documentary titled *Hillary: The Movie*, which criticized presidential hopeful Hillary Clinton. To promote its movie, *Citizens United* created television ads with short "pejorative" statements about Hillary Clinton followed by information concerning the documentary. *Citizens United* wanted to air the documentary and the ads within thirty days of the 2008 primary elections and so sought declaratory and injunctive relief against the FEC, arguing that these prohibitions on campaign spending violated its First Amendment right to free speech.

In yet another 5–4 decision, the Supreme Court held that the federal prohibitions on independent expenditures and electioneering communications violated the First Amendment. The Court rejected all three purported government interests in maintaining the ban: antidistortion, anticorruption, and shareholder protection. The Court did not examine the issue of direct campaign contributions because this was not at issue in the case, but the anticorruption rationale had previously been held sufficient to justify this type of limitation.[13]

Like *White*, the Court's decision in *Citizens United* quickly prompted speculation about its ultimate effects. In 2014, the Supreme Court extended its holding in *Citizens United* by striking down aggregate campaign contribution limits to all candidates and committees in *McCutcheon v. FEC*. Today, caps on direct contributions to a single campaign are still valid. Speculation persists about whether the Court will continue to preserve these limits or whether such caps are essentially meaningless, given the availability of independent expenditures.

The critical question for our purposes here is whether and to what extent *Citizens United* applies to judicial races. Shortly after the decision, former Justice Sandra Day O'Connor suggested that this decision could affect state judicial elections as well (O'Connor 2010). One reformer predicted that "the most severe impact of *Citizens United* may be felt in state judicial elections" (Skaggs 2010, 1).

The *Citizens United* Court did not make an exception for judicial races, and in the years since the case was decided, spending in supreme court races has increased significantly—as many predicted it would (Weiner 2015). The extent to which that increase can be attributed to *Citizens United* specifically, however, as opposed to the new politics of judicial elections generally, remains uncertain. That said, *Citizens United* was significant in part because it paved the way for the creation of so-called "Super PACs"—organizations that are permitted to spend "unlimited amounts of money to support or oppose candidates as long as they don't coordinate directly with any candidate's campaign" (Green 2015). There is some indication that "the revolution in financing political campaigns, with the surging role of 'super PACs' and other groups financed by corporations, unions and other interests, has entered what was the quieter arena of judicial elections" (Eckholm 2014).

If *Citizens United* is exerting an impact on campaign spending in judicial races, the issue becomes whether that impact can be blunted by regulations on independent expenditures that would be deemed unconstitutional in executive and legislative branch races (Brandenburg et al. 2010). Erwin Chemerinsky and James Sample have argued that the Supreme Court should find the "compelling interest in ensuring impartial judges is sufficient to permit restrictions on campaign spending that would be unconstitutional for nonjudicial elections" (Chemerinsky and Sample 2011; Sample 2011b). Although they acknowledge that *Caperton* provides a check after the fact via disqualification, they regard this as an insufficient remedy for a larger structural problem. Their argument proceeds on the assumption that a post-*Citizens United* infusion of money into judicial races would be deleterious. Others, such as Professor Chris Bonneau in Chapter 5 of this volume, have argued that increased spending in judicial races translates into increased advertising and corresponding voter interest that can be democracy-enhancing (Bonneau 2017).

## Implications

The implications of recent changes to the legal landscape of judicial elections are both trivial and profound. They are trivial in that—predictions to the contrary notwithstanding—none of these developments has caused the sky to fall or restored pieces of the fallen sky to their place in the firmament. They are simultaneously profound in that the ongoing debate over these developments reveals the great divide between disputants on the core question of whether judges are different enough from public officials in the legislative and executive branches of government to justify a different regulatory schema for judicial selection.

In the aftermath of *White*, critics of the decision worried that it would have a significant and deleterious effect on judicial campaigns. Proponents of the decision argued that *White* would simply add welcome transparency by enabling candidates to share with the public their policy predilections, which they would otherwise keep to themselves. To critics, however, this missed an important point:

When candidates tell voters how they will decide future cases, it constrains them from changing their minds later in light of operative facts and law without appearing duplicitous, to the ultimate detriment of their impartiality. As candidate position-taking became the new normal, critics warned, long-term erosion of impartiality norms would be inevitable.

Anecdotes aside, the dire predictions of *White* critics have not materialized; the decision has not yielded measurable effects on judicial campaigns (e.g., Bonneau, Hall and Streb 2011; Gibson 2012). That may be because the new era of candidate position-taking has produced no ill effects; or it may be because the new era never began, insofar as judicial candidates have clung to traditional impartiality norms and declined to telegraph their future rulings from the campaign stump, notwithstanding their right to do so. Either way, *White*'s threat or promise remains largely unrealized.

*Williams-Yulee*, viewed on its own, is a case destined for obscurity (e.g., Bonneau and Redman 2015). Its holding—in effect, that a state is within its authority to require that letters soliciting contributions to a judicial candidate's campaign be signed by the candidate's campaign chair rather than the candidate herself—resolves an arcane question in favor of the status quo. Had the decision gone the other way, as many predicted, it is unclear that the case would have been appreciably more consequential. Without disputing that it could spell trouble for judicial integrity, impartiality, and independence if judicial candidates had a First Amendment right to corner prospective litigants and their lawyers and shake them down for campaign contributions, the benignly worded mass mailing at issue in *Williams-Yulee* did not implicate those concerns in an especially troubling way.

As to *Caperton*, the majority opinion took pains to emphasize that it was an exceptional case reserved for exceptional circumstances. Hence, the perfect storm of factors that triggered the due process problem there are unlikely to recur often. The dissent conjured forty unanswered questions that would deluge the courts after *Caperton* opened the floodgates, but years later, drenching rains have yet to begin. The majority all but invited the states to avoid future due process problems by establishing disqualification rules above the constitutional floor that would require a judge to recuse herself from cases in which she had received so much campaign support from parties or lawyers who appeared before her as to call her impartiality into question. Had *Caperton* transformed disqualification rules in this way, it would have constituted an important if collateral impact of the decision, but those rules have not materialized either. Despite years of trying, the American Bar Association has failed to devise a model disqualification rule for the states to adopt that the ABA House of Delegates could agree upon.

The impact of *Citizens United* is more challenging to assess. The progress (or devolution, depending on one's point of view) of judicial campaign spending in the aftermath of *Citizens United* continues apace, as the data summarized at the beginning of this chapter show.[14] The extent to which the decision has accelerated these developments, however, is difficult to ascertain.

Ultimately, though, it would be a mistake to evaluate the impact of *Citizens United* in isolation. The same may be said for *White, Caperton*, and *Williams-Yulee*: the implications of the whole exceed the sum of its parts. The changing legal landscape of judicial elections follows the changing political landscape; these U.S. Supreme Court decisions, like the evolving politics of judicial campaigns, reveal an underlying struggle for the future of the American judiciary.

At the heart of this struggle is the question of whether judges are different enough from public officials in the other branches of government to justify a different system for managing their selection. This threatens to cue the tired "independence versus accountability" debate in which election opponents decry the threats elections pose to judicial independence whereas proponents tout the corresponding virtues of electoral accountability. But the underlying dispute at issue here is more tightly focused: Is what judges do different enough from what legislators or governors do to warrant a regulatory schema for the selection of judicial candidates that would be unacceptable for legislative and executive branch candidates?

No one would second-guess the propriety of gubernatorial or general assembly candidates announcing their views on the issues they will decide as governors or legislators. They are not supposed to be "impartial." They are expected to be partial to the preferences of their respective constituencies, and announcing their views to prospective voters enables voters to decide which candidate will better represent their views.

Judges, in contrast, are not supposed to represent the electorate's views; rather, judges are under an ethical directive to disregard "public clamor" and "uphold and apply the law" (American Bar Association 2010, Rules 2.2, 2.4). Unlike governors and assembly-people, then, judges are duty-bound to remain impartial. And since the earliest codes of judicial conduct were written in the 17th century, impartiality has subsumed an obligation to "reserve judgment until the entire matter be heard." Against this backdrop, announcing one's views before a matter is heard—and the holding of *White* entitling judicial candidates to announce their views on future cases—are sharply at odds with traditional conceptions of the judicial role.

Similarly, when it comes to soliciting campaign support from the public directly, few would argue that is improper for executive and legislative branch candidates to do so. But judicial candidates are arguably different, for reasons the Chief Justice offered on behalf of the Court in *Williams-Yulee* (2015, 1666): "Judges are not politicians, even when they come to the bench by way of the ballot ... Judges, charged with exercising strict neutrality and independence, cannot supplicate campaign donors without diminishing public confidence in judicial integrity." And because *Williams-Yulee* represents the Supreme Court's latest word on judicial campaigns (as of this writing), it acquires greater prominence in the ongoing "how different are judges?" debate.

The issue at stake in *Caperton* implicates differences between judicial and political branch candidates at least as starkly. In executive and legislative branch races, campaign support can reach levels that raise concerns about corrupting quid pro quos. But officeholders in the executive and legislative branches are not expected to be impartial, and few would argue that they should be barred from making or participating in decisions simply because they are biased in favor the causes of individuals or groups who support them. In *Caperton*, however, a state supreme court justice was disqualified for probable bias, despite the Court's explicit concession that the justice may not have been actually biased, let alone corrupted, by the campaign support he received. In short, judges, by virtue of their duty to remain impartial, are different.

*Citizens United*, in contrast to *White*, *Williams-Yulee*, and *Caperton*, did not arise in the context of a judicial campaign. But the application of *Citizens United* to judicial branch races raises similar questions concerning the differences between the judicial and political branches. In *Citizens United*, the Court ruled that the First Amendment prohibited the government from restricting independent corporate expenditures in support of political branch candidates. Is the same true of judicial candidates? Or could the state's interest in preserving judicial impartiality justify heightened regulation of independent expenditures in judicial races?

This recent series of 5–4 decisions by the United States Supreme Court reveals a sharp division over whether judicial campaigns are different enough from their counterparts in the political and legislative branches to be regulated differently. *White* and *Citizens United* (to the extent *Citizens United* is presumptively applicable to judicial campaigns) answer that question in varying shades of "no," whereas *Caperton* and *Williams-Yulee* seem to answer in the affirmative. This ongoing tension in the changing legal landscape mirrors some of the same tensions at issue in the development of positive and normative theories of judicial elections, to which the remainder of this volume is devoted.

## Notes

1 Minn. Code of Judicial Conduct, Canon 5(A)(3)(d)(i) (2002).
2 Canon 7(B)(1)(c) of the 1972 Code stated that a candidate, including an incumbent judge, should not "announce his views on disputed legal or political issues …"
3 See, e.g., *Duwe v. Alexander*, 490 F.Supp.2d 968 (WD Wis. 2007); *Republican Party of Minnesota v. White*, 416 F.3d 738 (8th Cir. 2005); *Republican Party of Minnesota v. White*, 361 F.3d 1035 (8th Cir. 2004).
4 *In re Watson*, 794 N.E.2d 1 (NY 2003); *Simes v. Arkansas Judicial Discipline & Disability Comm'n*, 247 SW 3d 876 (Ark. 2007).
5 Canon 2(A) of the old rules.
6 American Bar Association Model Code of Judicial Conduct Rule 2.11.
7 West Virginia Code of Judicial Conduct Canon 3E(1) called for disqualification in general when the judge's "impartiality might reasonably be questioned."
8 Justice Benjamin stated that "[a]ctual justice is based on actualities." *Caperton v. A.T. Massey Coal Co.*, 679 S.E.2d 223, 292–94 (W. Va. 2008) (Benjamin, J., concurring) (noting that neither appellants nor the dissent pointed to "any actual bias or prejudice on [Benjamin's] part which could be termed 'improper'" and calling the dissent's

advocacy for "appearance-driven" judging "disappointing"). Justice Benjamin believed that appearance-based judging ran contrary to Canon 3B(2), which "succinctly dispels any contention that appearance-based judging should supercede judging based on actualities."

9 Canon 3(E)(1)(e) of the 1999 Model Code provided that a judge shall disqualify himself from a case if "the judge knows or learns by means of a timely motion that a party or party's lawyer has within the previous [] year[s] made aggregate contributions to the judge's campaign in an amount that is greater than [[$] for an individual or [$] for an entity][[is reasonable and appropriate for an individual or an entity]]." The rule was retained, with a few small changes, in Rule 2.11(A)(4) of the 2007 Model Code.

10 As of the time of this writing, the Supreme Court has not addressed the issues raised in *Citizens United* in a judicial elections setting.

11 2 U.S.C. § 441b (2000).

12 2 U.S.C § 441b(b)(2) (2000).

13 *See Buckley v. Valeo*, 424 U.S. 1 (1976).

14 See also Chapter 5 of this volume.

## References


American Bar Association Commission on the 21st Century Judiciary. 2003. *Justice in Jeopardy*. Chicago: American Bar Association.

American Bar Association. 2010. *Model Code of Judicial Conduct, 2011 edition*. Chicago: American Bar Association.

Bannon, Alicia, Linda Casey, Lianna Reagan, and Eric Velasco. 2013. *The New Politics of Judicial Elections 2011–12*. Washington, DC: Justice at Stake.

Bonneau, Chris W. 2017. "Fundraising and Spending in State Supreme Court Elections." In *Judicial Elections in the 21st Century*, edited by Chris W. Bonneau and Melinda Gann Hall. New York: Routledge.

Bonneau, Chris W., Melinda Gann Hall, and Matthew J. Streb. 2011. "*White* Noise: The Unrealized Effects of *Republican Party of Minnesota v. White* on Judicial Elections." *Justice System Journal* 32: 247–268.

Bonneau, Chris W. and Shane M. Redman. 2015. "Much Ado About Nothing: The Irrelevance of *Williams-Yulee v. The Florida Bar* on the Conduct of Judicial Elections." *Vanderbilt Law Review En Banc* 68: 31–41.

Brandenburg, Bert, Andrew Siegel, Richard Hasen, Kathleen Sullivan, and David M. Skover. 2010. "Transcript: Session 1: One Symptom of a Serious Problem: *Caperton v. Massey*." *Seattle University Law Review* 33: 569–588.

Brennan, William J., Jr. 1977. "State Constitutions and the Protection of Individual Rights." *Harvard Law Review* 90: 489–504.

Carrington, Paul, Daniel Meador, and Maurice Rosenberg. 1976. *Justice on Appeal*. St. Paul: West Publishing Company.

*Caperton v. Massey Coal Co., Inc.* 2009. 556 U.S. 868.

Chemerinsky, Erwin and James Sample. 2011. "You Get the Judges You Pay For" *New York Times*. April 18, 2011.

*Citizens United v. Federal Election Commission*. 2010. 558 U.S. 310.

Cordray, Margaret Meriwether and Richard Cordray. 2001. "The Supreme Court's Plenary Docket." *Washington and Lee Law Review* 58: 737–794.

Eckholm, Erik. 2014. "Outside Spending Enters Arena of Judicial Races." *New York Times*. May 5, 2014.

Geyh, Charles Gardner. 2003. "Why Judicial Elections Stink." *Ohio State Law Journal* 64: 43–79.

Geyh, Charles Gardner. 2008. "The Endless Judicial Selection Debate and Why it Matters for Judicial Independence." *Georgetown Journal of Legal Ethics* 21: 1259–1281.

Geyh, Charles Gardner, Myles Lynk, Robert S. Peck, and Toni Clarke. 2015. "The State of Recusal Reform." *New York University Journal of Legislation and Public Policy* 18: 515–547.

Gibeaut, John. 2012. "Show Me the Money: States, ABA Try to Figure Out When Campaign Cash Leads to a Judge's Recusal." *ABA Journal*. March 1, 2012.

Gibson, James L. 2012. *Electing Judges: The Surprising Effects of Campaigning on Judicial Legitimacy*. Chicago: University of Chicago Press.

Green, Emma. 2015. "The Local Consequences of *Citizens United*." *The Atlantic*. July 2, 2015.

Greenhouse, Linda. 2002. "Justices Strike Down Minnesota Law Prohibiting Political Statements by Judicial Candidates." *New York Times*. June 28, 2002.

Hasen, Rick. 2007. "First Amendment Limits on Regulating Judicial Campaign." In *Running for Judge: The Rising Political, Financial, and Legal Stakes of Judicial Elections*, edited by Matthew J. Streb. New York: New York University Press.

Heller, Emily and Mark Ballard. 2000. "Hard-Fought, Big Money Judicial Races: U.S. Chamber of Commerce Enters Fray with Ad Money." *National Journal* 42.

*McCutcheon v. FEC*. 2014. 134 S.Ct. 1434.

Milord, Lisa L. 1992. *The Development of the ABA Judicial Code*. Center for Professional Responsibility. American Bar Association.

*Mississippi Commission on Judicial Performance v. Wilkerson*. 2004. 876 So. 2d 1006.

National Center for State Courts. 2015. "Judicial Selection in the States." Available at www.judicialselection.us/ (select a state; click on "selection of judges" and cursor down to "qualifications of judges").

O'Connor, Sandra Day. 2010. "Choosing (and Recusing) Our State Court Justices Wisely: Keynote Remarks by Justice O'Connor." *The Georgetown Law Journal* 99: 151–156.

*Republican Party of Minnesota v. White*. 2002. 536 U.S. 765.

Sample, James. 2011a. "Retention Elections 2010." *University of San Francisco Law Review* 46: 383–424.

Sample, James. 2011b. "Democracy at the Corner of First and Fourteenth: Judicial Campaign Spending and Equality." *New York University Annual Survey of American Law* 66: 727–782.

Schotland, Roy A. 2002. "*Republican Party of Minnesota v. White*: Should Judges Be More Like Politicians?" *Judges' Journal* 41: 7–10.

Shugerman, Jed Handelsman. 2012. *The People's Courts: Pursuing Judicial Independence in America*. Cambridge: Harvard University Press.

Skaggs, Adam. 2010. *Buying Justice: The Impact of Citizens United on Judicial Elections*. New York: Brennan Center for Justice.

Tarr, Alan G. 2003. "Appendix D: State Judicial Selection and Judicial Independence." *American Bar Association in Justice in Jeopardy: Report of the ABA Commission on the 21st Century Judiciary*. Chicago: American Bar Association.

Weiner, Daniel I. 2015. *Citizens United, Five Years Later*. New York: Brennan Center for Justice.

*Williams-Yulee v. The Florida Bar*. 2015. 135 S.Ct. 1656.

**SECTION 2**

# State Supreme Court Elections

# 3

# CONTESTATION AND COMPETITIVENESS IN STATE SUPREME COURT ELECTIONS, 1946–2015

## A State-Level Analysis

*Herbert M. Kritzer*

Have state supreme court elections become more competitive in recent years? That question has been an important part of the debate regarding those elections (e.g., Kang and Shepherd 2011, 2015; Shepherd and Kang 2014). Proponents of changing the role of elections in the process of selection and retention of judges, particularly judges on state supreme courts, argue that the claimed increase in competitiveness creates a range of problems for judges—dependence on campaign contributions, caution in decision making, etc.—and justifies reconsidering what role, if any, elections should play in staffing courts. However, in previous work (Kritzer 2011, 2015) I showed that while there has been some change both in the likelihood that state supreme court elections would be contested and in the competitiveness of those elections, those changes are largely limited to southern states. Moreover, the changes that occurred in those states coincided with broader political changes in the South: first the resistance to desegregation, then the end of the Democratic Party's overwhelming dominance in the southern states, and finally the current dominance of the Republican Party in most of those states. In this chapter, I revisit the question of whether there has been an increase in contestation and competitiveness by asking whether my previous description of change was too simplistic. I do this by examining individual state patterns for all thirty-eight states that currently employ popular elections to select and/or retain the justices of their courts of last resort, which I will refer to as "state supreme courts."[1]

Other aspects of my research on state supreme court elections suggest that patterns of change tend to be state specific. For example, to what degree do voting patterns in nonpartisan elections align with the partisan pattern in a state's gubernatorial elections? My analysis of this question (Kritzer 2015) showed that partisan alignment varies by state, with some states (e.g., Washington and Wisconsin) developing close alignments in many elections whereas others (e.g., Minnesota) continue to have mostly weak, if any, alignments. Similarly, in retention elections—those in which voters decide whether an incumbent will continue in office by casting ballots "yes" or "no"—I found that where there were partisan alignments, they varied substantially from state to state. Some states showed substantial changes over time, while others remained unchanged (Kritzer 2015). Generally, the variation and the nature of change reflected state-specific developments and state-specific issues.

A second reason to examine contestation and competitiveness at the individual state level is that during the period 1946 to 2015, many states changed the methods used for selecting and/or retaining the justices of their state supreme court (Kritzer 2015). For example, at the beginning of the period only two states used retention elections, but by the end of the period that number had increased to seventeen. An additional six states shifted from partisan to nonpartisan elections, with two of these states subsequently shifting to retention elections. At the beginning of the period, twenty-three states used partisan elections;[2] that figure is now down to nine states, three of which use partisan elections only for an initial term, using retention elections for subsequent terms. Looking at state-level patterns allows one to see what change, if any, occurs when the type of election changes.

This chapter proceeds as follows. The next section briefly discusses election formats and variations in those formats. The following section describes the data used in the analysis and the methods used for that analysis. The analysis section first discusses elections in eight of the southern states and then for each of the different types of election formats. The chapter ends with a brief conclusion.

## Election Formats

Judicial elections in the United States are typically described as following one of three formats:

- Partisan elections in which each candidate is listed on the ballot as being affiliated with a political party (or, occasionally, as an independent).
- Nonpartisan elections in which no party affiliations are listed on the ballot, even in states where nominations are made by party conventions.
- Retention elections in which candidates are listed without opponents and voters are asked simply to vote "yes" or "no" regarding a candidate.

As I have discussed elsewhere (Kritzer 2015), this type of categorization fails to reflect the variation that exists in how supreme court elections are conducted. In addition to the three states (Illinois, New Mexico, and Pennsylvania) that combine initial partisan elections with retention elections for subsequent terms, major variations include:

- Two states currently (Michigan and Ohio) and one state formerly (Arizona) combine party nominations either through primaries or conventions with nonpartisan general election ballots; I label these as "hybrid" elections in the analysis that follows.
- Two states (Montana and Utah) either do, or did, use nonpartisan ballots that revert to retention elections if an incumbent is unopposed. Uncontested elections in these states during the years that such elections become retention elections are included in both the analysis of nonpartisan elections (as uncontested) and in the analysis of retention elections.
- One state (Nevada) includes a "none of the above option" as part of its nonpartisan ballot. Whereas the "none of the above option" could be considered a form of retention vote, Nevada has not consistently reported the number of voters casting a "none of the above" vote, and hence I ignore these votes.
- One state (California) uses a retention-type ballot for persons nominated to succeed a justice leaving office at the end of the justice's term. This has happened three times (1970, 2010, and 2014); I treat those elections as retention elections for purposes of my analysis.
- One state (Louisiana) uses partisan elections but allows multiple candidates of the same party to run on a single ballot with a run-off for the top two candidates, regardless of party, if no candidate wins a majority in the first round. I treat Louisiana as a partisan election state.

Some of the other noteworthy variations in election structure include whether elections are for multiple seats (top X candidates win) or single seats, whether a straight-ticket voting option is provided in partisan elections, whether incumbency is indicated on the ballot, whether elections are statewide or district based, what percentage of "yes" votes is required for retention in a retention election, whether a candidate winning a majority in a nonpartisan primary faces opposition in the general election, and whether the election is scheduled in November to coincide with other statewide and national elections.

## Data and Methods

The unit of analysis I use is the supreme court seat up for election. This includes all 754 seats involving retention elections that occurred between 1946 and 2015, plus all but one of the 2,098 seats involving a partisan, nonpartisan, or hybrid election. The one seat omitted was a 1950 election in Oregon that involved only write-in candidates. Twenty-three elections from Utah and Montana appear twice in the analysis, once as an unopposed incumbent running in a nonpartisan election and once as an incumbent running in a retention election; this reflects the system that existed briefly in Utah and currently exists in Montana in which an unopposed incumbent runs in a retention election. For seats not subject to retention elections, up to five distinct elections could be involved: primaries for the Democratic and Republican Parties, run-offs for each of those parties, and a general election. A seat is counted as contested if any one of those five possible elections is contested other than by write-in candidates. Two seats from Tennessee for which the incumbents were denied re-nomination at the 1990 Democratic Party convention and then the nominee was unopposed in the general election are treated as uncontested open-seat elections.

My measure of competitiveness differs somewhat from the measure used in other studies (e.g., Hall 2001). In almost all cases, I compute vote share, measured as a percentage, based on the top two candidates, which generally affects only primaries but can affect partisan elections in which more than two parties put forth candidates. In an open-seat election, I use the closest election—general election, primary, or run-off—involving the eventual winner. Where an incumbent is running, I focus on the smallest top-two-candidate vote share received by the incumbent across the primary, run-off, or general election regardless of whether the incumbent won or lost except in the very small number of cases when the incumbent came in third in a primary; when the incumbent came in third, I used the percentage of the vote received by the incumbent across all candidates rather than just the top two. I ignore the primary and run-off results for the loser in the general election unless an incumbent loses in the primary or run-off. For multi-seat elections, I pair the top vote-getter with the bottom vote-getter to get a percentage; if there is fewer than twice the number of seats, the top vote-getter is treated as unopposed. No percentage is computed for candidates who are unopposed (ignoring write-in candidates) in partisan, nonpartisan, and hybrid elections.

This approach to measuring competitiveness tends to show elections as *more* competitive than the approach used by Hall (2001) in her analysis of incumbent vote shares. When an incumbent faced opposition in a primary, and possibly a run-off, but not in the general election, Hall used the incumbent's vote share in either the primary, or in the run-off if there was one; otherwise, she always used the vote share in a contested general election regardless of whether there was a primary and/or run-off that was more competitive than the general election. She used a similar approach for open seats, focusing on the vote share of the eventual winner. Thus, if the incumbent or eventual winner of an open seat handily won a contested general election but had squeaked through the primary and/or run-off, the election would be treated as noncompetitive in contrast to my measurement which would treat the election as very competitive. In a very small number of cases where an incumbent or the eventual winner of an open seat won a primary with three or more candidates without the need for a two-candidate run-off, Hall's method would potentially show a lower vote percentage than would my approach, which almost always restricts the calculation to the two top candidates.

The figures presenting my analysis below capture several key variations in the elections represented. Separate symbols indicate types of elections: circles for partisan elections, squares for nonpartisan elections, diamonds for hybrid elections (those in which candidates are nominated by parties but no party labels are shown on the general election ballot), and triangles for retention-type elections. Filled symbols indicate an election involving an incumbent, with black indicating that the incumbent lost and gray that the incumbent won. Hollow symbols indicate an election without an incumbent. The number of unopposed candidates each year is shown along the bottom of the figure for each state. Thus, the figures show indicators for all seats up for election in a state, either as points representing a percentage or a number indicating one or more uncontested seats. In some elections the ultimate winner came in second in a primary, and for those elections the percentage shown in the figure for the winner is less than 50 percent.

Vertical lines demark significant changes in the structure of a state's system for state supreme court elections. Horizontal lines indicate 50 percent, or the percentage required for retention (57% in New Mexico and 60% in Illinois). Where there are sufficient observations, the figures include a lowess line (Cleveland 1979) for contested partisan, nonpartisan, and hybrid elections, and for retention elections.[3] For states that employ multiple types of elections or have changed the type of election used since 1946, the figures show separate lines for each type of election for which there were sufficient observations to estimate the line. These lines provide a visual indication of whether the closeness of elections changed over time, with a downward sloping line indicating that elections became more competitive.

I used two types of statistical tests to assess whether the patterns in a state reflect something other than a purely random process. First, to check whether the likelihood that a seat would be uncontested changed over time, I split the period approximately in half: before 1980 and 1980 or later; for several states I used a different split to reflect a switch from partisan to nonpartisan elections that occurred within a few years of 1980. Using the time split, I computed a simple difference of proportions test. Second, for states where the lowess line suggested a change in the competitiveness of elections over time, I estimated either a simple linear regression or a quadratic regression to check whether the pattern was nonrandom. I make reference to these tests, most of which are reported in one of the tables, as appropriate in the discussion below.

## Results

Given the findings of my previous work that the bulk of change in contestation and competitiveness is to be found in partisan elections in southern states, I start by looking at the eight southern states that either continue to use partisan elections or did so up through at least 1990; the only other southern state using elections is Florida and that state shifted from partisan to nonpartisan elections in

1971 and then to retention elections in 1977.[4] I then look sequentially at (1) nonsouthern states currently using partisan or hybrid elections, (2) nonsouthern states currently using nonpartisan elections, and (3) all states currently using only retention elections. I conclude the analysis by comparing patterns for the separate courts of last resort for criminal and noncriminal matters in Oklahoma and Texas.

## *Southern States*

The columns on the left side of Table 3.1 show the percentage of elections contested in each state for two periods. The default division for the periods is 1946–1979 and 1980–2015. For states that switched to nonpartisan elections after 2000, the later period ends with the last year that partisan elections were used; for states that switched to nonpartisan elections prior to 2000, Period 1 consists of the years since 1946 when partisan elections were used and Period 2 consists of the years when nonpartisan elections were used. The table also shows a difference of proportions test of whether the likelihood of an election changed between the two periods. The numbers at the bottom of each state's part of Figure 3.1 indicate the annual number of uncontested elections for the state.

Consistent with my previous analyses, there are many uncontested elections, particularly through the 1980s. In the early period, much of the contestation that did occur was in primary elections. Contested elections were least likely in Georgia where only eight of 61 elections (13%) prior to 1984, at which time Georgia started using nonpartisan elections, were contested (all in the Democratic Party primary). Since Georgia changed to nonpartisan elections, nine of 32 elections (24%) have been contested, although the difference is not statistically significant ($p = 0.155$).[5] Mississippi, which shifted to nonpartisan elections starting in 1994, provides a striking contrast; there uncontested elections all but disappeared after the state shifted to nonpartisan elections starting in 1994—only three of 23 (13%) compared to 51 of 69 (74%) before the change ($p < 0.001$). In three of the southern states—Alabama, North Carolina, and Texas—uncontested elections had largely disappeared by some time in the 1980s, although there were three such elections in Alabama in 2012.[6] In Arkansas, uncontested elections did not occur for about fifteen years, between 1980 and 1994, but then reappeared and have continued since the state switched to nonpartisan elections. However, doing a simple comparison splitting at 1980 for either the entire period or just for the years when Arkansas used partisan elections does not show a statistically significant change. Importantly, in recent years, a significant proportion of the contested elections in these states occurred either in primaries or in general elections with only one major candidate who faced opposition from one or more minor-party candidates.

The eight states varied with regard to whether the competitiveness of contested elections changed over time (regression results are shown in the right side of Table 3.1). There were clear trends of increased competitiveness in Alabama

**TABLE 3.1** Contestation in Southern States, 1946–2015

| | *Percent Uncontested* | | | *Regression* | |
|---|---|---|---|---|---|
| *State* | *1946–1979* | *1980–2015* | *Z* (*p-value*) | *b [× (year)]* *b [× (year²)]* | $r^2$ *or* $R^2$ (*p-value*) |
| Alabama | 73% (48) | 24% (54) | 4.93 (p < 0.001) | -0.148 | 0.074 (p = 0.047) |
| Arkansas[a] | 50% (36) | 38% (21) | 0.87 (p = 0.384) | 0.146 | 0.099 (p = 0.096) |
| Georgia[b] | 87% (61) | 76% (37) | 1.42 (p = 0.155) | too few cases | |
| Louisiana | 64% (25) | 41% (29) | 1.66 (p = 0.097) | -0.010 | 0.001 (p = 0.906) |
| Mississippi[c] | 74% (69) | 13% (23) | 5.13 (p = 0.001) | 0.106 | 0.019 (p = 0.611) |
| North Carolina[d] | 56% (45) | 29% (31) | 2.29 (p = 0.022) | -0.334 | 0.377 (p < 0.001) |
| Tennessee[e] | 57% (28) | 58% (12) | -0.07 (p = 0.944) | -0.300 | 0.083 (p = 0.262) |
| Texas | 50% (82) | 5% (122) | 7.50 (p < 0.001) | -0.495 0.008 | 0.071 (p = 0.003) |
| Supreme Court | 54% (57) | 5% (66) | 6.16 (p < .001) | -0.009 | p 0.001 (p = 0.880) |
| Criminal Appeals | 40% (25) | 5% (56) | 3.92 (p < 0.001) | -0.595 0.010 | 0.133 (p = 0.010) |

Counts are shown in parentheses under percentages.

[a] Later period for Arkansas ends in 2000, after which Arkansas switched to nonpartisan elections; regression only for partisan elections.

[b] Split for Georgia is 1983, after which Georgia switched to nonpartisan elections; too few observations for regression analysis.

[c] Split for Mississippi is 1993, after which Mississippi switched to nonpartisan elections; regression only for partisan elections.

[d] Later period for North Carolina ends in 2002, after which North Carolina switched to nonpartisan elections; regressions only for partisan elections.

[e] Later period for Tennessee ends in 1992, after which Tennessee switched to retention elections.

and North Carolina, although the pattern for the latter state since its switch to nonpartisan elections is unclear; linear slopes for both of these states differed significantly from 0. The pattern in North Carolina is the most striking, with the two-candidate percentage for the winner decreasing by about a one-third percentage each year between 1946 and 2002, the years during which the state was using partisan elections. The amount of change in Alabama was about one-sixth of a percentage point per year. There were too few contested elections in Georgia to draw conclusions about changing competitiveness. In Arkansas, there may have

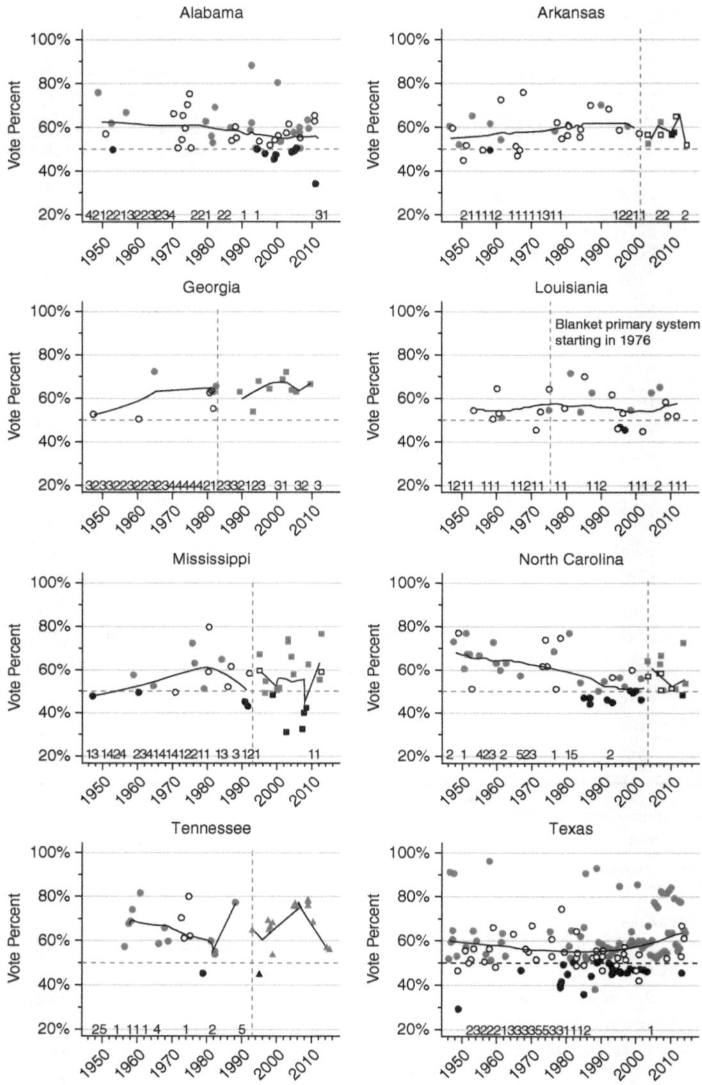


**FIGURE 3.1** Percent Winning Vote in Southern States

been a slight decline in competitiveness prior to the mid-1990s; looking only at the years prior to the change to nonpartisan elections, the winner's two-candidate percentage increased by about one-sixth of a percentage point per year (two-tailed $p = 0.096$). In Mississippi, there was a decline followed by an increase in the 1980s but there is no discernible pattern in the years since that state's switch to nonpartisan elections; however, the apparent pre-change decline could readily be explained as random variation. Texas saw an increase in competitiveness through the 1980s, but this then declined; the decline reflected in significant part Republican candidates who faced only minor party challengers after having been unopposed in the Republican primary. Fitting a linear model to the Texas data shows no significant change, but a quadratic model is statistically significant ($p = 0.003$).

This analysis confirms that there is a broad pattern of change in southern states. However, it also shows that the nature of the change varied substantially among those states. It also shows that in at least one state, Georgia, there has been relatively little change, even after that state switched to nonpartisan elections.

## *Partisan Elections in Nonsouthern States*

One issue that arises in comparing judicial elections is whether hybrid elections—those where parties nominate candidates but the general election ballot is nonpartisan—should be grouped with partisan election states or nonpartisan election states (Nelson, Caulfield, and Martin 2013). Here I group the two states currently using hybrid elections—Michigan and Ohio—with the nonsouthern states using partisan elections. I do this for two reasons. First, the involvement of the political parties in these two competitive states means that elections do not go uncontested, which is not true in fully nonpartisan states. Second, as an empirical matter, the patterns of competition in the hybrid states are essentially indistinguishable from those in the four partisan election states and again are very different from the pattern in nonsouthern states using nonpartisan elections. Hence, Figure 3.2 shows the patterns for four nonsouthern partisan election states plus the two hybrid election states. All but one of the partisan election states—West Virginia—shown in the figure combine partisan elections for an initial term with retention elections for subsequent terms. I do not show a table of statistics for the partisan election states because there is too little change to warrant reporting.

In the six states shown in the figure, very few elections go uncontested, and that does not change over time. This is not surprising given the role of the parties in selecting candidates and the fact that all of the states have a history of vibrant two-party systems unlike the southern states using partisan elections. The lowess lines do suggest some change in competitiveness in four of the states, although the nature of the change is not consistent. In three states—Illinois, West Virginia, and Michigan—the elections appear to have become slightly more competitive; however, only for West Virginia is the trend statistically significant (two-tailed $p = 0.052$, slope = -0.089). In contrast, in Pennsylvania, the partisan elections have become slightly *less* competitive (two-tailed $p = 0.002$, slope = +0.104). It is difficult to see any consistent change in either New Mexico or Ohio. While I will consider most of the retention states below (shown as triangles in the figure with separate lowess lines), I note here that retention elections in Illinois (slope = -0.204) and New Mexico (slope = +0.157) move in opposite directions, with the

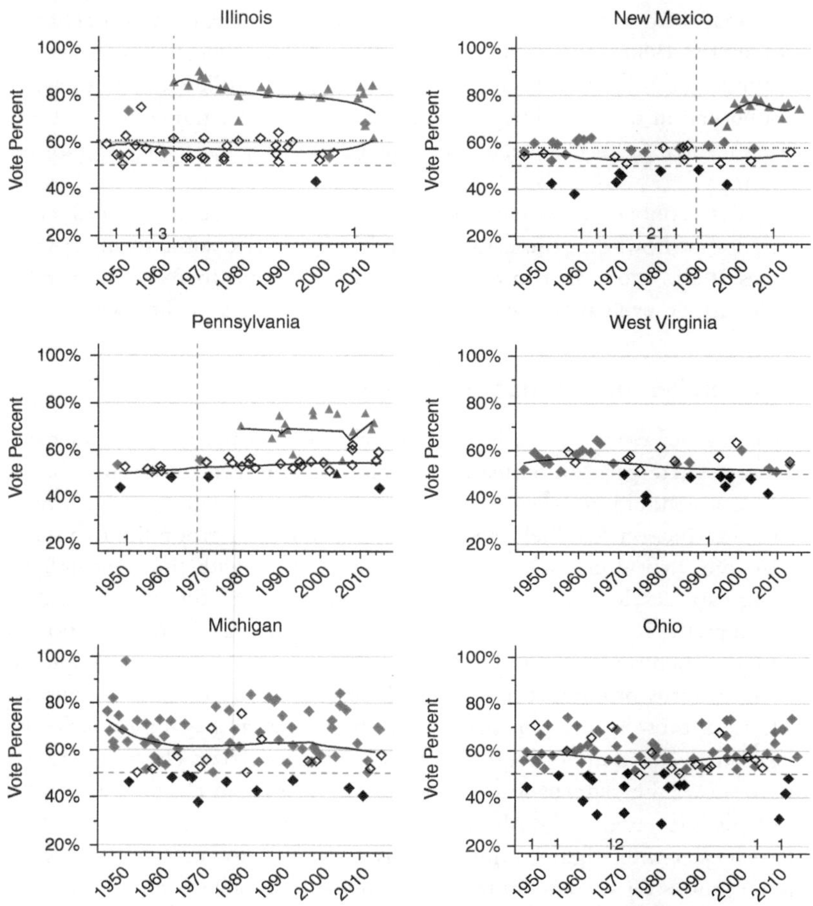


**FIGURE 3.2** Percent Winning Vote in Nonsouthern Partisan and Hybrid States

percentage voting to retain (the "yes-vote") declining in Illinois but increasing in New Mexico; however, only for Illinois can we conclude that the trend does not represent random variation ($p = 0.013$). There is no clear pattern in Pennsylvania.

Overall, there has been relatively little change in contestation and competition in these six states. Moreover, the small changes that have occurred are inconsistent.

## *Nonpartisan Elections in Nonsouthern States*

Figure 3.3 shows the eight nonsouthern states that use nonpartisan elections; Table 3.2 shows relevant statistics for those states. Seven of the states used nonpartisan elections over the entire period, although Montana adopted a variation in 1974 whereby uncontested elections involving incumbents become retention

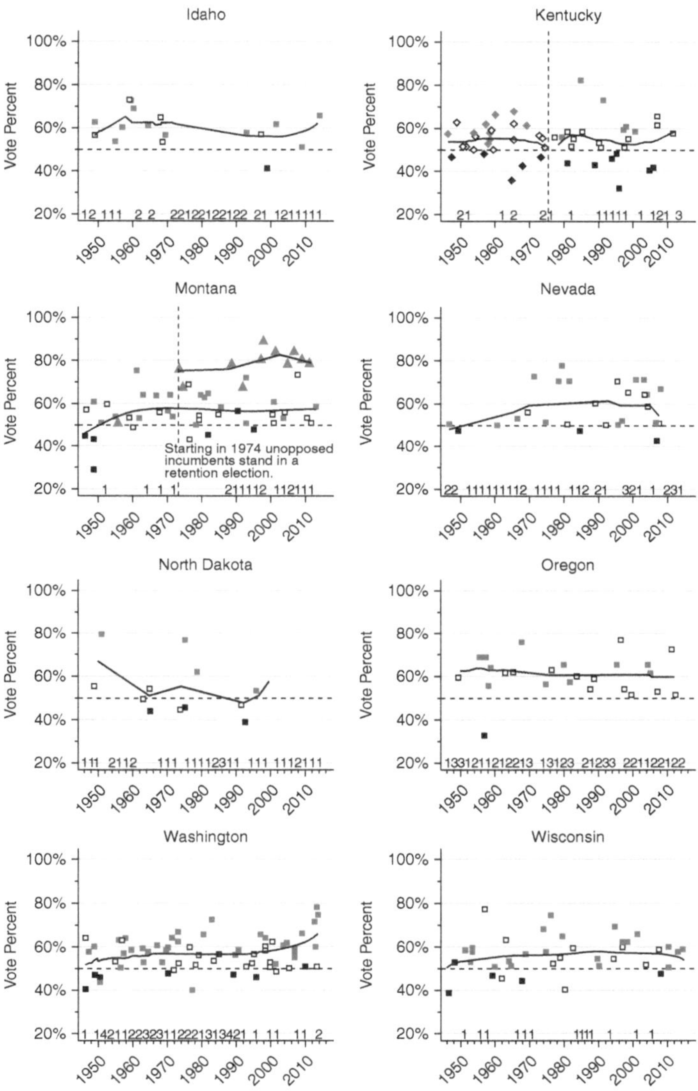


**FIGURE 3.3** Percent Winning Vote in Nonsouthern Nonpartisan States

elections. Among these states, only Kentucky switched from partisan to nonpartisan elections in the years since 1946.[7] The figure should make it immediately clear why I grouped the hybrid election states with the partisan election states: all of the states shown in this figure have many more uncontested elections than either of the hybrid election states. In four of the states—Idaho, Montana, North Dakota, and Wisconsin—that have used nonpartisan elections throughout the

**TABLE 3.2** Contestation in Nonpartisan Election States, 1946–2015

| | *Percent Uncontested* | | | *Regression* | | |
|---|---|---|---|---|---|---|
| *State* | *1946–1979* | *1980–2015* | *Z (p-value)* | *b* | *$r^2$ or $R^2$ (p-value)* | *n* |
| Idaho | 61% (28) | 77% (30) | -1.31 (p = 0.189) | -0.111 | 0.106 (p = 0.188) | 18 |
| Kentucky[a] | 24% (33) | 35% (43) | -1.00 (p = 0.317) | -0.010 | <0.001 (p = 0.869) | 53 |
| Partisan | | | | -0.039 | 0.002 (p = 0.823) | 26 |
| Nonpartisan | | | | -0.097 | 0.009 (p = 0.632) | 27 |
| Montana | 17% (30) | 39% (38) | -2.05 (p = 0.404) | 0.120 | 0.073 (p = 0.063) | 48 |
| Retention | | | | 0.176 | 0.153 (p = 0.149) | 15 |
| Nevada | 67% (27) | 50% (40) | 1.35 (p = 0.177) | 0.108 | 0.040 (p = 0.309) | 28 |
| North Dakota | 61% (23) | 83% (24) | -1.72 (p = 0.085) | -0.235 | 0.101 (p = 0.289) | 12 |
| Oregon | 70% (40) | 67% (46) | 0.26 (p = 0.795) | -0.061 | 0.026 (p = 0.443) | 25 |
| Washington | 49% (61) | 37% (60) | 1.39 (p = 0.164) | 0.086 | 0.060 (p = 0.042) | 69 |
| Wisconsin | 21% (29) | 31% (25) | -0.95 (p = 0.344) | 0.060 | 0.023 (p = 0.348) | 40 |

Counts are shown in parentheses under percentages.

[a] Split for Kentucky is 1975, after which Kentucky switched to nonpartisan elections.

period, the frequency of uncontested elections has actually increased, although only in Montana is the increase statistically significant (17% to 39%, p = 0.040) using 1980 as the split point. Kentucky has also experienced an increase in the proportion of elections that go uncontested in the years since it switched from partisan to nonpartisan elections (26% uncontested before, 33% after), although the change is not distinguishable from purely random variation (p = 0.517). In contrast, in Washington, the frequency of uncontested elections appears to have decreased, but the change was not statistically significant (p = 0.164). In the other two states, Nevada and Oregon, there were actually small decreases in the percentage of elections that were uncontested comparing before 1980 to 1980 or later, but neither decrease was statistically distinguishable from no change. It should not be surprising that looking in the aggregate at the seven states that have used nonpartisan elections throughout the period comparing the earlier and latter periods, the likelihood of an election going uncontested has, if anything, increased—50 percent uncontested early versus 53 percent late—although the small change is not statistically significant ($p = 0.464$).

Looking at Figure 3.3, it might be tempting to say that contested elections in one state (Oregon) became more competitive over time, in four states (Montana,[8] Nevada, Washington, and Wisconsin) they became less competitive, and in the remaining three it is difficult to discern any clear trend. Fitting linear and quadratic models (shown in the right portion of Table 3.2) produced only two results that are even marginally statistically significant, both in states where elections became *less* competitive (Montana, $p = 0.063$; Washington, $p = 0.042$). Regarding the retention elections held in Montana when an incumbent was unopposed, there may be a slight trend toward an increase in the "yes" vote, but the slope does not differ significantly from zero ($p = 0.149$).

As with the nonsouthern states using partisan and hybrid elections, there has been relatively little change in contestation and competition in the nonsouthern states using nonpartisan elections. Again, the small changes that have occurred are inconsistent.

## *Retention-Type Election States*

I turn now to the fifteen states that exclusively use retention elections. Research on retention elections, both those that covered elections for all levels of courts (Aspin 2011) and those that focused specifically on state supreme courts (Kritzer

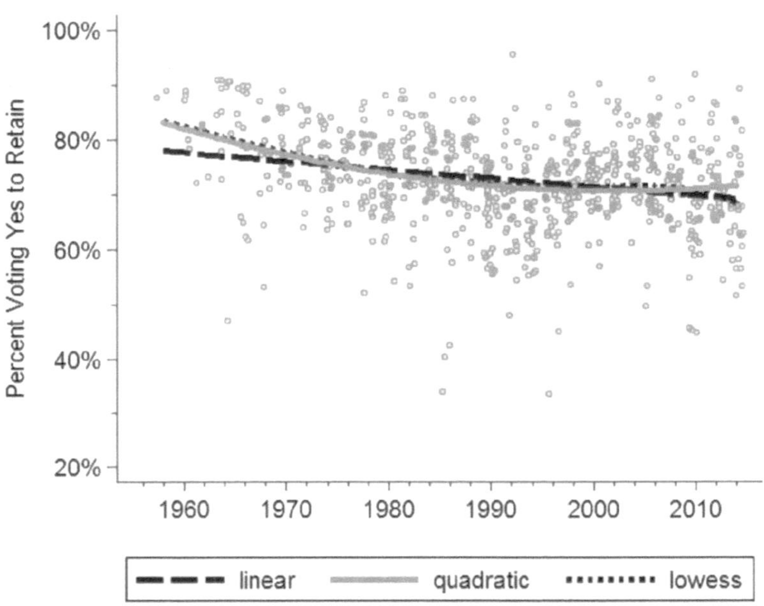


**FIGURE 3.4** Percent Vote to Retain in All Retention Elections, 1958–2014

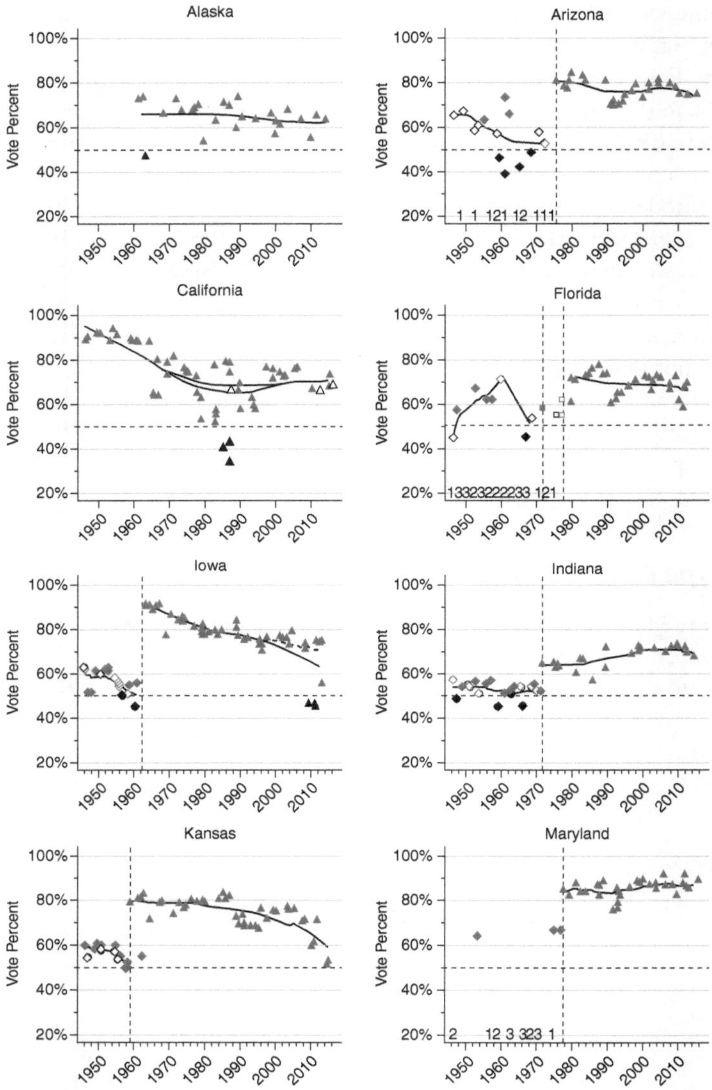


**FIGURE 3.5** Percent Vote to Retain by State

2015), has shown evidence of some drop-off over time in the percentage of votes cast in favor of retention (yes-votes). At one time a large proportion of incumbents received positive votes of 70 percent or more; positive votes of 80 percent or more were not uncommon. Figure 3.4 plots together the yes-no vote percentage for all state supreme court retention elections between 1958 and 2015; I limit the figure to this period because prior to 1958, only California and Missouri

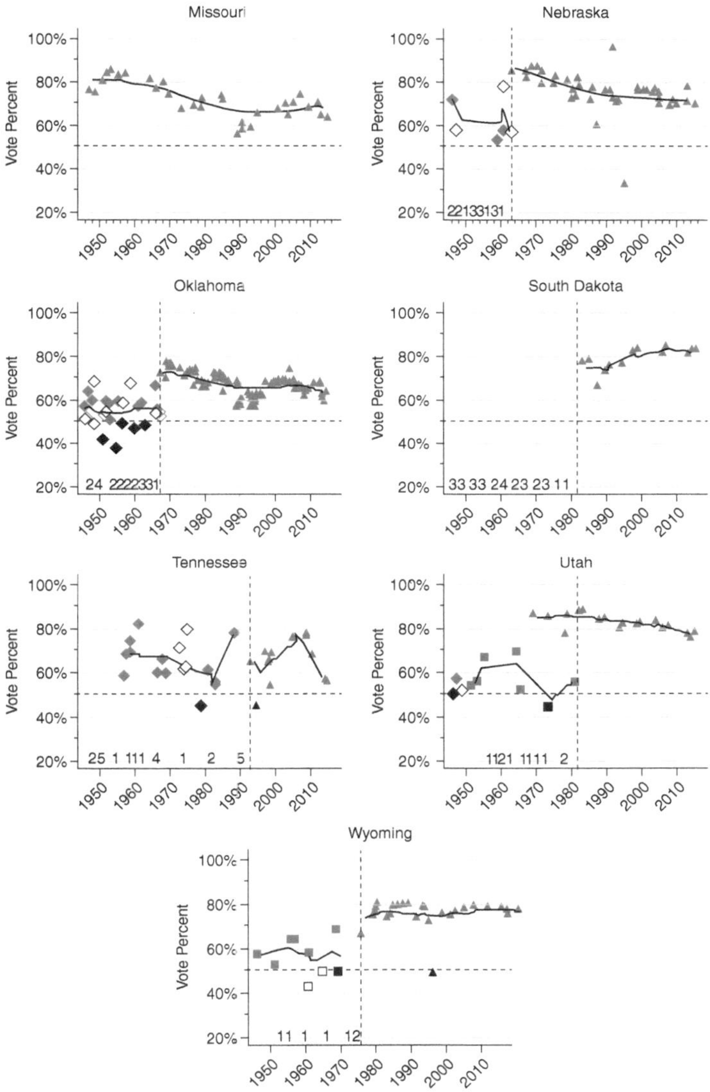


**FIGURE 3.5** *(Cont.)*

employed retention elections. The figure includes a straight-line fit, a lowess fit, and a quadratic fit. It shows clearly that there has been a drop-off in the yes-vote percentage, although the rate of decline flattened out around 1985; since then, the overall decline has been relatively minimal.

Figure 3.5 shows the percentage of yes-votes by state. These figures go back to 1946, showing patterns for partisan, nonpartisan, and hybrid elections used prior to the adoption of retention elections.[9] However, I limit my discussion to the pattern for the retention elections.

Unlike Figures 3.2 and 3.3, Figure 3.5 shows substantial change for many of the states. For California and Iowa, I have also included a dashed lowess line omitting the sets of three electoral defeats that occurred in each of those states: 1986 in California and 2010 in Iowa. The dominant pattern across a majority of states is a trend of a decline in the percentage voting in favor of retention (or confirmation in the case of the three California nominees). However, there is also substantial variation, in whether there is a trend, the direction of the trend, and the strength of the trend.

Table 3.3 shows the results of the simple linear regressions using a year counter (set at zero for 1946) as the predictor of the percentage voting yes. As the table shows, nine of the fifteen states have statistically significant downward trends; two additional states show downward trends that do not achieve statistical significance at the 0.05, two-tailed level although for one of those states, the trend would be statistically significant under a one-tailed test. Four states show positive trends, two of which (Indiana and Maryland) are statistically significant. Omitting the 1986 electoral defeats in California and the 2010 electoral defeats in Iowa reduces the slope for both states but increases the quality of the fit, particularly for Iowa.

Several of the lowess lines suggest that some of the trends may be nonlinear. For example, for California, the trend leveled out or possibly shifted to the positive

**TABLE 3.3** Trend Estimates for Percent Voting "Yes" to Retain

| *State* | *Slope* | *t* | *p-value (2-tailed)* | $r^2$ | *n* |
|---|---|---|---|---|---|
| Alaska | -0.102 | -1.26 | 0.219 | 0.062 | 26 |
| Arizona | -0.105 | -1.84 | 0.075 | 0.102 | 32 |
| California | -0.371 | -5.09 | <0.001 | 0.292 | 65 |
| California w/o 3 losers | -0.345 | -5.90 | <0.001 | 0.367 | 62 |
| Florida | -0.127 | -2.13 | 0.039 | 0.102 | 42 |
| Iowa | -0.496 | -10.06 | <0.001 | 0.620 | 64 |
| Iowa w/o 3 losers | -0.383 | -12.51 | <0.001 | 0.726 | 61 |
| Indiana | +0.213 | +4.65 | <0.001 | 0.484 | 25 |
| Kansas | -0.306 | -7.66 | <0.001 | 0.492 | 62 |
| Maryland | +0.127 | +2.20 | 0.036 | 0.138 | 32 |
| Missouri | -0.291 | -8.08 | <0.001 | 0.586 | 48 |
| Nebraska | -0.282 | -3.89 | <0.001 | 0.236 | 51 |
| Oklahoma | -0.147 | -4.70 | <0.001 | 0.163 | 115 |
| Supreme Court | -0.182 | -6.08 | <0.001 | 0.319 | 81 |
| Criminal Appeals | -0.044 | -0.58 | 0.568 | 0.010 | 34 |
| South Dakota | +0.333 | +4.32 | <0.001 | 0.508 | 20 |
| Tennessee | +0.135 | +0.37 | 0.719 | 0.010 | 16 |
| Utah | -0.194 | -4.66 | <0.001 | 0.509 | 23 |
| Wyoming | +0.047 | +0.52 | 0.606 | 0.009 | 31 |

direction in the late 1980s. To test for nonlinearity, I estimated quadratic models to the states where the lowess line suggested nonlinearity. The quadratic model produced improved fits for California (both with and without the 1986 defeats), Kansas, Missouri, and Oklahoma. The improvement was particularly striking for California, where the $R^2$ omitting the three justices defeated in 1986 went from 0.367 to 0.569 (from 0.292 to 0.508 including those justices). A quadratic model fit to the trend in Tennessee also produced a statistically significant fit ($p = 0.003$, $R^2 = 0.585$).

Clearly there is a general trend toward a declining percentage of voters casting ballots in favor of retention. That trend does not arise from the small number of elections where justices were not retained, nor can it be attributed to negative campaigns waged against justices in retention states because few elections have involved such campaigns. For example, whereas the defeats of justices in California in 1986 and in Iowa in 2010 in part reflected long-term trends of declining support for retention, similar trends were evident in states where there had been no nonretentions or only a single nonretention. With this said, it is important to note that the trend toward declining support for retention is by no means universal. In several states, Indiana most notably, there was a clear trend of increasingly positive votes.

## *Does the Kind of Court Matter?*

Oklahoma and Texas provide the opportunity to assess whether the types of cases a court deals with might have impacted changes in judicial elections vis-à-vis contestation and competitiveness. Figure 3.6 shows separate plots for each state's two courts of last resort, including the indication of uncontested elections for the entire period in Texas and prior to the switch to retention elections in Oklahoma. Statistics for the separate courts can be found in Tables 3.1 and 3.3. Interestingly, in both states, uncontested elections were less common in elections for their courts of criminal appeals (CCA) than in elections for the two supreme courts (SC). In Texas prior to 1980, 40 percent of CCA elections were not contested, compared to 54 percent of SC elections, although this difference can be attributed to random variation ($p = 0.230$). The corresponding figures for Oklahoma are 27 percent (CCA) and 49 percent (SC), but again a hypothesis of random variation cannot be rejected ($p = 0.210$). In Texas in 1980 and later, only 5 percent of elections for either court were uncontested; for neither court could the change be attributed to chance ($p < 0.001$ for both).

Turning to the competitiveness of the contested elections, the line for the Texas Supreme Court is effectively flat; neither the linear nor the quadratic model indicates systematic change. In contrast, there is clearly a parabolic trend for the Texas Court of Criminal Appeals; the test of a quadratic model is statistically significant ($p = 0.010$), although the overall fit is not particularly strong ($R^2 = 0.133$). Looking at the retention elections for the Oklahoma Supreme Court, there is a clear trend of a decreasing percentage of votes in favor of retention ($p < 0.001$, $r^2 = 0.319$); a quadratic model fits better ($p < 0.001$, $R^2 = 0.414$), presumably because it captures the

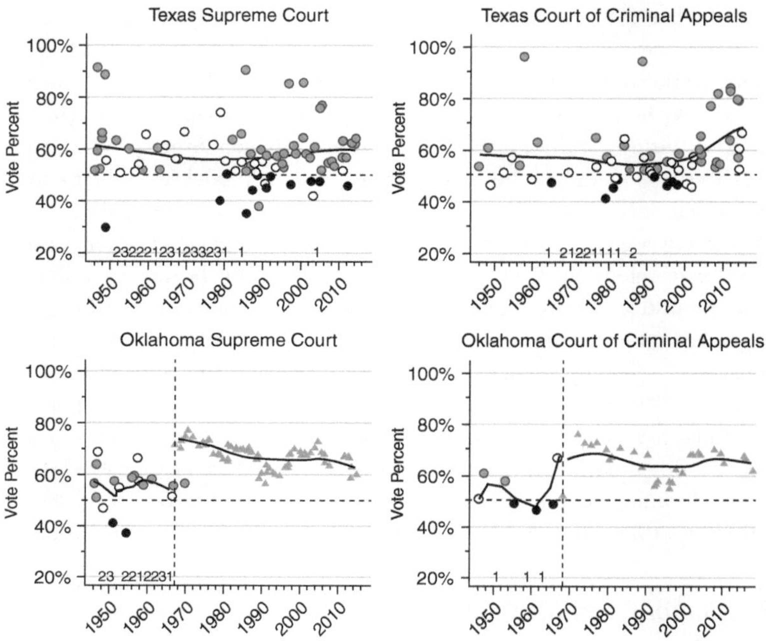


**FIGURE 3.6** Percent Winning Vote in the Texas and Oklahoma Supreme Courts and Criminal Appeals Courts

dip in the yes-vote percentages around 1990. Whereas the figure for the Oklahoma Court of Appeals might suggest a quadratic trend, fitting a quadratic model does not produce evidence of a statistically significant trend ($p = 0.245$).

Clearly the trends in voting patterns differ in Texas and Oklahoma depending on whether one looks at the state supreme court or the final appeals court for criminal matters. However, the two states differ in the trends that occurred. A trend is evident for the Court of Criminal Appeals in Texas but not for the Texas Supreme Court. In contrast, in Oklahoma there is no trend for the Court of Criminal Appeals but a clear trend for the Oklahoma Supreme Court. It is unclear what might account for the differences between the two states. It might reflect differences in how the citizens of the two states view their two courts of last resort. Or, it might reflect the use of partisan elections in Texas, which for most of the period examined was dominated by one party—albeit different parties in the earlier and later years. In contrast, Oklahoma switched to retention elections in the 1960s. Or, the differences between the two states might reflect something altogether different.

## Conclusion

Overall the analyses presented in this chapter are consistent with what I reported in my earlier work. However, by looking at the states separately, it becomes even more evident that one must be cautious in making broad claims about whether, and if so, in what ways, contestation and competitiveness have changed in state supreme court elections. Several contrasts demonstrate this clearly and raise interesting questions as to why the differences exist. For example, why did contestation change little in Georgia when it switched to nonpartisan elections, whereas there was a clear increase in Mississippi after it switched election type? Why has the percentage voting in favor of retention in Indiana increased when many states show a clear pattern of declining support for retention? Why have partisan elections in Pennsylvania become less competitive whereas in other nonsouthern states using partisan or hybrid elections there has been, if anything, a slight increase in competitiveness? Why has the frequency of uncontested elections increased in some nonsouthern states using nonpartisan elections while decreasing in others? These differences pose interesting questions for scholars of state politics.

The most important lesson to be taken from the state-by-state analysis presented in this chapter is that the claims of increasing contestation and competition in state supreme court elections have clearly been overstated. This does not mean that there have not been other changes in those elections—increased spending by both candidates and outside groups, a growing volume of television advertising in the supreme court elections with such advertising—but it does mean that those other changes cannot be explained by broad patterns of increased contestation and competition, nor is there a broad pattern of increased contestation and competition to be explained by factors such as spending and advertising.

The issue of spending and advertising has been the target of substantial criticism as represented by the series of reports produced by Justice at Stake and the Brennan Center for Justice at New York University (Goldberg, Holman, and Sanchez 2001; Goldberg et al. 2005; Sample, Jones, and Weiss 2007; Sample et al. 2010; Skaggs et al. 2011; Greytak et al. 2015). The implication of these reports is that spending and advertising have led to significant change in contestation and competitiveness of state supreme court elections. However, the analysis presented in this chapter raises questions about whether there has been as much change in this regard as implied by the Justice at Stake/Brennan Center reports, and whether—to the degree there has been change in contestation and competitiveness—that change could have been a result of increased spending and advertising. In fact, a stronger argument might be made that any change that has occurred in spending and advertising is a response to increased contestation and competitiveness rather than the causal direction going the other way. Moreover, it is likely that all of the changes—spending, advertising, contestation, and competitiveness—reflect the broader changes in American politics in terms of increased polarization and the nature of political campaigning.

## Notes

1 Oklahoma and Texas each have two courts of last resort, one for criminal matters and one for noncriminal matters; the former is called the Court of Criminal Appeals and

the latter the Supreme Court. Both courts in Oklahoma and Texas are included in my analysis. The court of last resort in New York is called the Court of Appeals; the supreme court in that state is a trial-level and intermediate appellate court. However, because New York ended elections for the Court of Appeals in the 1970s; I have omitted New York from the analysis presented in this chapter.

2 One of the states formerly using partisan elections is New York.
3 A lowess line uses a method of line fitting that allows for nonlinearity.
4 Between 1946 and 1970 only eight of 34 Florida Supreme Court elections were contested. In the other two southern states, Virginia and South Carolina, the legislature selects justices of the state supreme court.
5 Ignoring the change in election format and splitting at 1980 rather than 1984, there is a significant decrease in Georgia, from 94 percent uncontested to 69 percent uncontested ($p = 0.001$).
6 The tests of change for these three states are all statistically significant.
7 Two other states, Utah and Florida, switched from partisan to nonpartisan elections after 1946, but both subsequently switched to retention elections; they are included in the figure for retention elections.
8 There is no apparent trend in the percent voting in favor of retention in the Montana elections that defaulted for retention elections because the incumbent was unopposed.
9 The only state that used hybrid elections prior to switching to retention elections was Arizona.

## References


Aspin, Larry. 2011. "The 2010 Judicial Retention Elections in Perspective: Continuity and Change from 1964 to 2010." *Judicature* 94: 218–232.

Cleveland, William S. 1979. "Robust Locally-weighted Regression and Smoothing Scatterplots." *Journal of the American Statistical Association* 74: 829–836.

Goldberg, Deborah, Craig Holman, and Samantha Sanchez. 2001. *The New Politics of Judicial Elections: How 2000 Was a Watershed Year for Big Money, Special Interest Pressure, and TV Advertising in State Supreme Court Campaigns*. New York: Brennan Center for Justice.

Goldberg, Deborah, Sarah Samis, Edwin Bender, and Rachel Weiss. 2005. *The New Politics of Judicial Elections 2004: How Special Interest Pressure on Our Courts Has Reached a "Tipping Point" – and How to Keep Our Courts Fair and Impartial*. New York: Brennan Center for Justice.

Greytak, Scott, Alicia Bannon, Allyse Falce, and Linda Casey. 2015. *Bankrolling the Bench: The New Politics of Judicial Elections 2013–14*. New York: Brennan Center for Justice.

Hall, Melinda Gann. 2001. "State Supreme Courts in American Democracy: Probing the Myths of Judicial Reform." *American Political Science Review* 95: 315–330.

Kang, Michael S. and Joanna M. Shepherd. 2011. "The Partisan Price of Justice: An Empirical Analysis of Campaign Contributions and Judicial Decisions." *New York University Law Review* 86: 69–130.

Kang, Michael S. and Joanna M. Shepherd. 2015. "Partisanship in State Supreme Courts: The Empirical Relationship between Party Campaign Contributions and Judicial Decision Making." *Journal of Legal Studies* 44: 161–185.

Kritzer, Herbert M. 2011. "Competitiveness in State Supreme Court Elections, 1946–2009." *Journal of Empirical Legal Studies* 8: 237–259.

Kritzer, Herbert M. 2015. *Justices on the Ballot: Continuity and Change in State Supreme Court Elections*. New York: Cambridge University Press.

Nelson, Michael J., Rachel Paine Caulfield, and Andrew D. Martin. 2013. "OH, MI: A Note on Empirical Examinations of Judicial Elections." *State Politics and Policy Quarterly* 13: 495–511.

Sample, James, Lauren Jones, and Rachel Weiss. 2007. *The New Politics of Judicial Elections 2006: How 2006 Was the Most Threatening Year Yet to the Fairness and Impartiality of Our Courts – and How Americans Are Fighting Back*. New York: Brennan Center for Justice.

Sample, James, Adam Skaggs, Jonathan Blitzer, and Linda Casey. 2010. *The New Politics of Judicial Elections 2000–2009: Decade of Change*. New York: Brennan Center for Justice.

Shepherd, Joanna and Michel S. Kang. 2014. "Skewed Justice: *Citizens United*, Television Advertising and State Supreme Court Justices' Decision in Criminal Cases." Available at: http://skewedjustice.org/. Retrieved July 25, 2015.

Skaggs, Adam, Maria da Silva, Linda Casey, and Charles Hall. 2011. *The New Politics of Judicial Elections, 2009–10*. New York: Brennan Center for Justice.

# 4

# CAMPAIGNING FOR THE HIGH COURT BENCH

*Melinda Gann Hall and Matthew J. Zalewski*

In the 2012 Michigan Supreme Court races, the Judicial Crisis Network ran a televised advertisement featuring the mother of a soldier killed in Afghanistan, who found one of the candidates to be particularly troubling:

> When I heard Bridget McCormack volunteered to represent and help free suspected terrorists, I couldn't believe it. My son's a hero and fought to protect us. Bridget McCormack volunteered to help free a terrorist. How could you?[1]

Although Bridget McCormack ultimately prevailed in her bid for a seat on the Michigan Supreme Court, the content and tone of this advertisement epitomize criticisms that "judicial elections stink" (Geyh 2003) and have become "noisier, nastier, and costlier" (Schotland 1985). This spot is an excellent example of a "new style" judicial campaign that embraces televised advertising, significant expenditures, and sharp criticisms of candidates (Hojnacki and Baum 1992).

Although modern state supreme court campaigns as a whole are substantially more positive than their presidential, congressional, and gubernatorial counterparts (Kritzer 2015), any level of negativity exacerbates the criticisms of judicial elections opponents who see state court legitimacy as being threatened by, among other things, the need to engage in policy talk about issues that may reach the court and to accept campaign funds from donors whose interests may be affected by future court rulings (Brandenburg and Schotland 2008; Geyh 2003). Indeed, Justice at Stake's 2013–14 *New Politics of Judicial Elections* report warns that state judicial "campaigns are overwhelmingly supported by wealthy interests, enabling a system that may disproportionately elevate the preferences of wealthy spenders" (Greytak et al. 2015, 3).

Yet, while acknowledging that the public generally finds campaign finance and negative campaigning to be unsettling in judicial elections as well as many of the most visible political offices, Gibson (2012) has shown that any adverse effects of electioneering on judicial legitimacy are outweighed by the public's positive reactions to judicial institutions staffed through democratic electoral processes and by individuals who, through the campaigning process, are required to engage in policy conversations with state electorates. In short, there is a substantial disjunction between some of the projected fears about campaign politics and empirical research.

Despite evidence of the positive contributions of elections generally and policy conversations specifically to judicial legitimacy, opponents of judicial elections maintain that campaigns limit the quality and quantity of information reaching prospective voters. In contrast to the multifaceted campaigns and heightened media attention associated with presidential, gubernatorial, and even certain congressional campaigns, judicial candidates' interactions with voters in many races are limited to a few fleeting campaign ads, if any at all. Reflecting on the consequences of low-information campaigns and the general public's lack of training in the law, the legal community often portrays the electorate as not only uninformed but even unqualified to select justices for the high court bench (Geyh 2003; Pozen 2008).[2] In such an environment, even modest amounts of information delivered in campaigns "cannot help but educate voters" (Iyengar 2002, 695). A classic example of this phenomenon is found in the 1986 California Supreme Court retention elections, during which conservative politicians and interest groups mounted a coordinated campaign attacking Chief Justice Rose Bird for her record on death penalty cases. Overall, the Chief Justice failed to uphold even a single verdict of death imposed by the trial courts during her tenure on the Court. The 1986 race culminated in the ousting of Chief Justice Bird and two of her colleagues from the bench—the first time multiple justices had been removed from the California Supreme Court in a single election (Caufield 2007). At the time, polls indicated that the attacks on Chief Justice Bird's death penalty jurisprudence resonated with voters (Caufield 2007).

In these races, the advertising environment included not only information about candidates' positions but also more general emotional appeals. Two excellent examples are an anti-Bird ad featuring the mother of a murder victim whose killer's death sentence was set aside, and a pro-Bird ad depicting a person holding a machine gun made of money aiming at the justices to illustrate the fear of the Court being swayed by special interests (Kritzer 2015). Accordingly, one could easily ask whether, if ads have any effect on voters at all, is it because of their educational value or because of their poignant emotional appeals delivered in negative tones.

With these and many other questions in mind, the goal of this chapter is to review the current state of scholarship on campaign advertising in judicial elections and provide a comprehensive description of state supreme court campaigns from 2002 through 2013. We begin with a brief discussion of historical trends in campaign advertising and a caution about leaping to the conclusion that advertising of any sort in these races is a modern phenomenon.

## On the Evolution of "New Style" Judicial Campaigns

Though Rose Bird's defeat thirty years ago is reflective of today's judicial campaigning environment, we do not know the extent to which campaign practices historically were rancorous or issue-based. Information about televised advertising was not gathered systematically for judicial elections before 2000 (M. Hall 2015), and we have virtually no information about radio ads, newspaper ads, or other forms of advertising during any period of American history.

A rare exception is Kermit Hall's (1984) study of state supreme court elections in California, Ohio, Tennessee, and Texas from 1850 through 1920. In this intriguing analysis, Kermit Hall (1984) shows that these races were commonly characterized by intense partisan competition, electoral defeats, and levels of voter participation that not only outpaced modern levels but in some cases even exceeded turnout in elections for other statewide offices, including gubernatorial elections. Moreover, these early campaigns could be bruising and were centered on controversial issues, including specific criticisms of the justices' rulings (K. Hall 2005). Ohio provides a particularly striking example of the historical competitiveness of state supreme court elections; between 1850 and 1920, 20 percent of Ohio's justices seeking reelection were ousted from office (K. Hall 2005). Although the four states discussed by Kermit Hall (2005) could be exceptional (we simply do not know), they nevertheless demonstrate that attacks and other forms of keen competition are hardly the novel product of modern communication technology or recent campaign finance behaviors.

Against this context of partisanship, vigorous competition, and incumbent defeat, reforms to partisan judicial elections were enacted, including nonpartisan elections, the Australian ballot, and direct primaries (K. Hall 1984). Perhaps the most notable consequence of these reforms was a precipitous decline in voter turnout. In Ohio, for example, voter turnout dropped by 20 percent between 1910 and 1920 after the adoption of the nonpartisan ballot (K. Hall 1984).

In the end, the reforms did not ensure the absence of money and aggressive advertising, as "big money" from interest groups and enhanced fundraising activity began entering judicial campaigns at least as early as the 1970s (Champagne 2002). Likewise, so many campaigns featured interest group involvement and issue-based campaigning through the 1980s that Hojnacki and Baum (1992) coined the phrase "new-style" campaigns to describe the trend.

Although aggressive, competitive, and well-financed judicial campaigns clearly are not 21st-century inventions, developments in the early 2000s exacerbated concerns about the potential entrenchment of "new-style" campaigning on a national scale. Perhaps the most substantial catalyst in escalating concerns, especially in the legal community, about hotly contested races was the U.S. Supreme Court's decision in *Republican Party of Minnesota v. White* (2002). This landmark ruling held that "announce clauses" in state judicial codes of conduct violated the First Amendment by prohibiting judicial candidates from discussing their issue positions with voters. The timing of this ruling coincided with an increase in interest group funding of state supreme court campaigns beginning in 2000, which facilitated the adoption of sophisticated campaign strategies designed to assess and characterize candidates' policies, values, and even personal conduct.

## Voter Responses to Campaign Advertising

Among advocates and opponents of judicial elections, both praise and condemnation are rooted in an underlying recognition, supported by empirical evidence, that voters can and do respond to campaign advertising under certain circumstances. Of particular concern is the potential impact of harsh negativity on voters, judges, and courts. In this debate, three key questions about the possible consequences of modern campaign politics have dominated empirical research: does caustic advertising (1) demobilize the electorate, (2) threaten the incumbency advantage, or (3) diminish judicial legitimacy.

### *Campaign Advertising and Voter Participation*

Conventional criticisms of negative advertising in campaigns for the nation's most visible offices emphasize the view that attack ads disgust and ultimately demobilize the electorate. This is precisely the position advanced by Ansolabehere and Iyengar's (1995) foundational study, which forwarded the position that the most significant factor explaining the decline in voter turnout in the United States is attack advertising. However, Geer's (2006) examination of presidential campaigns from 1960 through 2004 counters Ansolebehere and Iyengar's conclusions with evidence that negative advertising enriches the information environment and that campaign negativity does not demobilize the electorate. Scores of additional scholars, both before and after Geer (2006), have sought to find conclusive evidence about the effects of negative campaigning on voter participation and the underlying attitudes necessary to a healthy democracy. Despite over one hundred studies being published on the subject, meta-analyses conducted by Lau et al. (1999, 2007) point convincingly to the conclusion that, although Americans purport to dislike negativity, such ads have no discernible adverse effects on voters, institutions, or the political system generally.

Just as the totality of the scholarship in political science largely rejects the demobilization hypothesis in elections to the most visible offices in the United States, specific findings about state supreme courts point to some of the advantages of negativity. First, consistent with Geer's (2006) suggestion that negativity enriches the information environment, Melinda Gann Hall (2015) shows that the attack ads aired from 2002–2008 in state supreme court elections had much higher issue content than did positive promotions. Additionally, in stark contrast to Ansolabehere and Iyengar's (1995) demobilization hypothesis, Melinda Gann Hall (2015) found that during the 2002–2008 period, attack airings were associated with reduced ballot-rolloff in nonpartisan races, thus indicating a mobilizing effect in nonpartisan states. Finally, ads drawing contrasts between candidates, which include both positive and negative elements, increased voter participation in both nonpartisan and partisan elections (M. Hall 2015). Accordingly, far from being a threat to efficacy and informed campaign discourse, campaign negativity appears to have some positive effects in state supreme court elections.

Overall, recent studies (M. Hall 2014, 2015; M. Hall and Bonneau 2013) on televised campaign advertising in state supreme court elections are consistent in rejecting the demobilization hypothesis while pointing to the advantages of attack advertising for voter turnout in some circumstances. Likewise, all of these results comport well with a sizable body of empirical research on state supreme courts showing that rather than being alienated by aggressive campaigns, the electorate is mobilized to vote by a variety of factors that increase the salience of the races and improve the volume and quality of information available to voters (e.g., Baum and Klein 2007; Bonneau and M. Hall 2009; Dubois 1980; M. Hall 2007a; M. Hall and Bonneau 2008; Hojnacki and Baum 1992; Klein and Baum 2001). Partisan elections, hotly contested seats, and substantial spending mobilize rather than demobilize voters. These well-documented patterns are manifestly inconsistent with an alienated, disaffected electorate brought about by rough-and-tumble campaign politics.

## *Campaign Advertising and the Incumbency Advantage*

Even if negative campaigns are mobilizing—or at least, not demobilizing—a substantial concern about contemporary campaign politics is that politically motivated actors can launch attacks against sitting judges, thereby exploiting public outrage about isolated opinions in an effort to unseat political opponents and shift the ideological balance of the bench in the attacker's favor (Geyh 2003). An excellent example of this strategy is the 2006 Nevada Supreme Court election, in which challenger Nancy Saitta successfully unseated Chief Justice Nancy Becker. During this hotly contested race, then-Judge Saitta ran a series of television ads criticizing specific opinions signed by Chief Justice Becker, including a case portrayed as paving the way for a massive tax increase in direct contradiction of a voter-approved constitutional amendment.[3] Similarly, in the 2010 Iowa Supreme Court retention elections, voters chose to remove Chief Justice Marsha Ternus and two of her colleagues from the bench in the wake of a campaign waged by an interest group attacking the justices as activists who purportedly ignored the will of the voters by invalidating Iowa's ban on same-sex marriage.[4]

Thus, anecdotal evidence supports the conclusion that disparaging televised campaign messages can undermine the incumbency advantage in state supreme courts and, in some cases, shift the ideological balance of a court. However, recent empirical evidence discounts this simple interpretation. As more systematic analysis (M. Hall 2014, 2015) indicates, harsh attacks have deleterious consequences for justices seeking reelection only when partisan labels are removed from ballots. In partisan elections, incumbents are relatively immune to negativity because partisanship mitigates the impact of brief events like campaign ads. Instead, voters select candidates largely on the basis of their partisan affiliations. However, nonpartisan elections significantly reduce the information immediately available to voters by removing the most important heuristic in American elections, thus exposing incumbents to idiosyncratic forces such as disparaging attacks. Stated differently, nonpartisan judicial elections facilitate some of the most serious consequences of hard-fought campaigns by altering the basic rules of the electoral game.

### *Campaign Advertising and Judicial Legitimacy*

The issue of state judicial legitimacy is considered in detail in Chapter 11 of this volume. We merely observe that recent evidence (Gibson 2012) shows that citizens do not perceive electioneering by judicial candidates unfavorably to the detriment of judicial legitimacy. Instead, the practice of electing judges is a powerful legitimizing force that eclipses the adverse effects of campaigning, including any harm stemming from judges accepting campaign contributions from attorneys, law firms, and organized interests who later may have business before the courts.

## The Informational Value of Campaign Advertising

Given the range of information presented to the electorate in campaigns, specific advertisements have not only been classified by their positive, negative, or mixed tone but also as presenting appeals focused on traits, values, and/or issues. In state supreme court elections, positive promotions tend to emphasize the candidates' traits (M. Hall 2015). These ads allow candidates to introduce themselves and present their qualifications for office. Interestingly, it is not uncommon for these types of messages to feature humor or mnemonic devices intended to help voters remember the candidate at the polls. An example is a spot aired by Justice Menis Ketchum in the 2008 West Virginia Supreme Court race. This ad featured two lawyers repeatedly exchanging the words "mumbo jumbo," followed by Justice Ketchum appearing and announcing that he is "tired of the mumbo jumbo in the legal system." The ad then alternates between conveying Ketchum's credentials and repeating the "mumbo jumbo" mantra.[5]

Negative appeals have different goals. Sometimes these messages contain derogatory personal remarks, as they all portray in some way a particular candidate as lacking the requisite experience, judgment, or character for a seat on the state supreme court. However, these types of ads frequently deliver substantive information relevant for selecting among judicial candidates, particularly in nonpartisan elections (M. Hall 2014, 2015; M. Hall and Bonneau 2013).

Consistent with Campbell et al.'s (1960) classic theory that voters filter newly acquired information through the lens of their partisan identifications, voters who have information about a judicial candidate's partisanship will structure their choices using that information (e.g., Bonneau and Cann 2015; Dubois 1979; Klein and Baum 2001; Rock and Baum 2010). Thus, it is not surprising that supreme court campaign ads often include direct references to partisanship or callout behaviors that can readily be identified as consistent with a conservative or liberal ideology. A notable example occurred in the 2004 Alabama Republican primary, in which incumbent Jean Brown faced criticism from challenger Tom Parker for complying with a federal court order to replace a standalone Ten Commandments display in the state courthouse with a larger display that included secular historical documents. A pro-Parker ad asserted that Brown had "been endorsed by every liberal newspaper in Alabama" and "removed the Ten Commandments and insulted us with her politically correct ACLU approved display."[6]

Of course, appeals to partisanship or ideology may not be so overt, particularly in a nonpartisan context. However, it is precisely in nonpartisan elections where the power of informational cues can be especially strong, where voters will examine whatever information is available about candidates for clues about the candidates' partisan orientations. Even in retention elections, voters are likely to seek partisan cues by ascribing the partisanship of the appointing governor to the judge standing for retention (Squire and Smith 1988). More broadly, voters can discern a candidate's partisanship from issue-based campaign information signaling partisan affiliation (Bonneau and Cann 2015). For example, conservative candidates will often tout a propensity to be "tough on crime" while decrying liberal candidates as siding with "trial lawyers." Even candidates who do not directly affiliate with the corresponding ideological classification may make such appeals in an effort to attract voters who will be structuring their party-aligned votes based on a specific issue.

Regardless of one's view of the desirability of partisan-based voting in judicial elections, the consistency of the empirical evidence showing that voters process informational cues from campaigns counters conventional portrayals of the judicial voter as uninformed and uninterested. Likewise, in light of the evidence that negative advertising disproportionately features issue-based content (M. Hall 2015), extant scholarship also challenges criticisms that such messages primarily appeal to raw emotion and thus lack any educational value.

Aside from partisanship, campaign advertising can facilitate conversations about a candidate's fundamental fitness for the bench. In this regard, critics may have some cause for concern, as these types of ads sometimes use dramatic flair to blur the line between fact and fiction. Such may have been the case in the 2008 Michigan Supreme Court election where challenger Diane Hathaway and the Michigan Democratic State Central Committee repeatedly aired spots featuring a dramatic reenactment of a justice falling asleep on the bench while alleging that Chief Justice Clifford Taylor fell asleep "several times" during oral arguments on a case involving the death of six children.[7] Although these allegations were never proven conclusively, the "sleeping judge" ad is credited in the popular press and in the legal community with allowing Hathaway to overcome an early disadvantage and defeat the Chief Justice. However, it is more likely that any such effect was merely complementary to the broader context of the 2008 election in which Republicans were resoundingly defeated in the wake of the financial crisis and the high Democratic voter turnout inspired by the candidacy of Barack Obama (Klemanski and Walters 2011).

Finally, substantive ads, including blistering attacks, can address significant pressing concerns, including scandalous examples of professional ethics breeches or plain poor judgment on the part of sitting justices. A prime example is the 2008 Democratic primary race for the West Virginia Court of Appeals, in which challenger Bob Bastress ran ads detailing Justice Spike Maynard's vacation "on the Riviera" with "coal baron" Don Blankenship, after which Justice Maynard ruled in favor of Blankenship's company in a $50 million case.[8] Maynard ultimately lost the primary and his seat on the Court. Whereas this example may invoke fears of justices voting in favor of the interests of those who fund them, it also demonstrates the power of televised campaign advertising to promote public debate about the proper role of a state supreme court justice.

## Data Sources and Measurement of Key Variables

With these various points in mind, we now turn to a comprehensive description of televised campaign advertising in contested partisan and nonpartisan state supreme court elections from 2002 through 2013. We begin our analysis in 2002 because of the absence of systematic data on television advertising in state supreme court elections before this election cycle. The analysis ends in 2013 only because of limits on the availability of advertising data at the time of writing. Retention elections, which are part of the Missouri Plan, are excluded because of the complete absence of any televised advertising in these races from 2002 through 2008 and the rarity of such ads after 2008.

In our investigation, we draw on two primary data sources. First, we utilize information about state supreme court elections gathered and coded from various official government sources, including reports from secretaries of state and state election commissions. Included are both the Texas Supreme Court and the Texas Court of Criminal Appeals.

Second, for specific details about televised campaign advertising, we utilize a variety of sources, starting with the storyboards and streaming videos collected by the Campaign Media Analysis Group (CMAG). CMAG, a commercial firm, captures every state supreme court campaign advertisement aired in the nation's one hundred largest media markets. All of these storyboards and videos are posted on the webpage of the Brennan Center for Justice. For detailed information about the content, cost, and sponsorship of each ad, we rely on reports in the *New Politics of Judicial Elections* series, advertising data coded by researchers at the Brennan Center for Justice, and information posted on the TV Ad Archive of the New Politics of Judicial Elections web page.[9] All televised advertisements are included regardless of sponsor, including spots purchased by political parties and other organizations. To simplify the various presentations, the small numbers of elections in any odd year are merged with those in the prior year, consistent with standard practice (e.g., M. Hall 2015).

Regarding tone, the Brennan Center for Justice categorized each advertisement as "promotion of one candidate," "contrasting two or more candidates," or "attack on the opponent." Collectively, these categories are mutually exclusive and exhaustive. Promotions are positive in tone, attack ads are negative, and contrast ads are mixed. Importantly, incumbents, challengers, political parties, and outside groups can sponsor each type of advertisement. Thus, attack ads are not directed solely at incumbents. Incumbents launch vitriolic attacks against their challengers, just as political parties and outside groups attack both incumbents and challengers. Collectively, these data will provide an interesting portrait of state supreme court campaigns in the post-*White* era.[10]

## State Supreme Court Advertising by Seat

Judicial reform advocates (e.g., American Bar Association 2003; Brandenburg and Schotland 2008; Geyh 2003; National Center for State Courts 2002; Sample et al. 2010) are stridently arguing that state judiciaries are facing crises of legitimacy brought about by rapid changes in the campaign context, including the rise of televised campaign advertising and the excoriating attacks that can be part of well-financed and strongly contested races. Just how prevalent are these practices and do there appear to be any upward trends in these figures? Also, are there significant differences between nonpartisan and partisan elections, or between incumbent–challenger races and open-seat contests?

Figure 4.1 begins this exploration by presenting some basic numbers about the presence (not volume) of televised campaign advertising on a race-by-race basis for each election cycle from 2002 through 2013. All elections, both with incumbents and for open seats, are counted. For each election cycle, Figure 4.1 shows the total numbers of elections, contested seats, races with television ads, and races with promote, contrast, and attack ads.

Included in the totals for 2006–2007 are three supreme court races from 2007 described briefly in the *New Politics of Judicial Elections* report for the 2000–2009 period (Sample et al. 2010). Although Sample et al. (2010) do not provide enough information for these three campaigns to be disaggregated by tone or sponsors, they discuss the high cost of televised advertising for two contested seats in Pennsylvania (not disaggregated by race) and another in Wisconsin. Thus, to avoid

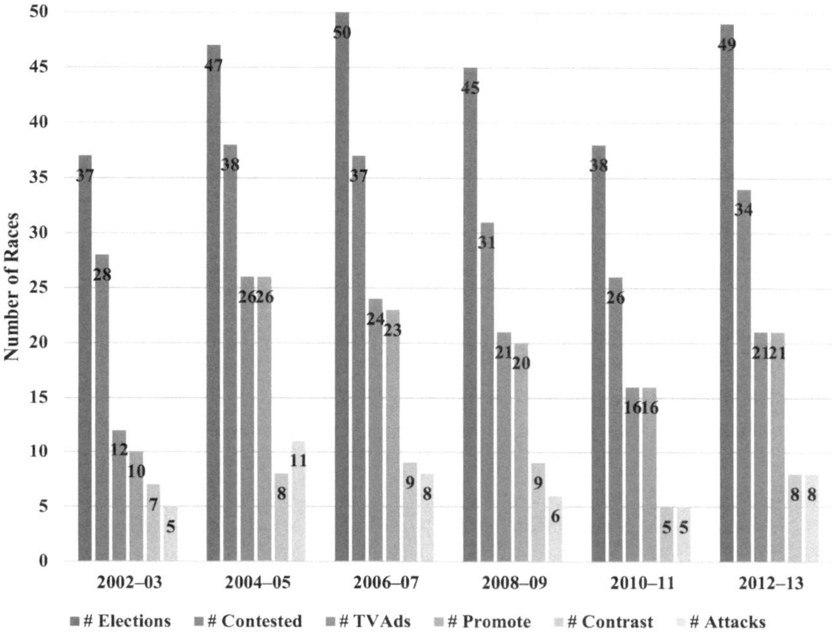


**FIGURE 4.1** The Number of Races with Televised Advertising by Election Cycle, 2002–2013

undercounting, we include these three elections in the various figures and assume that promote, contrast, and attack ads aired in each race.

Perhaps the most unanticipated finding in Figure 4.1, even with the addition of three 2007 elections just mentioned, is that television advertising is not used in a sizable proportion of state supreme court campaigns even when these races are contested. Of 194 contested elections from 2002 through 2013 (of 266 races total), only 120 (or 61.9%) resulted in televised airings of any sort. Given the power and importance of state supreme courts and claims in the advocacy literature that "candidates and groups now almost invariably rely on the airwaves to boost—or bash—contenders for judicial office" (Sample, Jones, and Weiss 2007, 1), this is a surprising finding but one consistent with previous research (e.g., M. Hall 2015).[11]

Moreover, the large majority of elections do not include messages of negativity, either in the form of contrast ads or attack ads. Over the twelve years being examined, only forty-six contested races (23.7%) included contrast ads and only forty-three (22.2%) involved attacks. Overall, neither televised campaign advertising nor negative messages are widely pervasive in contemporary state supreme court elections.

From the perspective of rates (calculated from Figure 4.1 but not shown), the percentage of contested races with television ads was 42.9 percent in 2002–2003, 68.4 percent in 2004–2005, 64.9 percent in 2006–2007, 67.7 percent in 2008–2009, 61.5 percent in 2010–2011, and 61.8 percent in 2012–2013. Certainly television broadcasts were used more commonly after 2002–2003 proportionally speaking, and a significant change appears to have occurred between 2002–2003 and 2004–2005. But even in the most active year, about one of every three contested elections did not motivate any candidates, political parties, or groups to take to the airwaves. In the last two election cycles, rates of television usage dropped to their lowest point since 2002–2003.

No pronounced increases in campaign negativity are obvious either. For the 2002–2003, 2004–2005, 2006–2007, 2008–2009, 2010–2011, and 2012–2013 election cycles, rates of attack advertising are, respectively, 17.9, 29.0, 21.6, 19.4, 19.2, and 23.5 percent. Although a higher percentage of races in 2012–2013 went negative than in previous years, the 2004–2005 elections were the peak point in outright attacks.

Contrast ads are a bit different. For the 2002–2003, 2004–2005, 2006–2007, 2008–2009, 2010–2011, and 2012–2013 election cycles, rates of contrast advertising on a seat-by-seat basis are, respectively, 25.0, 21.1, 24.3, 29.0, 19.2, and 23.5 percent. Thus, the 2012–2013 contrast rate falls short of 2002–2003, 2006–2007, and 2008–2009.

Graphing the data in Figure 4.1 over time would reveal only small fluctuations, except an increase from 2002–2003 in the use of televised advertising. A more meaningful depiction of trends is provided by Figure 4.2, which shows the percentage of contested races with televised advertising in incumbent–challenger races. The reform literature places a particular emphasis on the threats to incumbents posed by the current campaign climate, including depreciatory assaults and tabloid-like attempts at character assassination. Thus, examining the experiences of the justices seeking reelection is especially important.

As Figure 4.2 indicates, although there are interesting fluctuations in the extent to which contested nonpartisan and partisan supreme court elections attract the various types of advertising when incumbents are running, there are no dramatic trends from 2002 through 2013 in the use of particular types of messages in either election system except for the rise of promotions in partisan elections. At the same time, whereas the proportion of races with promotions has risen over time in partisan elections, rates have declined in the last two election cycles. In nonpartisan elections, the percentage of races with promotions has declined since 2004–2005 but still remains above the lowest point in 2002–2003. The percentage of contested nonpartisan elections with contrast ads also may be rising but has not yet reached 2002–2003 levels.

In a direct comparison of contested incumbent–challenger nonpartisan and partisan elections over time, rates in the use of promotions are higher in nonpartisan elections (in four election cycles compared with two for partisan elections). On

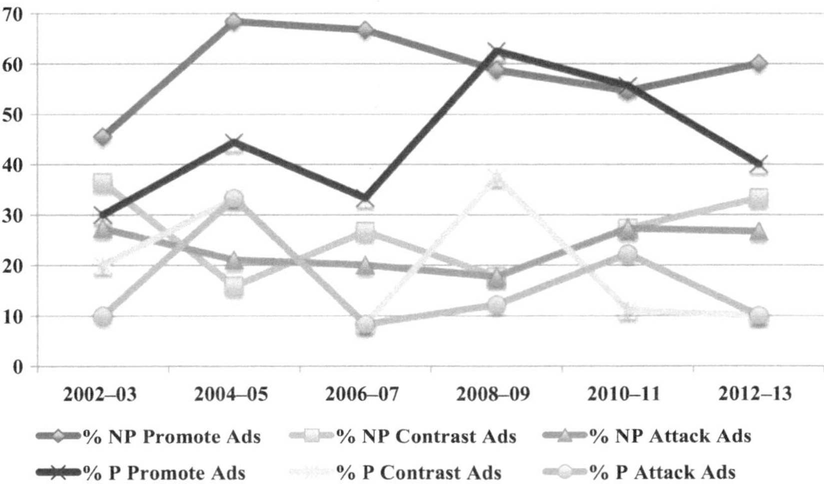


**FIGURE 4.2** The Percentage of Contested Incumbent–Challenger Races with Televised Advertising, 2002–2013

the use of contrast ads, nonpartisan and partisan elections tie, with three election cycles each. Finally, with attacks, nonpartisan elections clearly are more negative on a race-by-race basis than partisan elections. In five of six election cycles, larger percentages of nonpartisan elections drew attacks than did partisan elections.

Figure 4.3 takes a somewhat different look at the experiences of incumbents by comparing basic numbers for the four following types of races: nonpartisan incumbent–challenger, partisan incumbent–challenger, nonpartisan open seats, and partisan open seats. Figure 4.3 displays the numbers of races, contested races, races with television advertising, and races with promote, contrast, and attack ads disaggregated by selection system and incumbency status.

Overall, only 33 of 146 (22.6%) justices challenged for reelection from 2002 through 2013 were involved in campaigns characterized by the use of contrast advertising, and only 29 (19.9%) were in races with attack advertising. Clearly, most justices do not engage in or experience campaign negativity in state supreme court races.

However, percentages (not shown) calculated from Figure 4.3 document some interesting differences between nonpartisan and partisan elections. Generally, supreme court justices seeking reelection in nonpartisan elections are much more likely to be involved in campaign environments characterized by the use of televised advertising. Overall, the majority (64.8%) of all contested nonpartisan elections with incumbents but only a minority (43.1%) of all contested partisan elections drew televised advertising of any sort from 2002 through 2013. The figure for partisan elections is unexpected. Less than half of these races resulted in

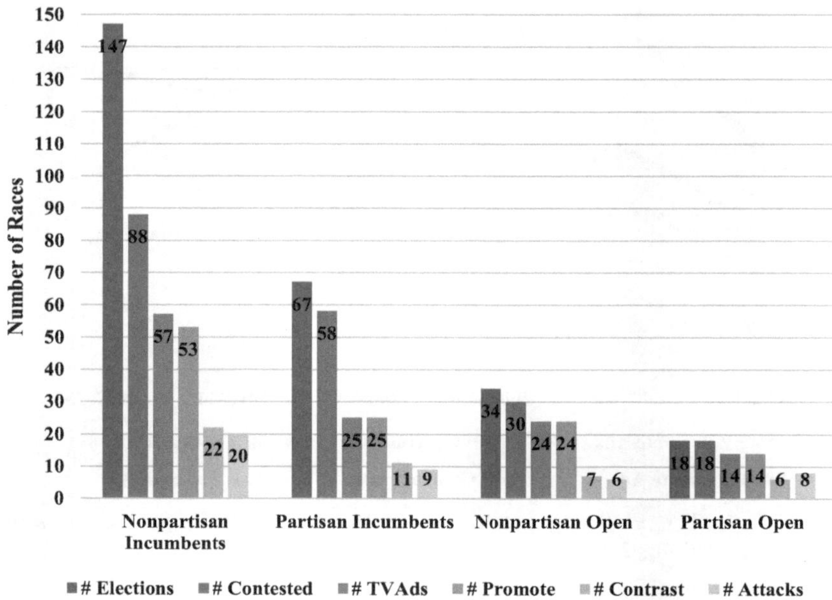


**FIGURE 4.3** The Number of Races with Televised Advertising by Incumbency Status, 2002–2013

televised advertising during the six election cycles being examined even though sitting justices were being challenged for reelection. From this perspective, advertising is not the norm in partisan races with incumbents though it is so in nonpartisan contests.

These same rankings are evidenced in the extent to which promote ads are used on a race-by-race basis. Overall, promote ads were broadcast to voters in 60.2 percent of contested nonpartisan elections with incumbents but in only 43.1 percent of contested partisan elections. When television advertising is employed as a strategy, these campaigns almost always involve positive messages.

Contrasts and attacks are used much less frequently than promotions in both types of elections. Proportions of contested elections with contrast ads for nonpartisan incumbent–challenger races and partisan incumbent–challenger races are, respectively, 25.0 and 19.0 percent. Attack ads were used in 22.7 percent of the nonpartisan elections and 15.5 percent of the partisan elections in which justices were seeking reelection. From 2002 through 2013, sizable majorities of contested elections simply did not prompt critical messages from candidates, political parties, or organized interests. Interestingly, partisan elections are the least likely to go negative.

Open-seat races are different. When seats are up for grabs on the states' highest courts, partisan elections are more negative proportionally speaking than nonpartisan elections. In partisan elections, contrast ads are used in 33.3 percent of the races and attacks are employed in 44.4 percent, compared with nonpartisan elections at 23.3 percent and 20.0 percent. However, both types of open-seat elections are likely to involve televised advertising: 80.0 percent of all open nonpartisan elections and 77.8 percent of all open partisan elections drew televised campaign advertising from 2002 through 2013. This makes perfect sense. Candidates seeking to reach the top court for the first time must educate voters about their credentials and engage in hard-fought challenges. Television advertising (positive and negative) is one tool for accomplishing these goals.

## State Supreme Court Advertising by Airings

A different way to conceptualize the scope of televised campaign advertising is to think in terms of volume, or saturation of airings, both with regard to average airings per race of promote, contrast, and attack spots and as the percentage of airings devoted to each category. Figure 4.4 provides this information by showing average airings by tone for the 2002–2003, 2004–2005, 2006–2007, 2008–2009, 2010–2011, and 2012–2013 election cycles, as well as percentages of total campaign effort dedicated to each of the three types of messages. These figures are calculated only for races with broadcast airings. Otherwise, average airings would be considerably lower in all categories.

Looking first at average numbers of airings for contested state supreme court elections, Figure 4.4 indicates that the volume of airings has increased substantially over the series in the races in which television advertising is utilized. However, this trend has not been monotonic. Total average airings are lower in 2004–2005 (1,757 average airings) and 2006–2007 (with 1,724 average airings) than in 2002–2003 (2,056 average airings) and all other years (3,147 in 2008–2009, 3,058 in 2010–2011, and 3,791 in 2012–2013). Even so, there is a discernable upward trend in these data. Thus, although the proportion of races with televised ads does not appear to be rising, the volume of airings is increasing in those races in which broadcast advertising is employed.

Regarding tone, average airings of promote ads are substantially higher than attack or contrast airings in all eight election cycles, illustrating that campaign airings tend toward the positive rather than the negative. Interestingly, the 2012–2013 races were the most positive to date, a trend sharply inconsistent with the notion of an increasingly nasty campaign climate. But when campaigns do go negative, average attack airings outnumber average contrast airings in each election cycle except 2002–2003.

From the perspective of the percentage of campaign effort, Figure 4.4 shows that promote airings are the largest proportions of messages when television advertising is introduced into state supreme court elections. Average promote airings as a percentage of total airings in televised campaigns are: 67.0 percent in 2002–2003, 62.8 percent in 2004–2005, 72.4 percent in 2006–2007, 61.1 percent

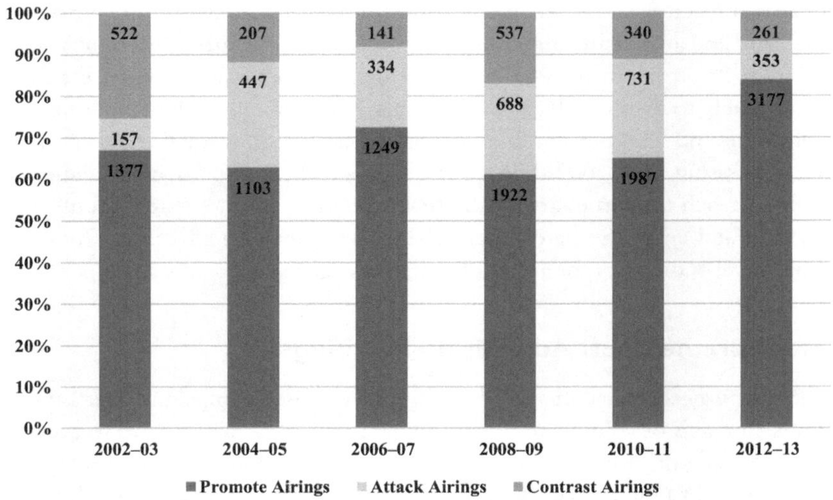


**FIGURE 4.4** Average Airings by Tone and Election Cycle as a Percentage of Total Airings, 2002–2013

in 2008–2009, 65.0 percent in 2010–2011, and 83.8 percent in 2012–2013. With campaign effort calculated as proportions of airings by tone, 2006–2007 was the most negative election cycle and 2012–2013 was the most positive.

The proportion of attack airings also shows no distinct upward trend except for a big change between 2002–2003 and 2004–2005. Figure 4.4 indicates that average attack airings were 7.6 percent in 2002–2003, 25.4 percent in 2004–2005, 19.4 percent in 2006–2007, 21.9 percent in 2008–2009, 23.9 percent in 2010–2011, and 9.3 percent in 2012–2013. However, the 2012–2013 elections resemble the 2002–2003 elections in their positivity, manifesting a pronounced downward turn in the reliance on attack airings as an overall advertising strategy. Overall, 2004–2005 was the most negative year for average attack airings as a percentage of advertising.

Contrast airings evidence different patterns. Generally, contrast advertising constituted a larger share of campaign advertising in 2002–2003 than in any other election cycle. In 2002–2003, contrast airings were 25.4 percent of the airings broadcast to voters on average, compared with 11.8 percent in 2004–2004, 8.2 percent in 2006–2007, 17.1 percent in 2008–2009, 11.1 percent in 2009–2010, and 6.9 percent in 2012–2013. Indeed, contrast airings appear to have declined overall as a proportion of campaign effort, reaching a new low in 2012–2013.

Figure 4.5 offers additional insights by displaying information about average airings of promote, attack, and contrast ads categorized by selection system and incumbency status rather than election cycle. As Figure 4.5 documents, overall

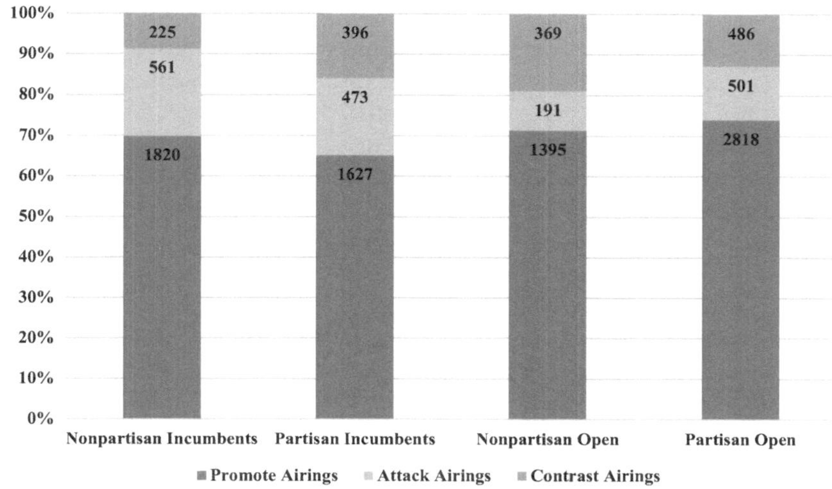


**FIGURE 4.5** Average Airings by Tone and Incumbency Status as a Percentage of Total Airings, 2002–2013

airings are the highest on average in partisan open-seat races, followed by nonpartisan elections with incumbents, partisan elections with incumbents, and nonpartisan open-seat races.

Regarding tone, the average airings of promote ads in all three types of races substantially outweigh negative airings, including in what are often intensely competitive elections for open seats. Regarding average promote airings, the highest levels of advertising are in partisan open-seat races (2,818 average airings per race), compared with nonpartisan incumbent–challenger races at 1,820 average airings, partisan incumbent–challenger elections at 1,627, and nonpartisan open seats with 1,395 average airings.

From the perspective of negativity and sheer volume alone, nonpartisan elections with incumbents have higher average levels of outright attacks (561 airings per race) than their partisan counterparts (473 airings per race), although partisan elections utilize contrast airings to a greater extent (396 average airings per race) than nonpartisan elections with incumbents (225 average airings). Overall, partisan elections with incumbents have the edge over nonpartisan elections in negativity when attack and contrasting airings are combined.

In open-seat races, attack airings are, on average, more prevalent in partisan (501 average attack airings) than nonpartisan elections (191 airings per race). This also is true of contrast airings (486 average airings in partisan elections and 369 in nonpartisan). Thus, partisan open-seat contests are more negative than nonpartisan open-seat elections when the average volume of airings is the comparative standard.

Examining airings as proportions of campaign advertising in each type of election further highlights these patterns. In partisan elections with incumbents,

65.2 percent of televised campaign airings were, on average, promotions, compared with 69.8 percent in nonpartisan elections with incumbents. In open seats, promote airings were 71.4 percent of the advertising content in nonpartisan races and 74.1 percent of partisan contests. Of course, these differences between election systems and incumbency status are not large.

Interestingly, average attack airings are highest as a proportion of overall campaign advertising in nonpartisan incumbent–challenger elections but again not by any great degree. The percentage of average airings of attacks in these races is 21.5 percent, compared with partisan elections at 19.0 percent. Alternatively, contrast airings are a small part of televised campaigns, proportionally speaking, when incumbents are seeking reelection in nonpartisan elections (8.6 percent of all airings in these types of races). In partisan elections, contrast airings are 15.9 percent of all airings broadcast to voters.

For open seats, average attack airings rates are 13.2 percent in partisan elections and 9.8 percent in nonpartisan elections. With average contrast airings, rates are 12.8 and 18.9 percent, respectively. Overall, partisan open-seat races are slightly less negative than nonpartisan elections when attack airings and contrast airings are combined and considered as proportions of overall campaign effort.

In sum, there are notable differences in the use of promote, attack, and contrast airings in nonpartisan incumbent-challenger elections, partisan incumbent–challenger elections, and nonpartisan and partisan open-seat contests. On balance, partisan elections in which justices are seeking to retain their seats are the most negative when airings are taken into account. Fewer partisan elections attract advertising and fewer have attack ads, but when televised advertising is introduced, partisan elections are nastier and noisier than nonpartisan elections. However, this does not mean that only incumbents are being attacked. Both incumbents and challengers sponsor toxic messages, as do political parties and other groups interested in the judicial selection process.

## State Supreme Court Advertising by Sponsors

One of the most serious concerns about contemporary state supreme court elections is the involvement of interest groups and other outside interests, including big-money players. Figures 4.6 and 4.7 provide some insight into this issue by examining the sponsorship of campaign advertising in recent races.

First, Figure 4.6 reports, in the aggregate, the overall share of total state supreme court airings by tone and sponsor from 2002 through 2013 in incumbent–challenger races. For each category, Figure 4.6 shows the percentage of total airings sponsored by incumbents, challengers, political parties, and interest groups. These figures are shown separately for nonpartisan incumbent–challenger races (127,555 airings in 56 elections) and partisan incumbent–challenger races (55,502 airings in 23 elections).[12] These data reveal the extent to which interest groups are responsible for what many consider to be

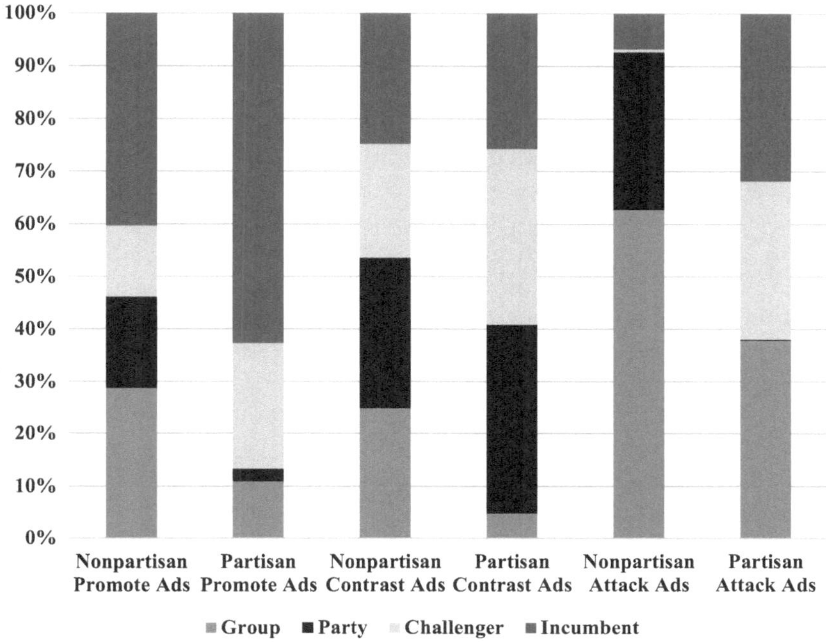


**FIGURE 4.6** The Sponsorship of Televised Airings by Tone in Incumbent–Challenger Races, 2002–2013

the gutter politics of campaign negativity and issue-based discourse in state supreme court elections.

Overall, as Figure 4.6 indicates, most of the promote airings, which are positive in tone, have been sponsored by the candidates; this is particularly true of partisan elections. In nonpartisan elections, 40.3 percent of the promotions came from incumbents and 13.6 percent from challengers, for a combined total of 53.9 percent. In partisan elections, the numbers are higher. In these races, 62.6 percent of all promote airings were sponsored by incumbents, along with another 24.2 percent from challengers, for a total of 86.8 percent. Thus, campaign positivity is largely a product of the candidates, although interest groups play a greater role in nonpartisan elections than in partisan elections and are more active in promoting candidates than are political parties in both types of races.

Contrast airings do not reflect these same patterns. In nonpartisan elections in which incumbents are seeking reelection, contrast airings are sponsored by all four types of participants: parties (28.6%), interest groups (24.9%), incumbents (24.7%), and challengers (21.9%). Collectively, political parties and interest groups rather than the candidates dominate these messages, at 53.5 percent. In partisan elections, interest groups contribute little to contrast airings. Only 4.8 percent of all contrast airings were sponsored by interest groups, compared with 36 percent by political parties, 33.5 percent from challengers, and 25.7 percent from incumbents. In partisan elections, these types of mixed messages are controlled largely by the candidates (at 59.2%).

The participation of interest groups in supreme court elections is most evidenced, and is of the greatest concern, in their sponsorship of attack airings. As Figure 4.6 reveals, 62.7 percent of all attack airings in nonpartisan incumbent races were sponsored by interest groups, compared with 37.9 percent in partisan elections. In nonpartisan elections, political parties come in second, with 29.9 percent of attack airings, followed by incumbents at 6.7 percent and challengers at 0.7 percent. The incredibly small proportion of attack airings by challengers is surprising. However, it may well be to the advantage of challengers not to attack when groups and parties have decided to assume this unpleasant task. The downside is that the challengers then cannot control the content of these messages.

Partisan elections with incumbents are different. Most of the attack airings in these elections are candidate-sponsored (31.7% by incumbents plus 30.3% by challengers). In fact, political parties were responsible for only a total of nineteen attack airings in partisan elections during this period. Consistent with attacks in nonpartisan elections, incumbents attack more than challengers as a proportion of these airings. Organized interests sponsored a sizable share of attacks (37.9%) in partisan elections but not in the same proportions as in nonpartisan elections.

In sum, organized interests actively sponsor attacks in partisan incumbent–challenger races but their most aggressive efforts have been in nonpartisan elections. Overall, interest groups sponsor larger shares of attack airings in nonpartisan elections than do other major political actors, including the candidates. This may reflect the practical reality that attacks against any state's partisan majority are less effective when partisan labels are on the ballot. Similarly, interest groups play a bigger role in sponsoring contrast airings in nonpartisan than partisan elections, resulting in a greater share of total campaign negativity when justices are running. In short, those concerned with the pernicious influence of organized interests and other financial high-rollers in state supreme court elections should look most carefully at nonpartisan elections.

Figure 4.7 displays these same data for nonpartisan and partisan open-seat contests from 2002 through 2013. In this figure, because there are no incumbents present, all candidates are grouped together in the "challenger" category.

As this figure illustrates, promote and contrast airings in both nonpartisan and partisan open-seat races are overwhelmingly the product of the candidates. Partisan elections draw the most involvement from groups and parties in the form of contrast airings sponsorship, but candidates still retain the dominant voice in these types of messages. Attack airings are a different case. Almost all attack airings in open-seat nonpartisan elections come from interest groups, whereas these types of messages are largely the product of political party sponsorship in

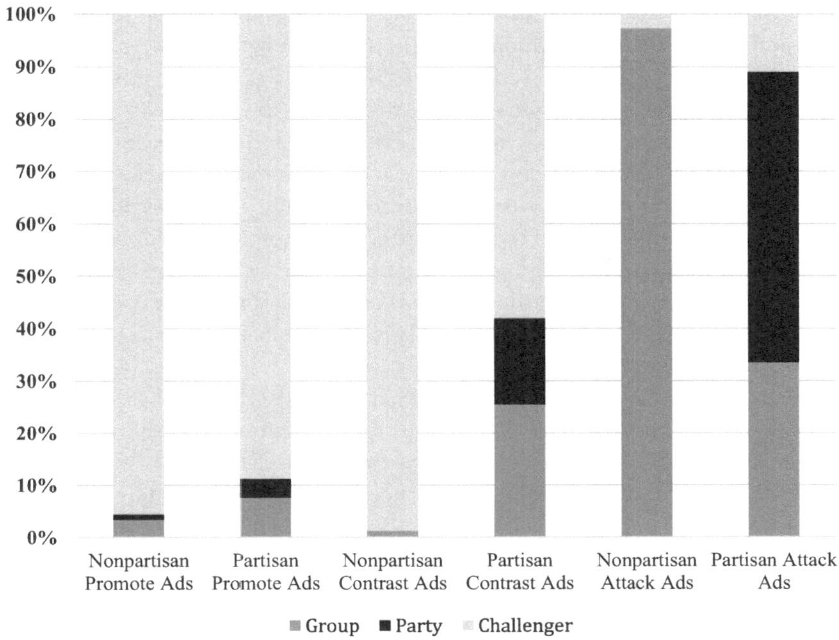


**FIGURE 4.7** The Sponsorship of Televised Airings by Tone in Open-Seat Races, 2002–2013

partisan elections. Again, those concerned with the impact of outside groups in state supreme court elections should be thinking carefully about the effectiveness of nonpartisan elections for stemming these effects.

## Conclusion

Whereas campaign negativity, issue-based discourse, and significant rates of contestation and electoral defeat were features of state supreme court elections long before the advent of "new style" campaigns (e.g., Bonneau and M. Hall 2009; Dubois 1980; M. Hall 2001, 2007b, 2011, 2015; Kritzer 2015), modern campaign techniques, especially televised campaign commercials, have helped to bring out changes in the contemporary electoral context. Among other things, televised advertising has significantly raised the costs of seeking office and heightened the visibility of judicial elections by bringing them directly into our homes while attracting significant involvement from moneyed players in American politics.

Nevertheless, claims that "noisier, nastier, and costlier" campaigns have overwhelmed the election process are overstated when considering the totality of judicial campaign advertising activity from 2002 through 2013. For instance, on the issue of noise, only 68.6 percent of all contested nonpartisan races and

51.3 percent of all contested partisan elections during this period featured any television advertising at all, which strikes us as quite low given the political and legal significance of state high courts. Notably, these figures do not include the 72 races (27.1%) never contested in the first place. On the issue of nastiness, there are no dramatic temporal trends indicating rises in proportions of races with campaign negativity or in the airings of attack and contrast ads, whether considered as averages per race or as the overall proportions of campaigns dedicated to these controversial messages. In fact, the 2012–2013 races were the most positive of all in tone over the series. Regarding the high cost of seeking office, we leave that discussion to other chapters in the volume. We merely note that televised advertising is very expensive, which helps to explain why campaign costs have escalated over the most recent decades.

For those who favor policy talk and other issue-based messages that provide valuable information to state electorates, these numbers may be discouraging given evidence that attack and contrast ads have the highest issue content (M. Hall 2015). However, for those concerned about the public's reaction to negative campaigning or its effects on judicial legitimacy and the incumbency advantage, it seems that a balance of sorts is being reached. Overall, the supreme court campaign advertising environment is dominated by innocuous promote ads but still features a quantity of ads promoting issue-oriented conversation. In the end, campaign dialogue may be sufficiently restrained so as to minimize the risk that the public's distaste for mudslinging and other forms of dirty politics will overpower the legitimizing function of policy talk and the election process.

Though aggregate data do not suggest a crisis in campaign trends, evidence does point toward marked differences in the advertising landscape between partisan and nonpartisan contests, as well as races for open seats versus those held by incumbents. Not surprisingly, contested campaigns for open seats feature the highest percentage of race-level advertising activity, with approximately 80 percent of all campaigns in both nonpartisan and partisan states conducted over the airwaves. Regarding incumbency, the differences are striking between partisan and nonpartisan elections. Among other things, televised advertising on a race-by-race basis is decidedly not the norm in partisan elections but is so in nonpartisan elections. But perhaps most significant is that parties and outside groups are dominating attack advertising in nonpartisan contests, both in races with incumbents and for open seats. Consequently, whereas the National Center for State Courts (2002, 14) has proposed that "nonpartisanship in judicial races will reduce the competitiveness of those races and thus the need for large campaign contributions," the opposite appears to be true.

However counterintuitive or unsettling this evidence may be to staunch critics of judicial elections or those who prefer nonpartisan elections, these results are perfectly consistent with empirically-supported theories pointing to the primacy of partisanship in structuring voting behavior in United States elections. Given that voters will seek to infer a candidate's partisanship from informational cues when partisanship is unavailable, it is unremarkable that political parties, interest groups, and candidates seek to provide this and other related information in nonpartisan elections. Moreover, the absence of the partisan cue opens the door to interest groups, political parties, and other political players, who then have a better chance of tipping an election by flooding the airwaves with emotionally charged high-profile ads. Partisanship strongly mitigates against the likelihood and effectiveness of these strategies.

Although the results in this chapter are intriguing, the study of campaign politics in the judicial context has only just begun. The great news is that empirical research on state supreme court elections, including campaigning and other forms of electioneering, is rapidly evolving into one of the most dynamic and theoretically significant areas of inquiry in political science. The new insights provided by recent and forthcoming works will illuminate the fascinating process of judicial selection and better delineate the exact nature of the complex linkages between the electorate and state court bench brought about by democratic processes. Broadly speaking, conventional wisdom often is wrong, and nowhere is this proposition better evidenced than in studies of judicial elections and the debate about the best methods for selecting and retaining the state court bench.

## Notes

1 This ad aired in the races between incumbent Stephen Markman and challengers Colleen O'Brien, Connie Kelley and Bridget Mary McCormack for two seats, one of which was open. The Campaign Media Analysis Group entitled the ad "STSUPCT_MI_JUDICIALCRISIS_MCCORMACK_FREED_TERRORIST." All ads referenced and analyzed in this chapter are accessible via the Brennan Center for Justice Buying Time website at www.brennancenter.org/analysis/buying-time.
2 An irony in this regard is that the judicial reform movement is responsible for convincing state governments to replace partisan elections with nonpartisan elections and to restrict campaign speech through codes of judicial conduct. It is little wonder that in some states there has been relatively little useful information available to voters.
3 CMAG entitled this ad "STSUPCT/NV Saitta Becker Denouncement."
4 See, for example, the ad labeled "STSUPCT/IA AFA Send Them a Message."
5 The CMAG identifier for this ad is "STSUPCT/WV Ketchum Mumbo Jumbo."
6 The CMAG label for this ad is "STSUPCT/AL Parker Liberal Newspapers."
7 See, for example, "STSUPCT/MI MIDSCC Taylor the Sleeping Judge."
8 See, for example, "STSUPCT/WV Bastress Warped Justice."
9 Data on airings, sponsors, cost, and tone for the messages televised from 2002 through 2008 were reported in Goldberg and Sanchez (2003), Goldberg et al. (2005), the Brennan Center webpage (www.BrennanCenter.org), and Sample et al. (2010). Additional information about the 2006 elections was found in Sample, Jones, and Weiss (2007). Information for the 2009 through 2013 elections was collected from http://newpoliticsreport.org/election-cycle/2011–12/, http://newpoliticsreport.org/election-cycle/2013–14/, Bannon et al. (2013), and Greytak et al. (2015).
10 The following figures, tables, and discussion essentially replicate M. Hall (2015). Essentially we have updated some of these initial findings with more recent data.

11 Even in the 2006 elections, which is the election cycle being discussed by Sample, Jones, and Weiss (2007), only 43.5 percent of all state supreme court elections involved television advertising, and only 60 percent of all contested races had television ads. This advocacy report exaggerates the extent of television advertising by discussing states rather than individual seats. Sample, Jones, and Weiss (2007) report that ten of eleven states (91%) in 2006 experienced television advertising, a figure significantly higher than the 60 percent figure for individual races but more consistent with their description of televised campaigning as "almost invariably" used in state supreme court elections.

12 There is not enough information to include the three 2007 elections in Pennsylvania and Wisconsin in these figures.

## References

Ansolabehere, Stephen and Shanto Iyengar. 1995. *Going Negative: How Political Advertisements Shrink and Polarize the Electorate.* New York: The Free Press.

Bannon, Alicia, Eric Velasco, Linda Casey, and Lianna Reagan. 2013. *The New Politics of Judicial Elections 2011–12: How New Waves of Special Interest Spending Raised the Stakes for Fair Courts.* Washington, DC: Justice at Stake Campaign.

Baum, Lawrence and David Klein. 2007. "Voter Responses to High-Visibility Judicial Campaigns." In *Running for Judge: The Rising Political, Financial, and Legal Stakes of Judicial Elections*, edited by Matthew J. Streb. New York: New York University Press.

Bonneau, Chris W. and Damon M. Cann. 2015. *Voters' Verdicts: Citizens, Campaigns, and Institutions in State Supreme Court Elections.* Charlottesville: University of Virginia Press.

Bonneau, Chris W. and Melinda Gann Hall. 2009. *In Defense of Judicial Elections.* New York: Routledge.

Brandenburg, Bert and Roy A. Schotland. 2008. "Justice in Peril: the Endangered Balance between Impartial Courts and Judicial Election Campaigns." *Georgetown Journal of Legal Ethics* 21: 1229–1258.

Brennan Center for Justice. 2006. "Buying Time 2006." Retrieved on June 19, 2007, from www.brennancenter.org/analysis/buying-time-2006-1.

Campbell, Angus, Philip E. Converse, Warren E. Miller, and Donald E. Stokes. 1960. *The American Voter.* Chicago: University of Chicago Press.

Caufield, Rachel. 2007. "The Changing Tone of Judicial Election Campaigns as a Result of *White*." In *Running for Judge: The Rising Political, Financial, and Legal Stakes of Judicial Elections*, edited by Matthew J. Streb. New York: New York University Press.

Champagne, Anthony. 2002. "Televised Ads in Judicial Campaigns." *Indiana Law Review* 35: 669–689.

Dubois, Philip L. 1979. "The Significance of Voting Cues in State Supreme Court Elections." *Law and Society Review* 13: 757–779.

Dubois, Philip L. 1980. *From Ballot to Bench: Judicial Elections and the Quest for Accountability.* Austin: University of Texas Press.

Geer, John G. 2006. *In Defense of Negativity: Attack Ads in Presidential Campaigns.* Chicago: University of Chicago Press.

Geyh, Charles Gardner. 2003. "Why Judicial Elections Stink." *Ohio State Law Journal* 64: 43–79.

Gibson, James L. 2012. *Electing Judges: The Surprising Effects of Campaigning on Judicial Legitimacy.* Chicago: University of Chicago Press.

Goldberg, Deborah, Sarah Samis, Edwin Bender, and Rachel Weiss. 2005. *The New Politics of Judicial Elections, 2004.* Washington, DC: Justice at Stake Campaign.

Goldberg, Deborah and Samantha Sanchez. 2003. *The New Politics of Judicial Elections, 2002.* Washington, DC: Justice at Stake Campaign.
Greytak, Scott, Alicia Bannon, Allyse Falce, and Linda Casey. 2015. *The New Politics of Judicial Elections 2013–15: Bankrolling the Bench.* Washington, DC: Justice at Stake Campaign.
Hall, Kermit L. 1984. "Progressive Reform and the Decline of Democratic Accountability: The Popular Election of State Supreme Court Judges, 1850–1920." *American Bar Foundation Research Journal* 1984: 345–369.
Hall, Kermit L. 2005. "Judicial Independence and the Majoritarian Difficulty." In *Institutions of American Democracy: The Judicial Branch*, edited by Kermit L. Hall and Kevin T. McGuire. New York: Oxford University Press.
Hall, Melinda Gann. 2001. "State Supreme Courts in American Democracy: Probing the Myths of Judicial Reform." *American Political Science Review* 95: 315–330.
Hall, Melinda Gann. 2007a. "Voting in State Supreme Court Elections: Competition and Context as Democratic Incentives." *Journal of Politics* 69: 1147–1159.
Hall, Melinda Gann. 2007b. "Competition as Accountability in State Supreme Court Elections." In *Running for Judge: The Rising Political, Financial, and Legal Stakes of Judicial Elections*, edited by Matthew J. Streb. New York: New York University Press.
Hall, Melinda Gann. 2011. "On the Cataclysm of Judicial Elections and Other Popular Antidemocratic Myths." In *What's Law Got to Do with It? What Judges Do, Why They Do It, and What's at Stake*, edited by Charles Gardner Geyh. Stanford: Stanford University Press.
Hall, Melinda Gann. 2014. "Televised Attacks and the Incumbency Advantage in State Supreme Courts." *Journal of Law, Economics, and Organization* 30: 138–164.
Hall, Melinda Gann. 2015. *Attacking Judges: How Campaign Advertising Influences State Supreme Court Elections.* Stanford: Stanford University Press.
Hall, Melinda Gann and Chris W. Bonneau. 2008. "Mobilizing Interest: The Effects of Money on Citizen Participation in State Supreme Court Elections." *American Journal of Political Science* 52: 457–470.
Hall, Melinda Gann and Chris W. Bonneau. 2013. "Attack Advertising, the *White* Decision, and Voter Participation in State Supreme Court Elections." *Political Research Quarterly* 66: 115–126.
Hojnacki, Marie and Lawrence Baum. 1992. "'New Style' Judicial Campaigns and Voters: Economic Issues and Union Members in Ohio." *Western Political Quarterly* 45: 921–948.
Iyengar, Shanto. 2002. "The Effects of Media-Based Campaigns and Candidate and Voting Behavior: Implications for Judicial Elections." *Indiana Law Review* 35: 691–699.
Klein, David and Lawrence Baum. 2001. "Ballot Information and Voting Decisions in Judicial Elections." *Political Research Quarterly* 54: 709–728.
Klemanski, John S. and Julie K. Walters. 2011. "Defeating an Incumbent Chief Justice: The 2008 Michigan Supreme Court Election." *Judicature* 94: 233–238.
Kritzer, Herbert M. 2015. *Justices on the Ballot: Continuity and Change in State Supreme Court Elections.* New York: Cambridge University Press.
Lau, Richard R., Lee Sigelman, Caroline Heldman, and Paul Babbitt. 1999. "The Effects of Negative Political Advertisements: A Meta-Analytical Assessment." *American Political Science Review* 93: 851–876.
Lau, Richard R., Lee Sigelman, and Ivy Brown Rovner. 2007. "The Effects of Negative Political Campaigns: A Meta-Analytic Reassessment." *Journal of Politics* 69: 1176–1209.

National Center for State Courts. 2002. *Call to Action: Statement of the National Summit on Improving Judicial Selection*. Williamsburg, VA: National Center for State Courts.
Pozen, David E. 2008. "The Irony of Judicial Elections." *Columbia Law Review* 108: 264–330.
*Republican Party of Minnesota v. White*. 2002. 536 *U.S.* 765.
Rock, Emily and Lawrence Baum. 2010. "The Impact of High-Visibility Contests for U.S. State Court Judgeships: Partisan Voting in Nonpartisan Elections." *State Politics and Policy Quarterly* 10: 368–396.
Sample, James, Lauren Jones, and Rachel Weiss. 2007. *The New Politics of Judicial Elections, 2006*. Washington, DC: Justice at Stake Campaign.
Sample, James, Adam Skaggs, Jonathan Blitzer, and Linda Casey. 2010. *The New Politics of Judicial Elections, 2000–2009*. Washington, DC: Justice at Stake Campaign.
Schotland, Roy A. 1985. "Elective Judges' Campaign Financing: Are State Judges' Robes the Emperor's Clothes of American Democracy?" *Journal of Law and Politics* 2: 57–167.
Squire, Peverill and Eric R.A.N. Smith. 1988. "The Effect of Partisan Information on Voters in Nonpartisan Elections." *Journal of Politics* 50: 169–179.

# 5

# FUNDRAISING AND SPENDING IN STATE SUPREME COURT ELECTIONS

*Chris W. Bonneau*

There is no topic more controversial in American politics than campaign fundraising and spending, and the same is true when applied to judicial elections. Indeed, since 2009, three cases decided by the U.S. Supreme Court involved campaign spending in judicial elections (either directly or indirectly): *Caperton v. Massey* (2009), *Citizens United v. FEC* (2010), and *Williams-Yulee v. State Bar of Florida* (2015).[1] Almost all of the current attacks on judicial elections focus on how judges need to raise money from lawyers and litigants who will appear before them and how expensive these races have become (e.g., Geyh 2003; Skaggs et al. 2011). In the words of Geyh (2005, 887): "The cost of judicial campaigns has skyrocketed as interest groups have challenged the retention or reelection of state judges as never before."

In this chapter, I examine and analyze recent data on campaign fundraising and spending in states that elect their judges in partisan and nonpartisan elections.[2] Whereas it is true that state supreme court elections are not cheap, they are not increasing in cost in any kind of linear or exponential fashion. Additionally, there is great variation among the states (and even within a state) in the costs associated with electing judges. This chapter provides a much-needed corrective to much of the conventional wisdom on campaign money and judicial elections.

## The Importance of Campaign Financing

The financing of judicial elections is important, both normatively and empirically, for three reasons. First, when attorneys and litigants appear before judges to whom they give campaign contributions, this can give rise to the appearance of impropriety. Specifically, judges may be making decisions based on the interests of their contributors rather than the law. It is worth noting that most states prohibit judicial candidates from soliciting or accepting money directly from contributors. Instead, donations are made to campaign committees that are run on behalf of candidates. The U.S. Supreme Court upheld restrictions on candidates directly soliciting funds from contributors in the *Williams-Yulee* (2015) case.

Empirical data show that the public is concerned with the linkage between campaign contributions and judicial outcomes. Indeed, in a survey of North Carolina voters in 2002, 78 percent of the respondents felt that campaign contributions had at least some influence over the decisions made by judges (Bonneau and Hall 2009, 109). A 2008 survey of Minnesotans found that 78 percent were at least somewhat concerned about the fact that judges need to raise money for their campaigns (Bonneau and Hall 2009, 121).[3] And in Wisconsin, 76 percent of those surveyed believed campaign contributions had at least some influence on judicial outcomes (Bonneau and Hall 2009, 126).

These findings are not just limited to these three states. A 2013 nationwide survey commissioned by Justice at Stake found that 87 percent of respondents felt that campaign contributions had at least some impact on the decisions judges make, and this is true whether the contributions were made directly to a judge's campaign or to an independent interest group supporting the judge.[4] Moreover, Cann and Yates (2008, 313) find that "individuals who express concern about campaign finance in judicial elections have substantially lower levels of support for their state courts."

Although there may concerns about the appearance of impropriety, there is little to no systematic evidence that there *is* impropriety. To be sure, there are a host of studies showing a correlation between campaign contributions and judicial decisions (Champagne 1988; McCall 2008; McCall and McCall 2006; Waltenburg and Lopeman 2000; Ware 1999). But this is precisely what we would expect: Campaign contributors are rational actors (e.g., Francia et al. 2003; Grant and Rudolph 2002; Rosenstone and Hansen 1993) and are going to donate to like-minded individuals. It would be shocking if there was not such a relationship. However, holding ideology constant, the evidence for a quid pro quo relationship is mixed. Cann (2002) found no evidence of a relationship in Wisconsin, but did find a relationship in Georgia (Cann 2007), despite both states utilizing nonpartisan elections.

Looking at decisions in civil cases in 2005, Cann, Bonneau, and Boyea (2012) find some evidence of a quid pro quo relationship between judges and contributors in Michigan but not in Texas or Nevada. While the authors are careful to qualify their conclusions, they find that judges in Michigan are less likely to issue unanimous rulings when campaign contributors are appearing before them. Moreover, even after controlling for case facts and matching judges on ideology, there is a significant relationship between contributions and judicial outcomes in Michigan. "For a judge who received $100 more from the liberal party's attorney(s), the odds of a liberal decision are more than double the odds (specifically 2.29 times greater) where the respective parties' contributions are at parity. For a judge who receives $100 more contributions from the conservative party, the odds of a liberal decision decrease by a factor of 0.44" (Cann, Bonneau, and Boyea 2012, 49).

What does all this mean? Clearly, there is a relationship between campaign contributors and judicial outcomes and the public finds this relationship troubling. However, it is far from clear that judges' votes are actually being bought by contributions. The most detailed study to date (Cann, Bonneau, and Boyea 2012) finds mixed evidence at best; even if one believes the empirical results, the authors are not able to explain why they find the result they do. Why is there a relationship in Michigan (a hybrid state) but not in Texas (a partisan state) or Nevada (a nonpartisan state)? Is it something about the specific judges in Michigan or is it something related to the electoral environment? Finally, it does seem odd that such a small amount of campaign contribution differential ($100) can have such a large effect, especially given how much money, on average, is spent on judicial elections in Michigan. All this is not to dismiss the Cann, Bonneau, and Boyea (2012) study; it does a rigorous job assessing the data available, but we still need to learn much more before we can be certain there is a quid pro quo relationship between contributors and judges.

Second, the financing could have implications for the perception of the legitimacy of the judicial system. Gibson (2012; Gibson et al. 2011) has done excellent work demonstrating that the net effects of judicial elections seem to be positive; that is, the good far outweighs the bad. But it is important to remember that legitimacy refers to a reservoir of goodwill that cannot be eroded overnight (Caldeira and Gibson 1992). Thus, it is possible that concerns over the financing of judicial elections could have a cumulative long-term effect and lead to the loss of legitimacy over time. However, Bonneau and Hall (2009) find that intense electoral competition and higher levels of campaign spending lead to increased voter participation. This increased voter participation under these conditions indicates that voters are not turned off by campaign spending and electing judges. This suggests they do not view state supreme courts as illegitimate. However, we simply do not have the longitudinal data necessary to assess this possibility directly.

Third, and finally, campaign fundraising and spending are important because the nature of campaigning for the state high court bench could deter highly qualified candidates from seeking office, though there has been no empirical evidence that this has actually occurred (Choi, Gulati, and Posner 2010). In a North Carolina survey, a whopping 85 percent of voters believed good candidates were deterred from running because of the high campaign costs (Bonneau and Hall 2009, 109). Moreover, given that we know women are more election-averse than men (Kanthak and Woon 2015), needing to raise significant funds of money could further deter candidates from minority groups from seeking office, leading to a lack of diversity on the bench. We have not yet seen this (Hurwitz and Lanier 2008), but if the cost of running for election becomes too high, we certainly could.

All of these concerns are legitimate (even if not borne out empirically), but it is also important to note the positives associated with campaign spending in elections. At its most basic, campaign spending is needed for candidates to get their message out to the voters; thus, spending money can help inform the electorate. Bonneau and Hall (2009) find that campaign spending helps lead to more competitive elections, presumably because candidates are able to disseminate their record to the voters (as well as pointing out the flaws in their opponent).

Likewise, Bonneau and Hall (2009; Hall and Bonneau 2008) find that campaign spending leads to increased voter participation in these elections. We know from the literature that voters are more likely to participate when they are informed (Coleman and Manna 2000), and campaign spending can help to provide this information. Thus, by spending money on their campaigns, judges can both help overcome the low-information nature of the electoral environment and eradicate voter ignorance.

For all these reasons, it is important to understand the landscape of campaign fundraising and spending in state supreme court elections. We do not expect elections for other offices to occur without campaign spending, and we should not have different expectations for judicial races. Whereas the data below do not shed light on whether campaign spending is good or bad, too high or too low, it does provide an empirical context in which this discussion should take place.

## The Past: What We Have Learned About Campaign Fundraising and Spending

### *Campaign Fundraising*

The first systematic look at campaign fundraising was done by Bonneau (2007a). Looking at campaign fundraising in constant dollars from 1990 through 2000, he found that incumbent candidates raised, on average, about $314,000 whereas nonincumbents raised about $205,000. Additionally, candidates in partisan elections raised slightly over $298,000 on average compared to almost $184,000 in nonpartisan elections. These amounts increased over the decade of the 1990s but not as much as one might think. For example, in 1990, candidates in partisan elections spent $196,450 on average; in 2000, this figure was $256,793.

Of course, these data are at least fifteen years old now. Bonneau and Hall (2009) report that in 2004, candidates in partisan elections raised over $1 million on average while those in nonpartisan elections raised over $491,000. The partisan election figures were heavily influenced by two races which were among the most expensive in history (Illinois and West Virginia), but partisan elections involved more fundraising than nonpartisan elections in every election cycle between 1990–2004, with the exception of 2002.

### *Campaign Spending*

In terms of campaign spending, unsurprisingly, many of the same conclusions hold: state supreme court races are becoming more expensive, although this rise is neither linear nor rapid. Bonneau (2005, 2007b) found that, on average, spending in partisan elections from 1990 through 2004 was just over $715,000, and for nonpartisan elections it was $419,000. Looking at all elections over that time period, the most expensive year was 1994, followed by 1998 and 2000. Moreover, 2002 was the second-least-expensive year of the time series; only 1990 involved less campaign spending. Thus, while these races are becoming more expensive, the data do not follow a neat, linear progression.

It is important to note that these figures only involve direct spending by the candidates themselves. Thus, any money spent by independent groups on behalf of candidates is not included in these figures. This is important because spending by independent groups has increased in recent years (e.g., Greytak et al. 2015) for a variety of reasons, including the U.S. Supreme Court's decision in *Citizens United* (2010).[5] In the current electoral environment, analyses that do not take into account the spending of independent groups risk being underinclusive in the accounting of campaign spending. Of course, disclosure requirements for these groups varies widely by state so oftentimes it is impossible for scholars to get a precise figure of how much is being spent and who is spending it.

## The Present: Campaign Fundraising and Spending in the 21st Century

The data for this chapter come from the *New Politics of Judicial Elections* reports that Justice at Stake publishes after each election cycle.[6] While Justice at Stake does an excellent job of collecting and compiling this data, they do not always collect the same data (or parse the data the same way) in each election cycle.[7] This presents some challenges for making comparisons across a long period of time. Thus, some of the data presented will go back to 2000, whereas others only start in 2008. There are two advantages to using the Justice at Stake data. First, the data are collected from a consistent and reliable source, using the same coding rules. Second, the data also include spending by independent interest groups, yielding a comprehensive picture of total spending in these elections.

Additionally, the data collected on campaign fundraising are far more comprehensive than the data collected on campaign spending. Thus, most of the analyses in this chapter will focus on campaign fundraising. However, the correlation between candidate fundraising and total spending for this period is 0.85; only in 2010 does it drop below 0.59 and not reach statistical significance. Indeed, in the two most recent years (the post-*Citizens United* election cycles), the correlation between candidate fundraising and campaign expenditures was 0.59 in 2012 and 0.96 in 2014. Thus, using the amount of money candidates raise can reasonably and fairly be thought of as equivalent to the amount of money they spend.

Table 5.1 displays the average amount of money raised by candidates (in constant year 2000 dollars) from 2000 through 2014, by method of selection.[8] I also present two adjusted measures of fundraising: the total amount raised by candidates in the state divided by the total number of seats and the total amount raised by candidates in the state divided by the total number of candidates running.

The story told in Table 5.1 is far from one of escalating costs. In fact, it is largely one of stability. Once we control for inflation by examining the data using constant dollars, candidates raised the *most* money in 2000 and the *least* amount of money in 2014. This is not just a function of candidates not needing to raise money themselves anymore because of the *Citizens United* case; recall that the correlation between fundraising and spending in 2014 is an extremely high 0.96.

In terms of spending by seat, the same pattern holds, although 2004 emerges as the year with the highest amount of money.[9] However, 2012 and 2014 remain relatively inexpensive compared with other years. With the exception of 2014, seats in partisan election states generally involve fundraising of a minimum of about $1 million, whereas nonpartisan states never top $487,000, on average.

Finally, when it comes to money raised per candidate, 2004 was again the most costly overall, followed closely by 2008. Unsurprisingly, partisan elections involve more fundraising than nonpartisan elections, with candidates in partisan elections raising from $245,000 to about $1.1 million, on average. In nonpartisan elections, the range is $89,376 to $236,032. Hybrid elections are generally the most expensive, although there are only two states in this category (Michigan and Ohio), and they have long had competitive and expensive races.[10]

The bottom line from Table 5.1 is that while state supreme court elections are not cheap, campaign fundraising in them is not changing in any kind of escalating manner. In fact, if anything, candidates are raising *less* money in recent years than they were at the beginning of the decade. State supreme court seats are extremely important and powerful offices; we should expect candidates to raise (and spend) significant amounts of money to obtain (and retain) them. Compared with other statewide offices such as U.S. Senator and Governor (Schill and Hendricks 2016), the amounts spent in races for the state high court bench are low.

Whereas Table 5.1 provides much interesting information about candidate fundraising by method of selection, it obscures the variation that exists among states within a method of selection. This data is provided in Table 5.2. For convenience, I only present the data of the total amount raised divided by the number of candidates.

As you can see, there is extraordinary variation within states: very few are uniformly expensive or inexpensive. Much has to do with the competitiveness of the race and the electoral environment. That said, candidates tend to raise higher amounts of money in Alabama, Illinois, Michigan, Ohio, Pennsylvania, and West Virginia (all partisan or hybrid election states), and candidates in Idaho, Minnesota, Montana, Oregon, and Washington (all nonpartisan election states) tend to raise lower amounts of money. Interestingly, Texas, which has long been a state with large amounts of campaign money (Champagne and Cheek 2001), is not one of the highest fundraising states when one considers money per candidate.

**TABLE 5.1** Average Fundraising per Number of Seats and Number of Candidates, 2000–2014

| | *All Elections* | | | *Partisan Elections* | | | *Nonpartisan Elections* | | | *Hybrid Elections* | | |
|---|---|---|---|---|---|---|---|---|---|---|---|---|
| *Year* | *Average* | *Avg/ Seat* | *Avg/ Candidate* | *Average* | *Avg/ Seat* | *Avg/ Candidate* | *Average* | *Avg/ Seat* | *Avg/ Candidate* | *Average* | *Avg/ Seat* | *Avg/ Candidate* |
| 2000 | $2,296,690 | $829,476 | $356,056 | $3,730,716 | $1,138,691 | $490,916 | $886,187 | $427,815 | $206,302 | $5,035,367 | $1,956,358 | $707,700 |
| 2002 | $1,301,102 | $769,622 | $300,692 | $2,302,933 | $1,407,123 | $496,407 | $358,716 | $238,599 | $101,178 | $3,449,011 | $1,724,506 | $812,775 |
| 2004 | $1,939,436 | $1,148,720 | $480,255 | $3,423,875 | $2,604,081 | $1,092,325 | $884,168 | $375,139 | $146,853 | $3,603,139 | $1,083,231 | $505,126 |
| 2006 | $1,688,864 | $448,650 | $180,728 | $4,850,365 | $970,073 | $333,594 | $903,890 | $255,032 | $124,076 | $1,656,452 | $828,226 | $291,344 |
| 2008 | $1,668,193 | $1,006,404 | $446,762 | $3,014,301 | $1,745,857 | $766,156 | $823,569 | $486,957 | $236,032 | $2,024,561 | $1,535,004 | $593,261 |
| 2010 | $1,063,147 | $637,307 | $244,085 | $2,338,908 | $1,533,891 | $440,950 | $643,822 | $463,115 | $220,275 | $2,056,659 | $839,732 | $411,332 |
| 2012 | $1,188,393 | $515,563 | $165,553 | $1,959,796 | $914,323 | $245,868 | $430,338 | $208,272 | $89,376 | $2,582,555 | $860,852 | $290,764 |
| 2014 | $965,201 | $378,580 | $191,345 | $1,086,851 | $420,515 | $257,632 | $531,179 | $211,870 | $110,120 | $2,735,826 | $1,065,870 | $457,424 |

**TABLE 5.2** Average Money Raised per Candidate, in Year 2000 Dollars, by State

| *State* | *2000* | *2002* | *2004* | *2006* | *2008* | *2010* | *2012* | *2014* |
|---|---|---|---|---|---|---|---|---|
| Alabama | $1,233,733 | $699,265 | $616,471 | $770,466 | $1,788,608 | $416,519 | $337,770 | $29,942 |
| Arkansas | $205,853 | $16,197 | $175,288 | $61,481 | $34,645 | $310,506 | $78,464 | $65,023 |
| Georgia | $12,963 | $114,509 | $371,716 | $306,409 | $155,603 | $154,848 | $45,851 | $66,214 |
| Idaho | $149,273 | $24,539 | $3,897 | – | $64,835 | $42,683 | – | $39,612 |
| Illinois | $746,796 | $633,762 | $4,268,336 | – | $872,659 | – | $342,789 | – |
| Kentucky | $194,917 | – | $218,160 | $181,072 | $103,117 | $2,724 | $136,200 | $19,519 |
| Louisiana | $125,978 | $549,539 | $412,108 | – | $737,194 | $394,697 | $220,362 | $565,265 |
| Michigan | $748,434 | $131,941 | $291,914 | $183,223 | $696,964 | $370,029 | $256,446 | $453,065 |
| Minnesota | $88,117 | $29,298 | $27,395 | $171 | $22,440 | $24,133 | $24,405 | $31,005 |
| Mississippi | $379,839 | $579,429 | $233,649 | – | $264,508 | $3,949 | $192,192 | – |
| Montana | $286,208 | $41,984 | $158,913 | $22,671 | $89,164 | $42,163 | $49,409 | $68,441 |
| Nevada | $112,636 | $246,824 | $281,352 | $244,058 | $417,926 | – | – | – |
| New Mexico | – | $43,567 | $212,719 | – | $41,315 | – | $62,392 | – |
| North Carolina | $512,334 | $128,794 | $115,531 | $212,458 | $71,292 | $64,645 | $64,881 | $317,166 |
| North Dakota | $6,963 | – | – | – | – | – | – | – |
| Ohio | $666,966 | $1,493,609 | $718,338 | $399,465 | $489,557 | $452,635 | $325,082 | $461,784 |
| Oregon | $93,600 | $41,407 | $55,737 | $241,105 | $3,010 | $26,465 | $118,830 | – |
| Pennsylvania | – | $1,088,271 | $507,586 | – | $1,081,445 | $1,070,882 | – | – |
| Texas | $190,125 | $331,650 | $365,332 | $230,315 | $313,445 | $155,399 | $200,419 | $177,690 |
| Washington | $73,345 | $96,253 | $96,913 | $171,877 | $55,591 | $98,869 | $107,368 | $21,242 |
| West Virginia | $871,457 | – | $1,263,722 | – | $528,427 | $121,002 | $311,480 | – |
| Wisconsin | $421,593 | $23,691 | $170,542 | $47,609 | $1,550,257 | $641,376 | $105,616 | $362,864 |

### *Who Is Spending the Money?*

Of all the campaign money being spent in state supreme court elections, what percentage is from the candidates compared to outside groups? Given the high correlation between money raised by candidates and the total spending in an election, we would expect to see most of the money being spent coming from the candidates themselves. Figure 5.1 displays these data.

Whereas over 90 percent of the campaign spending in 2002 was by candidates themselves, this has dropped to almost 60 percent in recent years. So, there has been a steady drop as spending by independent groups and political parties has increased. Indeed, in 2012 and 2014, almost 30 percent of the spending in judicial elections was by interest groups, according to the Justice at Stake data. Whereas spending has not increased dramatically when looked at in constant dollars, these data suggest the *sources* of spending have shifted,[11] although the majority of spending is still done by the candidates themselves.

This is both good news and bad news for those concerned with campaign spending. On the positive side, it means candidates may need to be less concerned with raising funds to support their campaigns, because interest groups will do it on their behalf. On the negative side, candidates will have less control over their campaigns, as they cannot dictate to groups how the money should be spent or the tone of the advertisements (Hall 2015). Whereas Gibson (2012) has shown that concerns over the tone of judicial campaigns have been overstated by many, there are certain types of ads that voters think "cross the line." To the extent that candidates lose control over the messages in their campaign, the proverbial line may be increasingly crossed. In fact, Hall (2015) shows that televised attack advertising has a negative impact on the electoral performance of incumbents in

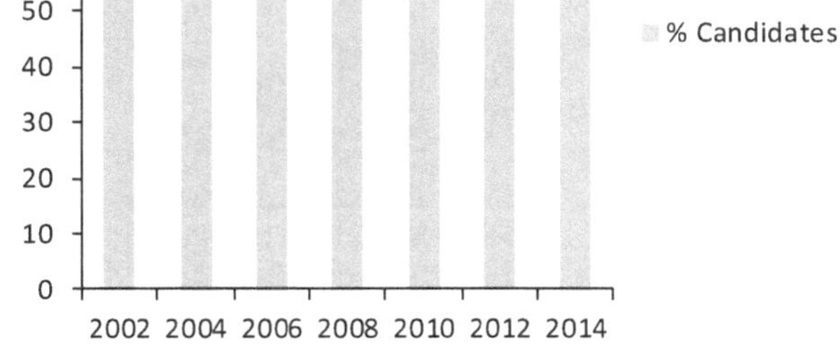


**FIGURE 5.1** Percent of Total Funds Spent by Candidates

nonpartisan elections, suggesting that outside spending on campaign negativity may have particularly adverse effects in nonpartisan races.

### On What Is Money Being Spent?

The primary reason why candidates need to raise money is to spend it on their campaigns. Yet, there are numerous things on which the money can be spent: overhead/infrastructure, staff, radio ads, television ads, direct mail, etc. While we do not have campaign spending data on all of these different options, we do have data on television advertising since 2008. I break these figures down by selection system in Figure 5.2.

When looked at in constant dollars,[12] the amount of spending on television advertising has been decreasing since 2008. Looking at all elections, spending on television advertisements was about $1.5 million, on average, in 2008; in 2014, it is around $500,000. Partisan election states and nonpartisan election states demonstrate the same trends. Indeed, spending on television advertising is only increasing in the two states that utilize hybrid elections: Michigan and Ohio. Both of these states have witnessed elections that could have swung the partisan majority of the court in recent years, so it is not surprising that candidates spent a lot of money on television advertising here. Whether or not this continues is an open question.

These results are surprising given all of the claims about the rise and importance of television advertising (see Hall 2015 for an excellent discussion of this).

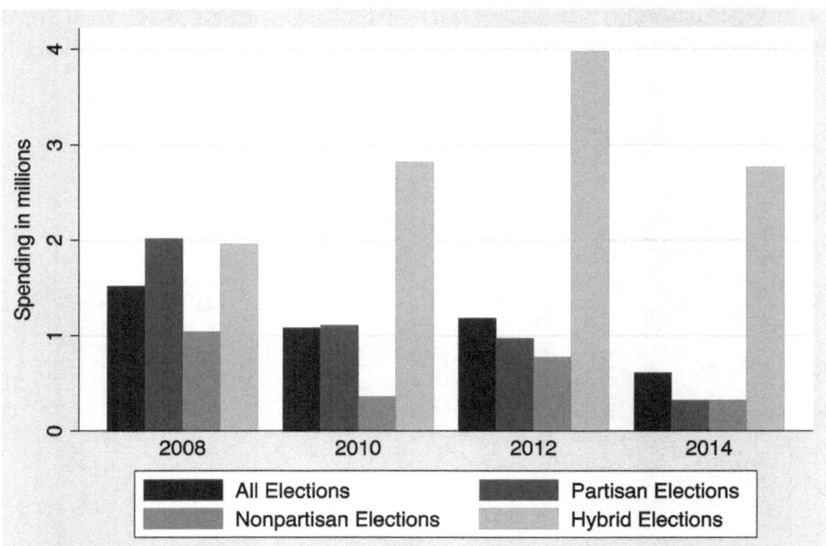


**FIGURE 5.2** Spending on TV Advertisements by Method of Selection

The data presented here make it difficult to sustain the claim that campaign spending on television is on the rise. If anything, television advertising has declined significantly, which is an unexpected and counterintuitive finding.

## The Future: Things to Watch

While state supreme court elections are not becoming more expensive over the first part of this decade, it is clear that campaign spending in judicial elections is not going away anytime soon. State supreme court seats are valuable and powerful offices; candidates and their supporters will continue to wage vigorous campaigns to obtain and retain them. This should be neither surprising nor troubling. Spending in any campaign is necessary to inform and engage voters. Higher levels of spending may be a public good as well as a democratic imperative, even in judicial elections.

However, the data presented here caution against judicial elections being treated as monolithic. There are important variations in campaign fundraising and spending both among methods of selection and between states within the same method of selection. One of the interesting things to monitor going forward is whether large amounts of campaign fundraising spreads to states that have yet to see them. The same holds true for television advertising. As Hall (2015) documents, and the data in this chapter and in Chapter 4 support, whereas television advertising is an important tool for campaigns, not all races involve television advertising (see also Hall and Bonneau 2013).

Another factor to watch in the future is whether the data stabilize at all and if there becomes less variation across states and races within a state. Right now, there is little empirical regularity in the data across years and across races. For many, this is comforting because it shows that elections do not necessarily have to be expensive affairs. Moreover, it shows that some candidates—presumably candidates with whom the voters are satisfied—do not have a lot of worry when it comes to expensive elections. Whether this continues or not bears observation.

Finally, as more and more states either change their method of selection (or consider doing so), the effect this has on campaign fundraising and spending ought to be studied. This is especially true for states that either institute or eliminate public financing of elections. Of particular interest in this regard are North Carolina and West Virginia.[13]

Overall, the picture of campaign fundraising and spending is more complex and nuanced than is typically portrayed. It is important moving forward that scholars examine data controlling for inflation and do not treat state supreme court elections as monolithic.

## Notes

1 See Geyh and Thrapp's (2017) excellent chapter in this volume for a discussion of these cases.

2 Both of these types of elections can involve multiple candidates. The only difference between them is that partisan elections have the candidates' political party affiliations listed next to their names, and nonpartisan elections do not provide the voters with that information.
3 It is also important that one does not take the results of a single survey question out of context. For example, the same poll shows that 78 percent of respondents consider the courts to be impartial, 82 percent believe that "fair" is an accurate way to describe the courts, and 74 percent have at least "some" confidence in the courts, a full eighteen percentage points higher than confidence in the legislature and twenty percentage points higher than confidence in the governor.
4 The survey is available at: www.justiceatstake.org/file.cfm/media/news/toplines337_B2D51323DC5D0.pdf
5 To be clear, *Citizens United* (2010) simply made it easier for these groups to spend money. It did not fundamentally change the landscape of who could spend money.
6 These reports are available at: www.justiceatstake.org/resources/the-new-politics-of-judicial-elections/.
7 While Texas has two courts of last resort, Justice at Stake only collects information for the Texas Supreme Court, not the Texas Court of Criminal Appeals.
8 Elections held in odd-numbered years are grouped with the subsequent even-numbered year. For example, the 2004 figures include elections held in 2003 and 2004.
9 Recall that there were two very expensive races in 2004 (Illinois and West Virginia) that are likely skewing the data for that year.
10 I refer to these elections as hybrids because candidates are nominated by political parties (either in a primary or caucus), but they run in the general election without their political party on the ballot. Thus, parties are involved to a much larger extent than they are in nonpartisan elections, but candidates do not have the advantage of having their political party next to their name on the ballot as in partisan elections.
11 In fact, Hall (2015) shows that much of the televised attack advertising in contested nonpartisan elections comes from interest groups. This is much less true in partisan elections.
12 For consistency with the rest of the chapter, I use 2000 as the base year, even though the data used here begin in 2008.
13 See Bonneau and Kane (2017) in this volume for more information on these states.

## References

Bonneau, Chris W. 2005. "What Price Justice(s)? Understanding Campaign Spending in State Supreme Court Elections." *State Politics and Policy Quarterly* 5: 107–125.

Bonneau, Chris W. 2007a. "Campaign Fundraising in State Supreme Court Elections." *Social Science Quarterly* 88: 68–85.

Bonneau, Chris W. 2007b. "The Dynamics of Campaign Spending in State Supreme Court Elections." In *Running for Judge: The Rising Political, Financial, and Legal Stakes of Judicial Elections*, edited by Matthew J. Streb. New York: NYU Press.

Bonneau, Chris W. and Melinda Gann Hall. 2009. *In Defense of Judicial Elections*. New York: Routledge.

Bonneau, Chris W. and Jenna Becker Kane. 2017. "Proposals for Reform: Successes and Failures." In *Judicial Elections in the 21st Century*, edited by Chris W. Bonneau and Melinda Gann Hall. New York: Routledge.

Caldeira, Gregory A. and James L. Gibson. 1992. "The Etiology of Public Support for the Supreme Court." *American Journal of Political Science* 36: 635–664.

Cann, Damon M. 2002. "Campaign Contributions and Judicial Behavior." *American Review of Politics* 23: 261–274.
Cann, Damon M. 2007. "Justice for Sale? Campaign Contributions and Judicial Decisionmaking." *State Politics and Policy Quarterly* 7: 281–297.
Cann, Damon M., Chris W. Bonneau, and Brent D. Boyea. 2012. "Campaign Contributions and Judicial Decisions in Partisan and Nonpartisan Elections." In *New Directions in Judicial Politics*, edited by Kevin T. McGuire. New York: Routledge.
Cann, Damon M. and Jeff Yates. 2008. "Homegrown Institutional Legitimacy: Assessing Citizens' Diffuse Support for State Courts." *American Politics Research* 36: 297–329.
*Caperton v. Massey Coal Co., Inc.* 2009. 556 U.S. 868.
Champagne, Anthony. 1988. "Judicial Reform in Texas." *Judicature* 72: 146–159.
Champagne, Anthony and Kyle Cheek. 2001. "The Cycle of Judicial Elections: Texas as a Case Study." *Fordham Urban Law Journal* 29: 907–940.
Choi, Stephen J., G. Mitu Gulati, and Eric A. Posner. 2010. "Professionals or Politicians: The Uncertain Empirical Case for an Elected Rather than Appointed Judiciary." *Journal of Law, Economics, and Organization* 26: 290–336.
*Citizens United v. Federal Election Commission*. 2010. 558 U.S. 310.
Coleman, John J. and Paul F. Manna. 2000. "Congressional Campaign Spending and the Quality of Democracy." *Journal of Politics* 62: 757–789.
Francia Peter L., John C. Green, Paul S. Herrnson, Lynda W. Powell, and Clyde Wilcox. 2003. *The Financiers of Congressional Elections*. New York: Columbia University Press.
Geyh, Charles Gardner. 2003. "Why Judicial Elections Stink." *Ohio State Law Journal* 64: 43–79.
Geyh, Charles Gardner. 2005. "The Judgment of the Boss on Bossing the Judges: Bruce Springsteen, Judicial Independence, and the Rule of Law." *Widener Law Journal* 14: 885–905.
Geyh, Charles Gardner and Katherine Thrapp. 2017. "The Changing Legal Landscape of Judicial Elections." In *Judicial Elections in the 21st Century*, edited by Chris W. Bonneau and Melinda Gann Hall. New York: Routledge.
Gibson, James L. 2012. *Electing Judges: The Surprising Effects of Campaigning on Judicial Legitimacy*. Chicago: University of Chicago Press.
Gibson, James L., Jeffrey A. Gottfried, Michael X. Delli Carpini, and Kathleen Hall Jamieson. 2011. "The Effects of Judicial Campaign Activity on the Legitimacy of Courts: A Survey-based Experiment." *Political Research Quarterly* 64: 545–558.
Grant, J. Tobin and Thomas J. Rudolph. 2002. "To Give or Not to Give: Modeling Individuals' Contribution Decisions." *Political Behavior* 24: 31–54.
Greyak, Scott, Alicia Bannon, Allyson Falce, and Linda Casey. 2015. *The New Politics of Judicial Elections 2013–14: Bankrolling the Bench*. Washington, DC: Justice at Stake Campaign.
Hall, Melinda Gann. 2015. *Attacking Judges: How Campaign Advertising Influences State Supreme Court Elections*. Stanford: Stanford University Press.
Hall, Melinda Gann and Chris W. Bonneau. 2008. "Mobilizing Interest: The Effects of Money on Citizen Participation in State Supreme Court Elections." *American Journal of Political Science* 52: 457–470.
Hall, Melinda Gann and Chris W. Bonneau. 2013. "Attack Advertising, the *White* Decision, and Voter Participation in State Supreme Court Elections." *Political Research Quarterly* 66: 115–126.

Hurwitz, Mark S. and Drew Noble Lanier. 2008. "Diversity in States and Federal Appellate Courts: Change and Continuity across 20 Years." *Justice System Journal* 29: 47–70.
Kanthak, Kristin and Jonathan Woon. 2015. "Women Don't Run? Election Aversion and Candidate Entry." *American Journal of Political Science* 59: 595–612.
McCall, Madhavi M. 2008. "The Politics of Judicial Elections: The Influence of Campaign Contributions on the Voting Patterns of Texas Supreme Court Justices, 1994–1997." *Politics and Policy* 31: 314–343.
McCall, Madhavi M. and Michael A. McCall. 2006. "Campaign Contributions, Judicial Decisions, and the Texas Supreme Court: Assessing the Appearance of Impropriety." *Judicature* 90: 214–225.
Rosenstone, Steven J. and John Mark Hansen. 1993. *Mobilization, Participation, and Democracy in America*. New York: MacMillan.
Schill, Dan and John Allen Hendricks. 2016. "Media, Message, and Mobilization: Political Communication in the 2014 Election Campaigns." In *Communication and Midterm Elections: Media, Message, and Mobilization*, edited by John Allen Hendricks and Dan Schill. New York: Palgrave.
Skaggs, Adam, Maria da Silva, Linda Casey, and Charles Hall. 2011. *The New Politics of Judicial Elections 2009–10*. Washington, DC: Justice at Stake Campaign.
Waltenburg, Eric N. and Charles S. Lopeman. 2000. "Tort Decisions and Campaign Dollars." *Southeastern Political Review* 28: 241–263.
Ware, Stephen J. 1999. "Money, Politics, and Judicial Decisions: A Case Study of Arbitration Law in Alabama." *Journal of Law and Politics* 25: 645–686.
*Williams-Yulee v. The Florida Bar*. 2015. 135 S.Ct. 1656.

# 6

# JUDICIAL RETENTION ELECTIONS

*Larry T. Aspin*

In recent election cycles, increased attention to judicial elections has focused on the high cost of races for state supreme courts. The high levels of campaign contributions in these elections have increased concerns about the independence and impartiality of the courts (e.g., Skaggs et al. 2011; Greytak et al. 2015). Commission selection and judicial retention elections have long been advocated as mechanisms to achieve and maintain judicial independence and impartiality.[1] Commission selection eliminates campaigns from the initial selection stage, and justices campaign in retention elections only when they are actively opposed. However, some of the most costly judicial elections in the last three election cycles have been retention elections for state supreme court justices (e.g., Illinois in 2010 and 2014, Florida in 2012, and Tennessee in 2014). Thus, in this chapter I address three questions: (1) Have judicial retentions changed of late? (2) Are supreme court retention elections representative of all judicial retention elections? (3) Do the recent high-cost supreme court retention elections foreshadow the future?

To provide an empirical base for answering such questions, recent judicial retention elections are examined within the context of the trends that have been captured by the Judicial Retention Project (JRP).[2] The comprehensive JRP database contains information about 9,919 judicial retention elections from 1964, when several states first adopted the commission-retention system, through to 2014. The database contains retention elections for the major trial, intermediate appellate, and supreme courts in the eighteen states that conduct retention elections in even numbered years.[3] To minimize the effect of inter-state variability, most of the long-term analysis herein focuses on the 7,845 retention elections in the 1984–2014 period, when most of the eighteen states had begun to hold retention elections. The JRP also began recording the existence and level of opposition with the 2010 elections; thus, the analysis of opposition reported here is confined to the 1,755 elections in the 2010–2014 period.

The overwhelming majority of recent judicial retention elections are found to be a continuation of past patterns. There continues to be significant inter-state variability in both the levels and trends of the affirmative vote; these differences are not easily explained. For example, given the frequency of conservative groups attempting to defeat judges with opposition campaigns in the 2010–2014 period, it could be hypothesized that party identification and ideological differences among the states might explain some of the inter-state variability. However, the persistent inter-state differences on the affirmative vote are related to the levels of political trust and support for the United States Supreme Court, not to the ideological and party identification differences among the states. Also of little consequence to the affirmative vote are election-specific variables such as the race, gender, and ethnicity of the judge.

The topic of opposition is explored in depth in the first systematic analysis of opposition in judicial retention elections employing the JPR data. Notable findings include the facts that low-level opposition never results in the defeat of a judge/justice; supreme court justices are much more likely to be a target of an opposition campaign than trial court judges; and all but one supreme court opposition campaign failed to defeat the targeted justices. Likewise, the 2010–2014 supreme court retention elections are clearly not representative of all retention elections. Major trial court judges had only a 1 in 100 chance of facing an opposition campaign, whereas supreme court justices had a 1 in 3 chance.

Given that opposition is recorded only for the 2010–2014 period, it is not possible to determine if this high proportion of opposition campaigns in supreme court retention elections is a significant break from the past or whether the opposition level in 2010–2014 will continue. On the one hand, given that in 2010–2014 only one opposition campaign was able to defeat a supreme court justice, it should not be assumed that all opposition groups are both willing and able to continue pouring significant resources into losing efforts. On the other hand, some of the opposition campaigns in judicial retention elections were but one element of an ongoing political struggle that may extend over several years and involve structural changes to judicial selection.

## Affirmative Vote

The national average affirmative vote in the 7,845 judicial retention elections during the 1984–2014 period is 73.3 percent, which is well above the 50 percent threshold employed in sixteen of the eighteen states. As can be seen in Figure 6.1, there is some yearly variation, with the national average peaking at 76.9 percent in 1988, dropping to the low point of 69.1 percent in the next election. Overall

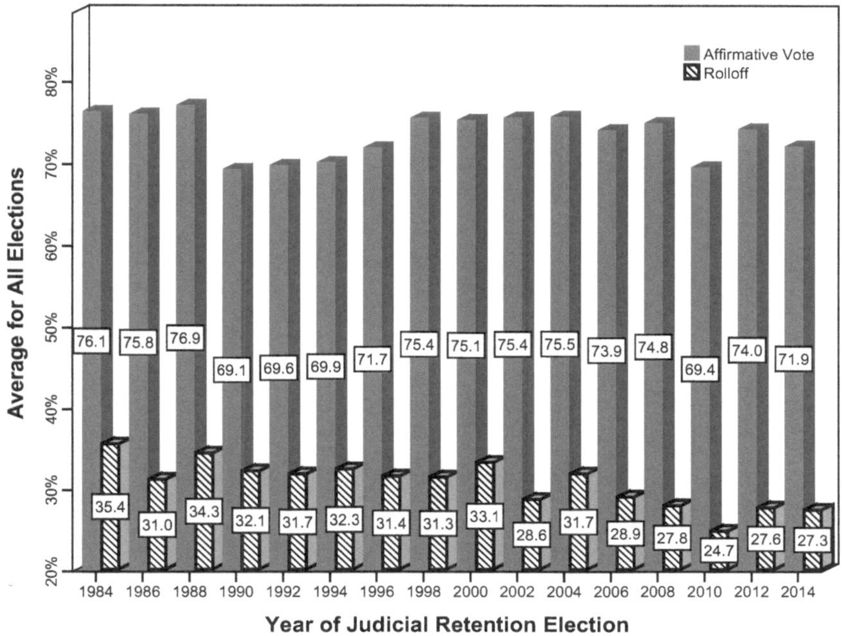


7,845 major trial court, intermediate appellate court, and supreme court retention elections held in the states of Alaska, Arizona, California, Colorado, Florida, Illinois, Indiana, Iowa, Kansas, Maryland, Missouri, Nebraska, New Mexico, Oklahoma, South Dakota, Tennessee, Utah, and Wyoming from 1984 through 2014

**FIGURE 6.1** Average Affirmative Vote and Rolloff in Judicial Retention Elections

there is no consistent upward or downward trend in the affirmative vote. The lower values beginning in 1990, and to a lesser extent those in 2010, correspond to a larger decline in trust in government.[4] The 1990 and 2010 elections also saw successful efforts to defeat judges, but opposition campaigns are so infrequent that their impact on the national average is relatively small.

The effect of efforts to defeat judges is more visible when retention elections are disaggregated by state. In Table 6.1, note for example the sharp drop in Wyoming's affirmative vote in 1992 when Justice Urbigkit and Judge Wolfe were defeated.

Finally with regard to yearly variation in the national mean affirmative vote, a statistically significant but very small part of the variation can be explained by the type of election year. The average affirmative vote in presidential election years is 74.8 percent, compared to 73.1 percent in midterm election years.

As just mentioned, there appears to be little evidence that nationally the affirmative vote in retention elections is trending upward or downward. Interestingly, the lack of a national trend may be the result of opposing trends at state level. Not only is there considerable variability in the affirmative vote from state to state, but there also are some conflicting trends. Thus, any sweeping conclusions about the future should be treated with caution. These patterns are shown in Table 6.1.

**TABLE 6.1** Mean Affirmative Vote by State by Election Year

| *State* | *1984* | *1986* | *1988* | *1990* | *1992* | *1994* | *1996* | *1998* | *2000* | *2002* | *2004* | *2006* | *2008* | *2010* | *2012* | *2014* |
|---|---|---|---|---|---|---|---|---|---|---|---|---|---|---|---|---|
| Alaska | 68.4 | 71.1 | 68.9 | 68.2 | 64.3 | 66.3 | 68.9 | 68.4 | 64.3 | 69.1 | 69.5 | 64.1 | 66.6 | 63.1 | 66.0 | 64.9 |
| Arizona | 81.0 | 79.8 | 78.7 | 69.2 | 66.8 | 72.7 | 72.4 | 73.4 | 76.1 | 73.6 | 75.4 | 73.6 | 73.4 | 65.8 | 71.1 | 69.4 |
| California | | 58.1 | | 65.8 | | 59.8 | | 75.3 | | 72.8 | | 72.9 | | 70.6 | | 71.5 |
| Colorado | 74.2 | 71.7 | 75.0 | 67.4 | 68.8 | 67.3 | 66.5 | 73.2 | 72.7 | 73.0 | 73.1 | 72.4 | 73.7 | 65.4 | 72.5 | 69.4 |
| Florida | 73.1 | 75.5 | 74.8 | 66.1 | 65.8 | 67.1 | 69.7 | 70.3 | 72.3 | 69.8 | 71.8 | 69.5 | 70.8 | 64.7 | 71.8 | 71.0 |
| Illinois | 77.2 | 75.5 | 76.7 | 69.7 | 72.8 | 75.3 | 75.0 | 78.6 | 78.9 | 79.1 | 78.9 | 79.4 | 78.7 | 75.8 | 76.7 | 76.9 |
| Indiana | 71.2 | 63.0 | 66.1 | 63.4 | 63.3 | 62.1 | 68.8 | 71.5 | 73.1 | 71.8 | 67.7 | 68.9 | 72.1 | 69.5 | 72.3 | 69.6 |
| Iowa | 77.4 | 80.2 | 79.1 | 76.5 | 74.2 | 73.7 | 74.1 | 77.0 | 76.9 | 76.8 | 76.4 | 74.3 | 74.3 | 63.4 | 75.8 | 72.8 |
| Kansas | 82.6 | 84.1 | 79.5 | 73.4 | 72.1 | 70.7 | 76.0 | 75.4 | 75.9 | 77.3 | 75.3 | 72.1 | 71.6 | 68.5 | 73.6 | 66.7 |
| Maryland | 84.4 | 87.9 | 87.1 | 77.6 | 82.1 | 76.5 | 84.1 | 85.6 | 85.9 | 88.1 | 86.3 | 87.3 | 85.3 | 85.4 | 86.9 | 85.2 |
| Missouri | 72.8 | 71.0 | 69.5 | 58.5 | 63.0 | 64.6 | 67.6 | 68.7 | 69.0 | 69.6 | 67.0 | 68.8 | 69.4 | 66.9 | 71.4 | 64.1 |
| Nebraska | 73.6 | 74.7 | 78.7 | 75.2 | 70.3 | 72.5 | 67.1 | 75.8 | 74.4 | 74.1 | 73.9 | 71.5 | 70.3 | 69.6 | 73.4 | 72.1 |
| New Mexico | | | | | | | 67.6 | 74.8 | 74.5 | 77.4 | 77.2 | 77.1 | 75.9 | 70.2 | 75.1 | 74.4 |
| Oklahoma | 69.5 | 67.9 | | 57.4 | 62.0 | 58.6 | 61.9 | 67.3 | 68.0 | 68.0 | 70.1 | 67.0 | 65.0 | 63.5 | 66.5 | 60.9 |
| South Dakota | 77.7 | 65.8 | | 74.9 | | 74.7 | | 82.2 | | | | 83.7 | | | | 82.5 |
| Tennessee | 69.1 | 69.7 | 75.9 | | 66.9 | 65.6 | 60.6 | 68.2 | 71.3 | | | 75.3 | 76.7 | 68.3 | 71.2 | 63.5 |
| Utah | | | 83.6 | 77.4 | 79.2 | 79.5 | 79.1 | 82.3 | 78.9 | 80.8 | 81.5 | 79.3 | 80.2 | 77.3 | 81.9 | 76.7 |
| Wyoming | 75.6 | 73.8 | 78.2 | 74.3 | 58.2 | 76.6 | 77.5 | 78.4 | 76.5 | 77.7 | 79.9 | 78.5 | 79.4 | 76.5 | 79.5 | 77.4 |

Some states have experienced a slight upward trend in the average affirmative vote over the 1984–2014 period (e.g., California, Illinois, Indiana, and South Dakota). In contrast, other states have experienced a downward trend in the affirmative vote (e.g., Alaska, Arizona, Iowa, and Kansas). The rest of the states have a relatively constant affirmative vote or oscillation with no overall movement up or down. In all cases any long-term trends are gradual. The fastest rate of change is in Kansas, where the affirmative vote is decreasing by an average of seven-tenths of a percent per election cycle.

The greatest variability in the affirmative vote is not from year to year but rather from state to state. As seen in Figure 6.2, the national aggregate pattern obscures differences among the states in terms of the typical affirmative vote for retention. The average vote ranges from the low of 64.9 percent in Oklahoma to the high of 85.2 percent in Maryland. Whereas accounting for this variability will be discussed shortly, these differences are a reminder that the judicial retention election is a mechanism that may be used differently by states and will elicit varying responses from different groups of voters.

Level of court is the second location for significant variability in the affirmative vote. Because they are fewer in number, supreme court retention elections have more yearly variability than the more numerous major trial court elections. More interestingly, with only two exceptions in each election year, the mean affirmative vote in supreme court elections has been lower than the mean affirmative

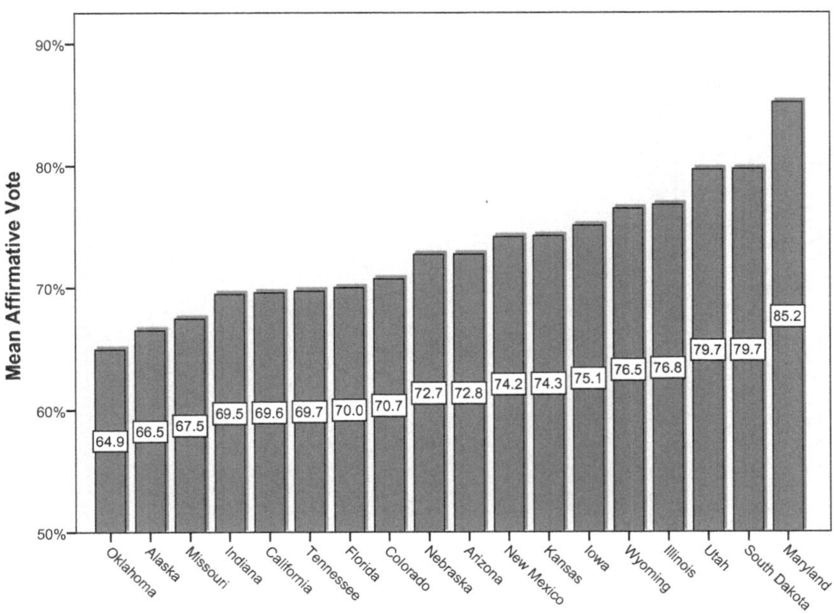


**FIGURE 6.2** Mean Affirmative Vote in 1984–2014 Retention Elections by State

vote in major trial court elections. Why might this be the case? This pattern is consistent with the observation to be discussed later that supreme court retention elections are much more likely to see opposition campaigns than are major trial court elections. Years with the greatest difference between the trial courts and the supreme courts saw major opposition campaigns and, in some cases, these successfully removed supreme court justices.

Whereas the recent big-budget campaigns in supreme court retention elections and the subsequent lower affirmative vote might tempt some to conclude that retention elections have entered a new era, caution should be the order of the day. Taking the long-term view reminds us there have been successful opposition campaigns against justices in the past (e.g., California 1986 and Tennessee 1996). As seen in Figure 6.3, the mean affirmative vote in supreme court elections in the 2010–2014 period is very similar to the 1990–1996 period. Furthermore, all of the recent declines in the supreme court vote cannot be attributed to the few opposition campaigns. In 2010 there were opposition campaigns against supreme court justices in only six states, but the affirmative vote in supreme court elections declined in all but one state holding elections. This is a reminder that the affirmative vote is a function of more than just election-specific variables but also of district, institutional, and temporal variables (e.g., trust in government). Figure 6.3 illustrates how the mean affirmative votes

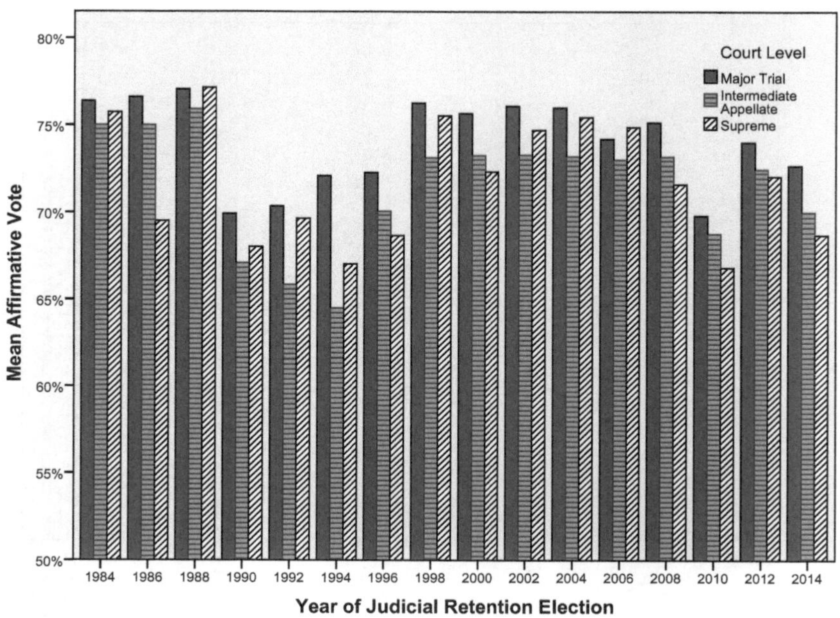


FIGURE 6.3 Mean Affirmative Vote by Year and Level of Court

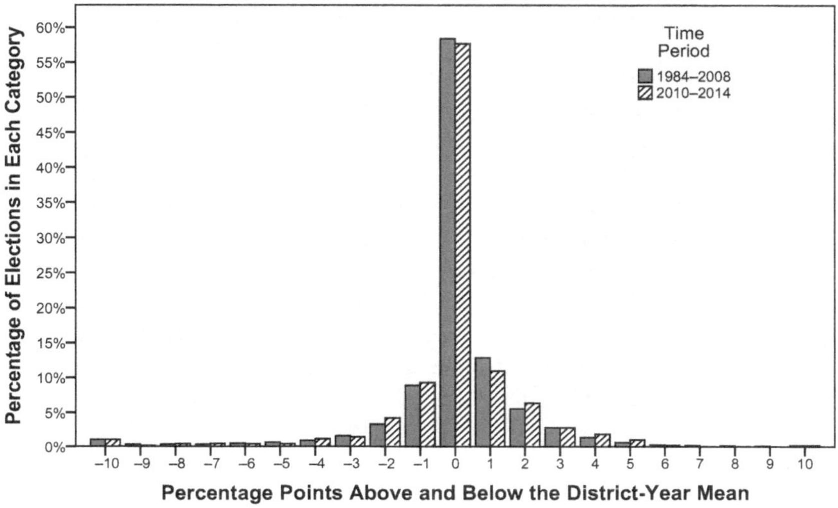


**FIGURE 6.4** Categorized Relative Distance of Affirmative Vote from District-Year Median

for each type of court move together across time. As will be discussed later, rarely is there significant opposition in major trial court elections, yet that mean affirmative vote declined in the 1990–1996 period and the 2010–2014 period just as in supreme court elections.

One of the hallmarks of judicial retention elections is that there is little intra-district variation in the affirmative vote—all the judges in a district are receiving very similar vote totals. Even when one or more judges on a ballot are defeated, the other judges are treated the same as each other rather than as the unsuccessful judge. It could be hypothesized that voter differentiation among the judges has increased recently because of factors such as the systematic communication of judicial performance evaluation commission materials or increased voter attention because of the high-profile judicial campaigns; however, this proves not to be the case. A counter-argument is simply that rarely do bar associations or judicial performance commissions recommend that a judge be defeated; thus, they are urging voters to treat all judges the same.

As there is significant inter-state and inter-district variation in the affirmative vote, voter differentiation among judges is assessed by calculating each judge's distance from the district-year mean affirmative vote. The sample is reduced to all elections where four or more judges were on the same ballot. In each election the average percent voting for retention for all judges in the district is calculated and then subtracted from each judge's affirmative vote. For the 4,882 elections with four or more judges on a ballot in the 1984–2014 period, the average absolute distance from the district mean is only 1.7 percentage points.

Figure 6.4 demonstrates both the lack of differentiation and the lack of any recent positive or negative changes. For the 1984–2014 period, 85.6 percent of all retention elections are within two percentage points of the district mean. There is only a small difference comparing recent elections to the long-term. The percentage of elections within two percentage points of the district year mean is 86 percent for 1984–2008 and 84 percent for 2010–2014. The percentage of elections that are three or more percentage points below the mean is 6.4 percent for 1984–2008 and 6.7 percent for 2010–2014.

Do the national values obscure any conflict trends within individual states? Looking at the 1984–2014 period by state reveals only small trends in five of the eighteen states. In Illinois and Missouri, there are slight long-term decreases in the average absolute difference from the district mean, and Arizona, Colorado, and Florida have slight long-term increases in the average absolute difference from the district mean.[5]

We know that voters differentiate among the judges when one is being targeted by organized opposition, but what other variables might cause them to vote for one judge and not another?[6] Whereas the judicial performance evaluation commissions and systematic bar evaluations produce information on individual judges, if voters do not retain the information they may be casting a vote with little knowledge of the judges on the ballot. In this case, one option is to rolloff and not vote in the judicial retention section of the ballot. Other voter options are to use cues about the judges found on their ballot or rely on their own attributes such as basic confidence in the political system. Gender, ethnicity, and (less so) race of the judge can be inferred from a judge's name, but during 1984–2014 none of these attributes is related to the affirmative vote. There is very little difference on the average affirmative vote between any of the gender, ethnic, and racial groups: women (73.5%), men (73.2%), Hispanic (72.2%), Non-Hispanic (73.3%), African-American (72.8%), and Non-African-American (73.1%). While these attributes may be important to some voters, overall they have no effect on the vote.[7]

Next to the lack of differentiation among judges, one of the other well-known patterns in judicial elections is that in every election there is always a certain percentage of voters in the district who do not support any judge standing for retention. In each election cycle, there are calls in the form of bloggers and letters to the editor for voters to reject all judges standing for retention. Apparently some voters heed the call, for no matter how highly rated and respected a judge is, there is always a significant "Do Not Retain" vote. For the last four decades, the average national affirmative vote has never been above 80 percent. One explanation for this shotgun no-vote is the lack of voter confidence in the political system or the courts. Attributes such as trust in political institutions, especially the courts, can guide voters when they lack information about the judges or justices. Thus, differences from state to state in confidence in the political system or in the courts may account for some of the interstate variation in the affirmative vote observed in Figure 6.2.

There is systematic empirical support for this hypothesis in the 1984–2014 period. Using the state as the unit of analysis, I conducted an empirical assessment of the eighteen states employing retention elections in the 1984–2014 period. Overall, I found moderate positive relationships between the average affirmative vote and (a) the state population's confidence in the United States Supreme Court; and (b) the state population's broader trust in government. The correlation between the mean affirmative vote and confidence in the U. S. Supreme Court was 0.52.[8] The correlation between the mean affirmative vote and the American National Election Study (ANES) trust in government index was 0.48 for election years 2000 through 2008.[9] In my analysis, the two trust variables had stronger relationships with the average affirmative vote than any of the other tested independent variables.

In my investigation, none of the other examined structural (e.g., whether the state utilizes a judicial performance evaluation commission) and population composition variables were related to the affirmative vote. With regard to the latter, neither political ideology nor the partisan identifications of the state's population were significant. Given that many conservative Republicans were involved in campaigns to defeat judges in the 2010–2014 period, I hypothesized that the mean affirmative vote would be related to these factors, but I observed no such relationships.

## Rolloff

Rolloff is the percentage of voters who cast ballots in the top races on the ballot but do not vote in the judicial retention election. Rolloff ranges from less than 5 percent in some judicial districts to over 60 percent in others, usually large urban districts. One clear trend across the entire 1984–2014 period is that an increasing percentage of voters are opting to vote in judicial retention elections. As reported in Figure 6.1, nationally there is a long consistent decline in rolloff, from 35.4 percent in 1984 to 27.3 percent in 2014. This pattern is repeated in most of the states with the notable exceptions of Arizona and Nebraska, which experienced increased rolloff during the 1984–2014 period. The declining rolloff occurs in states with and without judicial performance evaluation commissions, and with and without high-budget opposition campaigns. Also, for many states, rolloff is highest in the early years after the adoption of retention elections and then declines. Thus, the most plausible explanation for the long-term increased willingness to vote in retention elections is increased voter familiarity with judicial retention elections.

One of the most interesting characteristics of rolloff is how little it varies between presidential and midterm elections. From 1980 to 2012, average rolloff in retention elections is 31.6 percent in presidential election years and 29.8 percent in midterm elections. A long-held assumption has been that less-informed voters are those who are most likely to rolloff in judicial retention elections (Hall and

Aspin 1987a). Yet, research has demonstrated that presidential elections attract an influx of less-informed intermittent voters (PEW Research Center 2006). These voters seemingly would, if voting on the basis of information, be more likely to rolloff than the informed voters who are voting in both types of elections. Thus, the expectation should be for substantially more rolloff in presidential election years, but this does not occur. The decision to vote in retention elections appears to be driven by both specific knowledge of the judges and non-election-specific variables. Given that being informed is only one of the current motives for voting in retention elections, the implementation of a judicial performance evaluation system can create more informed voters but may not mean more voters in retention elections.

## Opposition

In the last few election cycles, there have been some contentious and very costly retention elections that have been the focus of much discussion and analysis. Are they a harbinger of what is to come? Should all judges standing for retention start gathering resources for their counter-campaigns? A review of opposition in the 2010, 2012 and 2014 retention elections reaffirms and expands some basic conclusions. Few judges standing for retention receive any opposition, and only a handful will face opposition of a level sufficient to result in their removal from the bench. A judge's probability of opposition and potential defeat increases if: (1) the judge's acts in or out of court are a substantial violation of the law or role expectations; (2) the judge made or was part of a controversial decision on a contentious issue; (3) the judge received a "Do Not Retain" recommendation from a state judicial performance evaluation commission; (4) the state has a high threshold for retention; (5) the judge sits on the supreme court; (6) the state typically has a low level of support in retention elections; and (7) there is a partisan struggle in the state over judicial selection.

For each retention election in 2010–2014, the existence and highest level of opposition is recorded. Instances of opposition were either directly observed on the internet or captured and reported by electronic media users (e.g., newspapers, bloggers, TV, group websites, etc.). Thus, some instances of low-level opposition were probably not captured, but it is highly unlikely that higher levels of opposition were missed. For those who experienced more than one type of opposition, the most intense was coded.

Of the 1,755 judges and justices who stood for retention, 1,557 (or 88.7%) experienced no observed opposition. All these judges were retained but with varying degrees of support depending upon the state in which the election occurred. The highest level of opposition experienced by the other 198 (or 12.3%) involved: (1) limited opposition (6.4%); (2) "Do Not Retain" recommendations by a bar association (1.8%); (3) "Do Not Retain" recommendation by a judicial performance evaluation commission (0.4%); or (4) full-out opposition campaigns (2.6%).

### *Types of Opposition*

*Limited.* Limited opposition includes actions (e.g., letters to the editor, editorials, blog postings, posted or circulated voting guides, etc.) that urge defeat of the judge. A total of 113 (6.4%) judges experienced this type of opposition. Increasingly, groups and individuals are generating voting guides and circulating them via electronic media. This practice varies considerably by state. For example, in 2014 there was no recorded opposition of any type in states such as Wyoming, Utah, Maryland, and Indiana, but in stark contrast, only 37.7 percent of the judges in Arizona did not have some type of opposition. In 2014, 44.9 percent of the Arizona judges standing for retention saw limited opposition, which most often was a negative recommendation in a voting guide.

*"Do Not Retain" recommendations by bar association(s).* "Do Not Retain" recommendations by bar associations were coded as more intense than instances of limited opposition. Although some voters distrust the legal profession and ignore them, bar association recommendations are a source of systematically gathered information from individuals with direct experience with the judges and justices standing for retention, something most voters do not have. In some states such as Missouri, bar associations are very comprehensive in their data gathering and dissemination. In states without formal judicial performance evaluation commissions, this is the highest level of opposition short of an opposition campaign. In the 2010–2014 period, only thirty-two (1.8%) of the judges and justices received a bar association "Do Not Retain" recommendation. All thirty-two of these recommendations occurred in the state of Illinois; twenty-seven were in Cook County, where multiple bar associations are making recommendations. None of the thirty-two judges faced an opposition campaign, and all were retained.

*"Do Not Retain" Recommendation of a Judicial Performance Evaluation Commission.* A "Do Not Retain" recommendation by a state judicial performance evaluation commission is considered a higher level of opposition than similar recommendations from bar associations because past research has demonstrated their use by voters (Esterling and Sampson 1998) and their effect on retention (Aspin 2007b).

Of the 1,775 major trial court, intermediate appellate court, and supreme court retention elections in the 2010–2014 period, there were only seven "Do Not Retain" recommendations, and these were all at the major trial court level (see Table 6.2 for details). The seven judges who received negative recommendations from their state judicial evaluation commissions also received some other opposition, but there were no opposition campaigns against any of them. The usual pattern was that the negative recommendations were publicized not only by the commissions but also by other groups in the state (e.g., newspapers, bloggers, civic groups). In some cases, the recommendations were simply reported, but in other cases they endorsed. Judges and their suppporters often responded to these recommendations. For example, suporters of Alaska Judge Estelle were very active in his defense. As one newspaper wrote in a followup editorial: "Supporters

**TABLE 6.2** Judges with a "Do Not Retain" Recommendation from a Performance Evaluation Commission 2010–2014

| *State* | *Year* | *Court* | *District* | *Judge* | *Affirmative Vote* | *Outcome* | *Affirmative Vote Prior Retention Election* | *District Mean Affirmative Vote W/O Judge* |
|---|---|---|---|---|---|---|---|---|
| Alaska | 2010 | Major Trial Court | 3 | Richard W. Postma | 46.0% | Not Retained | | 63.2% |
| Colorado | 2010 | Major Trial Court | 10 | Jill S. Mattoon | 56.9% | Retained | | 70.1% |
| Alaska | 2014 | Major Trial Court | 3 | William L. Estelle | 54.3% | Retained | 63.0% | 63.3% |
| Arizona | 2014 | Major Trial Court | 1 | Benjamin R. Norris | 42.0% | Not Retained | 55.6% | 67.9% |
| Arizona | 2014 | Major Trial Court | 2 | Catherine M. Woods | 59.2% | Retained | | 76.6% |
| New Mexico | 2014 | Major Trial Court | 1 | Sheri A. Raphaelson | 56.3% | Not Retained | | 80.1% |
| New Mexico | 2014 | Major Trial Court | 3 | Lisa Claire Schultz | 66.3% | Retained | 80.7% | 74.3% |

of District Court Judge William Estelle have embarked on a saturation bombing campaign of our Opinion page lately" (Our Words Matter, Too, 2014).

While judicial performance commissions are not without critics (e.g., the Kansas legislature effectively ended the Kansas commission by not funding it), voters do act on commission recommendations (Esterling and Sampson 1998). As will be discussed later, a negative recommendation often lowers levels of support by 10 to 20 percent. Whether this means defeat depends upon the general level of support in a state and the threshold for retention. Judge Raphaelson in New Mexico was supported by a majority of those voting but lost because New Mexico is one of two states with a retention threshold greater than 50 percent (in this case, 57%).

*Opposition Campaigns.* In contrast to situations with limited opposition, the more serious threat to retention is the presence of an opposition campaign. To be coded as an opposition campaign, there must be either formal or informal coordinated actions of multiple individuals with the purpose of defeating the judge. The creation of a registered reporting committee was neither necessary nor sufficient to establish the existence of a campaign. In some cases groups raised so little money they did not have to register (e.g., the opposition to Colorado Judge Munsinger in 2010 (Masich 2010)). In at least one instance, a formal committee registered and reported, but there was insufficient evidence to conclude more than a single individual was involved.[10] A single action (e.g., posting a formal or informal list of candidates to vote for and against) was insufficient to constitute a campaign. Multiple actions were required, such as signs, pamphlets, press conferences, dedicated websites, and social media communication.

Of the 1,755 judges and justices who stood for retention during the 2010–2014 retention elections, only forty-six, or 2.6 percent, faced an opposition campaign. There were only twenty-one separate campaigns, for half sought to defeat multiple judges. In eleven campaigns, only a single judge or justice was targeted.

Whereas, on average, campaigns constitute a greater threat to retention than the other forms of opposition, they vary tremendously in the degree of threat they pose. At the low end of the spectrum are the shoe-string efforts, often in the weeks just preceding the election. For example, the small group opposing Colorado Judge Munsinger in 2010 relied mainly on yard signs and flyers (Masich 2010), and the group opposing Nebraska Judge Gilbride in 2014 relied almost entirely on Facebook (Eye on the Bench 2014). Lower-intensity opposition campaigns also are present at the supreme court level. In the Arizona elections of 2012, both Justice Pelander and a supporter formed campaign committees to respond to materials being put out by the groups Williams Tea Party and Legislative District 18 Republican Committee (Fischer 2012). The opposition campaign never rose above the distribution of election materials. The 2011–2012 Report of the *New Politics of Judicial Elections* could not identify any money spent for and against Justice Pelander other than the $5,000 by his committee (Bannon, Velasco, Casey, and Reagan 2013). Likewise, the 2010 Fall campaign by Kansans for Life against Supreme Court Justices Beier, Biles, Luckert and Nuss never generated support from other groups and ultimately relied on lower-cost communication efforts. A post-election article in the *National Review* entitled "Kansas' 'Fire Beier' Campaign Disappears in a Cloud of Smoke" (Boyles 2010) deemed the Kansans for Life effort as modest and chastised Kansas conservatives for not seizing the opportunity to remove liberals from the Supreme Court.

It may be difficult at the first sign of opposition to determine its degree of threat, and this may be one reason for the differing responses by judges. Both Arizona Supreme Court Justice Pelander and Indiana Supreme Court Justice David (Stafford 2012) responded to low-threat opposition campaigns, but other judges and justices chose not to launch counter-campaigns. In seven of the twenty-one elections where opposition campaigns were present, neither the judges/justices nor their supporters engaged in campaign activity to check the opposition campaigns. In six elections with opposition campaigns, the judge or justice did not conduct a counter-campaign but instead relied upon supports to do so. The best-known examples of this are the supreme court justices in Iowa when in both 2010 and 2012 they steadfastly refused to run campaigns even in the face of intense opposition.

Standing in stark contrast to the low-budget low-threat campaigns are six high-budget, high-threat opposition campaigns, all of which involved supreme court justices: 2010 Illinois Justice Tom Kilbride; 2010 Iowa Justices Baker, Streit and Ternus; 2012 Florida Justices Perry, Lewis, Pariente and Quince; 2012 Iowa Justice Wiggins; 2014 Illinois Justice Lloyd Karmeier; and 2014 Tennessee Justices Clark, Lee and Wade. Except in Iowa, all the targeted justices engaged in counter-campaigns which, as reported in Table 6.3, raised significant amounts of money. These six opposition campaigns clearly threatened the retention of the targeted justices and are often discussed by the media and watchdog groups; however, they are neither representative of the other opposition campaigns nor of retention elections in general.

## *Motives for Opposition Campaigns*

Why the campaigns against judges and justices? Most opposition campaigns are motivated by one or more of the following: direct experiences prompting retaliation, controversial decisions or actions, financial self-interest, and political motivations.

*Direct Experience with the Court.* Behind some of the campaigns, especially against judges at the trial court level, are direct experiences with the court. The organizers often feel decisions or actions were unjust and launch a retaliatory campaign.

- One report of the 2010 campaign against Colorado Judge Munsinger said "Most of the complaints arise from probate cases. One woman involved in a dispute over her father's estate believes her brothers paid Munsinger to

**TABLE 6.3** Judges and Justices Opposed by Opposition Campaign 2010–2014

| *State* | *Year* | *Court* | *Judicial District* | *Judge/ Justice* | *Nature of Opposition* | *Opposition Issues* | *Outcome* | *Affirmative Vote* | *Affirmative Vote Prior Retention Election* | *N of Retention Elections in District* | *District Mean Affirmative Vote w/o Judge* | *Counter Organized Campaign by Judge/Others* | *Contributions to Judge's Committee* |
|---|---|---|---|---|---|---|---|---|---|---|---|---|---|
| Alaska | 2010 | Supreme Court | State wide | Dana A. Fabe | Social Conservatives: *Alaska Family Action, Alaskans for Judicial Reform* | Repeated "Activist Liberal Rulings" | Retained | 54.4 | 57.1 | 1 | | No/Yes | $0 |
| Alaska | 2012 | Superior Court | 3 | Sen K. Tan | Social conservatives: *Alaska Family Action* | Two decisions related to abortion | Retained | 55.1 | 58.8 | 10 | 63.4 | No/Yes | $0 |
| Arizona | 2012 | Supreme Court | State wide | A. John Pelander III | Republican & Tea Party Groups: *Williams Tea Party; Legislative District 18 Republican Committee* | Vote to allow Proposition 121 the November ballot | Retained | 73.9 | 80.3 | 1 | | Yes/Yes | $5,000 |

(continued)

**TABLE 6.3** (*cont.*)

| *State* | *Year* | *Court* | *Judicial District* | *Judge/ Justice* | *Nature of Opposition* | *Opposition Issues* | *Outcome* | *Affirmative Vote* | *Affirmative Vote Prior Retention Election* | *N of Retention Elections in District* | *District Mean Affirmative Vote w/o Judge* | *Counter Organized Campaign by Judge/Others* | *Contributions to Judge's Committee* |
|---|---|---|---|---|---|---|---|---|---|---|---|---|---|
| Arizona | 2014 | Major Trial Court | 1 | Dawn M. Bergin | Committee created by former attorney to address injustices in the judicial system: *Citizens for Clean Courts* | Actions in a child custody case | Retained | 67.8 | 60.2 | 46 | 67.3 | No/No | $0 |
| Arizona | 2014 | Major Trial Court | 1 | Mark Brain | " | Unjust acts with regard to other attorneys | Retained | 70.4 | | 46 | 67.3 | No/No | $0 |
| Arizona | 2014 | Major Trial Court | 1 | David O. Cunanan | " | Unjust actions in a trust case | Retained | 66.6 | | 46 | 67.3 | No/No | $0 |
| Arizona | 2014 | Major Trial Court | 1 | Norman J. Davis | " | Failed as presiding judge to insure proper actions by judges and attorneys | Retained | 70.1 | 65.9 | 46 | 67.3 | No/No | $0 |

| | | | | | | | | | | | | | |
|---|---|---|---|---|---|---|---|---|---|---|---|---|---|
| Arizona | 2014 | Major Trial Court | 1 | Sally S. Duncan | " | Conflict of interest and unjust decision | Retained | 65.7 | 63.2 | 46 | 67.4 | No/No | $0 |
| Arizona | 2014 | Major Trial Court | 1 | Dean M. Fink | " | Allowed violations of the rules in a trust case | Retained | 66.8 | 60.8 | 46 | 67.3 | No/No | $0 |
| Arizona | 2014 | Major Trial Court | 1 | J. Richard Gama | " | Series of charges with regard to the judge's compe-tence and thus flawed actions as judge | Retained | 67.4 | 61.7 | 46 | 67.3 | No/No | $0 |
| Arizona | 2014 | Major Trial Court | 1 | Rosa P. Mroz | " | President of the Center for Arizona Policy (CAP). | Retained | 68.7 | 61.3 | 46 | 67.3 | No/No | $0 |
| Arizona | 2014 | Supreme Court | State wide | Scott Bales | " | Actions related to disbarment of attorneys & inadequate supervision | Retained | 73.6 | 77.1 | 2 | 73.4 | No/No | $0 |
| Arizona | 2014 | Supreme Court | State wide | Robert M. Brutinel | " | Actions related to disbarment of attorneys & inadequate supervision | Retained | 73.4 | | 2 | 73.6 | No/No | $0 |

*(continued)*

**TABLE 6.3** (*cont.*)

| *State* | *Year* | *Court* | *Judicial District* | *Judge/ Justice* | *Nature of Opposition* | *Opposition Issues* | *Outcome* | *Affirmative Vote* | *Affirmative Vote Prior Retention Election* | *N of Retention Elections in District* | *District Mean Affirmative Vote w/o Judge* | *Counter Organized Campaign by Judge/Others* | *Contributions to Judge's Committee* |
|---|---|---|---|---|---|---|---|---|---|---|---|---|---|
| Colorado | 2010 | Major Trial Court | 1 | Stephen M. Munsinger | Informal group | Individual complaints about probate rulings | Retained | 64.6 | 71.2 | 3 | 63.8 | No/No | $0 |
| Colorado | 2010 | Major Trial Court | 8 | Jolene C. Blair | Independent Grassroots Group: *Committee for Judicial Justice* | Mistakes made when a prosecuter | Not Retained | 38.8 | 77.7 | 5 | 60.8 | No/Yes | $0 |
| Colorado | 2010 | Major Trial Court | 8 | Terence A. Gilmore | " | " | Not Retained | 37.8 | 77.4 | 5 | 61.0 | No/Yes | $0 |
| Colorado | 2010 | Supreme Court | State wide | Michael L. Bender | Conservative citizen group: *Clear the Bench Colorado* | Decisions allowing revenue increases | Retained | 60.4 | 72.3 | 3 | 60.7 | No/No | $0 |
| Colorado | 2010 | Supreme Court | State wide | Alex J. Martinez | " | " | Retained | 59.5 | 71.6 | 3 | 61.1 | No/No | $0 |
| Colorado | 2010 | Supreme Court | State wide | Nancy E. Rice | " | " | Retained | 61.9 | 74.7 | 3 | 59.9 | No/No | $0 |
| Florida | 2010 | Supreme Court | State wide | Jorge Labarga | Conservative Groups: *Citizen2 Citizen; Central Florida Tea Party Council; etc.* | Vote removing a proposed constitutional amendment from ballot | Retained | 59.0 | | 4 | 65.1 | No/No | $0 |

| | | | | | | | | | | | | | |
|---|---|---|---|---|---|---|---|---|---|---|---|---|---|
| Florida | 2010 | Supreme Court | State wide | James E. C. Perry | " | " | Retained | 61.7 | | 4 | 64.2 | No/No | $0 |
| Florida | 2012 | Supreme Court | State wide | R. Fred Lewis | Republican party and conservative groups: *Republican Party of Florida; Restore Justice 2012; SoutheasternLegal Foundation; Americans for Prosperity* | Several rulings of the liberal activists judges | Retained | 67.5 | 67.1 | 3 | 67.9 | Yes/No | $495,845 |
| Florida | 2012 | Supreme Court | State wide | Barbara J. Pariente | " | Several rulings of the liberal activists judges | Retained | 68.0 | 67.6 | 3 | 67.6 | Yes/No | $538,313 |
| Florida | 2012 | Supreme Court | State wide | Peggy A. Quince | " | " | Retained | 67.7 | 68.2 | 3 | 67.7 | Yes/No | $493,487 |
| Illinois | 2010 | Supreme Court | 3 | Tom Kilbride | Business Interests: *Illinois Civil Justice League* | Vote removing caps in malpractice cases | Retained | 65.9 | | 1 | | Yes/No | $2,789,649 |
| Illinois | 2012 | Major Trial Court | 3 | Ann E. Callis | Local citizens group *Citizens for Judicial Integrity* supported by the *Illinois Chamber of Commerce* | Campaign contributions from law firms linked to handling of asbestos cases | Retained | 68.6 | 73.7 | 4 | 64.3 | Yes/No | $154,988 |

(*continued*)

**TABLE 6.3** (*cont.*)

| *State* | *Year* | *Court* | *Judicial District* | *Judge/ Justice* | *Nature of Opposition* | *Opposition Issues* | *Outcome* | *Affirmative Vote* | *Affirmative Vote Prior Retention Election* | *N of Retention Elections in District* | *District Mean Affirmative Vote w/o Judge* | *Counter Organized Campaign by Judge/Others* | *Contributions to Judge's Committee* |
|---|---|---|---|---|---|---|---|---|---|---|---|---|---|
| Illinois | 2012 | Major Trial Court | 3 | Barbara L. Crowder | " | All four ran as a reform team in 2006 & have failed to deliver | Retained | 63.2 | | 4 | 66.1 | Yes/No | $63,970 |
| Illinois | 2012 | Major Trial Court | 3 | Dave Hylla | " | Campaign contributions from law firms linked to handling of asbestos cases | Retained | 65.3 | | 4 | 65.4 | Yes/No | $110,456 |
| Illinois | 2012 | Major Trial Court | 3 | John Knight | " | All four ran as a reform team in 2006 & have failed to deliver | Retained | 64.4 | 69.8 | 4 | 65.7 | Yes/No | $70,933 |
| Illinois | 2014 | Supreme Court | 5 | Lloyd A. Karmeier | Primarily plaintiffs' attorneys *Campaign for 2016* | Accused of a pro-business bias, especially financial contrbutors | Retained | 60.8 | 76.0 | 1 | | Yes/Yes | $309,331 |

| | | | | | | | | | | | | | |
|---|---|---|---|---|---|---|---|---|---|---|---|---|---|
| Indiana | 2012 | Supreme Court | State wide | Steven H. David | Tea party and libertarian activists, *The Indianapolis Tea Party* | Voted to overturn common law provision known as the 'Castle Doctrine'. | Retained | 69.1 | | 2 | 71.6 | Yes/No | $0 |
| Iowa | 2010 | Supreme Court | State wide | David L. Baker | Social Conservatives: *Iowa for Freedom; National Organization for Marriage; American Family Association* | Vote on Same Sex Marriage | Not Retained | 45.9 | 76.8 | 3 | 45.3 | No/Yes | $0 |
| Iowa | 2010 | Supreme Court | State wide | Michael J. Streit | " | " | Not Retained | 45.6 | 75.8 | 3 | 45.4 | No/Yes | $0 |
| Iowa | 2010 | Supreme Court | State wide | Marsha K. Ternus | " | " | Not Retained | 45.0 | 76.0 | 3 | 45.7 | No/Yes | $0 |
| Iowa | 2012 | Supreme Court | State wide | David S. Wiggins | Republicans & social conservatives: *Iowa Republican Party; Iowans for Freedom; National Organization for Marriage* | 2009 vote to overturn ban on same-sex marriage | Retained | 54.5 | 75.4 | 4 | 74.4 | No/Yes | $0 |
| Kansas | 2010 | Supreme Court | State wide | Carol A. Beier | Anti-abortion group: *Kansans for Life* | Rulings involving the former Attorney General | Retained | 63.3 | 76.5 | 4 | 62.5 | No/Yes | $0 |

*(continued)*

**TABLE 6.3** *(cont.)*

| *State* | *Year* | *Court* | *Judicial District* | *Judge/ Justice* | *Nature of Opposition* | *Opposition Issues* | *Outcome* | *Affirmative Vote* | *Affirmative Vote Prior Retention Election* | *N of Retention Elections in District* | *District Mean Affirmative Vote w/o Judge* | *Counter Organized Campaign by Judge/Others* | *Contributions to Judge's Committee* |
|---|---|---|---|---|---|---|---|---|---|---|---|---|---|
| Kansas | 2010 | Supreme Court | State wide | Dan Biles | " | Was law partner with head of the Democratic Party | Retained | 62.0 | | 4 | 62.9 | No/Yes | $0 |
| Kansas | 2010 | Supreme Court | State wide | Marla J. Luckert | " | Rulings involving the former Attorney General | Retained | 62.8 | 76.6 | 4 | 62.6 | No/Yes | $0 |
| Kansas | 2010 | Supreme Court | State wide | Lawton R. Nuss | " | Rulings involving the former Attorney General | Retained | 62.6 | 75.6 | 4 | 62.7 | No/Yes | $0 |
| Kansas | 2014 | Major Trial Court | 10 | Kevin P. Moriarty | Brian Baumgardner & *Pink Slips for Dishonorable Judges* | Ordered the court clerk to start issuing marriage licenses to same-sex couples | Retained | 61.7 | 64.4 | 11 | 64.5 | No/No | $0 |

| | | | | | | | | | | | | |
|---|---|---|---|---|---|---|---|---|---|---|---|---|
| Kansas | 2014 | Supreme Court | State wide | Lee A. Johnson | Family & friends of four murder victims: *Kansans for Justice;* Supported by *Gov Brownback & Kansans for Life* | Overturned death sentences of two brother who committed four murders | Retained | 52.7 | 70.3 | 2 | 52.7 | No evidence of campaigning | $0 |
| Kansas | 2014 | Supreme Court | State wide | Eric S. Rosen | " | " | Retained | 52.7 | 70.0 | 2 | 52.7 | No evidence of campaigning | $0 |
| Nebraska | 2014 | Major Trial Court | 5 | Mary C. Gilbride | Facebook group *Kids Have Rights Too* | Unfair in handling child custody cases | Retained | 70.7 | 66.6 | 1 | | No/No | $0 |
| New Mexico | 2014 | Major Trial Court | 10 | Albert J. Mitchell, Jr. | Victim's family & political opponent: *Committee for Law and Order* | Too lenient on criminals & slow making decisions | Not Retained | 51.8 | | 1 | | Yes/No | $10,050 |
| Tennessee | 2014 | Supreme Court | State wide | Cornelia A. Clark | *Republican Lt. Gov. Ron Ramsey; Tennessee Forum; Republican State Leadership Committee; Americans for Prosperity* | Liberal justices are soft on the death penalty and "anti-business". | Retained | 56.0 | 74.4 | 3 | 57.1 | Yes/Yes | $301,818 |
| Tennessee | 2014 | Supreme Court | State wide | Sharon G. Lee | " | " | Retained | 56.8 | 68.3 | 3 | 56.7 | Yes/Yes | $324,518 |
| Tennessee | 2014 | Supreme Court | State wide | Gary R. Wade | " | " | Retained | 57.3 | 77.1 | 3 | 56.4 | Yes/Yes | $526,014 |

rule in their favor. Another is a man who is denied contact with his mother" (Masich 2010).

- In 2014 Kids Have Rights opposed Nebraska Judge Gilbride "based on her record of deciding in the favor of one parent over another" in child custody decisions. According to a spokesman for the group, "the organization is not a result of 'sour grapes' but that the group's supporters have either been through the process or know someone who had" (Peirce 2014).
- Recently disbarred attorney Andrew Thomas, the creator of Citizens for Clean Courts opposing ten judges in 2014, announced the creation of the committee with several citizens involved probate court cases (Bentley 2012).
- The 2014 chair of the Committee for Law and Order was the father of an individual almost beaten to death by an individual New Mexico Judge Mitchell had released from jail (Cole 2014).

*Controversial Decision or Action.* Occasionally the actions or decisions by a judge/justice are met with widespread disapproval, which then leads to defeat in the next retention election (e.g., Utah Judge Leslie Lewis 2006 (Fattah and Thomson 2006)). In the 2010–2014 period, several decisions and actions clearly motivated specific groups to launch opposition campaigns:

- Justice Pelander in Arizona 2012—the decision allowing Proposition 121 on the ballot upset his fellow Republicans and the Tea Party (Kiefer 2012).
- Justice David in Indiana 2012—the decision overturning the "Castle Doctrine" angered the Tea Party and libertarians (Stafford 2012).
- Justices Baker, Streit, and Ternus in Iowa 2010 and Justice Wiggins in Iowa 2012—the positive decision on same-sex marriage was opposed by social conservatives (Simon 2010).
- Judge Moriarty Kansas 2014—an order for the clerk to issue marriage licenses to same-sex couples also upset social conservatives (Associated Press 2014).
- Justices Johnson and Rosen Kansas 2014—the decision overturning the death sentences of two brothers outraged the families and friends of the victims (Margolies 2014).

While there were multiple motives by the opposing groups, the immediate trigger for the 2010 campaign to defeat Florida Supreme Court Justices Labarga and Perry was their vote to remove a proposed constitutional amendment from the ballot (Musgrave 2010). At least one other opposition campaign may have stemmed from specific decisions, but it is not clear that the decisions were necessary for the opposition. The group opposing Alaska Judge Tan in 2012 because of two abortion-related decisions had opposed Supreme Court Justice Fabe in the previous election for her repeated "activist liberal rulings" (Feidt 2012).

Some cited decisions or rulings appear to be part of a strategy rather than motivational factors. Although Clear the Bench cited several objectionable decisions in their 2010 effort to oust Colorado Justices Bender, Martinez, and Rice, this campaign was probably more ideologically or politically motivated and not the result of any one decision (Arnold 2010). The goal of Clear the Bench is reflected in their name and mission to "bring back balance to the bench," especially the Supreme Court which they portrayed as the "most activist, partisan state Supreme Court in the nation."[11] Whereas the 2010 campaign by Kansans for Life against Supreme Court Justices Beier, Biles, Luckert and Nuss cited specific rulings involving the former Attorney General, their political agenda was clear. One example is a statement on their blog that "Kansas is a 'red' conservative state with a 'blue' state Supreme Court and a liberal media supporting the latter" (Ostrowski 2014).

*Financial Self-Interest.* Two opposition campaigns stand apart from the others because financial self-interest appears to be a major driving force for the opposition and in some cases supporters. This was clearly the case in the 2014 campaign against Illinois Supreme Court Justice Lloyd Karmeier. Illinois employs partisan elections for the initial selection of judges and then retention elections thereafter. Justice Karmeier attained his seat on the supreme court via an expensive partisan campaign in 2004. Justice Karmeier's campaign received substantial donations from business, insurance, and medical industry interests, whereas his opponent was largely funded by trial lawyers. Subsequently, Justice Karmeier provided a key vote to overturn a $10.1 billion dollar class action judgment against Phillip Morris, *Price v. Philip Morris*, and a $1 billion dollar judgment against State Farm, *Avery v. State Farm*. Both cases promoted the creation of the Campaign for 2016 for the purpose of defeating Justice Karmeier, thus increasing the chances the Supreme Court would reinstate the initial judgments. Especially in the *Phillip Morris* case, plaintiff attorneys stood to gain substantially if the Supreme Court reinstated the judgment. Among the four people and three law firms that bankrolled Campaign for 2016, all but one had direct ties either to the *State Farm* or *Philip Morris* cases (Maher 2014; Mackey 2015).

The 2010 campaign against Illinois Supreme Court Justice Kilbride also had financial motives, but this was less a case of direct individual financial gain. Justice Kilbride voted to overturn limits on medical malpractice claims. The Illinois Civil Justice League, a pro-business group that advocates for liability caps and other restrictions on civil lawsuits, then launched the campaign to defeat Justice Kilbride. This was not the first effort by the group to shape the Supreme Court as it had supported Justice Karmeier in 2004. The Illinois Civil Justice League did not oppose two other justices up for retention even though they had also voted with Justice Kilbride. Justices Fitzgerald and Freeman's judicial district, Cook County, is a Democratic Party stronghold and thus a safe district for Democrats (Sachdev 2010). In neither of the campaigns against the Illinois justices could the opponents use their self-interest as the reason for voters to defeat the justices. In the campaign against Justice Karmeier, questions of ethical conduct were raised given his campaign contributors, but this was not possible with Justice Kilbride.

The Illinois Civil Justice League instead followed the conservative playbook of charging the Democrat with being soft on crime by running very negative television ads accusing the Justice of siding with violent felons.

*Political Motives*. Campaigns motivated by direct experience or a judge's specific action are often reactive and retaliatory in nature—"throw the bum out." Such campaigns are not oblivious to the replacement's future actions, but that is a secondary concern. However, financially and politically motivated campaigns are much more concerned with future decisions. Furthermore, politically motivated campaigns may be just one component of a struggle for political control.

Three campaigns by ongoing citizens groups—2010 Alaska Justice Fabe; 2010 Colorado Justices Bender, Martinez and Rice; and 2010 Kansas Justices Beier, Biles, Luckert, and Nuss—were ideologically motivated efforts to shift the court balance to the conservative end of the continuum. In contrast, two of the most expensive opposition campaigns were partisan contests, with the political parties either leading (Tennessee) or assisting (Florida) the opposition.

The 2014 Tennessee retention elections occurred in an ongoing struggle for control of the courts via what was to be the method of judicial selection. The statutory basis of the judicial selection system had expired and a political compromise system known as Amendment 2—appointment by the Governor, confirmation by the Legislature, followed by regular retention elections—was on the ballot in the November 2014 election. Given that the Republicans controlled the executive branch and had supermajority control of the legislature, approval of Amendment 2 would give Republicans the ability to appoint conservative justices. In this setting, three supreme court justices appointed by a Democrat stood for retention during the August 2014 primary. The loss of any one of their seats would have given the court a majority of Republican appointees. Seizing the opportunity, Republican Lt. Gov. Ron Ramsey spearheaded the opposition campaign to defeat Justices Clark, Lee, and Wade. While supported by the Republican State Leadership Committee and Americans for Prosperity, Ramsey's Tennessee Forum, a national conservative group dedicated to electing Republicans and conservative issue advocacy groups founded by David Koch led the opposition campaign. Lacking a highly controversial mobilizing case as in the 2010 Iowa election, the campaign turned to the familiar tactic of portraying the three justices as soft on the death penalty and as "anti-business." While this clearly was one of the most partisan efforts in judicial retention elections, not all Republicans supported the effort (e.g., Republican Governor Bill Haslam (Humphrey 2014; Srikrishnan 2014)). In the end, voters retained all three justices.

The 2012 campaign against Florida Justices Lewis, Pariente, and Quince occurred in a less visible partisan struggle for control of the courts. The Supreme Court had made a series of rulings upsetting the Republican Party (e.g., the ruling removing the Affordable Care Act amendment from the ballot that sparked the 2010 opposition campaign). In 2011, then-House Speaker Dean Cannon (R-Winter Park) and Representative Eric Eisnaugle, an Orlando lawyer angling to be Speaker, pushed an amendment to split up the high court, but the measure failed. Since his election in 2011, Republican Governor Rick Scott had been consistently appointing conservatives to Florida's judicial nominating commissions (Jackson 2014). While individual Republicans had participated in the 2010 opposition campaign, the Republican Party held back. This would not be the case in 2012. The 2012 opposition campaign began with the familiar cast of characters: another Tea Party group Restore Justice 2012 and their ideological brethren Americans for Prosperity. The Republican Party soon directly entered the opposition campaign when the executive board voted unanimously to oppose Justices Lewis, Pariente, and Quince. The partisan struggle did not end in 2012, for Republicans placed Amendment 3 on the 2014 ballot, which would give the outgoing governor in 2019, presumably Scott if reelected, the authority to appoint replacements for Supreme Court Justices Lewis, Pariente, and Quince, all Democrats, who will be forced to retire in 2019 because of age (Deslatte 2014).

The 2014 supreme court retention elections in Kansas also occurred with a backdrop of partisan struggles over judicial selection. The state removed commission selection from its Court of Appeals in 2013, replacing it with gubernatorial appointments. Republican Governor Sam Brownback had threatened to re-examine the commission system for selecting supreme court justices. However, in contrast to the opposition campaigns in Tennessee and Florida, the 2014 campaign against Kansas Supreme Court Justices Johnson and Rosen also had an element of partisan self-interest. The main opposition campaign was initiated and carried out by Kansans for Justice. The organization was formed by the family and friends of the Carr brothers' five victims after the Supreme Court overturned their death sentence, although the underlying convictions were upheld. Subsequently, Republican Governor Brownback attempted to save his then-struggling reelection campaign by using the Carr brothers' case (Fasbinder 2014; Bush 2014). He opposed the retention of Justices Johnson and Rosen, and his commercials suggested his opponent, Paul Davis, would appoint more liberal justices who would make the same objectionable decisions. Both the clear use of victims for political purposes and the loophole that allowed Kansans for Justice not to reveal its contributors probably diminished the effectiveness of the opposition campaign (Faturechi 2014).

There are at least four major types of motives for opposition campaigns, but motive alone is not a sufficient condition for an opposition campaign. Ultimately any group desiring the defeat of a judge must make a decision about whether to launch an opposition campaign. Some may be so motivated by anger or strong belief even when there is little chance of success. For many, however, these decisions involve calculating the benefits of defeating the judge, the costs of failing, and most importantly the probability of success. The opponents of Illinois Justice Kilbride did not campaign against the other justices up for retention because of the low probability of success—they were standing for retention in a very safe district. Likewise, observers reported that the Kansas Republican Party did not enter the 2010 campaign against Supreme Court Justices Beier, Biles, Luckert, and Nuss because there was little chance of success (Smith 2010).

Numerous structural, political, and behavioral factors affect the probability of successfully defeating a judge and thus must be weighed in the decision of whether to launch an opposition campaign. The retention threshold is a good example of not only an important determinant of the probability of success but also the need to consider all the determining factors. In Illinois with the 60 percent threshold for retention, Justice Kilbride was structurally more vulnerable than judges in any other state. Yet, this structural vulnerability was partially offset by a behavior pattern: The affirmative vote in Illinois is typically higher than most other states. Whereas Alaska has a 50 percent threshold for retention and Illinois a 60 percent threshold, the typical affirmative vote in Illinois is 77 percent but 66 percent in Alaska. Activists seeking to raise the retention threshold in their state so as to ease their task of defeating judges may not have the success they desire if the voters typically have a high level of support for the judiciary. Conversely, raising the retention threshold in states such as Alaska with their typically low affirmative vote would make it much easier for even a modest campaign to defeat a judge.

## *Anticipating an Opposition Campaign*

The potential effects of opposition go beyond the question of whether a judge or justice is retained. Some judges and justices may be anticipating a serious opposition campaign and planning a response, including the raising of funds even before the opposition campaign begins or its level of threat is clear. Preplanning is understandable given the concern that a last-minute opposition campaign would allow only limited time for them to respond. If the effort goes beyond planning to the raising of funds and campaigning and then the opposition fails to materialize, the judge or justice is in a very awkward position of having accepted contributions for which there is no political need.

The 2012 case of Arizona Supreme Court Justice Pelander illustrates this dilemma. Justice Pelander, concerned that the negative information starting to be distributed would affect his retention, was torn between doing nothing and responding. He ultimately decided to create and self-fund the political committee Retain Justice John Pelander. An independent committee called Save Our Judges was also created by his supporters (Kiefer 2012). Ultimately the opposition never intensified into a serious threat and could have been safely ignored, as other justices had done.

There are other examples. In 2014, Wyoming Supreme Court Justice Burke received $9,600 in donations, but there was no observed opposition in the election (Greytak et al. 2015). In 2012, Illinois Circuit Judge Gorman received $5,124 in contributions to support her retention. Judge Gorman was one of eight Cook County judges to receive a "Do Not Retain" recommendation from a bar association in 2012 but the only one to raise funds. Possibly because he refused to reopen the *Price v. Philip Morris* case in 2012, Illinois 3rd Circuit Court Judge Dennis Ruth formed a campaign committee in 2014, which received over $70,000 in contributions. While no active opposition campaign was observed, Illinois 18th Circuit Judge Kenneth Popejoy formed a last-minute campaign committee that collected over $7,000 in contributions after the Illinois Judicial Inquiry Board filed a complaint against him for fleeing the scene of an accident. Finally, in 2014, the Committee to Retain Your Will County Circuit Judges received over $66,000 in donations to support the retention of the seven judges of the 12th Circuit. The only opposition was the Illinois State Bar Association recommendation that one of the seven judges not be retained. Illinois allows judges to raise money to advertise that they are up retention, and there had been substantial campaign activity in the past by judges standing for retention (Aspin and Hall 1994, 1996; Aspin 1998).

## Opposition Patterns and Sources

*State and Temporal Variability.* The number of judges and justices who were the targets of opposition campaigns each election year was relatively stable, with sixteen in 2010, eleven in 2012, and nineteen in 2014. However, levels of opposition are not constant across states. In over a third of the states, the 2010–2014 period was very quiet for there was little, if any, opposition. In seven of the eighteen states, there was either no or only limited opposition in the 2010–2014 retention elections. At the other end of the continuum, the twenty-one opposition campaigns occurred in eleven different states with differing degrees of regularity. In five of the eleven states there were campaigns in only one of the three election years. Alaska, Arizona, Kansas, Iowa, and Florida witnessed opposition campaigns in two of the three election cycles; only Illinois experienced opposition campaigns in all three election years.

The 2010–2014 time period is too short to make inferences about trends or to conclude that some states are consistently more contentious than others. A safer conclusion is that a high-level opposition is possible in every state and, given the motives for opposition, generally sporadic. For example, Wyoming is one of the states for which no opposition was recorded in the 2010–2014 period, yet it has removed five judges via retention elections. This is more than Arizona, Florida, Iowa, Kansas, and Tennessee, which witnessed some of the more intense campaigns in the 2010–2014 period. No justice in Florida, only one judge in Kansas, and one supreme court justice in Tennessee have been defeated. Even Illinois, which accounts for 40 percent of all judges removed via retention elections, has long periods of calm. Only one Illinois judge was defeated from 1996 through 2014.

*Level of Court Variability.* The existence and level of opposition is anything but distributed equally across the types or levels of courts. All of the "Do Not Retain" recommendations by bar associations and judicial performance commissions were directed at major trial court judges. In contrast, appellate and supreme court justices received a disproportionate share of both limited opposition and,

**TABLE 6.4** Level of Opposition by State, 2010–2014

| | *Level of Opposition* | | | | | |
|---|---|---|---|---|---|---|
| *State* | *None* | *Limited* | *DNR* by Bar Association* | *DNR by JPEC*** | *Campaign* | *Total* |
| Alaska | 64<br>94.1% | 0<br>0.0% | 0<br>0.0% | 2<br>2.9% | 2<br>2.9% | 68<br>100.0% |
| Arizona | 141<br>67.8% | 54<br>26.0% | 0<br>0.0% | 2<br>1.0% | 11<br>5.3% | 208<br>100.0% |
| California | 63<br>71.6% | 25<br>28.4% | 0<br>0.0% | 0<br>0.0% | 0<br>0.0% | 88<br>100.0% |
| Colorado | 160<br>89.4% | 13<br>7.3% | 0<br>0.0% | 1<br>0.6% | 5<br>2.8% | 179<br>100.0% |
| Florida | 59<br>83.1% | 7<br>9.9% | 0<br>0.0% | 0<br>0.0% | 5<br>7.0% | 71<br>100.0% |
| Illinois | 351<br>90.2% | 0<br>0.0% | 32<br>8.2% | 0<br>0.0% | 6<br>1.5% | 389<br>100.0% |
| Indiana | 34<br>97.1% | 0<br>0.0% | 0<br>0.0% | 0<br>0.0% | 1<br>2.9% | 35<br>100.0% |
| Iowa | 128<br>95.5% | 2<br>1.5% | 0<br>0.0% | 0<br>0.0% | 4<br>3.0% | 134<br>100.0% |
| Kansas | 148<br>93.1% | 4<br>2.5% | 0<br>0.0% | 0<br>0.0% | 7<br>4.4% | 159<br>100.0% |
| Maryland | 18<br>100.0% | 0<br>0.0% | 0<br>0.0% | 0<br>0.0% | 0<br>0.0% | 18<br>100.0% |
| Missouri | 101<br>100.0% | 0<br>0.0% | 0<br>0.0% | 0<br>0.0% | 0<br>0.0% | 101<br>100.0% |
| Nebraska | 64<br>98.5% | 0<br>0.0% | 0<br>0.0% | 0<br>0.0% | 1<br>1.5% | 65<br>100.0% |
| New Mexico | 76<br>95.0% | 1<br>1.3% | 0<br>0.0% | 2<br>2.5% | 1<br>1.3% | 80<br>100.0% |
| Oklahoma | 20<br>74.1% | 7<br>25.9% | 0<br>0.0% | 0<br>0.0% | 0<br>0.0% | 27<br>100.0% |
| South Dakota | 3<br>100.0% | 0<br>0.0% | 0<br>0.0% | 0<br>0.0% | 0<br>0.0% | 3<br>100.0% |
| Tennessee | 24<br>88.9% | 0<br>0.0% | 0<br>0.0% | 0<br>0.0% | 3<br>11.1% | 27<br>100.0% |
| Utah | 73<br>100.0% | 0<br>0.0% | 0<br>0.0% | 0<br>0.0% | 0<br>0.0% | 73<br>100.0% |
| Wyoming | 30<br>100.0% | 0<br>0.0% | 0<br>0.0% | 0<br>0.0% | 0<br>0.0% | 30<br>100.0% |
| Total | 1557<br>88.7% | 113<br>6.4% | 32<br>1.8% | 7<br>0.4% | 46<br>2.6% | 1755<br>100.0% |

* "Do Not Retain" Recommendation

** Judicial Performance Evaluation Commission

**TABLE 6.5** Level of Court and Type of Opposition, 2010–2014

| | *Level of Court* | | | |
|---|---|---|---|---|
| *Opposition* | Major Trial | Appellate | Supreme | *Total* |
| None | 1214<br>91.2% | 289<br>87.6% | 54<br>57.4% | 1557<br>88.7% |
| Limited | 60<br>4.5% | 41<br>12.4% | 12<br>12.8% | 113<br>6.4% |
| DNR* by Bar Association | 32<br>2.4% | 0<br>0.0% | 0<br>0.0% | 32<br>1.8% |
| DNR by JPEC** | 7<br>.5% | 0<br>0.0% | 0<br>0.0% | 7<br>0.4% |
| Campaign | 18<br>1.4% | 0<br>0.0% | 28<br>29.8% | 46<br>2.6% |
| Total | 1331<br>100.0% | 330<br>100.0% | 94<br>100.0% | 1755<br>100.0% |

* "Do Not Retain" Recommendation
** Judicial Performance Evaluation Commission

more importantly, opposition campaigns. Whereas 29.8 percent of supreme court justices were targeted by opposition campaigns, only 1.4 percent of trial court judges were; no appellate justice was targeted by an opposition campaign. Stated otherwise, a major trial court judge had a 1 in 100 chance of facing an opposition campaign; a supreme court justice had a 1 in 3 chance.

*Additional Sources of Opposition.* The above discussion of opposition campaigns addressed some of the reasons voters may oppose a judge or justice in a retention election. However, during the 2010–2014 period, the gender, race, and ethnicity of the judge or justice had very little to do with the presence or level of opposition.

Given the large number of elections (1,755), finding statistically significant but weak relationships is relatively easy. First, the statistically significant relationship between race and opposition is extremely weak and inconsistent. Of the 104 African-American judges, 8.7 percent received limited opposition whereas 6.3 percent of the 1,651 non-African-American judges received limited opposition. This small difference is reversed for opposition campaigns. Only 1 percent of African-American judges were campaign targets compared to 2.7 percent of non-African-American judges and justices. Although the differences between African-American and non-African-American judges are statistically significant, they are very small, offering little help in explaining why some judges are opposed and others are not.

The pattern for gender is only slightly different. Of the 481 female judges and justices, 8.3 percent received limited opposition; of the 1,270 male judges and justices, 5.7 percent received limited opposition. The difference is even smaller for opposition campaigns. Of women, 3.1 percent were targets of opposition campaigns and a very similar 2.4 percent of the men were targets.

Turning to ethnicity, although the percentage differences may be slightly larger than for gender, the pattern is the same: There is some difference with regard to limited opposition but no meaningful difference when examining opposition campaigns. Of the seventy-nine Hispanic judges and justices, 16.5 percent saw limited opposition, compared to 6 percent of the 1,675 non-Hispanic judges and justices. Of Hispanic judges, 3.8 percent were campaign targets, compared to 2.6 percent of non-Hispanic judges. Simply stated, neither race, gender, nor ethnicity contributes much to explaining why some judges and justices are opposed while others are not.

Two variables that need to be considered for more systematic study are the party affiliations of judges and justices and the political party of the appointing governor. Neither variable is presently recorded by the JRP so systematic empirical tests are not possible at this time. Given the previous discussion of the political motives for opposition campaigns, the potential explanatory power of these variables is significant. Their importance may extend well beyond opposition campaigns. Numerous times when recording the instances of limited opposition, the party identification of the judge and/or appointing governor were cited as reasons for voting against the judge. These instances occurred both with and without the presence of an opposition campaign. In many situations under retention systems, the party affiliation of the judge or justice is unknown; however, this is not always the case. Illinois and New Mexico used hybrid judicial selection relying on partisan elections for the initial selection and then retention elections for continuation. In other states, a judge may move to the appellate level via commission-retention, but an initial trial court position came via a partisan or nonpartisan election that revealed party identification. Not surprisingly, the groups frequently citing party identification as a reason for opposition were political parties.

## *Opposition Effects*

Turning from the reasons for opposition to the effects of opposition reveals that many past patterns continue through the 2010–2014 period. Lower levels of opposition may affect the affirmative vote but are not enough to defeat a judge or justice. Opposition campaigns also affect the affirmative vote, but they must be more than a narrow or low-budget effort to have a chance of removing a judge. Well-funded opposition campaigns have the best chance of success; however, they can be nullified by counter-campaigns by the judges/justices and/or their supporters.

*Lowering the Affirmative Vote.* Opposition's effect on the affirmative vote depends upon the type of opposition. The average affirmative vote received by judges and justices with no opposition was 72.3 percent for the 2010–2014 period. The

**TABLE 6.6** Type of Opposition and Attributes of the Judges/Justices Standing for Retention, 2010–2014

| | *Race* | | *Gender* | | *Ethnicity* | | |
|---|---|---|---|---|---|---|---|
| *Type of Opposition* | Non-African-American | African-American | Male | Female | Non-Hispanic | Hispanic | Total |
| None | 1470<br>89.0% | 87<br>83.7% | 1150<br>90.6% | 404<br>84.0% | 1494<br>89.2% | 62<br>78.5% | 1557<br>88.7% |
| Limited | 104<br>6.3% | 9<br>8.7% | 72<br>5.7% | 40<br>8.3% | 100<br>6.0% | 13<br>16.5% | 113<br>6.4% |
| DNR* by Bar Association | 25<br>1.5% | 7<br>6.7% | 14<br>1.1% | 18<br>3.7% | 31<br>1.9% | 1<br>1.3% | 32<br>1.8% |
| DNR by JPEC** | 7<br>0.4% | 0<br>0.0% | 3<br>0.2% | 4<br>0.8% | 7<br>0.4% | 0<br>0.0% | 7<br>0.4% |
| Campaign | 45<br>2.7% | 1<br>1.0% | 31<br>2.4% | 15<br>3.1% | 43<br>2.6% | 3<br>3.8% | 46<br>2.6% |
| Total | 1651<br>100.0% | 104<br>100.0% | 1270<br>100.0% | 481<br>100.0% | 1675<br>100.0% | 79<br>100.0% | 1755<br>100.0% |

* "Do Not Retain" Recommendation
** Judicial Performance Evaluation Commission

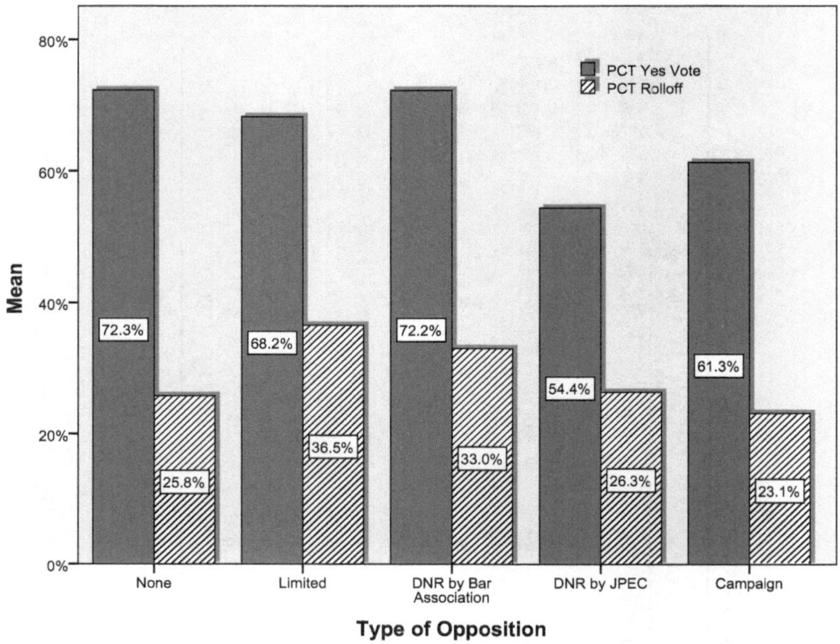


**FIGURE 6.5** Mean Affirmative Vote and Rolloff by Type of Opposition

average affirmative vote for those who faced only limited opposition is slightly lower at 68.2 percent, which is far above the 50 percent retention threshold used in most states. This is consistent with previous research findings that limited opposition can reduce the affirmative vote, but the effects are usually too small to threaten retention. No judge or justice was defeated by limited opposition alone. The group opposing the judge is often such a small part of the electorate that it cannot produce much of a decrease in the affirmative vote. Narrow issues affecting just one group or those that are unimportant to a large percentage of voters are unlikely to garner the necessary support from other voters to defeat the judge or justice.

Note that rolloff is higher (36.5%) when there is limited opposition than when there is none (25.8%). This should not be interpreted as opposition causing fewer voters to cast ballots. Rather, both limited opposition and "Do Not Retain" recommendations by bar associations are more common in states with numerous elections and traditionally high rolloff (e.g., Arizona and Illinois) than in states with very low rolloff (e.g., Wyoming).

The overall average affirmative vote for those who received a "Do Not Retain" recommendation from one or more bar associations (72.2%) is the same as those who faced no opposition (72.3%); however, the negative bar association recommendation can affect the affirmative vote. As previously noted, in the 2010–2014 period, all of the bar association "Do Not Retain" recommendations were in Illinois, which traditionally has a high affirmative vote. For the 2010–2014 period, the average affirmative vote for all Illinois retention elections was 77.1 percent, whereas the average for judges opposed by at least one bar association was 72.2 percent. The bar association's "Do Not Retain" recommendations only produced a small reduction in the affirmative vote. Again, as in previous elections, even multiple "Do Not Retain" recommendations by bar associations lower the affirmative vote only a few percentage points below that received by other judges in the district.

A "Do Not Retain" recommendation from a judicial performance evaluation commission has the most consistent and largest negative impact on the average affirmative vote.[12] The average affirmative vote for the seven judges recommended for removal was 54.4 percent, whereas the average for the other judges in their districts was 70.8 percent. In every case a "Do Not Retain" recommendation resulted in a significantly lower affirmative vote for the judge. Furthermore, judicial evaluation commission reports can have a negative impact on the affirmative vote even when they recommend retention. If the 2014 Arizona pattern is at all representative, voters use more than the bottom line "Retain" or "Do not Retain" recommendation from judicial performance evaluation commissions.[13] In Arizona, the commission's vote and the resulting recommendation are reported together. For example, in 2014, the commission reported the vote was three for and twenty-five against the retention of Judge Norris, hence the "Do Not Retain" recommendation. In 2014, every judge evaluated in Arizona who received less than a unanimous vote for retention also received a lower affirmative vote than their unanimously recommended colleagues. The extreme case is Judge Porter, who was almost defeated when his affirmative vote was only 50.9 percent whereas the district average was 67.3 percent. The reported commission vote on Judge Porter was eighteen for retention and eleven against.

*Defeating Judges.* Figure 6.6 provides a long-term perspective from which to view the defeated judges/justices in the 2010–2014 period. Judges/justices were defeated in only seventy-four or 0.7 percent of the 9,919 judicial retention elections from 1964 to 2014. In the seventy-four elections when the judge/justice lost, sixty-two were major trial court judges, two were intermediate appellate level justices, and ten were supreme court justices.

In the 2010–2014 period, nine (0.5%) judges and justices were not retained. Three of the nine who were defeated were supreme court justices; six were major trial court judges. No judge or justice whose opposition was either just limited or a bar association "Do Not Retain" recommendation was defeated. All the defeated judges/justices faced significant opposition in the form of either an opposition campaign or a "Do Not Retain" recommendation from a judicial performance evaluation commission, but they are the minority of judges who faced these types of opposition. Of the twenty-one opposition campaigns, only three

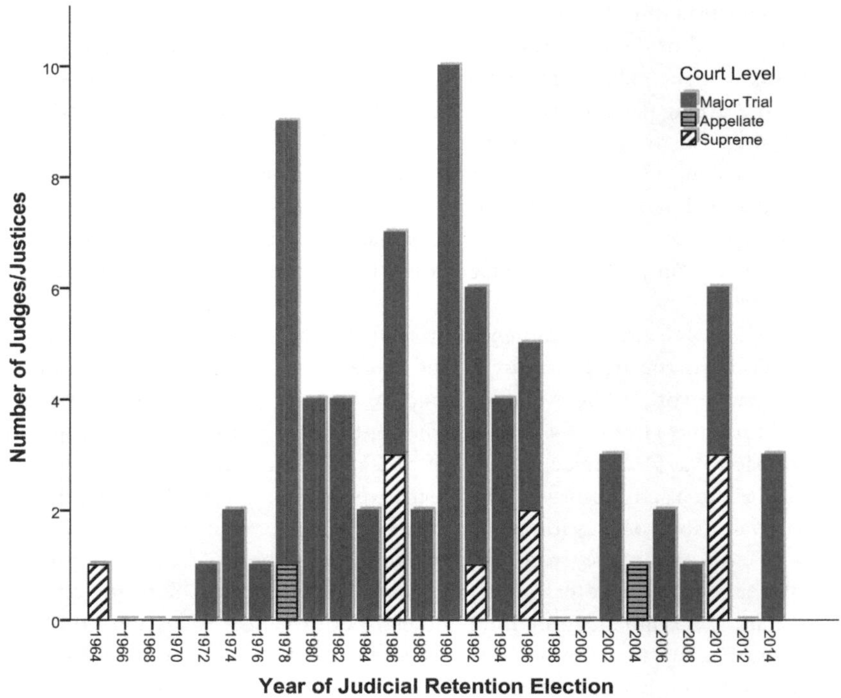


**FIGURE 6.6** Number of Judges Not Retained in Retention Elections, 1964–2014

were successful in defeating judges or justices: one in 2010 that defeated Colorado trial court judges Blair and Gilmore; one in 2010 that defeated Iowa Supreme Court Justices Baker, Ternus, and Streit; and one in 2014 defeating New Mexico trial court Judge Mitchell. Of the seven judges who received "Do Not Retain" recommendations from their performance evaluation commissions, only Judges Postma, Norris, and Raphaelson were not retained.

"Do Not Retain" recommendations from judicial performance evaluation commissions consistently lowered the affirmative vote, but in just three of the seven cases was it sufficient to push the judge's affirmative vote below the threshold for retention.[14] Judges Postma (46%), Norris (42%), and Raphaelson (56.3%) all lost their bids for retention.[15] In contrast, Judges Mattoon, Estelle, Woods, and Schultz were all retained. Whereas a "Do Not Retain" recommendation from a judicial evaluation commission has a much larger effect on the average affirmative vote than either limited opposition or a negative bar association recommendation, such a recommendation, by itself, may not be sufficient to remove a judge from the bench. Conversely, a recommendation for retention, by itself, will not assure a judge's retention. All the judges and justices defeated in the 2010–2014 period by opposition campaigns were recommended for retention either by bar associations

**TABLE 6.7** Judges and Justices Defeated in Judicial Retention Elections, 2010–2014

| *State* | *Year* | *Court* | *District* | *Judge/Justice* | *Opposition* | *Affirmative Vote* | *Affirmative Vote Prior Retention Election* | *District Mean Affirmative Vote W/O Judge* |
|---|---|---|---|---|---|---|---|---|
| Alaska | 2010 | Major Trial | 3 | Richard W. Postma | DNR* by JPEC** | 46.0% | | 63.2% |
| Colorado | 2010 | Major Trial | 8 | Jolene C. Blair | Campaign | 38.8% | 77.7% | 60.8% |
| Colorado | 2010 | Major Trial | 8 | Terence A. Gilmore | Campaign | 37.8% | 77.4% | 61.0% |
| Iowa | 2010 | Supreme | State | David L. Baker | Campaign | 45.9% | 76.8% | 45.3% |
| Iowa | 2010 | Supreme | State | Marsha K. Ternus | Campaign | 45.0% | 76.0% | 45.7% |
| Iowa | 2010 | Supreme | State | Michael J. Streit | Campaign | 45.6% | 75.8% | 45.4% |
| Arizona | 2014 | Major Trial | 1 | Benjamin R. Norris | DNR by JPEC | 42.0% | 55.6% | 67.9% |
| New Mexico | 2014 | Major Trial | 1 | Sheri A. Raphaelson | DNR by JPEC | 56.3% | | 80.1% |
| New Mexico | 2014 | Major Trial | 10 | Albert J. Mitchell, Jr. | Campaign | 51.8% | | |

* "Do Not Retain" Recommendation

** Judicial Performance Evaluation Commission

(i.e., Iowa) or judicial performance evaluation commissions (i.e., New Mexico, Colorado).

There are significant differences between low- and high-budget opposition campaigns, but, as with other forms of opposition, any type of campaign is neither necessary nor sufficient for a judge not to be retained. Most of the low-budget campaigns were not responded to by the targeted judge/justice who was almost always retained. Low-budget campaigns have the greatest possibility of success at the trial court level where they only have to contend with a judicial district and not the entire state. This was the case in the 2010–2014 period where the only successful low-budget campaigns were against trial court judges Mitchell in New Mexico ($8,350) and Blair and Gilmore in Colorado ($11,266). The latter is noteworthy because Judges Blair and Gilmore were opposed for their behavior before taking their seats on the bench (Dickman 2010). The former illustrates that, even at the trial court level, low-budget efforts may require additional factors for success. The campaign against Judge Mitchell tried to reach every voter in the district with postcard mailers and newspaper ads; however, the task of defeating the judge was made easier by two structural factors in New Mexico's selection system. First, New Mexico's retention threshold is 57 percent whereas most other states use 50 percent. With his affirmative vote of 51.8 percent, Judge Mitchell would have been retained in all other states except Illinois, which used a 60 percent threshold. Second, because of the initial partisan selection in the New Mexico system, there was an existing base of opposition to Judge Mitchell. In the 2008 partisan election, Republican candidate Mitchell defeated by the relatively small margin of 56 to 44 percent the appointed incumbent Democrat Judge Shutte, who would later be a contributor to the 2014 campaign opposing Judge Mitchell. Thus, there was a degree of past opposition to Judge Mitchell in the district that usually is not the case in a retention system.[16]

In contrast to the low-budget opposition campaigns, the six high-budget opposition campaigns against supreme court justices all stimulated a response by the targeted justices and/or their supporters. Only in Iowa did the justices themselves not actively campaign to retain their seats. In the other cases, the justices engaged in numerous campaign activities, sometimes over an extended period of time (e.g., Illinois Justice Kilbride). In all six cases, the justices and/or their supporters raised large sums of money to conduct their campaigns supporting the targeted justices. Even though the targeted justices and their supporters responded vigorously, the opposition campaigns still significantly lowered the affirmative vote close to the retention threshold in five of the six cases with big-budget campaigns. Had the targeted justices and their supporters not responded, the justices probably would not have been retained.

All six large-opposition campaigns reduced the justices' affirmative votes but only in Iowa in 2010 was it enough to defeat the justices. Why the success in Iowa and not elsewhere? If there has been no outrageous action by a judge or justice, then opposition campaigns are most likely to succeed when there is a clear issue important to a large portion of voters, specific action(s) upon which to focus voter attention, and resources to conduct a full campaign. In the 2010 Iowa election, same-sex marriage was an issue important to a large portion of voters, a specific court decision provided for marriage equality, and substantial monetary resources were involved, especially from outside the state. While the other five opposition campaigns had resources, they lacked a significant issue focus and related judicial acts. Opposition efforts based on narrow self-interest, as were the campaigns in Illinois, or lacking a clear act to serve as a mobilizer find it very difficult to sway enough voters to oppose retention.

Was not the 2012 election in Iowa where Justice Wiggins, who did not campaign and was retained, identical to the 2010 election when three justices were defeated? Yes on the surface, but there were significant differences between the two elections. Probably the most important difference was the rapidly growing acceptance of same-sex marriage in the entire country. Second, supporters of retention were quicker to respond and more aggressive so as to prevent another loss by giving voters multiple reasons to vote yes. Supporters of same-sex marriage defined the vote as important in that struggle; the legal community had criticized the 2010 outside interference in Iowa and advocated proper place of the courts and retention elections in the political system. Finally, the opposition campaign in total spent significantly fewer resources in 2012 than 2010 (Greytak et al., 2015).

## Looking Forward

The long-term stability in how judicial retention elections have been used by states and responded to by voters suggests more of the same for the future. On the other hand, some 2010–2014 events create uncertainties for supreme court justices, at least in the short term.

### *Continuity and Change?*

As long as the level of confidence in political institutions remains unchanged and judges carry out their duties professionally, most major retention election patterns are likely to continue for trial courts. Few judges will face any opposition and will thus be retained. Nationally the affirmative vote is not moving up or down; however, there are very slight downward trends in some states. Some temporal variation in the affirmative vote is to be expected as is a continuation of the substantial inter-state variation in the affirmative vote.

The judicial retention election as a mechanism for attaining judicial accountability will be used sparingly to remove judges at the trial court level, but it will be used. For example, Utah Judge Johansen's 2015 order to remove a foster child from the home of a same-sex couple stimulated an immediate attempt to remove him from the bench, which will probably be carried over to his upcoming retention election (Winslow 2015).

Unless there is a major change, such as raising the retention threshold, low-level opposition and "Do Not Retain" recommendations by bar associations will continue to have only limited effects on whether a judge is retained. "Do Not Retain" recommendations by judicial performance evaluation commissions have consistently had greater effects on voter behavior, but even they may require additional complementary conditions to result in the removal of a judge. How the recommendation is communicated, why the negative recommendation was made, the general level of support for the judiciary, and the particular political structures in the state also have a role in determining the election outcome.

It is not clear if the 2010–2014 campaigns against supreme court justices, especially the big-budget efforts, represent a significant change and signal a future where justices will be more frequently challenged and will have to respond in order to remain on the bench.[17] Even if the level of opposition in the 2010–2014 period was higher than in the past, the future is uncertain. Almost all of the 2010–2014 campaigns failed to remove the targeted justices. How long will the groups that have failed to remove justices keep trying? The level of recent opposition has created at least a short-term expectation of future opposition. For example, opposition is already anticipated for the 2016 Kansas elections:

> Two cases that will be heard in Kansas courts this week could put a political spotlight on the judges and justices hearing them, potentially threatening the careers of any who vote contrary to how activist groups think they should. All 14 judges of the Kansas Court of Appeals on Wednesday will hear the state's appeal of a lower court ruling striking down a new abortion law. The next day, the state Supreme Court will consider a case that involves the court's own power to supervise lower courts. A majority of the jurists will be up for retention votes next year, and some experts are predicting the elections will draw a flood of money from outside interest groups seeking to change the makeup of the state's highest courts reported (SFGate 2015).

What of the longer term? Will the opposition to justices continue at 2010–2014 levels, increase, or decrease? Most of the previously discussed motives for opposition are more short term in duration; thus, as in the past, this opposition will likely be irregular and passing. There are few reasons to expect increases or decreases in upset court participants, controversial cases, or flawed behavior. Politically motivated opposition was a significant component of the 2010–2014 opposition, and its future is less predictable. It will probably continue in those states currently experiencing partisan struggles over control of the courts, (e.g., Kansas (Merritt 2016)). Whether or not it expands to other states may be shaped by variables such as the balance of political control in a state and the perceptions of how partisan the supreme court is.

## *Altered Institutional Environment*

There is a similar degree of certainty about the institutional environment for judges and/or justices whose states employ judicial retention elections. In many states it will be more of the same for there are few, if any, significant reform efforts underway.[18] In other states, however, there are a variety of proposed changes. For example, there are efforts to make it easier for political groups to influence both the selection of judges and their removal via the retention election. If the past is any guide, the probability of a proposed reform being adopted is in part a function of the obstacles that must be overcome.

Current efforts to add retention elections range from calls to completion. After a very expensive 2014 partisan election for the Circuit Court, there are (thus far unheeded) calls to move Cole County to the list of counties in Missouri that employ commission-retention systems (Watson 2014). In 2015, Pennsylvania lawmakers began a multi-year task to change the state constitution to replace the practice of electing judges to the Supreme, Superior, and Commonwealth courts with a commission-retention system. Supporters argued it would end the fundraising in the current partisan election system, which may create the perception that judges are unfairly influenced by campaign contributors (Jackson 2015). North Carolina has recently added judicial retention elections to its system as an option. A state supreme court justice can now opt for an up-or-down retention election to determine continuation in office rather than run again in a nonpartisan election. While supporters claim this will help stem the flow of money and campaigns and their threat to the independence of the court, critics respond that it was simply an effort to keep conservative justices on the bench (Hardin 2015).

The best-known call for adopting judicial retention elections was by United States Senator Ted Cruz with regard to the United States Supreme Court; however, in this case, the motive was not to get politics out of the court and reduce the role of campaign contributions. Senator Cruz proposed ending lifetime tenure for the U.S. Supreme Court by introducing a system of judicial retention elections. Obviously such a change would not only make the justices accountable to the voters for the first time, but it would also reduce the court's independence and open the door to campaign contributions on a level not seen in any state retention election.

It should come as no surprise that given the low success rate of opposition campaigns there would be efforts not only to increase control over the initial appointment process but also to make it easier to remove a judge by modifying retention elections. A common theme in the proposed modifications is to raise the retention threshold, thus reducing the burden on those who want to remove a judge.[19] In 2015, several members of the Arizona legislature advanced HCR 2002 that will change the state's constitution so that Arizona would require a 60 percent threshold (Raftery 2015a). Also in 2015, two different constitutional amendments proposed in Indiana would raise the retention threshold from

50 to 60 percent or 67 percent (Raftery 2015b). One of the several 2015 Kansas bills proposing changes in the selection of supreme court justices is HCR 5009, which increases the retention threshold to 67 percent. The proposed changes in Kansas also include additional proposals that would decrease merit and increasingly politicize the selection process (e.g., removing the selection commission and requiring legislative confirmation (Raftery 2015c)). Obviously raising the retention threshold to 67 percent makes it much easier for an organized opposition campaign to defeat a judge; however, it also increases the probability of loss caused by the other variables that affect the retention vote (e.g., a significant drop in trust in government).

Whereas currently there are a significant number of proposed changes to retention elections, in the past many proposed changes were not adopted; this will probably be the case as the future unfolds. The probability of a proposal being adopted varies with the nature of the change and the requirements for adoption. Changing an entire selection system has always been a hard-fought political struggle. Less sweeping changes (e.g., constitutional changes, voter approval, legislative approval, and administrative change) face a series of potential hurdles, each slightly less difficult to overcome. Proposals requiring only administrative changes (e.g., Tennessee easing of the rules governing what supreme court justices could do when faced with an opposition campaign) (Humphrey 2015) have a high probability of adoption and can occur quickly. Reforms proposing fundamental changes are both less likely to be adopted and will require a more long-term effort by proponents.

## Notes

1 This form of selection is also referred to as "merit selection" or the "Missouri Plan."
2 Project details can be found in previous reports from JRP, including Hall and Aspin (1987b), Aspin (1999), Aspin et al., (2000), Aspin (2007a), and Aspin (2011).
3 Some states use retention elections for courts below the major trial level. Given the variability from state to state in both use and structure of these lower level courts, their retention elections are not included in any statistical analysis. However, in data gathering the JRP regularly observes the lower level courts and thus is confident that many but not all patterns which apply to major trial courts also apply to lower level courts. One exception is that Colorado voters are far less likely to follow judicial performance commission recommendations for county judges than for higher courts (Aspin 2007b). Judicial retention elections in Pennsylvania are not included for they are conducted in odd-numbered years and thus inhibit the use of temporal variables in analysis.
4 See the American National Election Studies Guide to Public Opinion and Electoral Behavior: Trust in Government Index 1958–2012.
5 Voter differentiation cannot be examined by level of court for seldom are there four or more intermediate appellate or supreme court justices on the same ballot.
6 A demonstration of voter differentiation in 2010 occurred in the 8th judicial district in Colorado when two targeted judges were defeated and the others in the district were easily retained. The affirmative votes for the five judges on the ballot were 38.8, 37.8, 68.2, 68.9, and 68.3 percent.

7 An additional attribute that proved to be unimportant is whether or not the judge had stood in a previous retention election.
8 The values for each state on confidence in the U.S. Supreme Court index were generated from a pooled sample of Cooperative Congressional Election Study (CCES) Common Core datasets. See http://projects.iq.harvard.edu/cces/home.
9 The average trust index value for each state was generated from a pooled sample of the ANES Time Series Studies. See www.electionstudies.org/studypages/download/datacenter_timeseries_NoData.htm.
10 Other than financial reports, there are only two brief references to "Vote No for Judge Amico" (Taibo 2014; Johansson 2014). Taibo suggests that the yard signs were placed by a disgruntled litigant. This would not be the only opposition "campaign" conducted by a single individual (Paul 2015).
11 Retrieved from Clear the Bench Colorado website 9/2/2010.
12 Previous research on JPEC recommendations found that high percentages of Alaska, Arizona, Colorado, and Utah voters who professed familiarity with the judicial performance evaluation recommendations also claimed the recommendations either aided their decision or were the sole basis for their decision (Esterling and Sampson 1998).
13 Previous research found positive relationships between the affirmative vote and the numeric score of the judicial performance evaluation commission in Arizona, Alaska, and Colorado (Aspin 2007b).
14 Judicial retention elections below the major trial court level are not included herein and as noted earlier their patterns can diverge from higher courts, but in this case they are similar. In 2014, Colorado County Judges Haynes, McClelland, and Moore received "Do Not Retain" recommendations. Judges Haynes (62.9%) and Moore (60.8%) were retained, but Judge McClelland (46.8%) was not.
15 One of the unusual occurrences in the 2014 retention elections involved Judge Raphaelson. After her loss, Judge Raphaelson initially refused to step down, arguing that her name should not have been on the ballot. Ultimately the New Mexico Supreme Court rejected her arguments and ordered her to vacate the bench.
16 Judge Mitchell's defeat is noteworthy in that it only temporarily removed him from the bench. Both Mitchell and Shutte applied to the nominating committee for the vacancy created by Mitchell's defeat. The Committee for Law and Order that had defeated Judge Mitchell in the retention election opposed his effort to regain his seat, but ultimately he was appointed to his former seat by the governor (Hansen 2015).
17 The lack of significant changes in rolloff and differentiation among judges on the affirmative vote do not support the conclusion that there has been a significant change. Successful opposition campaigns can both lower rolloff and increase differentiation, as voters treat the targeted judge substantially differently than the other judges on the ballot. If there were a significant increase in successful opposition campaigns in retention elections, rolloff in recent elections should be lower than its long-term trend would predict and there should be more differentiation than in previous periods. While rolloff in 2010 might be below the long-term trend line, rolloff in 2012 and 2014 was slightly greater than expected. Only in Arizona is differentiation in the 2010–2014 period, as measured by the average absolute difference from the district year mean, higher than previous periods. The corroborating evidence for increased opposition is not observed.
18 For a summary of types of changes, see Raftery (2013); for a summary of reform efforts by state, see Raftery (2015d).
19 While not the first time it has happened, some Illinois judges have a strategy to circumvent the 60 percent threshold for retention. Judges John Baricevic, Robert Haida, and Robert LeChien of the 20th Circuit will retire at the end of 2016, and thus are not required to run for retention in November 2016. Instead each will run in the partisan November 2016 election used to fill their soon-to-be-empty seats and only need 50 percent to continue on the bench (Maher 2015).

## References

American National Election Studies. 2012. *Guide to Public Opinion and Electoral Behavior: Trust in Government Index 1958–2012*. http://electionstudies.org/nesguide/toptable/tab5a_5.htm.

Arnold, Matt. 2010. "The Case against Three Justices." *Boulder Dailey Camera*, October 17, 2010.

Aspin, Larry. 1998. "Campaigns in Judicial Retention Elections: Do They Make A Difference?" *Justice System Journal* 20: 1–15.

Aspin, Larry. 1999. "Trends in Judicial Retentions Elections, 1964–1998." *Judicature* 83: 79–81.

Aspin, Larry. 2007a. "Judicial Retention Election Trends 1964–2006." *Judicature* 90: 208–213.

Aspin, Larry. 2007b. "Retention Elections and Evaluations: A Response to Current Trends in Contested Judicial Elections?" In *Future Trends in State Courts*, edited by Carol Flango. Williamsburg, VA: National Center for State Courts.

Aspin, Larry. 2011. "The 2010 Judicial Retention Elections in Perspective: Continuity and Change in Retention Elections from 1964 to 2010." *Judicature* 94: 218–233.

Aspin, Larry and William K. Hall. 1994. "Retention Elections and Judicial Behavior." *Judicature* 77: 306–315.

Aspin, Larry and William K. Hall. 1996. "Campaigning for Retention in Illinois." *Judicature* 80: 84–87.

Aspin, Larry, William K. Hall, Jean Bax, and Celeste Montoya. 2000. "Thirty Years of Judicial Retention Elections: An Update." *Social Science Journal* 37: 1–17.

Associated Press. 2014. "Drive Underway To Oust Judge in Gay Marriage Case." October 25, 2014. Available at: www.washingtontimes.com/news/2014/oct/25/drive-under-way-to-oust-judge-in-gay-marriage-case/.

Bannon, Alicia, Eric Velasco, Linda Casey, and Lianna Reagan. 2013. *The New Politics of Judicial Elections: How New Waves of Special Interest Spending Raised the Stakes for Fair Courts*. Washington, DC: Justice at Stake.

Bentley, Linda. 2012. "Andrew Thomas Rolls Out Citizens for Clean Courts." *Sonoran News*, June 6, 2012.

Berry, Kate. 2015. *How Judicial Elections Impact Criminal Cases*. New York: Brennan Center for Justice.

Boyles, Denis. 2010. "Kansas' 'Fire Beier' Campaign Disappears in a Cloud of Smoke." *National Review Online*, October 16, 2010.

Bush, Kent. 2014. "Kansans for Justice, or Politicizing Victims?" *Leavenworth Times*, October 30, 2014.

Cole, Thomas. 2014. "Bounced Judge Tries to Bounce Back." *Albuquerque Journal*, December 8, 2014.

Deslatte, Aaron. 2014. "Amendment 3 Could Reshape Florida's High Court." *Orlando Sentinel*, October 5, 2014.

Dickman, Pamela. 2010. "Retention of Judges Gilmore, Blair in Question." *Reporter Herald*, October 18, 2010.

Esterling, Kevin M. and Kathleen M. Sampson. 1998. *Judicial Retention Evaluation Programs in Four States: A Report with Recommendations*. Chicago: American Judicature Society.

Eye on the Bench. 2014. "Group Effort to Oust Judge Mary Gilbride." *Eye on the Bench*, September 17, 2014.

Fasbinder, Devon. 2014. "Former DA Responds to Campaign Ad Featuring Carr Brothers' Case." *KWCH12*, October 21, 2014.

Fattah, Geoffrey and Linda Thomson. 2006. "Judge Lewis is Ousted by 54% of Voters: Controversial Jurist Only the 2nd Utah District Judge to Lose Seat." *Utah News*, November 8, 2006.

Faturechi, Robert. 2014. "A Kansas Group's Push to Oust Judges Reveals a Gap in Campaign Finance Rules." *ProPublica*, October 17, 2014.

Feidt, Annie. 2012. "Group Targeting Superior Court Judge Up for Retention." *alaskapublic.org*, November 1, 2012.

Fischer, Howard. 2012. "Groups Campaign to Oust Arizona Supreme Court Judge." *East Valley Tribune*, October 23, 2012.

Greytak, Scott, Alicia Bannon, Allyse Falce, and Linda Casey. 2015. *The New Politics of Judicial Elections: Bankrolling the Bench*. Washington, DC: Justice at Stake.

Hall, William K. and Larry Aspin. 1987a. "The Roll-Off Effect in Judicial Retention Elections." *Social Science Journal* 24: 415–427.

Hall, William K. and Larry Aspin. 1987b. "What Twenty Years of Judicial Retention Elections Have Told Us." *Judicature* 70: 340–347.

Hansen, Steve. 2015. "Albert Mitchell Reappointed as Judge." *Clovis News Journal*, January 9, 2015.

Hardin, Peter. 2015. "Effectively Canceling a Judicial Election in North Carolina." *GavelGrab*, June 18, 2015.

Humphrey, Tom. 2014. "Ads Stoke State Justices' Retention Debate." *Knoxville News Sentinel*, July 28, 2014.

Humphrey, Tom. 2015. "New Rules Relax Campaign Restrictions for Tenn. Judges." *Knoxville News Sentinel*, December 7, 2015.

Jackson, Jay. 2014. "Governors Battle to Shape the Judiciary without Merit Selection." *ABA Journal*, February 1, 2014.

Jackson, Peter. 2015. "Correction: Merit Selection-Judges Story." *Washington Times*, June 17, 2015.

Johansson, Brandon. 2014. "Judicial Ballot Questions: You Be the Judge of Who Gets to Stay on the Bench." *Aurora Sentinel*, October 24, 2014.

Kiefer, Michael. 2012. "Arizona Supreme Court Justice Pelander Fights Effort to Oust Him –Pelander's Rare Campaign a Response to 'Tea Party' Anger Over Court Ruling." *Arizona Republic*, October 27, 2012.

Mackey, Brian. 2015. "Supreme Tort: The Campaign to Fire Justice Lloyd Karmeier." *NPR Illinois*, February 1, 2015.

Maher, Ann. 2014. "Karmeier Files Retention Papers for November Election." *Madison Record*, May 5, 2014.

Maher, Ann. 2015. "Judicial Races Take Shape in Twentieth Judicial Circuit." *Madison Record*, December 2, 2015.

Margolies, Dan. 2014. "Kansas Judges Targeted for Ouster Retain Seats." *KCUR 89.3*, November 4, 2014.

Masich, Matt. 2010. "Small Groups Emerge to Oppose Retention of Judges in Denver." *Jeffco. Law Week Colorado*, October 29, 2010.

Mat-Su Valley Frontiersman. 2012. "Our Words Matter, Too." *Mat-Su Valley Frontiersman*, October 25, 2012.

Merritt, Davis. 2016. "Right Takes Aim At Judicial Independence." *Wichita Eagle*, January 4, 2016.

Musgrave, Jane. 2010. "Florida Judges may be on Political Hot Seat." *Palm Beach Post*, November 14, 2010.

Ostrowski, Kathy. 2014. "Media Selective About Kansas Supreme Court Partisanship." *Kansans for Life Blog*, September 24, 2014.

Paul, John. 2015. "Man's $20,000+ Bid to Unseat Judge Deborah Kunselman Was Unsuccessful but Had an Impact." *Beaver Countian*, November 21, 2015.

Peirce, Larry. 2014. "Group Seeks to Oust Judge." *The Banner-Press*, September 5, 2014.

PEW Research Center. 2006. *Who Votes, Who Doesn't, and Why: Regular Voters, Intermittent Voters, and Those Who Don't*. October 18, 2006. Available at: www.people-press.org/2006/10/18/who-votes-who-doesnt-and-why/.

Raftery, Bill. 2013. "Judicial Selection in the States." *National Center for State Courts*, Available at: www.ncsc.org/sitecore/content/microsites/future-trends-2013/home/Monthly-Trends-Articles/Judicial-Selection-in-the-States.aspx.

Raftery, Bill. 2015a. "Arizona: Con Amendment Would Require Judges in Retention Elections Receive 60% Yes Votes; NM uses 57%, IL 60%." *Gavel to Gavel*, January 8, 2015.

Raftery, Bill. 2015b. "Indiana: End State's Merit Selection System, Require 67% Yes Vote for Retention Elections, Repeal Judicial Canons, Diminish Role of Lawyers." *Gavel to Gavel*, January 13, 2015.

Raftery, Bill. 2015c. "Kansas: A Look at the Bills Seeking to Change Supreme Court Selection." *Gavel to Gavel*, February 13, 2015.

Raftery, Bill. 2015d. "Review of 2015 Efforts to Change, Alter, or End Merit Selection/Commission Based Judicial Appointment Systems." *Gavel to Gavel*, August 13, 2015.

Sachdev, Ameet. 2010. "Conservatives Gunning for Illinois Judge Kilbride." *Chicago Breaking Business*, August 23, 2010.

SFGate. 2015. "Court Cases Put Political Spotlight on Kansas Judges." December 6, 2015.

Simon, Mallory. 2010. "Iowa Voters Oust Justices Who Made Same-Sex Marriage Legal." *CNN Politics*, November 3, 2010.

Skaggs, Adam, Maria da Silva, Linda Casey, and Charles Hall. 2011. *The New Politics of Judicial Elections: How Special Interest "Super Spenders" Threatened Impartial Justice and Emboldened Unprecedented Legislative Attacks on America's Courts*. Washington, DC: Justice at Stake.

Smith, Holly. 2009. "Republicans Won't Campaign Against Justice Beier in 2010." *Kansas Liberty*, August 21, 2009.

Srikrishnan, Maya. 2014. "Conservatives Nationwide Target Tennessee Supreme Court Justices." *Los Angeles Times*, August 6, 2014.

Stafford, Dave. 2012. "Tea Party Radio Ad Opposes David's Retention; Shepard Gives Backing." *Indiana Lawyer*, November 2, 2012.

Taibo, Alisha. 2014. "Voting on Judges." *Alisha Taibo's Family Law Blog*, Available at: www.taibolaw.blogspot.com/2014/10/voting-on-judges.html.

Watson, Bob. 2014. "*Election Aftermath: Some Suggest Nonpartisan Court Plan for Cole County*." News Tribune, November 9, 2014.

Winslow, Ben. 2015. "*Judge Targeted for Removal from the Bench for Decision on Same-Sex Foster Parents*." Fox 13 Salt Lake City, November 16, 2015.

# SECTION 3

# State Lower Court Elections

# 7

# THE LATEST TRENDS IN INTERMEDIATE APPELLATE COURT ELECTIONS

*Matthew J. Streb, Brian Frederick, Casey LaFrance, and Kimberly Rice*

As the preceding chapters make clear, there has been an increased and substantial focus on judicial elections over the past two decades largely because of the so-called "new politics of judicial elections." Most of this research indicates that judicial elections are taking on many of the same characteristics as elections for higher-profile offices, such as the U.S. Senate or governor. In other words, the campaigns are becoming more expensive and quite political. Outside groups are spending, in many cases, substantial amounts of money to try to influence the makeup of the bench, including sponsoring televised attack ads, as shown in Chapter 4. Even some judicial candidates, who for so long resisted the opportunity to look like other politicians, have become vocal on the campaign trail regarding their positions on issues and their opponents' weaknesses.

Moreover, much of this research on judicial elections indicates that the same systematic trends that exist in elections for other offices do so for the judiciary as well. For example, quality challengers are often strategic when deciding to run and usually obtain a greater percentage of the vote than those challengers who are not as experienced (Bonneau and Hall 2009; Hall and Bonneau 2006).

Yet, almost all of the research on judicial elections has focused on the courts of last resort—state supreme courts. Scholars have conducted far less research on levels below that of the supreme court. This lack of research is problematic because (1) there are many more lower-level courts and judges than state supreme courts, and (2) these lower-level judges are still making decisions that affect substantial numbers of people.

In this chapter, we build upon our previous work examining intermediate appellate court (IAC) elections. In particular, we extend our earlier work by adding several years of new data to our analyses. To our knowledge, this is the most comprehensive data set on IAC elections assembled to date. Examining all IAC elections from 1999 through 2014 (473 partisan elections, 617 nonpartisan elections, and 792 retention elections), we focus on whether the new politics of judicial elections has trickled down to lower-level judicial races. Consistent with our previous work, we find that, in general, it has not done so. Although the data do not exist for us to do a complete analysis (e.g., we do not have access to data on campaign commercials or independent spending at the IAC level), most IAC elections continue to be uncontested, few people participate, and campaign spending is not substantial. When IAC elections are contested, they do appear to be competitive but do not necessarily take on the same characteristics as competitive elections for other offices. Participation is still low (or, conversely, voter rolloff is high) largely because the campaigns tend to continue to fly below most people's radar and do not occur under conditions that optimize voter incentives to cast ballots.

However, the fact that the new politics of judicial elections has not trickled down to IAC elections does not mean that the characteristics of those races are completely random. In fact, in several cases, the results indicate that there are systematic forces that explain what is going on in these races. To illustrate, we examine the following aspects of IAC races: contestation, competition in the form of reelection rates and vote shares, campaign spending, and voter participation. Before doing so, however, we discuss briefly why one might (or might not) expect the new politics of judicial elections to have seeped into IAC contests.

## The New Politics of Judicial Elections and IACs

For quite some time, judicial elections—even at the supreme court level—were low-profile contests. Campaign contributions to candidates were minimal. In partisan races, labor or trial lawyers often would make small contributions to Democratic candidates, and the general business community would do the same for Republicans. Often these groups provided donations to parties, who, in turn, would contribute to their candidates. Rarely were these sums of money large and almost never were they spent independently on behalf of candidates. Due to lack of money, many candidates did not run campaign commercials, either on radio or television.[1] Media coverage of the races was scarce. Due to judicial canons, candidates were often prohibited from discussing substantive issues on the campaign trail, instead focusing on their qualifications or experience. Even if candidates were permitted to make their positions clear on substantive issues, such as criminal justice or tort reform, many would have resisted doing so because of the norms of the office. Judges are supposed to be impartial interpreters of the law, not politicians. In short, judicial elections were fairly boring affairs from these perspectives.

However, that understanding began to change in the 1980s, when longtime judicial scholar Roy Schotland (1985, 76) famously noted that judicial elections were becoming "nosier, nastier, and costlier." The changing makeup of judicial elections was most evident in California and Ohio. In California, three supreme court justices were defeated in retention elections in 1986 on the grounds that they voted consistently to overturn death sentences (Wold and Culver 1987). In the same year in Ohio, the controversial Chief Justice Frank Celebrezze lost a particularly nasty race in which his opponent tied his political contributions to the mafia. In both cases, substantial money was spent and media coverage was frequent.

Certainly not all judicial races reflected the California and Ohio elections, as most supreme court contests still flew below the radar.[2] However, more races were starting to take on the characteristics of elections for other high-profile offices (Goldberg, et al. 2002). What led to the rise in visibility of some supreme court elections? Essentially, groups began to realize they could seek to affect policy easier by turning their attention to the courts of last resort. To influence the legislature, interest groups had to elect dozens of people (or potentially more) who supported their position, in some cases only to see their favored legislation overturned by the state supreme court. Interest groups learned that supreme courts also affect policy and have far fewer members for a group to attempt to sway.

Ohio provides an excellent example of the increased attention by interest groups. In the 1990s, a Republican-controlled legislature and a Republican governor passed and signed into law several bills regarding tort reform, such as limiting Ohioans' ability to sue for personal injury. Yet, the Ohio Supreme Court was a plaintiff-friendly court and often struck down these laws.[3] The business community became increasingly frustrated with what they viewed as an activist court and spent substantial money in competitive elections in 2002 and 2004 to help elect justices who held their points of view on tort reform. As a result, the court's record on tort-related issues moved from being pro-plaintiff to strongly pro-defendant and has remained that way ever since.[4]

Like a few other states, Ohio has been home to some relatively high-profile campaigns for the IAC bench in recent years. For instance, in 2014, former Ohio Congresswoman Mary Jo Kilroy unsuccessfully challenged appointed incumbent Betsy Luper Schuster for a seat on the Franklin County Court of Appeals in a spirited race in which the two candidates combined to spend over $450,000. The question is whether examples like this one have become more commonplace in recent years or whether they represent the exception to the general pattern characterizing IAC elections of the past.

It is certainly possible that the new politics of judicial elections has trickled down to the IAC level. As we have written elsewhere, "Although the state supreme courts are technically 'the courts of last resort,' they hear only a limited number of cases. At the appellate level in most states, it is IACs that carry the workload of the state court systems" (Streb and Fredrick 2009, 522). Moreover, according to state court experts, "Generally speaking, the jurisdiction of intermediate appellate courts is mandatory because Americans hold to the view that parties in a case are entitled to at least one appeal. In numerous instances, then, these are the courts of last resort for litigants in the state court system" (Carp, Stidham, and Manning 2004, 65). As a result, political parties and interest groups often find their interests before an IAC and may want to try to influence the makeup of that court.

Yet, the conditions that have led to the new politics of judicial elections at the supreme court level do not necessarily apply to lower courts. There are two clear differences between supreme court elections and lower court elections that might lead to different impacts. First, there are substantially greater numbers of elections at the IAC level than at the supreme court level because there are more seats. For example, in 2014, the state of Ohio held elections for two positions on the state supreme court whereas there were 23 elections for positions on the state's IACs. The sheer number of seats at the IAC level leads to a few possible results. It is plausible that more races go uncontested because parties need to recruit more candidates to run. Also, the fact that there are so many races means that there is keener competition for money, which may limit campaign spending. Finally, the number of races makes it difficult for the media to cover these elections, which may make it harder for people to vote.

From a different perspective, elections for IAC judges are not likely to be viewed as important as races for the supreme court by interest groups, voters, the media, and members of the legal community. Although the workload of IACs is much greater than that of state supreme courts, the influence of the supreme courts is more substantial. State lower courts are often bound by precedent in their rulings, but even when IAC judges have some leeway in their rulings, the cases may be appealed to and heard by the supreme courts. To go back to the Ohio example, the supreme court will have the final say on the major tort-related decisions. What lower level courts might rule, while not unimportant, is not nearly as important as how the supreme court rules. Even when lower court judges have some discretion (e.g., presiding over settlements), they are constrained by the rulings of the state supreme court and are subject to reversal. As a result, parties and interest groups will put more focus on the supreme court contests, which, in turn, could lead to fewer contested elections, less campaign spending, and lower political participation in IAC elections.

The remainder of this chapter will allow us to determine if IAC elections have been transformed in a meaningful way over the past decade. Have these races become vigorously contested along the same lines as state supreme court elections? Or do they continue to feature low rates of contestation, competition, campaign spending, and citizen participation?

## Contestation

Our first set of analyses begins with an examination of the degree to which IAC races are contested. Figure 7.1 presents the percentage of IAC incumbents facing an opponent by election cycle from 1999 through 2014 in both partisan and

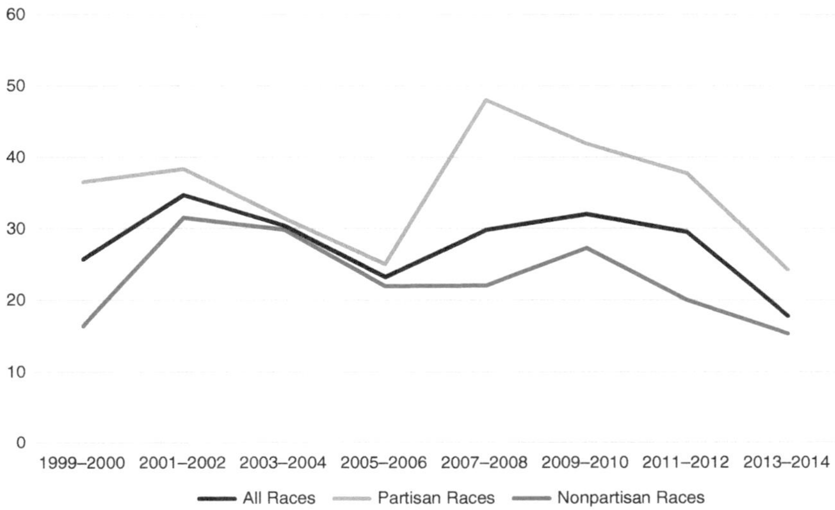


**FIGURE 7.1** Incumbent Contestation Rates in Non-Retention IAC Elections, 1999–2014

nonpartisan races. Overall, the results are consistent with earlier research showing that very few incumbents (27.5% over this period) face a challenger. The contestation rate ranges from a high of 34.7 percent in the 2001–2002 cycle to a low of 17.8 percent in the 2013–2014 cycle. Contrary to the idea of a newfound era of vigorous electoral competition, IAC elections are actually less contested over time.

Figure 7.1 also compares these trends for partisan and nonpartisan elections,[5] supporting the proposition that incumbents in partisan races are more likely to face opponents in every election cycle. In partisan races, incumbents faced a challenger in 24.2 percent of races for the 2013–2014 cycle compared to a high of 48 percent in 2007–2008. Nonpartisan incumbents have a lower probability of running against an opponent, with a rate of only 15.3 percent in 2013–2014, down from a high of 31.5 percent in 2001–2002. These results bolster the notion that partisan ballots can play a critical role by imposing greater electoral accountability in judicial elections, but even that stimulus has its limits at the IAC level.

Figure 7.2 reveals that another crucial factor influencing contestation in IAC elections is whether the race lacks an incumbent. Across the board, open-seat races are more likely to be contested, although 2013–2014 marked a low point in the time series, with only 57.1 percent of IAC races contested. That number is down from a high of 80 percent in both the 2003–2004 and the 2007–2008 cycles. We urge caution in drawing too many inferences from a single election period, but contestation rates for open IAC seats are not on an upward trajectory.

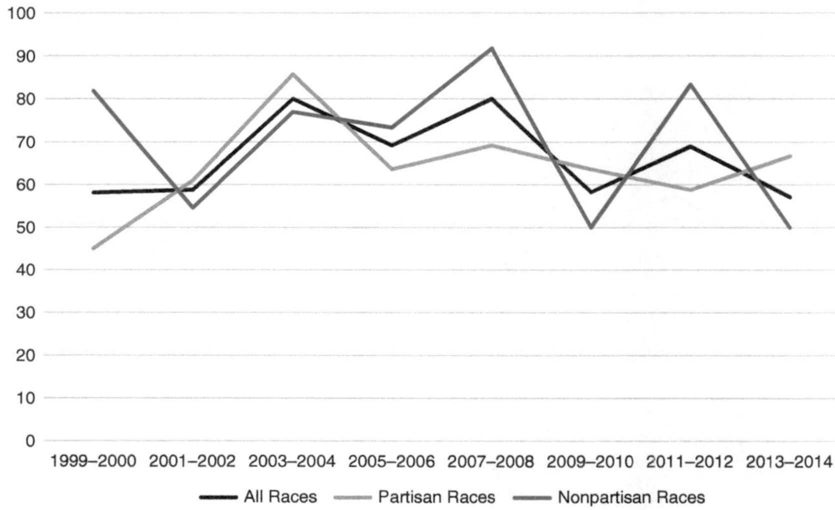


**FIGURE 7.2** Open Seat Contestation Rates in Non-Retention IAC Elections, 1999–2014

One significant difference between races involving incumbents and those for open seats is that election format matters less in determining rates of contestation. In three of the eight election cycles examined, contestation rates were higher in nonpartisan states compared to states using the partisan ballot. In the 2007–2008 cycle, 91.7 percent of nonpartisan races were contested, which is 22 percentage points higher than the contestation rate for partisan open-seat races in the same period. These results serve as a reminder that the impact of partisan ballots on electoral competition is conditional upon incumbency status. Political parties are instrumental in helping to encourage challengers against the power of incumbency, but that role proves less critical in an open-seat context.

## Competition: Reelection Rates and Vote Shares

The data on contestation demonstrate that the vast majority of incumbent IAC judges get a free pass to reelection. However, as indicated below, those incumbents unfortunate enough to attract an opponent are typically going to be involved in a highly competitive race. Figure 7.3 displays the percentage of incumbents winning reelection from 1999 through 2014 in all races and races where an IAC incumbent faced a challenger. In all races, incumbent IAC judges won 92.5 percent of the time, jumping to a high of 95.8 percent in 2013–2014. However, the overall reelection rate drops to 74.7 percent when an incumbent faces a challenger, with only 65.7 percent incumbents in contested races winning in the 1999–2000 period compared to a high of 80.6 percent in 2009–2010. Incumbent

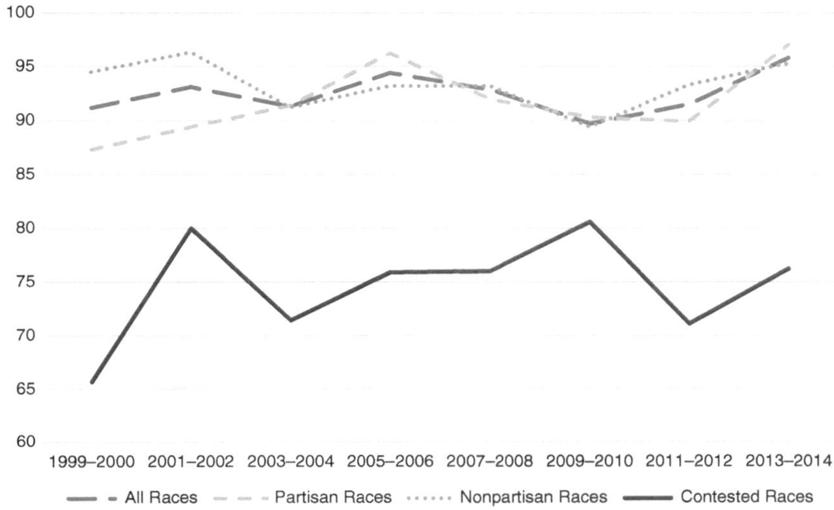


**FIGURE 7.3** Incumbent Success Rates in Non-Retention IAC Elections 1999–2014

reelection rates vary slightly based on election type, with incumbents in partisan elections performing about two percentage points better, although the relationship is not statistically significant.

To supplement this analysis of electoral competition, we analyze the average percentage of the vote received by incumbents in contested races, which was 54.6 percent overall during the 1999–2014 period. Interestingly, the 54.6 percent average is nearly identical to the rate for 2000 through 2006 (Streb, Frederick and LaFrance 2007). Figure 7.4 documents the pattern across each election cycle and depicts a reasonable level of level of stability, with a mean of 52.3 percent in the 2007–2008 cycle and 56.7 percent in 2013–2014. Sitting IAC judges seeking reelection confront a difficult battle when facing challengers, but that struggle is magnified in partisan elections. The overall mean for IAC judges in partisan races is 52.9 percent, which reached its nadir in 2007–2008 at 50.9 percent. The path to reelection for nonpartisan incumbents is a bit less treacherous, with an overall mean percentage of 56.3 and a range with no clear trend, from a low of 53.5 percent in 2007–2008 to a high of 59.3 percent in 2001–2002.

Apart from the institutional context in which the election occurs, Streb and Frederick (2009) have established that the individual characteristics of the candidates themselves will factor heavily in determining the degree of competitiveness in judicial elections. For instance, not all sitting judges are equally situated to enjoy the advantages of incumbency. Earlier research at both the state supreme court and IAC levels has shown that judges initially appointed fare demonstrably worse than judges who have previously been elected (Bonneau and Hall 2009; Streb and Frederick 2009). The same findings apply to challengers and open-seat candidates,

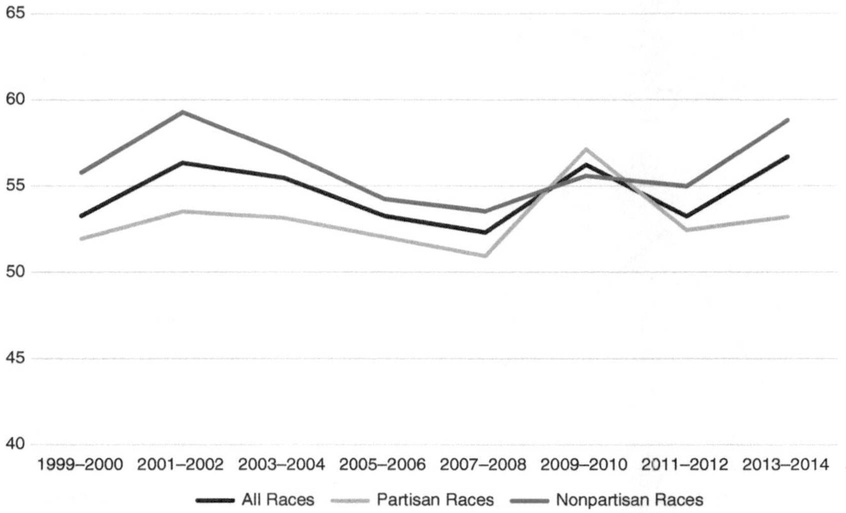


**FIGURE 7.4** Incumbent Vote Shares in Non-Retention IAC Elections, 1999–2014

as well as candidates with no prior judicial experience (Bonneau 2006; Hall and Bonneau 2006). On this last measure, Streb and Frederick (2009) find that the relationship between judicial experience and electoral performance is more tenuous for IAC challengers.

In order to assess the effects of candidate attributes, Figure 7.5 provides the mean percentage of the vote in IAC elections received by six types of candidates previously identified by Frederick and Streb (2011): (1) elected incumbents, (2) appointed incumbents, (3) quality challengers, (4) non-quality challengers, (5) quality open-seat candidates, and (6) non-quality open-seat candidates. Quality in this analysis simply denotes whether the non-incumbent candidates had any prior judicial experience. Unsurprisingly, incumbents garner greater support than challengers, and appointed incumbents are less successful than elected incumbents. Incumbents facing voters for the first time receive an average of 52.0 percent of the vote whereas incumbents previously on the ballot receive 56.1 percent. While this difference is not massive, it is statistically significant at the 0.001 level.

Prior experience appears to be a meaningful indicator of success among non-incumbents in IAC races over the time frame of this study. On average, quality IAC challengers received 48.2 percent of the vote whereas non-quality challengers received 44.3 percent, a difference also statistically significant at the 0.001 level. These results depart from Streb and Frederick's (2009) earlier analysis of IAC elections, which indicated that quality challengers did not perform significantly better than inexperienced challengers. There are a couple of reasonable explanations for this discrepancy. Unlike Streb and Frederick's study, these results do not

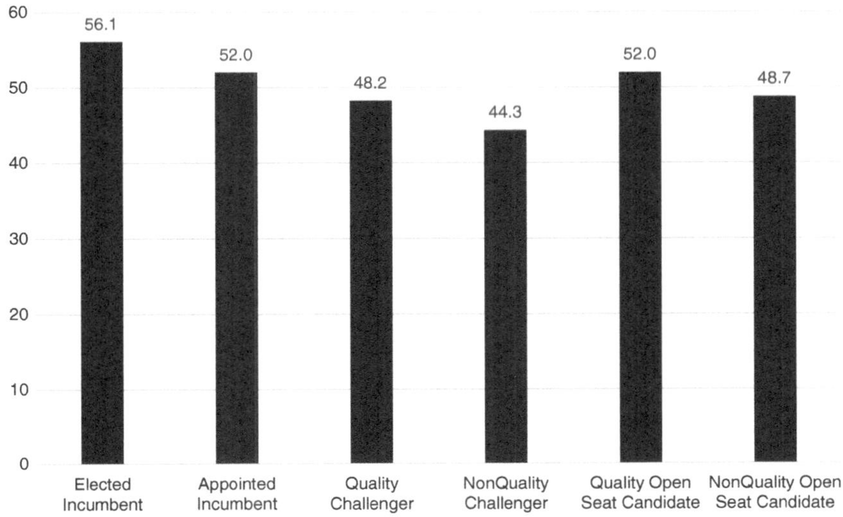


**FIGURE 7.5** Vote Shares in Non-Retention IAC Elections by Candidate Type, 1999–2014

control for other factors that might influence the success of IAC challengers, such as the general level of electoral competition in the state or district or the ratio of incumbent to challenger spending in the race. Additionally, Streb and Frederick's study developed a model predicting incumbent vote shares that included an independent variable indicating whether the incumbent faced a quality challenger. The results in Figure 7.5 include the mean vote share for each type of challenger with no accounting for other variables. Nevertheless, it does supply some critical evidence that judicial experience matters at both the state supreme court and IAC levels. Of course, this conclusion will still need to be tested more rigorously with a fully-specified model in future research.

In contested open-seat IAC races, experienced candidates outperform inexperienced candidates. This finding is consistent with Bonneau's (2006) research on open-seat state supreme court elections. Over the life of this study, quality open-seat IAC candidates averaged 52.0 percent of the vote whereas non-quality open seat candidates averaged 48.7 percent. This gap is modest but statistically significant at the 0.001 level, offering further empirical validation that prior service as a judge provides a boost in the electoral fortunes of candidates at multiple levels in state judicial elections.

Collectively, these results show that IAC elections can be highly competitive when incumbents face an opponent and when open seats are contested. Moreover, the evidence also bolsters the claim that IAC races are not random affairs but instead are characterized by systematic outcomes. Each race has its own idiosyncrasies but there are predictable sets of institutional and individual variables influential in understanding the dynamics of these races. Furthermore, these patterns have remained consistent over the course of the study despite the changing electoral landscape that emerged in the past decade.

Before concluding this section on competition in IAC elections, a brief note about retention elections is in order. We devote limited attention to this subject because the story here is in accord with earlier retention elections at the IAC level (Streb, Frederick, and LaFrance 2007). We calculated the percentage of the vote to retain judges in 792 retention elections from 1999 through 2014 for each election cycle covered in this study. The results display remarkable stability over this period, with a high of 73.3 percent in the 2001–2002 cycle to a low of 68.9 percent in 2009–2010. Although there are occasional instances of voter ire toward individual judges that draw headlines in other state judicial elections, in IAC retention elections, the overwhelming majority of judges on the ballot keep their jobs with relative ease. In theory, retention elections at the IAC level present an opportunity for voters to impose accountability; in reality, there is scant evidence that they actually do so.[6]

## Campaign Spending

The topic of how state judicial elections are financed has generated enormous controversy in recent years. This normative debate has unfolded while empirical understanding of how much money gets raised and spent in judicial campaigns has expanded enormously. Whereas the bulk of this research has been devoted to state supreme court races (e.g., Bonneau 2007) there have been advances in understanding these dynamics at the IAC level as well (Frederick and Streb 2008, 2011; Streb and Frederick 2011). This section of the chapter updates the findings of Streb and Frederick through the 2014 election cycle.

Earlier research uncovered no noticeable increase in the level of campaign spending for IAC elections in the aftermath of the U.S. Supreme Court's decision in *Republican Party of Minnesota v. White* (2002), which declared unconstitutional judicial canons that prevented judicial candidates from announcing their views on issues (Bonneau, Hall, and Streb 2011). The concern among some scholars and judicial reform organizations was that the *White* ruling would usher in a new era of increased campaign spending because campaigns would be overtly political. The data in Figure 7.6 include the mean amount of campaign spending by individual candidates in contested IAC races adjusted for inflation (in 2014 dollars) for the 1999–2014 period.[7] These data corroborate previous research that spending has not increased noticeably over the past few cycles and, if anything, is on a downward trajectory. The high point for campaign spending in the series occurred during the 1999–2000 cycle, with a mean of $248,554 for candidates in that period (ironically before the *White* ruling in 2002). That average fell to $113,119 in the 2011–2012 cycle and only slightly increased to $131,473 in

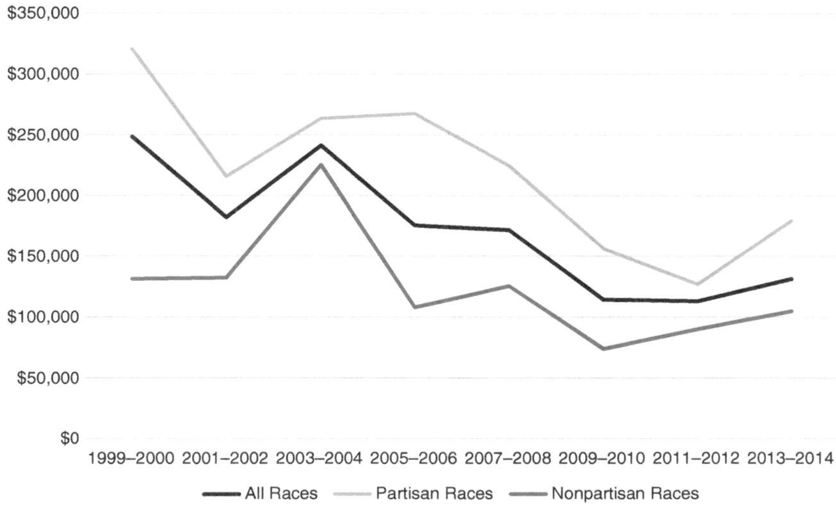


**FIGURE 7.6** Campaign Spending by Candidates in Contested Non-Retention IAC Elections, 1999–2014

2013–2014. While there may be year-to-year variations in the amount of money candidates in IAC races spend, there is no consistent pattern that emerges from the data.

Although the post-*White* period may not have ushered in a new avalanche of spending in IAC elections, there are systematic factors that do cause campaign spending to vary in predictable ways. As Figure 7.6 demonstrates, partisan IAC elections are consistently more costly than nonpartisan elections. In every election cycle examined in this chapter, average individual candidate spending was higher in partisan races than in nonpartisan contests. Average individual candidate spending in partisan races ranged from $126,729 in the 2011–2012 cycle to $320,538 in the 1999–2000 cycle. The comparative range for nonpartisan IAC candidates was $73,881 in 2009–2010 to $225,082 in 2003–2004. It should be noted that most of this disparity in spending levels can be accounted for by the fact that partisan races tend to be more competitive. Previous studies have shown that once this variable is controlled for, there are negligible differences in rates of spending for partisan and nonpartisan IAC races. In other words, partisanship drives up competitiveness which, in turn, leads to increased levels of spending (Frederick and Streb 2011).

Just as individual candidate characteristics carry great weight in determining the degree of electoral competition in IAC elections, they are also vital in ascertaining why certain candidates spend more than others. Figure 7.7 plots the mean level of campaign spending for the six types of candidates identified previously. Not surprisingly, elected incumbents outspent appointed incumbents by a margin of $187,864 to $159,290. Similarly, quality challengers outspent non-quality

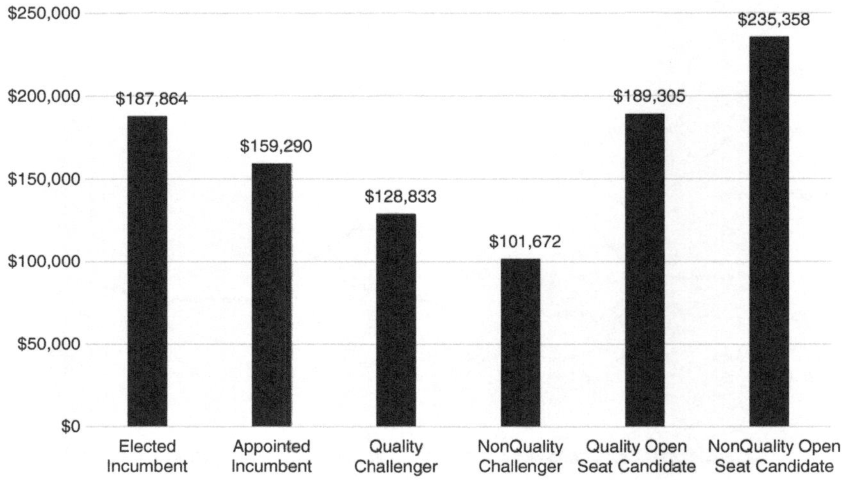


**FIGURE 7.7** Campaign Spending by Candidate Type in Contested Non-Retention IAC Elections, 1999–2014

challengers by a margin of $128,833 to $101,672. Spending by open-seat candidates was the highest, which is logical considering that these races constitute the most competitive IAC contests. However, what runs slightly counter to the conventional wisdom is the finding that non-quality open-seat candidates outspent quality open-seat candidates by a margin of $235,358 to $189,305.

What accounts for the spending gap between inexperienced and experienced candidates for open seats? Most likely these differences can be attributed to the fact that many successful lawyers looking to become judges tap their networks of well-connected legal supporters in open-seat races in which they may have the best opportunity to emerge victorious. Additionally, these candidates may use their own money on the campaigns. Sitting lower court judges may not have the same level of personal wealth to spend and might feel constrained about appealing to wealthy members of the legal community who have business before their courts.

## Voter Participation

The final aspect of IAC elections we examine is voter participation. Doing so for IAC elections is a big challenge because there are no individual-level survey data available or any reliable way of estimating voter turnout in judicial elections. However, following the lead of previous studies of judicial elections, we use ballot rolloff in IAC elections as a means of estimating variation in participation (Bonneau and Loepp 2014; Hall 2007, 2015; Hall and Bonneau 2008, 2013; Shortell 2013; Streb, Frederick, and LaFrance 2009; Streb and Frederick 2011). Rolloff is the percentage of people in an election who cast votes in the top race but fail to do so in the IAC race. Hypothetically, if 100,000 voters cast a ballot in a presidential election and 90,000 cast a ballot in an IAC race, rolloff in that race is 10 percent. Of course, rolloff is not a perfect measure of voter participation in judicial elections because it only indicates voters who actually show up to the polls. However, as previous studies note, the measure does allow researchers to gain critical insight into why some races generate more interest from voters than others.

Figure 7.8 contains the percentage of ballot rolloff in 1,458 IAC elections from 1999 through 2014 with a presidential, gubernatorial, or U.S. Senate race at the top of the ballot in five types of races: (1) contested partisan races, (2) uncontested partisan races, (3) contested nonpartisan races, (4) uncontested non partisan races, and (5) retention races. Overall during this period, ballot rolloff in IAC contests averaged 27.9 percent, with a low of 24.8 percent in the 2011–2012 cycle and a high of 30.8 percent in the 1999–2000 cycle. Once again, we see fluctuations from one election cycle to the next but no clear directional pattern based on time.

What really matters when untangling the amount of rolloff in IAC elections is the electoral context of the race. By far, the optimal conditions for voters to cast a ballot is in a contested partisan race. In such races, rolloff averaged under 8 percent for each election cycle, dropping as low as 4.8 percent in the 2005–2006 cycle. Whereas voters may express little knowledge of, or interest in, contests for the IAC bench, under the right circumstances they can overcome the electoral barriers to participation. At the other end of the spectrum, voter participation is most inhibited in uncontested nonpartisan races. In all but one election cycle, rolloff is

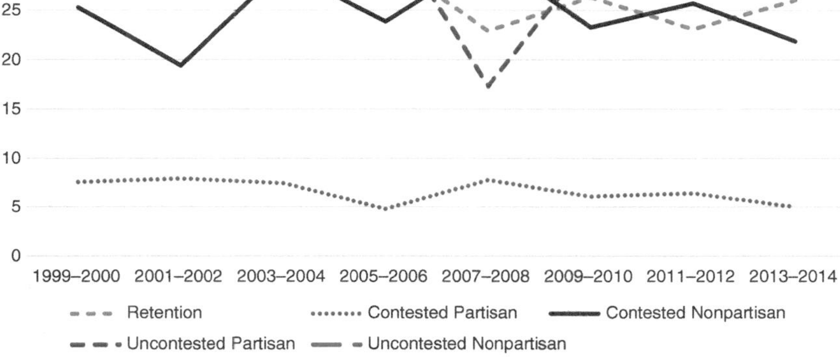


**FIGURE 7.8** Ballot Rolloff Percentage in IAC Elections, 1999–2014

highest under these circumstances, with a low of 32.2 percent in the 2001–2002 period and a high of 40.9 percent in 2011–2012. Two central observations can be made from these results, consistent with previous studies of ballot rolloff in judicial elections (Hall 2007, 2015; Streb, Frederick, and LaFrance 2009). First, as political scientists have highlighted for decades, the partisan cue is essential for voters to make decisions in a low-information environment. Second, many voters will not bother to cast a vote when the outcome of the race is virtually certain.

The results in Figure 7.8 also reveal that retention elections provide a mixed set of conditions for participation in IAC elections. Voters always have an up or down choice of whether to retain the incumbent judge, but they always lack the partisan affiliation of the candidate on the ballot as a stimulus to participate. The percentage of rolloff consistently hovers in the middle of the graph, ranging from a high of 30.2 percent in 2011–2012 to a low of 22.9 percent in 2007–2008. Retention elections give voters more incentive to participate than uncontested elections but do not come anywhere close to approximating the motivation and information of contested partisan elections.

## Conclusion

Detailed research on IAC elections has been in short supply until the past decade. This chapter has built on the work of Streb and his colleagues by updating aggregate trends in IAC races through 2014, largely confirming the findings of previous research. Most notably, the new politics of judicial elections, at least as we measure the concept here, has not trickled down to the IAC level. Most IAC races go uncontested, and various indicators of electoral competition have not changed much over the life of this study. If any conclusion can be drawn it is that there has been a slight decline in electoral competitiveness. Moreover, neither candidate spending nor political participation has increased.

Second, this chapter has also shown that while IAC races may lack the competitive zeal of more high-profile elections on the ballot, there is nonetheless a set of institutional and individual candidate characteristics that explain variance in levels of contestation, competition, campaign spending, and voter participation in IAC races. These systematic relationships include: (1) higher levels of competition and contestation in partisan and open-seat races, (2) superior electoral performance by elected incumbents and experienced non-incumbents, (3) higher levels of campaign spending in partisan elections, and (4) higher levels of voter participation in partisan and contested races.

Although our understanding of the dynamics involved in IAC elections has expanded tremendously over the past decade, there are still avenues of research that can be pursued on this topic. Streb (2009) has highlighted the need for individual-level data for all judicial elections. While Bonneau and Cann (2015) have taken up that challenge in examining supreme court races, there is still a huge void in lower court elections. Aggregate data can only explain so much in our understanding of why voters behave the way they do in IAC elections. Individual-level data are critical for untangling the causal mechanisms at work.

Another area where there is a notable absence of knowledge about IAC elections is the role of independent expenditures. As we report in this chapter, overall campaign spending by individual candidates in IAC elections has remained stable over time. However, can the same be said about the spending of outside groups? It is the increased involvement of outside groups often most associated with the new politics of judicial elections. Anecdotal evidence indicates that interest groups have not been active participants independently in IAC elections, but systematic evidence is unavailable. Given the wide variance in the quality and consistency of campaign finance disclosure at the state level, answering this question is a daunting task. However, a full accounting of the state of IAC elections requires some empirical understanding of independent expenditures in these contests.

One final area where information about IAC elections is lacking is the tone of the races. Are candidates running primarily biographical advertisements highlighting their accomplishments or are there increasing numbers of contrast or negative advertisements attacking the weaknesses of their opponents? It is not possible to rule out fully the emergence of a new politics of judicial elections at the IAC level until hard data are presented on the nature of candidate advertisements in these races. Systematic television campaign commercial data at the supreme court level have been made available regularly since 2000, which Hall (2014, 2015) analyzes extensively for recent elections. However, no such data (at least of which we are aware) exist at the IAC level. Indeed, it is not even clear how often candidates at the IAC level are advertising, either on radio or television.

Additional research is necessary to gain a complete picture of what is going on in elections for the IAC bench. Despite empirical gaps, we have a much more comprehensive understanding than was the case just a few years ago. The data presented in this chapter will serve as a critical foundation for the next line of research into IAC elections for years to come. As the focus on judicial elections by the media, judicial organizations, and scholars continues to grow and the normative debate becomes more heated, having a clearer understanding of elections for all levels of courts becomes even more important.

## Notes

1 However, Hall (2015) shows that attack advertising in various media has been a staple of many state supreme court elections going back to the mid-1850s.

2 This was true even in California and Ohio. Not all judicial elections in these states were high-profile affairs. For a discussion of the variability in visibility in Ohio, see Baum, Klein, and Streb (2007).

3 Although Republicans held a 5–2 advantage on the court during most of this time, two of the Republican justices (Douglas and Pfeifer) often voted with their Democratic colleagues on tort-related issues.

4 For more on interest group involvement in Ohio Supreme Court elections and the court's shift to the right on tort-related cases, see Baum, Klein, and Streb (2007).
5 Unlike Streb, Frederick, and LaFrance (2007), we code elections Ohio and Michigan as nonpartisan races. This approach is consistent with subsequent studies of IAC elections (e.g., Streb and Frederick 2009). For a careful discussion of this issue in state supreme court races, see Hall (2015).
6 In fact, over 99 percent of IAC judges were retained over this period. The exception was Illinois Court of Appeals Judge Gordon Maag who was denied retention in 2004.
7 For less than 1 percent of the candidates, there was no publicly available report of how much money they spent in their races. Hence, they are excluded from the analysis.

## References


Baum, Lawrence, David E. Klein, and Matthew J. Streb. 2017 *Influencing the Court: The Relationship between Judicial Elections and Judicial Policy*. Charlottesville: University of Virginia Press.

Bonneau, Chris W. 2006. "Vacancies on the Bench: Open-Seat Elections for State Supreme Courts." *Justice System Journal* 27: 143–159.

Bonneau, Chris W. 2007. "The Effects of Campaign Spending in State Supreme Court Elections." *Political Research Quarterly* 60: 489–499.

Bonneau, Chris W. and Damon M. Cann. 2015. *Voters' Verdicts: Citizens, Campaigns, and Institutions in State Supreme Court Elections*. Charlottesville: University ofVirginia Press.

Bonneau, Chris W. and Melinda Gann Hall. 2009. *In Defense of Judicial Elections*. New York: Routledge.

Bonneau, Chris W. and Eric Loepp. 2014. "Getting Things Straight: The Effects of Ballot Design on Electoral Structure and Participation." *Electoral Studies* 34: 119–130.

Bonneau, Chris W., Melinda Gann Hall, and Matthew J. Streb. 2011. "*White* Noise: The Unrealized Effects of *Republican Party of Minnesota vs. White* on Judicial Elections." *Justice System Journal* 32: 247–268.

Carp, Robert A., Ronald Stidham, and Kenneth L. Manning. 2004. *Judicial Process in America*, 6th edition. Washington, DC: CQ Press.

Frederick, Brian and Matthew J. Streb. 2008. "Paying the Price for a Seat on the Bench: Campaign Spending in Contested Elections for State Intermediate Courts of Appeals." *State Politics and Policy Quarterly* 8: 410–429.

Frederick, Brian and Matthew J. Streb. 2011. "The Cost of Going For The Gavel: Individual Candidate Spending in Intermediate Appellate Court Elections." *Justice System Journal* 32: 25–43.

Goldberg, Deborah, Craig Holman, and Samantha Sanchez. 2003. *The New Politics of Judicial Elections*. Washington, DC: Justice at Stake.

Hall, Melinda Gann. 2007. "Voting in State Supreme Court Elections: Competition and Context as Democratic Incentives." *Journal of Politics* 69: 1147–1159.

Hall, Melinda Gann. 2014. "Televised Attacks and the Incumbency Advantage in State Supreme Courts." *Journal of Law, Economics, and Organization* 30: 138–164.

Hall, Melinda Gann. 2015. *Attacking Judges: How Campaign Advertising Influences State Supreme Court Elections* Stanford: Stanford University Press.

Hall, Melinda Gann and Chris W. Bonneau. 2006. "Does Quality Matter? Challengers in State Supreme Court Elections." *American Journal of Political Science* 50: 20–33.

Hall, Melinda Gann and Chris W. Bonneau 2008. "Mobilizing Interest: The Effects of Money on Citizen Participation in State Supreme Court Elections." *American Journal of Political Science* 52: 457–470.

Hall, Melinda Gann and Chris W. Bonneau. 2013. "Attack Advertising, the *White* Decision and Voter Participation in State Supreme Court Elections." *Political Research Quarterly* 66: 115–126.

*Republican Party of Minnesota v. White*. 2002. 536 US 765.

Schotland, Roy A. 1985. "Elective Judges' Campaign Financing: Are State Judges' Robes the Emperor's Clothes of American Democracy?" *Journal of Law and Politics* 2: 57–167.

Shortell, Christopher. 2013. "Voting in Trial Court Elections: Ballot Roll-Off in Partisan, Nonpartisan, and Retention Elections in High-Population Counties." *Justice System Journal* 34: 153–170.

Streb, Matthew J. 2009. "The Need for More Individual-Level Judicial Election Data." *Justice System Journal* 30: 307–314.

Streb, Matthew J. and Brian Frederick. 2009. "Conditions for Competition in Low-Information Judicial Elections: The Case of Intermediate Appellate Court Elections." *Political Research Quarterly* 62: 523–537.

Streb, Matthew J. and Brian Frederick. 2011. "When Money Can't Encourage Participation: Campaign Spending and Rolloff in Low Visibility Judicial Elections." *Political Behavior* 33: 665–684.

Streb, Matthew J., Brian Frederick, and Casey LaFrance. 2007. "Contestation, Competition, and the Potential for Accountability in Intermediate Appellate Court Elections." *Judicature* 91: 70–78.

Streb, Matthew J., Brian Frederick, and Casey LaFrance. 2009. "Voter Roll-Off in a Low-Information Context: Evidence from Intermediate Appellate Court Elections." *American Politics Research* 37: 644–669.

Wold, John T. and John H. Culver. 1987. "The Defeat of the California Justices: The Campaign, the Electorate, and the Issue of Judicial Accountability." *Judicature* 70: 348–355.

# 8

# TRIAL COURT CAMPAIGN MESSAGING IN A POST-*WHITE* ENVIRONMENT

## An Analysis of Candidate Websites in Contested Elections*

*Mark Jonathan McKenzie and Ryan J. Rebe*

State trial courts are the judicial institutions Americans are most likely to experience directly. These courts handle millions of cases every year, and thus any political conditions that threaten the impartiality and independence of these courts have a direct bearing on the strength of our justice system and democracy. Governments that operate without a strong rule of law struggle to maintain a fully fledged democracy. Some judicial observers have identified the politicization of judicial elections as one possible threat to the impartiality and independence of our courts, and hence, our democracy.

Certainly, the popular mythology within many law schools and state bars suggests that judicial election campaigns are awash in negative personal attacks and heated political rhetoric focusing on "baby killers," frivolous lawsuits, and the like. Furthermore, critics of judicial elections typically attribute the source of these supposed "realities" to either the 2002 United States Supreme Court decision *Republican Party of Minnesota v. White*, or the "scourge" of partisan judicial elections, or both.

As *White* presumably liberalized state judicial campaign speech laws in judicial elections, it remains to be seen whether judicial candidates have taken advantage of these changing legal dynamics to engage in unduly negative personal attacks against opponents or discuss polarizing policy issues such as abortion or same-sex marriage. How often is it the case that trial court candidates resort to negative rhetoric and wedge issues to polarize unsuspecting judicial voters? Unfortunately, there are very few studies that have actually tried to measure the extent of rhetoric present in the current post-*White* climate, particularly in trial court campaigns. Moreover, it is unclear whether *White* has had any effect whatsoever on the range of speech occurring in judicial elections.

In this chapter, we investigate the extent of polarizing and issue-related rhetoric being propagated by major trial court candidates across the country in the recent 2012 and 2013 elections. To gauge politicization levels, our study relies on the campaign websites of all contested trial court candidates in the general elections of 2012 and the off-year judicial elections of Wisconsin and Pennsylvania in 2013. The results of our study show that most major trial court candidates use their websites primarily to promote their résumé (i.e., their legal experience and qualifications and their biography). Even more remarkable, out of the hundreds of websites examined in this study, only a handful of candidates even mention such issues as abortion, same-sex marriage, or tort reform. Few candidates take the opportunity to attack or even mention their opponents on their websites. In addition, we show that there is virtually no difference in the content of rhetoric between partisan and nonpartisan judicial elections. Finally, our analyses suggest that states with more robust campaign speech regulations in their judicial canons tend to have websites with less polarizing rhetoric or substantive issue discussions.

## What we know about judicial elections after *White*

Before the 1980s, most judicial campaigns across America, even state supreme court races, were very low-profile affairs. Candidates spent sparse amounts of money in these races and voters knew little about the candidates (Dubois 1980, 1986). To the extent that candidates were visible to voters, their campaigns tended to focus on mundane messages such as legal qualifications and experience (Dubois 1980). The last three decades have brought substantial changes to some aspects of state supreme court elections. Beginning in the 1980s, state supreme court races became more vibrant and issue-oriented, and these trends only continued in the 1990s (e.g., Hojnacki and Baum 1992; Rock and Baum 2010). These races are now marked by competitiveness (Hall 2001), higher levels of campaign spending (Bonneau 2007), and participation by voters (Hall and Bonneau 2008).

In response to growing levels of perceived politicization of the judiciary, many states modeled their judicial codes after the American Bar Association's *Model Code of Judicial Conduct*, adopting provisions limiting campaign speech by judicial candidates (Caufield 2007). These judicial canons were intended to preserve the impartiality of elected state court judges by prohibiting them from appearing to take positions on disputed legal or political issues during their campaigns. They also had the effect of limiting voter information about the candidates and their positions (Caufield 2007), prohibiting judicial candidates from seeking endorsements from political parties, endorsing other candidates themselves, or soliciting campaign contributions (Bonneau, Hall, and Streb 2011). Some of these canons were viewed by many as unconstitutional limits on free speech.

In *Republican Party of Minnesota v. White* (2002), the United States Supreme Court invalidated Minnesota's "announce" clause on First Amendment grounds. In theory, the case loosened speech restrictions on judicial candidates. Now candidates are allowed to provide ideological positions, party affiliations, and positions on controversial issues openly to voters (Caufield 2007). After the *White* decision, nearly every state reevaluated its code of judicial conduct (Caufield 2007). North Carolina repealed its "pledges or promises" clause and changed its code to allow candidates to endorse other candidates and directly seek campaign contributions; Texas repealed a provision prohibiting statements that disclosed candidates' opinions on issues subject to judicial interpretation; and the Alabama Judicial Inquiry Commission withdrew an advisory opinion suggesting judicial candidates should not respond to questionnaires from the Christian Coalition (Caufield 2005). Similar trends have happened in other states.

In the wake of the Court's decision, scholars and court watchers believed judicial campaigns would become longer, more contentious and more costly (Caufield 2005). The freedom to speak out on disputed political issues would allow judicial candidates to attract more special-interest money; consequently, campaign donors would pressure candidates to adopt controversial opinions consistent with the donors' interests (Caufield 2005). Pennsylvania Supreme Court Justice Ronald D. Castille worried that judicial elections would "go negative" in his state, arguing that the "Minnesota case was a disaster as far as I'm concerned.... Once that came down, you could kind of see the handwriting on the wall" (Ove 2007). Many legal advocacy groups like Justice at Stake have joined Justice Castille in pronouncing concern that the *White* decision will lead to a qualitative change in the nature of judicial campaigning, with attacks and the use of "hot-button" political issues increasing. "The conventional wisdom in contemporary court reform advocacy is that *White* will have disastrous consequences for the state court bench by radically transforming the conduct of elections" (Bonneau, Hall, and Streb 2011, 249).

## *White* Effects in Judicial Campaign Rhetoric?

Several studies have looked at the impact of *White* on campaign advertising (Caufield 2007; Goldberg et al. 2004; Sample et al. 2007). In their report for Justice at Stake, Goldberg et al. (2004) assert that four times as many states in 2004 attracted network television ads in Supreme Court campaigns than in 2000. "These trends reveal that the era of low-budget state Supreme Court campaigns has come to an end, as an increasing number of campaigns are now built around television advertising as a primary means of winning seats on the bench" (Goldberg et al. 2004, 1). Moreover, the number of negative ads in 2004 doubled from 2000. Sample et al.'s (2007) report on the 2006 elections reiterates concerns about the tone and messaging of supreme court campaigns, but parts of the study offer conflicting findings. At one point, the 2006 study claims that many supreme court candidates "return[ed] to traditional themes ... focused on the candidate's qualifications, experience, or temperament" (Sample, Jones, and Weiss 2007, 9). The report also concludes that *White* has produced an increase in candidates speaking out on the campaign trail, and that "... nasty and misleading ads ... have become the new normal" (Sample et al. 2007, 1).

In her analysis of state supreme court advertising during the 2002 and 2004 elections, Caufield (2007) finds that states imposing a narrow interpretation of *White* (by only removing their announce clause) had a much higher percentage of positive ads focusing on one candidate than states imposing a broad interpretation (by removing their announce clause as well as other speech restrictions). States with a narrow interpretation also had a much lower percentage of contrast ads with other candidates. Thus, states implementing a broad interpretation saw more politicized judicial campaigns.

However, a growing consensus suggests *White* has done little substantively to change the state of affairs of judicial elections (Arbour and McKenzie 2011; Bonneau and Hall 2009; Bonneau, Hall, and Streb 2011; Gibson 2008, 2009, 2012; Hall 2014, 2015; Peters 2008). According to Bonneau and Hall (2009), there is no objective evidence that states with competitive high court elections are experiencing crises in their judiciaries. The institutional legitimacy of state courts remains unaffected by policy pronouncements and debates between candidates (Gibson 2008, 2009), and rates of contestation, quality challengers, vote shares of incumbents, campaign spending, and citizen participation have not radically changed since the *White* decision (Bonneau, Hall, and Streb 2011). Even if the situation has changed, further evidence from Hall and Bonneau (2013; Hall 2015) shows that attack advertising and liberalized speech codes in state supreme court races actually energize voters rather than demobilize them.

## Trial Court (or District Court) Campaign Messaging

The question remains, though, whether and how *White* has affected the tone and content of trial court campaign messaging. Hall (2015) performed an extensive study of the effects of campaign rhetoric at the state supreme court level. At the trial court level, however, evidence about campaign messaging is sparse (notwithstanding Arbour and McKenzie 2010, 2011). Still, the evidence suggests that trial court campaigns have not undergone significant changes in practice, organization, or rhetoric (Abbe and Herrnson 2002; Arbour and McKenzie 2010, 2011). Rates of contestation across most states remain relatively low (Nelson 2011), as does the level of voter knowledge about trial court candidates (Champagne and Thielemann 1991; McKenzie and Rebe 2013; McKenzie, Rugeley, Bailey, and McKee, n.d.; Sheldon and Lovrich 1983). Furthermore, trial court campaigns tend to be amateur operations, relying on friends and neighbors for volunteer help (Arbour and McKenzie 2010). The research indicates that trial court campaigns focus on traditional themes such as experience and qualifications while avoiding negative attacks and substantive policy appeals (Abbe and Herrnson 2002; Arbour and McKenzie 2010, 2011).

These findings regarding lower court elections are not definitive. The Abbe and Herrnson (2002) study was conducted before the *White* case was decided. The Arbour and McKenzie (2010, 2011) studies were limited in geographic scope and were based on a mail survey that relied on the subjective impressions of the survey participants.

## *Campaign Websites*

One of the best ways to look at the issue of campaign rhetoric is to focus on the candidates' campaign websites. In the digital age, the internet is becoming a prominent venue for political information and an important way for candidates to communicate with constituents (Dulio, Goff, and Thurber 1999; Niven and Zilber 2001; Wilson 2009). It is estimated that two-thirds of internet users obtain information from the government through the internet (Larson and Rainie 2002), and according to a 2004 survey by the Pew Center for People and the Press, 35 percent of Americans regularly or sometimes get campaign news from the internet, an increase from 24 percent in 2000 (Dolan 2005).

Campaign websites are a good way to measure the state of judicial campaign rhetoric because, as Druckman, Kifer and Parkin note, websites "offer an unmediated, holistic, and representative portrait of campaigns" (2009, 343). Unlike surveys of candidates or the filtered editing of news mediums, websites present at least one aspect of the "reality" of judicial campaign rhetoric rather than a secondhand report (see also Dolan 2005). Candidates have unlimited space to present themselves in whatever manner or style they choose, with the ability to list their endorsements, talk to voters about issues and experience, and post photos and videos. Moreover, websites are readily accessible to voters, journalists, policymakers, and researchers.

## *Campaign Strategy*

In examining the effects of *White* on campaign rhetoric, it is important to understand the factors influencing the rhetorical strategies used by judicial campaigns, factors that possess importance both before and after the *White* decision. A vital factor in down-ballot campaigns is familiarity. When voters are able to recall or recognize the name of their congressional candidate, that candidate wins more votes (Jacobson 1978, 2007; McKee 2008). Judicial elections often produce high levels of ballot rolloff (Hall and Bonneau 2008), but quality candidates can overcome some of these obstacles (Hall and Bonneau 2006).

The first goal for any candidate is simply to get voters to recognize their name. The second is to get voters to develop positive thoughts associated with that name. To build up familiarity, campaigns often focus on the biography of their candidate in an effort to demonstrate to voters how much the candidate has in common with them. Thus, references to a candidate's parents or local upbringing, pictures of the candidate's spouse and children, and discussions of life lessons learned from hard work and sacrifice are common parts of congressional campaign discourse (Arbour 2014). We expect judicial campaigns to be no different and therefore expect candidates to focus much of their rhetorical effort on their own biography and qualifications for the job. Such rhetoric helps build up voter familiarity with not only the name of the judicial candidate, but also the positive accomplishments of the candidate. These appeals serve as a rhetorical résumé, demonstrating how the past accomplishments of the candidate make them well suited for the position they are seeking.

Candidates also focus on the issue agenda they present to voters and have several different goals in employing their issue agenda. First, they may seek to position themselves at the ideal place along the ideological spectrum to attract the most votes, and highlight their positions on issues as a means to do this (Ansolabehere, Snyder and Stewart 2001; Burden 2004; Downs 1957). Empirical studies of campaign messaging show that such positioning does not happen with great frequency, as this requires a greater amount of voter knowledge than usually displayed (Sides 2006). Instead, campaigns prefer to "frame" their rhetoric by highlighting particular aspects of favorable issues, values, or biographical details and making these the primary basis for consideration by voters (Arbour 2014; Entman 2003; Jacoby 2000). One way that campaigns do this is by highlighting "valence" issues on which there is universal agreement to a broad set of goals, thus connecting their candidate to these goals (Stokes 1963).

Candidates for executive and legislative office have the ability to connect issues to the perceptions of their party. For judicial candidates, the task is more difficult because such actions are potentially circumscribed by legal culture, the norm of impartiality, a state's judicial campaign speech regulations, the expectations of voters, and even the method of the state's judicial selection. Thus, we would expect that some candidates for trial court will be reluctant to engage in controversial issues that cleave the two parties. Instead, these candidates have an incentive to focus on valence issues on which there is broad agreement among voters. Such valence messages include legal qualifications, experience, vague judicial values of impartiality and fairness, and promoting efficient court administration. Everyone thinks courts should be administered efficiently and effectively, and proposals to deal with these issues do not run afoul of either pre-*White* canons of judicial conduct or norms of voters, bar associations, or other judicial elites. If trial court candidates are going to focus on hot-button issues, they will most likely focus on crime. Although policy appeals to be tough on crime can sometimes run afoul of judicial canons,[1] they can also signal a candidate's policy views without straying too far from the norms of judicial campaigning.

## Judicial Campaign Website Data

The data relied upon for the analyses in this chapter come from contested major trial court races for the general election in states with judicial races in 2012 and 2013. With the help of two student researchers, we endeavored to collect all website pages for any judicial candidate running in a contested major trial court race.[2] We downloaded these websites about a week before the election, or in a few instances, immediately after the election. We then coded each website for information on the rhetorical strategy used by each candidate. In conducting our coding, we relied heavily on the coding rubric used by James Druckman, Michael Parkin, and Martin Kifer as a guide (cf. Druckman, Kifer, and Parkin 2009, 2010; Druckman, Hennessy, Kifer, and Parkin 2010). In sum, our analysis contains 398 judicial candidate websites from twenty-seven partisan and nonpartisan states.[3] The descriptive breakdown of our data appear in the Appendix of this chapter. Our data contain roughly equal numbers of partisan and nonpartisan races as well as Republican (30.4%) and Democratic (29.6%) candidates. About 40 percent of all candidates were nonpartisan (or independent). About two-thirds of the candidates in our sample were male. In terms of the racial and ethnic breakdown, about 10 percent of our sample were African-American candidates, 5 percent Hispanic, and 1 percent Asian. In the sections that follow, we employ descriptive and multivariate analyses to investigate the state of judicial campaign messaging a decade after the *White* decision.

## *Front Page Candidate Messages*

We begin with an examination of messages on the front page of each website, as this represents the one place a candidate is assured that a voter will look when they click on it. Presumably, strategic candidates should emphasize messages they find most salient on the front page.

We categorized the front page messages primarily as issues, biography, experience, or values. Throughout this analysis, we refer to "issues" strictly in terms of substantive policy appeals (e.g., court administration, crime, abortion). Court administration issues include candidate claims to provide greater efficiency in case processing, instituting e-filing, implementing cost-saving measures at the courthouse, etc. Experience refers to messages about legal qualifications and legal experience. Biography encompasses a candidate's discussion of their life. Values rhetoric consists of amorphous candidate affirmations of "fairness" and "impartiality" and the desire to ensure "justice" or "follow the law." Finally, judicial philosophy refers to a candidate's ideological beliefs, employing language that is devoid of any substantive policy appeals.

As the breakdown in Figure 8.1 illustrates, experience and values are by far the two most common messages displayed. Approximately eight out of ten candidates discussed experience and six out of ten discussed values. In fact, they are the only types of messages found on a majority of the front pages; none of the other types of messages exceed 40 percent. Notably, almost 70 percent of websites did not even mention an issue on the front page, whereas only 5 percent featured an attack on an opponent and 10 percent mentioned religion. Moreover, there appears to be little difference in candidate messaging on the front page between partisan and nonpartisan races.

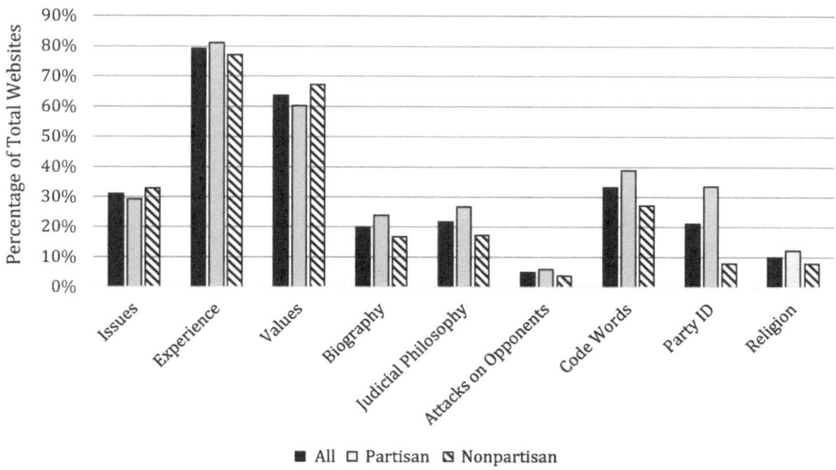


**FIGURE 8.1** District Court Websites, Front Page Content, 2012 and 2013

### *Messages across All Pages of the Website*

In this next section, we catalog the content of messages that appeared across all pages of the website. As is evident in Table 8.1, nearly all candidates (about 98%) provided some kind of legal experience somewhere on their website, whereas almost 89 percent mentioned biographical information.[4] Clearly, most candidates take the opportunity to convey some amount of qualifications and biography.

The contrast between candidates' focus on qualifications and biography on the one hand, and substantive policy appeals on the other, is starkly illustrated in Figure 8.2. All of the columns representing issues are simply indications of whether a website mentioned one of these issues. For example, close to 30 percent of candidates mentioned a court administration issue on their website, whereas a little over 25 percent of candidates focused on crime policy and protecting the community.[5]

However, 5 percent or less of candidates used their websites to focus on the issues that operate as the boogeyman of judicial reform advocates (i.e., abortion, gay marriage, God in the courtroom, gun rights, etc).[6] There are candidates who promote views on these controversial legal issues, but they constitute a minute contingent of the sample. The columns on hot-button issues (a little over 30%) refer to websites that either mentioned crime policy or one of the other controversial policy issues. The columns entitled "issues" combine court administration issues with hot-button issues. About 55 percent of all websites in this sample—the "issues" columns—mentioned a hot-button issue and/or a court administration issue. The last set of three graphs in Figure 8.2 indicates whether the candidate used the majority of her website to promote her legal experience and/or

**TABLE 8.1** Experience and Biographical Messages

| | *All Websites* |
|---|---|
| Prior legal work noted | 97.7% |
| Biography noted | 88.9% |
| Education mentioned | 81.3% |
| Family of candidate mentioned | 76.2% |
| Endorsements listed | 64.1% |
| Newspaper endorsements | 18.5% |
| Bar poll numbers listed | 13.9% |
| Military service | 10.1% |
| Church or religious activities | 42.3% |
| Works or support for charity | 54.9% |
| Candidate's local roots | 47.8% |

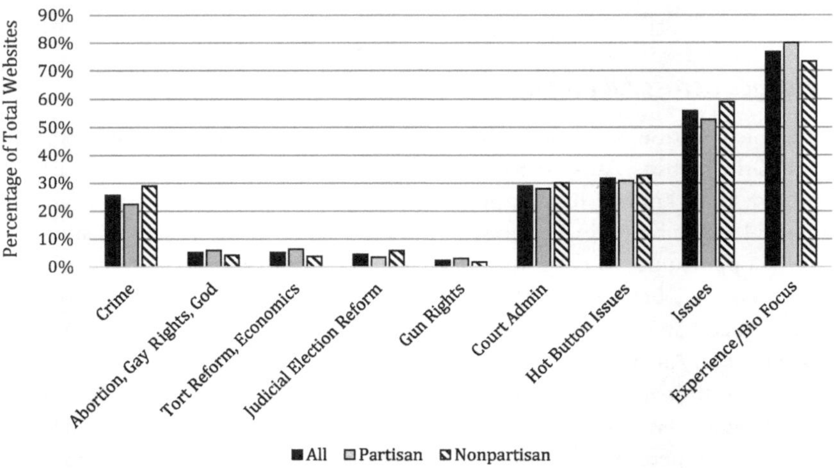


**FIGURE 8.2** District Court Websites, Content from All Pages, 2012 and 2013

biography ("Experience/Bio Focus").[7] It suggests that most trial court candidates are preoccupied with telling voters about their legal qualifications and life story rather than taking positions on polarizing policy issues. Finally, Figure 8.2 also suggests that there is little difference overall between the messaging of candidates in partisan states versus nonpartisan states.

Next we examine a breakdown of polarizing rhetoric and ideological philosophies provided in Table 8.2.

**TABLE 8.2** Judicial Philosophy and Faith

| *Across the entire website* | *All Websites* | *Partisan* | *Nonpartisan* |
|---|---|---|---|
| Conservative philosophy touted | 11.4% | 14.1% | 8.4% |
| Liberal philosophy touted (such as rights of the accused and diversity) | 7.8% | 5.4% | 10.5% |
| Faith discussed (as a philosophy, not as a policy employed in the courtroom) | 6.8% | 7.8% | 5.8% |
| Family values, Christian values | 3.0% | 2.9% | 3.2% |
| God in the courtroom | 1.5% | 1.5% | 1.6% |
| Pro-Life | 1.3% | 2.0% | 0.5% |
| Gay marriage | 0.8% | 1.0% | 0.5% |
| Pro-Life; Gay marriage; Family values; God in the courtroom – combined | 5.1% | 5.9% | 4.2% |
| *N* | 395 | 205 | 190 |

As Table 8.2 illustrates, partisan states offer no more polarizing rhetoric than do nonpartisan states. The only apparent difference between the two types of selection systems is in the substance of judicial philosophies promoted. Candidates in partisan systems tend to tout their conservative philosophy whereas candidates in nonpartisan systems are slightly more likely to promote principles rooted in leftist philosophy. These differences are, perhaps, only a function of the relative conservatism or liberalism of partisan and nonpartisan states found in the study.

The negative attacks that scholars were so worried about after the *White* case are also virtually nonexistent in our data (see Table 8.3). Admittedly, a website is perhaps the most unlikely place for a judicial candidate to launch a negative attack. However, even contrast messages—mild statements such as "I am the most experienced candidate in the race"—fail to appear in more than a handful of websites.

These findings are consistent with those found by Arbour and McKenzie (2011), in which the authors gave survey respondents at the trial court level a chance to complain about any unfair attacks made by their opponents, and very few respondents offered any complaints about the behavior of their opponents. So far, no study has found any substantial amount of negativity by candidates whatsoever in any set of trial court campaigns since the *White* case was decided.

## Multivariate Analysis Modeling Judicial Messages

To investigate further why some judicial candidates occasionally focus on polarizing issues whereas the vast majority tout their biography, experience, and qualifications, we ran four logistic regressions modeling the presence of four types of

**TABLE 8.3** Attacks on Opponents

| *Across the entire website* | *All Websites* | *Partisan* | *Nonpartisan* |
|---|---|---|---|
| Opponents mentioned | 20.0% | 19.5% | 20.5% |
| Criticism of opponent on issues | 5.6% | 3.9% | 7.4% |
| Criticism of opponent on qualifications | 11.4% | 11.8% | 11.1% |
| Rebuttal of charges made by opponent | 0.8% | 0.0% | 1.6% |
| Other | 1.3% | 2.0% | 0.5% |
| *N* | 395 | 205 | 190 |

messaging behavior (presence = 1 and absence = 0). The independent variables in each of these models consisted of:

(1) a three-point measure of judicial speech regulation (with 2 representing the strictest judicial canons on speech and 0 representing the loosest regulations on speech);[8]
(2) whether the candidate website came from a partisan election state (1) or not (0);
(3) the gender of the candidate, with female coded as 1 and male coded as 0; and
(4) whether the candidate was an ethnic or racial minority (1) or white (0).

Our first model contains a dependent variable examining whether candidates mostly emphasized either experience or biography across the whole of their website. As the reader may recall, this variable is more impressionistic than mathematical. Nevertheless, the model indicates that neither speech regulations nor the type of judicial selection method appear to affect whether judicial candidates choose to emphasize experience and biography. The second model attempts to account for instances where judicial candidates make some sort of substantive policy appeal on their website—either a noncontroversial court administration claim or a more polarizing hot-button issue such as crime or abortion. The third and fourth models provide different dependent variable measures of what constitutes a polarizing issue—hot-button issues (a) with crime policy included and (b) with crime policy excluded. The regression results appear in Table 8.4.

What is most striking about the findings is the failure of the judicial selection system variable to affect judicial candidate messaging in campaign websites. A fifth model (not included) using the mentioning of an opponent on a website as a dependent variable also failed to show any connection to the type of judicial selection system from whence the website came. The findings indicate that neither partisan nor nonpartisan judicial selection systems have any significant statistical relationship to the type of messaging produced in judicial campaigns by the candidates themselves—at least as it relates to messaging on websites in 2012 and 2013. However, the findings suggest that heavy judicial regulations on speech

**TABLE 8.4** Logit Regression Models Predicting Messages on Judicial Campaign Websites

| *Independent Variables* | *Experience & Biography Emphasis* | *Substantive Issues* | *Hot Button Issues (includes crime)* | *Hot Button Issues (excluding crime)* |
|---|---|---|---|---|
| Strong campaign speech regulations | -0.074 | -0.497** | -0.506*** | -0.588*** |
| | (0.177) | (0.197) | (0.188) | (0.213) |
| Partisan election | 0.325 | -0.413 | -0.274 | 0.017 |
| | (0.214) | (0.328) | (0.335) | (0.362) |
| Female | -0.002 | -0.051 | -0.471* | -0.471 |
| | (0.220) | (0.276) | (0.255) | (0.350) |
| Minority candidate | 0.165 | -0.592** | -0.634** | -1.54** |
| | (0.348) | (0.236) | (0.260) | (0.605) |
| Constant | 1.18** | 1.84*** | 0.906 | -0.376 |
| | (0.475) | (0.667) | (0.598) | (0.598) |
| *N* | 395 | 395 | 395 | 395 |

*Notes*: Dependent variables in these four logistic regressions are dichotomous. Robust standard errors clustered on states. * $p < 0.10$ ** $p < 0.05$ *** $p < 0.01$

do appear to tamp down candidate appeals to polarizing policies. An alternative explanation is that states with more traditional legal cultures—where social costs are high for judicial candidates who venture into campaign speech considered inappropriate—also happen to enact more speech regulations. Regardless of the causal connection, there potentially is a link between the regulation environment and the types of appeals made by candidates. Finally, it appears that minority candidates and women are less keen on making appeals on hot-button issues. Furthermore, it is worth noting that more liberal-minded candidates never once made any appeals to support same-sex marriage, protect abortion rights, or advocate gun control. The few liberal appeals to substantive policy on "hot-button" issues tended to be within the area of crime and civil rights or supporting access to the courts.

## Conclusions

The findings in this chapter echo previous findings by Arbour and McKenzie (2010, 2011) and Abbe and Herrnson (2002) demonstrating that most trial court candidates focus their messaging on rather noncontroversial topics such as the candidates' legal experience and qualifications, biography, and views on promoting efficient court administration. There is simply no evidence among studies of trial court campaigns to suggest that the speech environment in these races has devolved into nasty attacks or denouncements of "baby killers." Despite the repeated claims of certain segments of the American Bar Association and the legal community, partisan judicial elections are not contributing to an unhealthy campaign environment in trial court races. Undoubtedly, partisan judicial elections and elections for judges in general can have their downsides. No selection system is perfect, and selecting judges on a partisan basis could encourage those same judges to later decide certain cases in a partisan manner (particularly electoral-related issues, see McKenzie 2012). Selection systems that rely heavily on gubernatorial appointment, state bar association influence, or the state legislature also have their own drawbacks in terms of the incentives for judges that those systems create. Nevertheless, when it comes to the campaign speech environment, partisan elections for judges appear no better or worse than nonpartisan elections. Finally, our descriptive analyses of the 2012 and 2013 judicial candidate websites suggest that there is relatively little overall controversial rhetoric occurring in state trial court elections.

**Appendix:** *Summary Statistics, District Court Candidates, 2012 and 2013*

| | *All Websites* | *Partisan* | *Nonpartisan* |
|---|---|---|---|
| **Selection Method** | | | |
| Partisan | 51.76% (206) | | |
| Nonpartisan | 48.24% (192) | | |
| **Political Party** | | | |
| Republican | 30.40% (121) | 48.06% (99) | |
| Democrat | 29.65% (118) | 48.54% (100) | |
| Other | 39.95% (159) | 3.40% (7) | |
| **Race** | | | |
| White | 84.17% (335) | 83.01% (171) | 85.42% (164) |
| African-American | 9.80% (39) | 9.71% (20) | 9.90% (19) |
| Hispanic | 5.03% (20) | 6.80% (14) | 3.13% (6) |
| Asian | 1.01% (4) | 0.49% (1) | 1.56% (3) |
| **Sex** | | | |
| Male | 64.57% (257) | 66.50% (137) | 62.50% (120) |
| Female | 35.43% (141) | 33.50% (69) | 37.50% (72) |

## Notes

* We would like to thank Texas Tech student researchers Peyton Craig and Chana Elgin for their hard work in helping us collect data on trial court candidate websites in 2012. We thank Texas Tech University for helping fund the collection of the data used in this research. This research was also supported in part by a summer stipend from the Research Center for the Humanities and Social Sciences at William Paterson University. Finally, we would like to thank Brian Arbour for his contribution to some of the ideas about what information to code from judicial websites, as well as his contributions to early variants of work that spawned from this data collection project.

1 See, for example, the case of *In the Matter of Watson* 794 N.E.2d 1 (New York 2003). In that case, the judicial candidate got in trouble for, among other things, writing a letter

to law enforcement asking them to "put a real prosecutor on the bench" and stating that "[w]e are in desperate need of a judge who will work with the police, not against them. We need a judge who will assist our law enforcement officers as they aggressively work towards cleaning up our city streets." Thus, policy appeals for being tough on crime can have the potential to violate judicial norms and canons.

2 The states included in this analysis are Alabama, Arizona, Arkansas, California, Florida, Georgia, Illinois, Indiana, Kansas, Kentucky, Louisiana, Michigan, Minnesota, Missouri, Montana, Nevada, New Mexico, New York, North Dakota, North Carolina, Ohio, Oregon, Pennsylvania, Texas, Washington, West Virginia, and Wisconsin.

3 Despite our best efforts, we were unable to locate any trial court candidate websites from states that only have retention races for this office. In fact, some states with retention races made it quite difficult for the average person to find out who was running for these offices. Our data are not able to speak to the content of rhetoric employed by retention candidates. Furthermore, our dataset is missing the state of Tennessee. No trial court candidate list could be found on governmental websites, and despite repeated calls to Tennessee's Secretary of State, we were unable to determine whether and to what extent trial court races occurred in this state at the time of our data collection in 2012. A handful of candidates in our sample who had websites ended up as missing data because they went down or a technical glitch developed when downloading the website pages. For three websites, we only have front page data and are missing other pages. Thus the analyses in the latter sections contain 395 websites instead of 398.

4 Though we collected a wide variety of information on biography and experience, we only provide a small portion here due to space constraints.

5 For illustrative purposes, the following is a small sample of the crime policy messages that appeared on candidate websites in our sample: (1) "dedicated to protecting the community"; (2) "law and order candidate"; (3) "Madelyn Fudeman has prosecuted criminals in Dade County, Florida and will continue to be tough on crime"; (4) "a tough but fair conservative judge who strives to keep our community safe by punishing those who break the law and putting dangerous criminals behind bars"; and (5) "Janet has 25 years of experience keeping Milwaukee streets safe .... She's tough."

6 A few concrete examples of these rare but highly polarized messages in our sample include the following: (1) "I am Pro-Life, I firmly believe in Traditional Marriage and I am a strong supporter of our 2nd Amendment Rights. But most importantly, I will not remove the Name of God from my platform. To me, these values are the basic foundation of what it means to be a true conservative. Values are important when it comes to a judge exercising 'judicial discretion' in his rulings."; (2) One Illinois candidate wrote "Frivolous lawsuits cost jobs" and "Obama Care coercively mandates individuals to purchase health insurance and requires religious organizations to condone actions that violate their faith and teachings ... Mayor Rahm Emanuel in Chicago is pressing for a statewide gun registration for law abiding citizens ... Will Democrat judges owing allegiance to Obama and Gov. Quinn, be willing to question the constitutionality of these measures? Or, will they pride themselves on their 'more enlightened' interpretation that will eviscerate the constitution? We need judges with core conservative values. Burkart is the choice to stop the madness."

7 The alternative measure that is not shown would be websites that mostly promoted substantive policy issues or some combination of issues and experience or issues and biography. The reader should keep in mind that this particular measure in this last coumn that we call Experience/Bio Focus is more impressionistic in nature, assigned to a website after the authors finished coding a website.

8 The construction of this variable is a derivative based on a simple tabulation of the different types of speech regulations in the 2012 judicial canons of the states included in this study. The authors do not assert that this variable is mathematically precise. Instead, it is supposed to represent a rough approximation of the speech regulation

environment based on the existing canons of the time. States' positions in our measure were based on the presence of the following canons: a type of false statements canon, a rule on solicitations of campaign donations, endorsements—either received or given—restrictions on being a member of or associating with political organizations, and finally, a two-part tabulation on whether a state has a pledges and promises clause, and whether the state has any other additional restrictions on speech beyond the standard pledges and promises clause. This tabulation yielded scores of up to 6 for each state. Because this construction can only roughly approximate the speech environment, states were divided into three categories based on the 1 to 6 scores. States in the low regulation 1–2 range were coded as 1 (including states such as Alabama and North Carolina). In the medium 3–4 range (coded as 2) there are states such as Texas, Oregon, New Mexico, Kansas and Wisconsin. States in the high speech regulation 5–6 range (coded as 3) include California, Florida and Ohio, among others.

## References

Abbe, Owen G. and Paul S. Herrnson. 2002. "How Judicial Election Campaigns Have Changed." *Judicature* 85: 286–295.

Ansolabehere, Stephen, James M. Snyder, and Charles Stewart. 2001. "Candidate Positioning in US House Elections." *American Journal of Political Science* 45: 136–159.

Arbour, Brian. 2014. *Candidate-Centered Campaigns: Political Messages, Winning Personalities, and Personal Appeals*. New York: Palgrave MacMillan.

Arbour, Brian K. and Mark J. McKenzie. 2010. "Has the 'New Style' of Judicial Campaigning Reached Lower Court Elections?" *Judicature* 93: 150–160.

Arbour, Brian K. and Mark J. McKenzie. 2011. "Campaign Messages in Lower-Court Elections after *Republican Party of Minnesota vs. White*" *Justice System Journal* 32: 1–24.

Bonneau, Chris W. 2007. "Campaign Fundraising in State Supreme Court Elections." *Social Science Quarterly* 88: 68–85.

Bonneau, Chris W. and Melinda Gann Hall. 2009. *In Defense of Judicial Elections*. New York: Routledge.

Bonneau, Chris W., Melinda Gann Hall, and Matthew J. Streb. 2011. "*White* Noise: The Unrealized Effects of *Republican Party of Minnesota v. White* on Judicial Elections." *Justice System Journal* 32: 247–268.

Burden, Barry C. 2004. "Candidate Positioning in US Congressional Elections." *British Journal of Political Science* 34: 211–227.

Caufield, Rachel P. 2004. "In the Wake of *White*: How States Are Responding to *Republican Party of Minnesota v. White* and How Judicial Elections are Changing." *Akron Law Review* 38: 625–647.

Caufield, Rachel P. 2007. "The Changing Tone of Judicial Election Campaigns as a Result of *White*." In *Running for Judge: The Rising Political, Financial, and Legal Stakes of Judicial Elections*, edited by Matthew J. Streb. New York: New York University Press.

Champagne, Anthony and Greg Thielemann. 1991. "Awareness of Trial Court Judges." *Judicature* 74: 271–276.

Dolan, Kathleen. 2005. "Do Women Candidates Play to Gender Stereotypes? Do Men Candidates Play to Women? Candidate Sex and Issues Priorities on Campaign Websites." *Political Research Quarterly* 58: 31–44.

Downs, Anthony. 1957. *An Economic Theory of Democracy*. New York: Harper and Row.

Druckman, James, Cari Lynn Hennessey, Martin J. Kifer, and Michael Parkin. 2010. "Issue Engagement on Congressional Campaign Websites (2002–2006)." *Social Science Computer Review* 28: 3–23.

Druckman, James, Martin J. Kifer, and Michael Parkin. 2009. "Campaign Communications in US Congressional Elections." *American Political Science Review* 103: 343–366.

Druckman, James, Martin J. Kifer, and Michael Parkin. 2010. "Timeless Strategy Meets new Medium: Going Negative on Congressional Campaign Websites." *Political Communication* 27: 88–103.

Dubois, Philip L. 1980. *From Ballot to Bench: Judicial Elections and the Quest for Accountability*. Austin: University of Texas Press.

Dubois, Philip L. 1986. "Penny for Your Thoughts: Campaign Spending in California Trial Court Elections, 1976–1982." *Western Political Quarterly* 39: 265–284.

Dulio, David A., Donald L. Goff, and James A. Thurber. 1999. "Untangled Web: Internet Use during the 1998 Election." *PS: Political Science and Politics* 32: 53–59.

Entman, Robert. 2003. *Projections of Power: Framing News, Public Opinion, and U.S. Foreign Policy*. Chicago: University of Chicago Press.

Gibson, James L. 2008. "Challenges to the Impartiality of State Supreme Courts: Legitimacy Theory and 'New-Style' Judicial Campaigns." *American Political Science Review* 102: 59–75.

Gibson, James L. 2009. "'New-Style' Judicial Campaigns and the Legitimacy of State High Courts." *Journal of Politics* 71: 1285–1304.

Gibson, James L. 2012. *Electing Judges: The Surprising Effects of Campaigning on Judicial Legitimacy*. Chicago: University of Chicago Press.

Goldberg, Deborah, Sarah Samis, Edwin Bender, and Rachel Weiss. 2004. *The New Politics of Judicial Elections*. Washington, DC: Justice at Stake.

Hall, Melinda Gann. 2001. "State Supreme Courts in American Democracy: Probing the Myths of Judicial Reform." *American Political Science Review* 92: 315–330.

Hall, Melinda Gann. 2014. "Televised Attacks and the Incumbency Advantage in State Supreme Courts." *Journal of Law, Economics, and Organization* 30: 138–164.

Hall, Melinda Gann. 2015. *Attacking Judges: How Campaign Advertising Influences State Supreme Court Elections*. Stanford: Stanford University Press.

Hall, Melinda Gann and Chris W. Bonneau. 2006. "Does Quality Matter: Challengers in State Supreme Court Elections." *American Journal of Political Science* 50: 20–33.

Hall, Melinda Gann and Chris W. Bonneau. 2008. "Mobilizing Interest: The Effects of Money on Citizen Participation in State Supreme Court Elections." *American Journal of Political Science* 52: 457–470.

Hall, Melinda Gann and Chris W. Bonneau. 2013. "Attack Advertising, the *White* Decision, and Voter Participation in State Supreme Court Elections." *Political Research Quarterly* 66: 115–126.

Hojnacki, Marie and Lawrence Baum. 1992. "'New Style' Judicial Campaigns and the Voters: Economic Issues and Union Members in Ohio." *Western Political Quarterly* 45: 921–948.

Jacobson, Gary C. 1978. "The Effects of Campaign Spending in Congressional Elections." *American Political Science Review* 72: 469–491.

Jacobson, Gary C. 2007. *The Politics of Congressional Elections*, 7th ed. New York, NY: Longman.

Jacoby, William G. 2000. "Issue Framing and Public Opinion on Government Spending." *American Journal of Political Science* 44: 750–756.

Larson, Elena and Lee Rainie. 2002. *The Rise of the E-citizen: How People Use Government Agencies' Web Sites*. Washington, DC: Pew Internet and American Life Project.

McKee, Seth C. 2008. "Redistricting and Familiarity with US House Candidates." *American Politics Research* 36: 962–979.

McKenzie, Mark Jonathan. 2012. "The Influence of Partisanship, Ideology, and the Law on Redistricting Decisions in the Federal Courts." *Political Research Quarterly* 65: 799–813.

McKenzie, Mark Jonathan and Ryan Rebe. 2013. "Political Knowledge of Local Courts: Are Rural Voters More Informed than Urban Voters?" *Judicature* 96: 169–177.

McKenzie, Mark Jonathan, Cynthia R. Rugeley, Daniel Benjamin Bailey, and Seth C. McKee. n.d. "Americans' Knowledge of the Local Judges." *Political Behavior*. Forthcoming.

Nelson, Michael J. 2011. "Uncontested and Unaccountable? Rates of Contestation in Trial Court Elections." *Judicature* 94: 208–217.

Niven, David and Jeremy Zilber. 2001. "Do Women and Men in Congress Cultivate Different Images? Evidence from Congressional Web Sites." *Political Communication* 18: 395–405.

Ove, Torsten. 2007. "Door Opened for Judicial Candidates to Speak Out." *Pittsburgh Post-Gazette*. May 21, 2007.

Peters, C. Scott. 2008. "Campaigning for State Supreme Court 2006." *Justice System Journal* 29: 166–186.

*Republican Party of Minnesota v. White*, 536 U.S. 765 (2002).

Rock, Emily and Lawrence Baum. 2010. "The Impact of High-Visibility Contests for U.S. State Court Judgeships: Partisan Voting in Nonpartisan Elections." *State Politics and Policy Quarterly* 10: 368–396.

Sample, James, Lauren Jones, and Rachel Weiss. 2007. *The New Politics of Judicial Elections, 2006: How 2006 Was the Most Threatening Year Yet to the Fairness and Impartiality to Our Courts – and How Americans Are Fighting Back*. Washington, DC: Justice at Stake.

Sheldon, Charles H. and Nicholas P. Lovrich, Jr. 1983. "Knowledge and Judicial Voting: The Oregon and Washington Experience." *Judicature* 67: 235–245.

Sides, John. 2006. "The Origins of Campaign Agendas." *British Journal of Political Science* 36: 407–436.

Stokes, Donald E. 1963. "Spatial Models of Party Competition." *American Political Science Review* 57: 368–377.

Wilson, Walter. 2009. "Latino Representation on Congressional Websites." *Legislative Studies Quarterly* 34: 427–448.

# 9

# DO JUDICIAL PERFORMANCE EVALUATIONS INFLUENCE RETENTION ELECTION RESULTS?

*Rebecca D. Gill*[1]

At present, thirteen American states retain some or all of their judges via retention elections.[2] These retention elections have long been plagued by low voter participation. It is exceedingly difficult for voters to determine whether nonpartisan judges ought to keep their jobs. Few voters have specifically formed ideas of what makes for a good judge. In addition, most voters lack information about the incumbents in uncontested races. This is bad news, of course, if we are to see retention elections as providing a measure of democratic accountability.

In an attempt to provide voters with reliable information upon which to make a decision, a number of retention election states developed official programs of judicial performance evaluation (JPE). These JPE systems rely upon expert assessments of judicial performance, and most of them generate official recommendations about how voters should judge the qualifications of the incumbent judges. However, the relationship between JPEs and retention vote share is woefully understudied. At present, we have only hints about the effect that these programs have on the electoral support of incumbent judges. In this chapter, I attempt to provide some more solid answers. I analyze retention vote shares in five states with robust, state-sponsored JPE programs. I find some evidence that the JPE recommendations matter. I also find some support for the proposition that voters react to specific negative assessments of judges by lawyers, even when these assessments do not cause JPE commissions to issue overall negative retention recommendations.

## Predicting Retention Vote Share

Retention elections serve as the primary accountability mechanism in many "merit plan" (Missouri Plan) judicial appointment systems, although the role of voters in the process has usually been "very small and usually insignificant" (Glick

1983). In some important ways, the retention election is designed to minimize the impact of voters by making it decidedly difficult to vote out any but the most terrible judges (Geyh 2012). In the most visible judicial races, though, retention elections may no longer insulate state supreme court judges from public accountability on highly salient political issues (Canes-Wrone, Clark, and Park 2012).

Critics of the merit plan complain that retention elections are still insufficient for promoting a reasonable amount of public accountability, especially when it concerns the election of state supreme court justices. Media coverage of high-profile retention election ousters tends to obscure the fact that the vast majority of these judges are retained. The affirmative retention vote has generally remained extremely high and stable over time (Aspin 2007). Retention elections show a "pronounced tendency against incumbent defeat relative to other types of elections" (Hall 2007a; see also Hall 2001a). From 1980 to 2000, the state supreme court incumbent defeat rate was a mere 2 percent in retention elections, which is much lower than in contested elections (Hall 2007a). The pattern was similar in intermediate appellate courts, where between 2000 and 2005 only two of 524 judges facing retention elections were defeated (Streb, Frederick, and LaFrance 2007).

The judicial selection literature has identified a number of key predictors of judicial election vote share. Many of these focus on a relative comparison between candidates vying for a seat in a contested race. Close elections in previous election cycles lead to decreased incumbent vote share (Bonneau 2007a; Hall 2014, 2015; Hall and Bonneau 2006). First-term incumbents get a lower percentage of the vote share (Bonneau 2007b; Hall and Bonneau 2006; Streb and Frederick 2009). Murder rates may (Hall 2001a) or may not (Bonneau 2007a) lower incumbent vote share, perhaps depending upon whether one considers the effect of campaign expenditures. These expenditures, when spent by challengers *against* incumbents, drive incumbent vote share down (Bonneau 2007a; Hall 2014, 2015). Female candidates may also have a vote-share advantage in contested judicial elections (Frederick and Streb 2008; Streb and Frederick 2009).

In competitive elections, a key predictor of vote share is the relative quality of the candidates. This is true in research on congressional elections (Carson, Engstrom, and Roberts 2007; Jacobson 1989), state legislative elections (Van Dunk 1997), and judicial elections (Bonneau 2007a; but see Streb and Frederick 2009). Hall and Bonneau (2006), Bonneau and Hall (2009), and Hall (2014, 2015) find that high-quality state supreme court challengers reduce the vote share of the incumbent, supporting the idea that voters in these elections reward high-quality challengers and thus have some capacity to distinguish among candidates. Streb and Frederick fail to find this relationship in intermediate appellate court elections, surmising that "voters simply do not have enough information about candidates" in these lower-information elections to distinguish levels of candidate quality (2009, 533). However, Lim and Snyder (2015) find that, in the absence of party cues in trial court judge elections, judicial quality does predict vote outcomes.

## The Information Problem

It is likely, though, that retention elections work significantly differently than competitive elections when it comes to vote share. A big contributor to the high retention rate is the dearth of information available to voters, and this is somewhat unique to retention elections. One of the key reasons voters cite for failing to vote in judicial elections is a lack of information about the candidates. To provide real accountability, voters need relevant information about candidates. Local newspapers provide some coverage, but rarely is it information that helps voters make informed decisions (Schaffner and Diascro 2007). Where more information is available, voters participate at higher rates (Klein and Baum 2001).

Partisan elections provide voters with a very important piece of information: the candidates' party identification (Bonneau and Hall 2009; Hall 2007b; Streb, Frederick, and LaFrance 2009). In contested elections, the campaign is the other key source of information for voters (Hall 2014, 2015). Judicial campaigns have evolved of late (Hojnacki and Baum 1992). Higher spending rates in election campaigns serve to increase voter participation (Bonneau 2007b; Bonneau and Hall 2009; Hall 2015), likely by providing voters with relevant information to guide their choices in the voting booth.

Retention elections generally obscure the political party affiliation of the incumbent judge, encouraging some voters to rely instead upon the party of the appointing governor as a voting cue (Squire and Smith 1988). Party identification information is available in some retention elections, although it is often quite difficult to glean. An exception to this is New Mexico, where the initial selection to the bench takes place via partisan elections. Although the judge's political party does not appear on the retention ballot, voters can make quick work of determining their party identification by looking through their original appearance on the partisan ballot. In the other states, though, this information is difficult for voters to determine.

Retention election campaigns generally fail to supplement the minimal to non-existent voter cues on the ballot. Uncontested retention elections provide little incentive for candidates to spend money to provide voters with information (Volcansek 1981). On rare occasions, independent groups have taken advantage of this to attack under-prepared merit plan judges unfriendly to their policy goals. A recent example of this is the series of "vote no" campaigns against Iowa Supreme Court judges, who were targeted in 2010 for striking down the state's same-sex marriage ban (Skaggs et al. 2011). However, most retention elections—particularly those for trial or intermediate appellate judges—provide essentially no campaign information upon which voters can base their decision.

In response to this dearth of information in retention elections, judicial performance evaluation systems began to spring up in these states (Bernick and Pratto 1995; Esterling 1999; W. Hall 1985). These systems drew inspiration from a 1985 publication of the American Bar Association (ABA), which outlined some best practices for evaluating judicial performance (American Bar Association 1985). Although the details of judicial performance evaluation systems vary widely, the key feature in most of these evaluation systems is the attorney survey (Brody 2000; Esterling and Sampson 1998; Olson and Batjer 1999).

States generally adopted evaluation language directly from these guidelines (Gill, Lazos, and Waters 2011; Gill 2014a), despite the ABA's admonishments to produce evidence-based, behaviorally anchored evaluation questions derived from the general performance dimensions outlined in the report (American Bar Association 1985, 2005). The characteristics of the resulting surveys have come under scrutiny for problematic design (Elek and Rottman 2013; Elek, Rottman, and Cutler 2012; Gill 2014a) and their propensity to manifest gender and race biases (Elek and Rottman 2014; Gill, Lazos, and Waters 2011).

Despite these problems, many states publicize the results of these surveys as part of the commission's overall assessment of incumbent judge quality. These assessments often include a narrative discussion of the judge's performance on the bench, along with the committee's official recommendation about whether voters should retain the judge. These voter guides are intended to provide the kind of information that comes more naturally in contested campaigns; in that way, the voter guides function like a kind of campaign advertisement coming directly from the state (Gill 2013; Tarr 2009).

## Retention Vote Share and JPEs

Despite the fact that retention elections are seen as "poor mechanisms for fostering accountability" (Bruhl and Leib 2012, 1232), judges do appear to believe that retention elections have the potential for rewarding or punishing judicial behavior (Aspin and W. Hall 1994). Research has shown that trial court judges facing their first retention elections impose steeper sentences (Huber and Gordon 2004) than elected judges, although competitively elected judges impose steeper sentences overall (Gordon and Huber 2007). Judges also seem to bend toward public opinion in their constituency about abortion, more so than their partisan-elected counterparts (Canes-Wrone, Clark, and Park 2012). Shepherd (2009) finds that judges facing retention elections may shift their behavior slightly in torts cases, but this is a much narrower and smaller magnitude of behavior change than she finds in judges facing competitive elections. In all, it seems that judges generally see retention elections as holding them accountable, despite the fact that few judges lose their retention elections.

Judicial performance evaluations are seen as a way to improve incentives for judges, such that they will be held accountable by voters for the quality of their decisions, not their content. Some scholars have argued that judges themselves believe that judicial performance evaluations are a strong accountability mechanism in the retention election context (Brody 2008; Esterling and Sampson 1998). This is partly due to the fact that voters in low-information elections grasp at any voting cue available (Dubois 1984; Hall 2001a, 2014, 2015; Squire and Smith 1988). Proponents of JPEs certainly hope that voters will rely heavily upon the evaluation results when they make their choice in the voting booth (Kourlis and Singer 2007; Paynter and Kearney 2010; White 2009).

Given the documented problems with existing JPE systems (Elek, Rottman, and Cutler 2012, 2014; Gill 2014a; Sterling 1993), judge trepidation about the process is not unfounded. Although overall negative recommendations are fairly rare, the presence of one outlying negative score in the publicized reports could have a disproportionate effect on the voter's impression of the incumbent judge. These negative ratings may not be reflections of systematic underperformance, given the likelihood that "individuals who have an interest in whether a judge is retained will be more apt to respond to surveys tha[n] others" (Brody 2000, 339). The organizational psychology research has long found that negative information disproportionately influences performance evaluations (Anderson 1966; Feldman 1981). Indeed, research show that vote share totals reflect strong negativity bias when summary performance information of elected officials is made available to voters (James and John 2007).

## Judicial Performance Evaluation: Five Cases

Although candidate quality is a key consideration in predicting vote share in contested elections, it has been little studied in the context of retention elections. This is in part because, by and large, much of the existing research focuses on comparing the different electoral systems. As only retention election systems tend to conduct state-sponsored judicial performance evaluations (Goelzhauser 2012)—for good reason (Gill and Lazos 2009)—judicial performance evaluation scores cannot be used to compare candidate quality across electoral systems. Although other measures of judicial performance exist (Choi, Gulati, and Posner 2013), these measures are not generally available to voters in advance of the election. As such, they can link "objective" judge quality to election outcomes, but they cannot help us understand how JPE-inspired voter guides impact judicial and voter behavior.

A key exception to this is the recent study by Lim and Snyder (2015), which finds evidence that their measure of candidate quality is related to vote share, especially in retention election states (Lim and Snyder 2015, 118). Their measure, though, is admittedly imprecise. This is necessitated by the fact that they attempt to capture the results of state-sponsored JPE recommendations and locally administered bar polls using a single measure. The resulting dummy variable of "qualified" versus "unqualified" mirrors—although not perfectly—the nominal-level recommendation typical of state-sponsored JPE committees. Proponents of state-sponsored JPE programs would protest this choice loudly, though, given that they see JPEs as a much more nuanced, rigorous, and apolitical assessment of judicial performance than informal bar polls (Aynes 1981; Brody 2000; Esterling 1999; Mahoney 1989; White 2001).

In this chapter, I get around this problem by focusing on a subset of states with retention elections and state-sponsored JPE programs, all of which follow the general outline of the ABA's guidelines (American Bar Association 1985, 2005). All of these states evaluate judges on the basis of five key categories: legal ability, communication skills, impartiality and integrity, judicial temperament, and administrative capacity. Some states organize their categories differently, but the survey questions intended to measure these concepts track closely to the language in the ABA guidelines (Gill, Lazos, and Waters 2011).

Here, I attempt to determine the effect of these multidimensional JPE programs on the retention elections of the evaluated judges. Although a number of retention election states engage in formal judicial performance evaluations for judge self-improvement purposes, there is a growing number of states that actively publicize the results of their JPEs for the purposes of voter education. Among these states are Alaska, Arizona, Colorado, New Mexico, and Utah. Currently, each of these states uses anonymous attorney surveys as a key part (Brody 2003) of their overall assessment of judges. Below is a brief introduction to each of these five systems.

*Alaska.* Alaska's judicial performance evaluation system was the nation's first (Brody 2008). Its inaugural year was 1975, well ahead of the publication of the ABA's first set of guidelines a decade later. Alaska's judges serve terms of four to seven years, depending upon the court. The Alaska Judicial Council (AJC)[3] evaluates judges when their current term is about to expire. At present, the AJC's final recommendation is based upon information gathered from surveys of attorneys and others who interact with the judge professionally. Also considered are the analyses of a sample of the judge's cases, a questionnaire filled out by the judge, public hearings, other public records, and optional interviews with the judge. From the beginning of the program in 1976, the AJC recommended against retention a dozen times. Only four judges have lost their retention elections since the AJC was established. All four were among the dozen judges who drew negative recommendations from the AJC.

Aside from these examples, there is reason to believe that Alaskan voters are likely aware of the AJC's recommendation (Andersen 2000). Alaskan law requires the AJC to provide a summary recommendation for inclusion in the voter information pamphlet. This recommendation appears after the candidate's own one-page statement, should the candidate opt to purchase space in the voter guide.[4] The voter guides are mailed to each registered voter in advance of the election.

*Arizona.* The Arizona Commission on Judicial Performance Review (ACJPR)[5] has evaluated some—but not all—of Arizona's judges since its creation by constitutional amendment in 1992.[6] Judges subject to the performance reviews are those retained through the retention election process. These include judges on the appellate courts, as well as some trial court judges. The ACJPR conducts two performance reviews of each judge during their term. The publicized evaluation takes place in advance of the election year. This features surveys of attorneys and others who interacted with the judge professionally. The commission also holds public hearings and accepts written comments for consideration in the evaluation.

As in Alaska, the results of the ACJPR's evaluations are distributed widely (Esterling and Sampson 1998) and are included in the state's official voter information pamphlet. The ACJPR does not explicitly make recommendations about how voters should cast their ballots, instead indicating that the judge "meets" or "does Not meet" the relevant judicial performance standards. As of 2014, only three judges have received a "Does Not Meet" rating. Just one of these three lost a retention bid. The only other retention election defeats were two judges removed by voters in 1978.

*Colorado.* Judicial performance evaluations in Colorado are conducted by a number of separate commissions operating under the Colorado Office of Judicial Performance Evaluation (COJPE). These commissions and the COJPE were established in 1988. All of Colorado's judges are subject to the COJPE performance evaluations in advance of their retention election. The commissions gather information using surveys of attorneys and laypeople, self-evaluations, interviews with the judge, reviews of opinions/decisions, courtroom observation, and judicial statistics.

Since its establishment, the commissions have evaluated more than 1,300 judges. The commissions are tasked with providing one of three recommendations: "Retain," "Do Not Retain," or "No Opinion." The COJPE commissions have given "Do Not Retain" recommendations to a total of twenty judges as of 2014. A total of eleven judges were not retained, although only seven were judges who had garnered a negative recommendation from the commissions (Colorado Office of Judicial Performance Evaluation 2014). The COJPE commission recommendations are published widely (Andersen 2000) and are included in the Legislative Council's Blue Book (the state's official voter guide).

*New Mexico.* Since 1988, New Mexico's judicial selection system has been a hybrid of partisan elections and the merit system. Candidates compete for open seats in contested partisan elections. After this first election, retention elections are used. The threshold for success is 57 percent affirmative vote share. New Mexico's Judicial Performance Evaluation Commission (JPEC)[7] was created in 1997 in part to provide voters with information about judicial performance. New Mexico provides midterm self-improvement evaluations as well as publicized evaluations in advance of retention elections. The JPEC gathers information from surveys of lawyers and others who have interacted with the judge professionally during the evaluation period. The JPEC also conducts interviews with the judges and requires self-assessments. Finally, the JPEC has a mechanism for courtroom observations, although these do not appear to be administered in a systematic way. The resulting recommendations are "Retain," "Do Not Retain," "No Opinion," or "No Recommendation."

Since 2002, the JPEC has given "Do Not Retain" recommendations to nine judges. Of these nine, five were not retained by voters. An additional judge lost his retention election in 2014 despite garnering a "Retain" recommendation from the commission. The JPEC's evaluations are not included in information mailed to registered voters because there is no state-sponsored voter information pamphlet. The JPEC produces a "Report to Voters" that it publicizes through newspaper articles, paid advertisements, and the like. It also produces public service announcements for television.

*Utah.* In 2008, the Judicial Performance Evaluation Commission (JPEC) was created by the Utah legislature.[8] The JPEC evaluates all of Utah's judges in advance of their retention elections, but it also conducts one or two midterm evaluations (depending upon the length of the judge's term). The JPEC collects survey data from attorneys, court staff, and jurors. It invites public comment on the judges. It also collects data about participation in judicial education programs and disciplinary records. Additionally, the JPEC is mandated by law to conduct a courtroom observation program.

The JPEC makes recommendations for each judge: "Retain," "Do Not Retain," or "No Recommendation." Under the current JPEC system, all of the 71 judges evaluated have gotten positive recommendations, and all of them have been retained by voters. The results of the evaluations are included in an official Utah Voter Information Pamphlet that is sent to registered voters in the state.

## Understanding Retention Election Vote Share

Voters in retention elections receive precious little information. This is likely the reason that so few voters participate in these elections, even when they already have the ballot in their hand (W. Hall and Aspin 1987; Hall 2007b). Those who do vote in retention elections are given an up-or-down vote on an array of judges. Unfortunately, we know little about what drives these votes. Although some research suggests JPE results are related to vote outcomes (Brody 2008; Esterling 1999), there is little systematic evidence linking JPE scores with retention vote shares (see Lim and Snyder 2015 for an important exception).

The data for this analysis were collected as part of a larger project on judicial performance evaluations in the American states.[9] Data on 1,011 judicial performance evaluations were collected from Alaska (1996–2012), Arizona (2010–2014), Colorado (2002–2012), New Mexico (2010–2012), and Utah (2012–2014). Descriptive statistics for the sample are included in Table 9.1. For each performance evaluation in the sample, the committee's recommendation was recorded. In all, "Do Not Retain" recommendations were given in just 8 percent of the evaluations, and "No Opinion/No Recommendation" ratings were given in 32 percent of evaluations.

The aggregate-level results of the attorney surveys across the range of available questions were recorded and the five-point scales were adjusted to range from one to five. Each of these states reports average scores by ABA performance category (with some variation in terms of the number and content of the categories), so

**TABLE 9.1** Descriptive Statistics for Retention Vote Share Models

| | *Vote Share* | *Law School Prestige* | *Supreme Court* | *Female Judge* | *Lowest Score* | *JPE Recommend* |
|---|---|---|---|---|---|---|
| **Alaska** | | | | | | |
| N | 101 | 101 | 101 | 101 | 101 | 101 |
| Mean | 64.84624 | 4.425743 | 0.039604 | 0.19802 | 3.968152 | 1.980198 |
| Std. Dev. | 5.364255 | 1.143211 | 0.196 | 0.400495 | 0.378022 | 0.140014 |
| Minimum | 45.97 | 2 | 0 | 0 | 2.85 | 1 |
| Maximum | 78 | 6 | 1 | 1 | 4.5 | 2 |
| **Arizona** | | | | | | |
| N | 202 | 202 | 202 | 202 | 202 | 202 |
| Mean | 68.80693 | 4.856436 | 0.019802 | 0.287129 | 4.085743 | 1.990099 |
| Std. Dev. | 6.41868 | 0.854711 | 0.139665 | 0.453546 | 0.372905 | 0.099256 |
| Minimum | 42.1 | 2 | 0 | 0 | 3.06 | 1 |
| Maximum | 79.7 | 6 | 1 | 1 | 4.84 | 2 |
| **Colorado** | | | | | | |
| N | 618 | 618 | 618 | 618 | 618 | 618 |
| Mean | 72.16585 | 4.197411 | 0.011327 | 0.265372 | 4.141872 | 2.977346 |
| Std. Dev. | 6.226179 | 1.063553 | 0.105909 | 0.441889 | 0.390443 | 0.195918 |
| Minimum | 37.80272 | 1 | 0 | 0 | 2.3 | 1 |
| Maximum | 91.09589 | 6 | 1 | 1 | 4.875 | 3 |
| **New Mexico** | | | | | | |
| N | 21 | 21 | 21 | 21 | 21 | 21 |
| Mean | 69.14238 | 4.095238 | 0.142857 | 0.52381 | 4.198016 | 1.857143 |
| Std. Dev. | 5.767847 | 0.995227 | 0.358569 | 0.511766 | 0.471654 | 0.358569 |
| Minimum | 55.35 | 2 | 0 | 0 | 2.916667 | 1 |
| Maximum | 76.42 | 6 | 1 | 1 | 4.741667 | 2 |
| **Utah** | | | | | | |
| N | 69 | 69 | 69 | 69 | 69 | 69 |
| Mean | 78.7 | 4.782609 | 0.043478 | 0.217391 | 4.194179 | 1 |
| Std. Dev. | 3.58592 | 0.872278 | 0.205425 | 0.415493 | 0.256086 | 0 |
| Minimum | 71.2 | 1 | 0 | 0 | 3.467742 | 1 |
| Maximum | 87.8 | 6 | 1 | 1 | 4.711765 | 1 |
| **Total** | | | | | | |
| N | 1011 | 1011 | 1011 | 1011 | 1011 | 1011 |
| Mean | 71.14664 | 4.389713 | 0.020772 | 0.265084 | 4.118038 | 2.522255 |
| Std. Dev. | 6.777553 | 1.056078 | 0.142689 | 0.441596 | 0.38354 | 0.640428 |
| Minimum | 37.80272 | 1 | 0 | 0 | 2.3 | 1 |
| Maximum | 91.09589 | 6 | 1 | 1 | 4.875 | 3 |

this method was followed. In keeping with the likely negativity bias engendered by these survey scores, the lowest average score was isolated. This score varies little by state (see Figure 9.1(a)) or by overall JPE commission recommendation (see Figure 9.1(b)). Recommendation narratives all feature average attorney ratings by performance category prominently in their promotion materials, and the narratives associated with negative recommendations tend to rely heavily upon these attorney survey results as justification. General committee reluctance to assign low

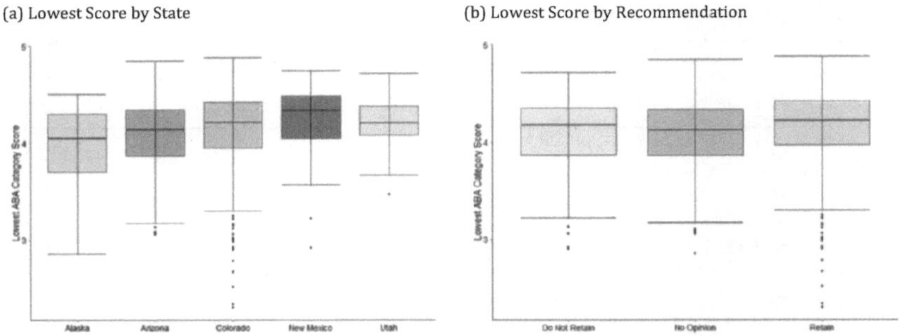


**FIGURE 9.1** Boxplots of Lowest ABA Category Score

ratings may drive voters to look to additional salient information about the judge. The lowest average attorney survey rating might be just such a cue.

Vote share data come from the relevant election officials in the five states. This value represents the percentage of ballots cast in favor of retention. Here, the vote share variable is negatively skewed, ranging from 37.8 to 91.1 percent. The distributions vary by state (see Figure 9.2). In addition, individual judge-level data were collected for the 385 judges who appear in this sample. Data about gender were derived from official judge biographies. Law school attendance was also collected this way and was supplemented with data from the Martindale-Hubbell directory of lawyers[10] and the *American Bench* online directory.[11] The law school alma mater prestige variable is an ordinal variable ranging from 1–6.[12]

The generalized linear models with random effects presented in Table 9.2 attempt to explain vote share in retention elections across five states. The first model, shown in Table 9.2(a), isolates the effects of the various possible retention JPE recommendations on vote share. Here, the JPE recommendations are interacted with the lowest average ABA category score in order to capture the way that these two variables combine to shape vote totals.

The downside of this specification is the resulting difficulty in interpreting the parameter estimates in Table 9.2. As such, Figure 9.1(a) presents the predicted vote share, with 90 percent confidence intervals, over levels of the lowest category score for each of the three possible JPE recommendations. Here, we see that having a "Do Not Retain" evaluation essentially mutes the effect of the lowest category score. However, the effects of the lowest category score are more pronounced when the JPE recommendation is not so firm. This supports the idea that voters may look for additional negative evidence in the JPE narratives when overall negative recommendations are scarce.

The model in Table 9.2(b) estimates the effects of lowest category scores across the five different samples. Here, the JPE recommendation variable is included as a dummy variable, and the inclusion of the positive recommendation has a strong and positive effect on retention vote share. Again, the relationship is made clearer

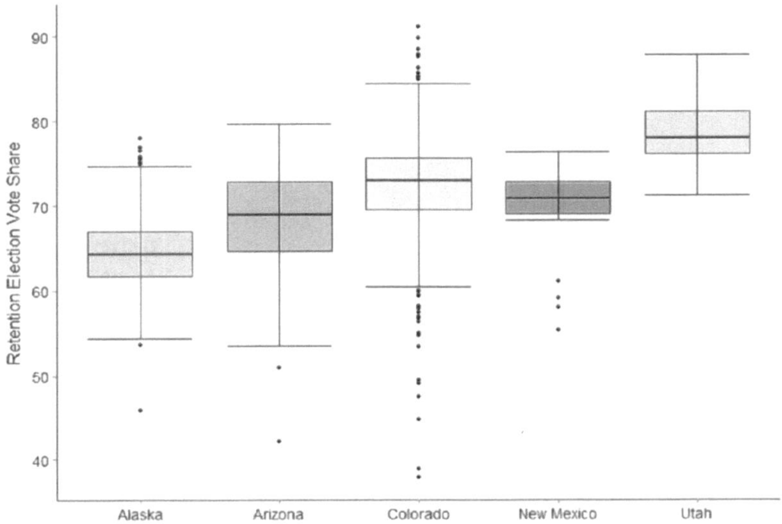


**FIGURE 9.2** Boxplot of Retention Vote Share by State

by the plot in Figure 9.3(b), where the predicted vote share is plotted for each state with 90 percent confidence intervals against the lowest category score. All else being equal, the lowest category score seems to have the strongest relationship to vote share in New Mexico and Arizona. Utah sees essentially no effect of lowest category score, and the predicted vote share here is consistently high and impervious to low category scores. Some of this may be due to the extremely truncated 1.25 point range of category scores in Utah (see Table 9.1).

Across both models in Table 9.2, law school prestige has little independent effect on vote share. Some of this may be attributable to some endogeneity, whereby law school prestige may be (inappropriately)[13] driving the scores in the attorney surveys. More likely, however, is the clustering of observations in our dataset at a single level of prestige. Of the 701 judges in the dataset, 45 percent attended a law school ranked between 15th and 50th in the 2014 *U.S. News* rankings; another 28 percent attended schools ranked from 51st to 100th.

Similarly, it is reasonable to suspect an endogenous relationship between the lowest ABA category score and the JPE commission's overall recommendation. Clearly, the predicted vote shares in Figure 9.3 show pronounced differences in the slopes when plotted against the lowest category score, and the joint F-tests of the interactions are significant. A difference of means test shows that judges with a "Do Not Retain" recommendation have only slightly and insignificantly lower lowest scores than judges without negative recommendations.[14] In addition, the JPE recommendation variable is not significantly related to the error term. That said, it is likely that there is a causal relationship—indeed, there

**TABLE 9.2** Models of Retention Vote Share by JPE Results in Five States

| | *(a)* | | *(b)* |
|---|---|---|---|
| Law School Prestige | -0.705*** | Law School Prestige | -0.697*** |
| | (0.177) | | (0.180) |
| Supreme Court | -0.963 | Supreme Court | -0.789 |
| | (1.155) | | (1.173) |
| Female Judge | 0.536 | Female Judge | 0.603 |
| | (0.404) | | (0.409) |
| Lowest Score | 1.690 | Lowest Score | -0.918 |
| | (2.035) | | (2.282) |
| JPE "No Opinion" | -0.929 | JPE "Retain" | 13.182*** |
| | (7.642) | | (1.493) |
| JPE "Retain" | 12.426 | Alaska | -32.255** |
| | (7.454) | | (11.761) |
| Lowest*No Opinion | 3.363 | Arizona | -36.326*** |
| | (2.183) | | (10.661) |
| Lowest*Retain | 1.660 | Colorado | -35.002*** |
| | (2.086) | | (10.240) |
| Interaction $\chi^2(5)$ | 254.15*** | New Mexico | -48.626*** |
| | | | (14.130) |
| Alaska | -25.712*** | AK*Lowest | 4.560 |
| | (2.2451) | | (2.846) |
| Arizona | -21.227*** | AZ*Lowest | 6.738** |
| | (2.424) | | (2.549) |
| Colorado | -26.551*** | CO*Lowest | 3.454 |
| | (2.285) | | (2.432) |
| New Mexico | -18.727*** | NM*Lowest | 9.873*** |
| | (2.560) | | (3.357) |
| | | Interaction $\chi^2(9)$ | 423.11*** |
| Constant | 84.747*** | Constant | 92.772*** |
| | (9.868) | | (11.174) |
| N(Judges) | 1.011 (701) | N(Judges) | 1,011 (701) |
| Wald $\chi^2(21)$ | 860.56*** | Wald $\chi^2(21)$ | 789.27*** |
| $\sigma_u$ | 3.661 | $\sigma_u$ | 3.658 |
| $\sigma_e$ | 3.131 | $\sigma_e$ | 3.244 |
| $\rho$ | 0.578 | $\rho$ | 0.560 |
| $R^2 = 0.444$ (within = 0.447, between = 0.483) | | $R^2 = 0.431$ (within = 0.411, between = 0.471) | |

Both models are random-effects generalized linear regression models grouped by judge. In models (a) and (b), the omitted state category is Utah. In model (a), the omitted JPE recommendation is "Do Not Retain." Models were estimated with fixed effects for election years, which are unreported here but are available from the author upon request. F-tests showed that the year variables were jointly significant in both models.

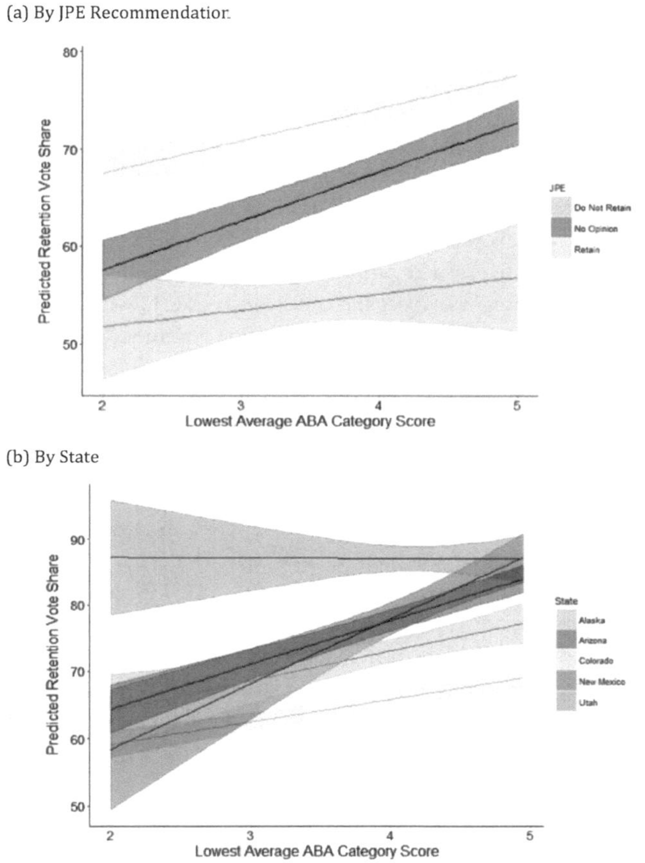


**FIGURE 9.3** Predicted Vote Share over Lowest ABA Category

ought to be—between the lowest category score and the overall JPE committee recommendation.

Overall, though, the results show that the effects of the JPE process on retention election vote share are highly sensitive to context. Certainly, being branded with the "Do not Retain" recommendation makes it much more difficult to win a retention election, regardless of the content of the category scores. However, these scores *do* seem to matter in the absence of the strong negative signal from the JPE commission.

## Discussion

Of course, the findings discussed above leave a lot of questions unanswered. The analyses indicate that there *is* a link between JPE results and retention election vote share, but it has not established a mechanism for that link. Although there is some evidence that voters do pay attention to JPE recommendations (Brody 2008; Esterling 1999), it is a hard sell to think that a large proportion of voters commit the JPE results to memory before entering the voting booth. The five states in this analysis all have among the strongest mechanisms for communicating JPE results to voters, so perhaps these relationships do represent voter attentiveness to JPEs. However, it is more plausible to think that voters may be responding to impressions about candidates as opposed to fully formed assessments of judicial performance (Lim and Snyder 2015). Local media coverage may certainly play a key role in conveying the content of these impressions to the mass public, as might lawyers and other local elites. However, more research needs to be done in order to isolate the effects of JPE recommendations and the accompanying narratives. Another possibility, of course, is that the relationship is driven by a third, unmeasured variable, such that attorney respondents, JPE committees, and voters are all independently assessing judge quality to be similar.

Future research also needs to address the question of selection bias, which may be obscuring the most important way in which JPEs affect retention elections. Research on state supreme court judges has shown that weak incumbents may retire instead of subject themselves to an election they may lose (Hall 2001b). If judges do believe that JPEs matter to voters, they may also decline to stand for retention election in the face of poor JPE marks. If this is the case, then JPEs might be the primary tool in holding judges accountable in retention election systems. Reformers will need to think carefully about what it means to have judges be at least as accountable to government commissions as they are to the electorate.

## Notes

1 This research was sponsored by generous research grants from the National Science Foundation [SES: 1354544], the University of Nevada, Las Vegas Faculty Opportunity Award Program, and the Black Mountain Institute-College of Liberal Arts Humanities Fellowship Program. The author thanks Benjamin Nruyneel, Kate Eugenis, Justin Ponkow, Kenneth J. Retzl, Rafael Oganesyan, Kate Eugenis, and Mallory Waters for invaluable research assistance on this project.
2 These states are Alaska, Arizona, California, Colorado, Florida, Illinois, Indiana, Iowa, Kansas, Maryland, Missouri, Nebraska, New Mexico, Oklahoma, Pennsylvania, South Dakota, Tennessee, Utah, and Wyoming.
3 Information about Alaska's current JPE system can be found on the Alaska Judicial Council's website. Available at: www.ajc.state.ak.us/retention/retproced.
4 These voter pamphlets dating back to 1974 are archived on the Alaska Elections website, available at: www.elections.alaska.gov/pub_oep.php. AJC recommendations begin appearing on these pamphlets in 1984.
5 Information about the Arizona Commission on Judicial Performance Review are available at: www.azcourts.gov/jpr.
6 Prior to this, attorney surveys of judicial performance were performed by a variety of state bar associations (Klumpp 2008). Unfortunately, all of these records appear to have been destroyed.
7 Information about the New Mexico Judicial Performance Evaluation Commission is available at: www.nmjpec.org/.

8 Information about the Utah Judicial Performance Evaluation Commission is available at: www.judges.utah.gov/.
9 Data used in these analyses come from a project funded by the National Science Foundation (Gill 2014b) and an internal grant by the University of Nevada, Las Vegas (Gill 2012).
10 This directory is avaialable at: www.martindale.com.
11 *The American Bench* by Forster-Long, LLC is a directory of judges in American state and federal courts. Available at: www.forster-long.com/americanbench.
12 The prestige of the law school was measured using the *U.S. News and World Report* law school rankings from 2014. Note that the *U.S. News* rankings are such that prestigious schools have lower numbers. The categories in the prestige variable are: 1 = no degree, 2 = unranked, 3 = ranked higher than 100, 4 = ranked from 51–100, 5 = ranked from 15–50, and 6 = top 14 school. More information is available at: www.usnews.com/education.
13 I say that this would be inappropriate because the JPE survey instruments purport to be measures of the judge's observable behavior during the evaluation term in question. Although we should expect some overlap here (such that students who attend prestigious law schools may end up being better judges than other students), we should not expect the law school alma mater to *drive* or *cause* the JPE scores or recommendations.
14 The mean lowest category score for those with "Do Not Retain" recommendations is 4.07, while that for other judges is 4.12 ($t(1009) = 1.07, p = 0.28$).

## References


American Bar Association. 1985. *Guidelines for the Evaluation of Judicial Performance.* Washington, DC: American Bar Association.

American Bar Association. 2005. *Guidelines for the Evaluation of Judicial Performance with Commentary*. Chicago: American Bar Association.

Andersen, Seth S. 2000. "Judicial Retention Evaluation Programs." *Loyola of Los Angeles Law Review* 34: 1375–1389.

Anderson, Norman H. 1966. "Component Ratings in Impression Formation." *Psychonomic Science* 6: 279–280.

Aspin, Larry. 2007. "Trends in Judicial Retention Elections, 1964–2007." *Judicature* 90: 208–213.

Aspin, Larry T. and William K. Hall. 1994. "Retention Elections and Judicial Behavior." *Judicature* 77: 306–315.

Aynes, Richard L. 1981. "Evaluation of Judicial Performance: A Tool for Self-Improvement." *Pepperdine Law Review* 8: 255–312.

Bernick, E. Lee and David J. Pratto. 1995. "A Behavior-based Evaluation Instrument for Judges." *Justice System Journal* 18: 173–184.

Bonneau, Chris W. 2007a. "The Effects of Campaign Spending in State Supreme Court Elections." *Political Research Quarterly* 60: 489–499.

Bonneau, Chris W. 2007b. "The Dynamics of Campaign Spending in State Supreme Court Elections." In *Running for Judge: The Rising Political, Financial, and Legal Stakes of Judicial Elections*, edited by Matthew J. Streb. New York: New York University Press.

Bonneau, Chris W. and Melinda Gann Hall. 2009. *In Defense of Judicial Elections.* New York: Routledge.

Brody, David C. 2000. "Judicial Performance Evaluations by State Governments: Informing the Public While Avoiding the Pitfalls." *Justice System Journal* 21: 333–356.

Brody, David C. 2003. "The Relationship between Judicial Performance Evaluations and Judicial Elections." *Judicature* 87: 168–192.

Brody, David C. 2008. "The Use of Judicial Performance Evaluation to Enhance Judicial Accountability, Judicial Independence, and Public Trust." *Denver University Law Review* 86: 115–157.

Bruhl, Aaron-Andrew P. and Ethan J. Leib. 2012. "Elected Judges and Statutory Interpretation." *University of Chicago Law Review* 73: 1215–1283.

Canes-Wrone, Brandice, Tom S. Clark, and Jee-Kwang Park. 2012. "Judicial Independence and Retention Elections." *Journal of Law, Economics and Organization* 28: 211–234.

Carson, Jamie L., Erik J. Engstrom, and Jason M. Roberts. 2007. "Candidate Quality, the Personal Vote, and the Incumbency Advantage in Congress." *American Political Science Review* 101: 289–301.

Choi, Stephen J., G. Mitu Gulati, and Eric A. Posner. 2013. "How Well do Measures of Judicial Ability Predict Judicial Performance? A Case Study Using Securities Class Actions." *International Review of Law and Economics* 33: 37–53.

Colorado Office of Judicial Performance Evaluation. 2014. *Judicial Performance Fact Sheet*. Denver, CO.

Dubois, Philip L. 1984. "Voting Cues in Nonpartisan Trial Court Elections: A Multivariate Assessment." *Law and Society Review* 18: 395–436.

Elek, Jennifer K. and David B Rottman. 2013. "Improving Judicial-Performance Evaluation: Countering Bias and Exploring New Methods." *Court Review* 49: 140–200.

Elek, Jennifer K. and David B. Rottman. 2014. "Methodologies for Measuring Judicial Performance: The Problem of Bias." *Onati Socio-Legal Series* 4: 863–879.

Elek, Jennifer K., David B. Rottman, and Brian L. Cutler. 2012. "Judicial Performance Evaluation: Steps to Improve Survey Process and Measurement." *Judicature* 95: 65–75.

Elek, Jennifer K, David B. Rottman, and Brian L. Cutler. 2014. "Judicial Performance Evaluation in the States: A Re-Examination." *Judicature* 98: 12–19.

Esterling, Kevin M. 1999. "Judicial Accountability the Right Way." *Judicature* 82: 206–215.

Esterling, Kevin M. and Kathleen M. Sampson. 1998. *Judicial Retention Evaluation Programs in Four States: A Report with Recommendations*. Chicago: American Judicature Society.

Feldman, Jack M. 1981. "Beyond Attribution Theory: Cognitive Processes in Performance Appraisal." *Journal of Applied Psychology* 66: 127–148.

Frederick, Brian and Matthew J. Streb. 2008. "Women Running for Judge: The Impact of Sex on Candidate Success in State Intermediate Appellate Court Elections." *Social Science Quarterly* 89: 937–954.

Geyh, Charles G. 2012. "Judicial Selection Reconsidered: A Plea for Radical Moderation." *Harvard Journal of Law and Public Policy* 35: 623–643.

Gill, Rebecca D. 2012. *Assessing Judicial Performance Evaluations for Race and Gender Bias*. University of Nevada, Las Vegas: Office of Research and Economic Development.

Gill, Rebecca D. 2013. "Beyond High Hopes and Unmet Expectations: Judicial Selection Reforms in the States." *Judicature* 96: 278–295.

Gill, Rebecca D. 2014a. "Implicit Bias in Judicial Performance Evaluations: We Must Do Better than This." *Justice System Journal* 35: 271–294.

Gill, Rebecca D. 2014b. "Objective Measures and Implicit Bias in Evaluating Public Officials." University of Nevada, Las Vegas: Law & Social Science Program, National Science Foundation.

Gill, Rebecca D. and Sylvia R Lazos. 2009. "Reflections in Response to the Nevada Judicial Evaluation Pilot Project." *UNLV William S. Boyd School of Law Legal Studies Research Paper* (10–36).

Gill, Rebecca D., Sylvia R. Lazos, and Mallory M. Waters. 2011. "Are Judicial Performance Evaluations Fair to Women and Minorities? A Cautionary Tale from Clark County, Nevada." *Law and Society Review* 45: 731–759.

Glick, Henry R. 1983. *Courts, Politics, and Justice*. New York: McGraw Hill.

Goelzhauser, Greg. 2012. "Accountability and Judicial Performance: Evidence from Case Dispositions." *Justice System Journal* 33: 249–261.

Gordon, Sanford C. and Gregory Huber. 2007. "The Effect of Electoral Competitiveness on Incumbent Behavior." *Quarterly Journal of Political Science* 2: 107–138.

Hall, Melinda Gann. 2001a. "State Supreme Courts in American Democracy: Probing the Myths of Judicial Reform." *American Political Science Review* 95: 315–330.

Hall, Melinda Gann. 2001b. "Voluntary Retirements from State Supreme Courts: Assessing Democratic Pressures to Relinquish the Bench." *Journal of Politics* 63:1112–1140.

Hall, Melinda Gann. 2007a. "Competition as Accountability in State Supreme Court Elections." In *Running for Judge: The Rising Political, Financial, and Legal Stakes of Judicial Elections*, edited by Matthew J. Streb. New York: New York University Press.

Hall, Melinda Gann. 2007b. "Voting in State Supreme Court Elections: Competition and Context as Democratic Incentives." *Journal of Politics* 69: 1147–1159.

Hall, Melinda Gann. 2014. "Televised Attacks and the Incumbency Advantage in State Supreme Courts." *Journal of Law, Economics, and Organization* 30: 138–164.

Hall, Melinda Gann. 2015. *Attacking Judges: How Campaign Advertising Influences State Supreme Court Elections*. Stanford: Stanford University Press.

Hall, Melinda Gann and Chris W. Bonneau. 2006. "Does Quality Matter? Challengers in State Supreme Court Elections." *American Journal of Political Science* 50: 20–33.

Hall, William K. 1985. *Judicial Retention Elections: Do Bar Association Polls Increase Voter Awareness?* Urbana, IL: Institute of Government and Public Affairs, University of Illinois.

Hall, William K. and Larry T. Aspin. 1987. "The Roll-Off Effect in Judicial Retention Elections." *Social Science Journal* 24: 415–427.

Hojnacki, Marie and Lawrence Baum. 1992. "'New-Style' Judicial Campaigns and the Voters: Economic Issues and Union Members in Ohio." *Western Political Quarterly* 45: 921–948.

Huber, Gregory A. and Sanford C. Gordon. 2004. "Accountability and Coercion: Is Justice Blind When it Runs for Office?" *American Journal of Political Science* 48: 247–263.

Jacobson, Gary C. 1989. "Strategic Politicians and the Dynamics of US House Elections, 1946–86." *American Political Science Review* 83: 773–793.

James, Oliver and Peter John. 2007. "Public Management at the Ballot Box: Performance Information and Electoral Support for Incumbent English Local Governments." *Journal of Public Administration Research and Theory* 17: 567–580.

Klien, David and Lawrence Baum. 2001. "Ballot Information and Voting Decisions in Judicial Elections." *Political Research Quarterly* 54: 709–728.

Klumpp, Albert J. 2008. "Arizona Judicial Retention: Three Decades of Elections and Candidates." *Arizona Attorney* November: 12–18.

Kourlis, Rebecca Love and Jordan M. Singer. 2007. "Using Judicial Performance Evaluations to Promot Judicial Accountability." *Judicature* 90: 200–207.

Lim, Claire S. H. and James M. Snyder, Jr. 2015. "Is More Information Always Better? Party Cues and Candidate Quality in U.S. Judicial Elections." *Journal of Public Economics* 128: 107–123.

Mahoney, Anne Rankin. 1989. "Citizen Evaluation of Judicial Performance: The Colorado Experience." *Judicature* 72: 210–216.

Olson, Susan M. and Christina Batjer. 1999. "Competing Narratives in a Judicial Retention Election: Feminism versus Judicial Independence." *Law and Society Review* 33: 123–160.

Paynter, Sharon and Richard C. Kearney. 2010. "Who Watches the Watchmen? Evaluating Judicial Performance in the American States." *Administration and Society* 41: 923–953.

Schaffner, Brian F. and Jennifer Segal Diascro. 2007. "Judicial Elections in the News." In *Running for Judge: The Rising Political, Financial, and Legal Stakes of Judicial Elections*, edited by Matthew J. Streb. New York: New York University Press.

Shepherd, Joanna M. 2009. "The Influence of Retention Politics on Judges' Voting." *Journal of Legal Studies* 38: 169–206.

Skaggs, Adam, Maria da Silva, Linda Casey, and Charles Hall. 2011. *The New Politics of Judicial Elections 2009–10: How Special Interest 'Super Spenders' Threatened Impartial Justice and Emboldened Unprecedented Legislative Attacks on America's Courts.* Washington DC: Justice at Stake.

Squire, Peverill and Eric R.A.N. Smith. 1988. "The Effect of Partisan Information on Voters in Nonpartisan Elections." *Journal of Politics* 50: 169–179.

Sterling, Joyce S. 1993. "The Impact of Gender Bias on Judging: Survey of Attitudes Toward Women Judges." *Colorado Law Review* 22: 257.

Streb, Matthew J. and Brian Frederick. 2009. "Conditions for Competition in Low-Information Judicial Elections: The Case of Intermediate Appellate Court Elections." *Political Research Quarterly* 62: 523–537.

Streb, Matthew J., Brian Frederick, and Casey LaFrance. 2007. "Contestation, Competition, and the Potential for Accountability in Intermediate Appellate Court Elections." *Judicature* 91: 70–79.

Streb, Matthew J., Brian Frederick, and Casey LaFrance. 2009. "Voter Roll-off in a Low Information Context: Evidence from Intermediate Appellate Court Elections." *American Politics Research* 37: 644–669.

Tarr, G. Alan. 2009. "Do Retention Elections Work?" *Missouri Law Review* 74: 605–633.

Van Dunk, Emily. 1997. "Challenger Quality in State Legislative Elections." *Political Research Quarterly* 50: 793–807.

Volcansek, Mary L. 1981. "An Exploration of the Judicial Election Process." *Western Political Quarterly* 34: 572–577.

White, Penny J. 2001. "Judging Judges: Securing Judicial Independence by Use of Judicial Performance Evaluations." *Fordham Law Review* 29: 1053–1077.

White, Penny J. 2009. "Using Judicial Performance Evaluations to Supplement Inappropriate Voter Cues and Enhance Judicial Legitimacy." *Missouri Law Review* 74: 635–664.

# SECTION 4

# The Impact of Judicial Elections

# 10

# MEASURING THE IMPACT OF ELECTION OUTCOMES ON VOTING IN STATE SUPREME COURTS

*Lawrence Baum, Thomas R. Gray, and David E. Klein*

Judicial elections fascinate observers for many reasons, but what ultimately matters most about them is whether and how they affect courts' outputs. Through their decisions and opinions, state supreme courts shape policy in significant ways on a wide range of issues. To the extent that elections influence those courts' actions, the elections have a real impact on the lives and work of the people and organizations governed by the law.[1]

Scholars have given considerable attention to one potential effect of elections on supreme court decision making. The prospect of facing voters in the future may influence justices' votes and opinions by leading them to take positions that they perceive as popular and, in particular, to avoid taking positions that electoral opponents could use to attack them in a campaign. Because of the salience of criminal justice to voters, judges might be especially concerned about avoiding the appearance of pro-defendant leanings. Indeed, studies have demonstrated that effect in capital punishment cases (Hall 1992, 1995; Canes-Wrone, Clark, and Kelly 2014), just as studies of trial judges have found some tendency for sentencing behavior to change as judges move closer to their next election (Huber and Gordon 2004; Gordon and Huber 2007). There is also evidence that elections affect justices' positions on other issues such as abortion (Caldarone, Canes-Wrone, and Clark 2009).[2]

Observers of supreme court elections have also expressed concern about the possibility that campaign contributions or independent spending on behalf of candidates may affect the choices of elected justices. That concern is symbolized by the U.S. Supreme Court's decision in *Caperton v. A.T. Massey Coal Co.* (2009), in which the Court held that massive spending by a coal company executive on behalf of a successful candidate for the West Virginia Supreme Court required recusal of that justice in a case with large stakes for the company. Several studies have taken on the difficult task of measuring the independent impact of contributions on justices' votes in cases relevant to the contributors (e.g., Cann 2002, 2007; Cann, Bonneau, and Boyea 2012), although together, these studies do not provide the basis for firm conclusions (see Kritzer 2015, 79–84).

Almost certainly, however, the most powerful effect of elections on supreme court policy is the most straightforward: elections determine who sits on a court, and the policy preferences of election winners are a powerful determinant of their choices as decision makers. This linkage between elections and legal policy is widely acknowledged, but it has been the subject of relatively little systematic analysis in state supreme courts. One reason is uncertainty about how to measure the effects of a court's membership on its decisions.

In this chapter we introduce an analytic strategy for measurement of those effects. This strategy makes use of information provided by the votes of other judges on a court to generate comparisons between a judge's actual votes and the votes we would have expected to be cast by another judge holding the same seat. Thus, this strategy concerns voting by the holder of a single seat on a court, and that will be the focus of our analysis in this chapter. But as we will discuss, estimates of the effect of an election outcome on a single seat can be used to estimate the effect of that outcome on the court's collective decisions.

Although our primary purpose is to present this analytic strategy for scholars to consider, we also make use of it to begin inquiry into possible sources of variation in the impact of election outcomes. We do so with a four-state comparison of that impact over a sixteen-year period between the two fields of policy most closely connected with supreme court election campaigns: tort law and criminal law and procedure.[3] Tort law has been the most powerful motivator for interest groups that participate in supreme court campaigns; criminal law has been the most prominent issue in those campaigns. The impact of election outcomes on supreme court policy in those two fields, including the relative magnitude of its impact between them, has important implications for our understanding of how judicial elections work.

## Election Outcomes and Judicial Policy

In the U.S. Supreme Court, in which justices act largely on the basis of their policy preferences (e.g., Segal and Spaeth 2002), we are accustomed to the effects of appointments on the Court's collective preferences and thus on Supreme Court policy. To take one example, commentators frequently point to cases in which the Court's decisions likely result from the appointment of Samuel Alito to succeed Sandra Day O'Connor (e.g., Wolf 2016). The effects of judges' preferences on their choices may be more limited in lower federal courts, because of the constraint of Supreme Court precedent and the high proportion of "easy" cases, but those effects are still substantial.

The absence of life terms in nearly all states reduces the impact of judges' policy preferences by creating a significant constraint. Just as judges who face future elections may depart from their preferred positions with an eye to electoral opponents and voters, judges whose tenure depends on reappointment may temper their positions with that prospect in mind (Shepherd 2009a). Still, judges on supreme courts and other state courts have considerable freedom to cast votes and write opinions on the basis of their conceptions of good policy.

Moreover, judges' interest in continuing tenure may reinforce the impact of policy preferences in some respects, rather than reduce, that impact. Supreme court candidates are likely to attract support on the basis of perceptions of where they stand on issues. After they win election or re-election, justices have an incentive to maintain the stands that supporters found attractive. For instance, a successful supreme court candidate whose pro-plaintiff leanings in tort law brought support from interest groups on that side of the tort wars can please those supporters and maintain their support by taking pro-plaintiff positions in decisions.

Elections can have a direct effect on the collective policy preferences of a supreme court only if they are contested by candidates whose preferences differ. A substantial proportion of nonpartisan supreme court elections are uncontested, especially when incumbents run for re-election (Hall 2015, 46–47; Kritzer 2015, 117–22), and even contested elections might feature candidates with similar views about the policy questions that supreme courts address. But competing candidates are likely to differ in their policy preferences. In states with partisan elections, by definition the general election candidates come from different political parties. Even in states that use nonpartisan elections, the competing candidates frequently differ in their party affiliations. These partisan differences tend to carry ideological differences with them, and in turn, those differences are reflected in candidates' views about at least a large share of the issues that state supreme courts address.[4]

This linkage between elections and supreme court policy undoubtedly has strengthened with changes in judicial elections and in the larger political world. In that larger world the key change is the partisan sorting that has taken place at the elite level. Republicans and Democrats are more distinct ideologically than they were a few decades ago (e.g., Theriault 2008). As a result, supreme court contests between candidates from different parties are more likely to pit liberal and conservative against each other.

At the same time, the growing involvement of issue-oriented groups in supreme court elections fosters the recruitment of candidates who differ in their ideological positions. The competing economic groups that are typically the largest spenders in supreme court campaigns want candidates who reflect their own positions. Accordingly, political party organizations and the groups themselves are more likely than in the past to seek out candidates who have distinctly conservative or liberal positions, at least on economic issues.

To a considerable degree, then, the changes that have occurred in U. S. Supreme Court appointments at the federal level are paralleled in the states. Just as presidents have become more likely to choose Supreme Court nominees who share their party's dominant ideological orientation, competing candidates in state supreme court elections are more likely to give voters a choice between a conservative and a liberal. In turn, the outcomes of those elections have a heightened potential to shift the collective policy preferences of supreme courts and thus the policies they adopt.

As we noted earlier, the two policy areas that we consider in this chapter play key—though quite different—roles in electoral contests for state supreme court seats. Tort is a common law field in which state supreme courts traditionally were the dominant policy makers, although state legislatures have increasingly intervened to supersede judicial doctrines with their own legal rules. The significance of state supreme courts in this field was underlined by the slow but revolutionary change in tort law from the late nineteenth century to the 1970s, in which longstanding rules that favored tort defendants were supplanted by rules that favored plaintiffs across the states (Baum and Canon 1982; Canon and Baum 1981).

By the 1980s, interest groups with a stake in the decisions of state supreme courts on economic issues were playing an active part in campaigns for supreme court seats in some states.[5] The involvement of those groups has broadened and deepened since then. Among the issue areas that motivate interest group involvement, tort law is by far the most prominent. On the plaintiffs' side are labor unions and trial lawyers (lawyers who represent plaintiffs in tort cases). On the defendants' side are businesses and business groups, especially insurance companies, and sometimes medical professionals. Groups on the defense side have had an especially strong incentive to participate in supreme court elections because of the long-term movement toward doctrines favoring tort plaintiffs in many courts. Defense-oriented groups such as the U.S. Chamber of Commerce increasingly undertake major independent expenditures in support of candidates they favor (e.g., Champagne 2005).

Even if economic interest groups were not involved in campaigns, we would expect election outcomes to have a substantial effect on tort policy in state supreme courts. At the elite level, conservatives and liberals typically take quite different positions on economic issues such as liability for personal injuries. To the extent that supreme court contests are between candidates with different ideological orientations, then, the position that the winning candidate takes in a tort cases are likely to differ considerably from those the loser would have taken. Interest group involvement strengthens this tendency by increasing the likelihood that competing candidates will have different ideological orientations and by creating incentives for candidates to vote and write opinions consistent with those orientations.

If tort law is the most powerful motivator for interest group involvement in supreme court contests, criminal law and procedure is the most visible issue in those contests (see Berry 2015). High as the stakes in tort law are for interest groups, personal injury law is not necessarily a good issue on which to campaign;

for one thing, public opinion is divided. Thus, whereas campaigns sometimes emphasize tort issues, more often groups and candidates that care about those issues choose other emphases. Among policy issues, criminal law is especially attractive because it is a valence issue: the great majority of voters favor pro-prosecution policies. If a candidate can be depicted as soft on crime, the opposing candidate gains a substantial advantage. For this reason, interest groups sometimes focus their supreme court campaigns on criminal law rather than the economic issues that they really care about.[6]

Analysis of the impact of election outcomes in tort and criminal law allows us to compare the magnitude of that impact between the two fields. Our expectations are uncertain. On the one hand, among political elites, Republicans and Democrats as a whole differ considerably in their views about both torts and criminal justice. Thus we might expect Republican and Democratic justices to differ to about the same degree in the two fields.

On the other hand, elected judges have strong incentives to avoid the reputation of being soft on crime, incentives that affect their decisions. At the supreme court level, those incentives have strengthened with the growing frequency of large-scale campaigns in which challengers and their supporters can publicize any evidence that an incumbent justice is unduly favorable to defendants. Even justices who take strongly liberal positions on other issues such as torts might curb their liberal tendencies in criminal law to avoid electoral vulnerability. As a result, differences between Democratic and Republican justices might be muted.

These competing possibilities have important implications. Because the general public is generally more conscious of, and concerned about, criminal justice than tort policy, from one perspective it would be reassuring if voters' collective choices have a substantial impact on criminal justice rather than only on a field that is more important to interest groups than to voters. Moreover, the extent to which candidates from the two parties diverge in their decisional tendencies in criminal law will tell us something about the extent of their self-perceived freedom to take positions that are consistent with their own preferences but (in the case of liberals) diverge from the voters' preferences.

Although potential differences between these two policy areas are our major substantive concern, we can also consider possible variation in the impact of election outcomes across states. Interstate variation undoubtedly reflects several different factors. Among them are the magnitude of ideological differences between the two parties, the configuration of interest groups and the pattern of group activity in politics, the level of campaign activity, and the strength of consensual norms on the supreme court.

Perhaps the most important factor is the role of parties and partisanship in supreme court elections. The more substantial this role is, the more likely it is that competing candidates differ substantially in their ideological positions. In turn, partisan elements in supreme court contests are fostered by formally partisan elections, which ensure that competing candidates in a general election are nearly always from different parties. Among states with formally nonpartisan supreme court elections, there is more room for variation in the degree to which competing candidates represent the two parties and differ ideologically.

We selected states for this study primarily on the basis of the availability of usable data on supreme court decisions and the frequency of contested elections within the period for which we have appropriate decisional data (1995–2010). However, the states we chose do differ in their formal selection systems.[7] Arkansas used partisan elections through 2000, when its voters approved a ballot measure adopting nonpartisan elections. Michigan has a hybrid system in which the general election is nonpartisan but candidates are nominated in partisan conventions.[8] Wisconsin and Georgia have nonpartisan elections.

During the study period, all four states had several contested races for the supreme court contests, in some of which policy issues played a role.[9] In the latter part of that period, there were contests that featured high levels of spending and considerable heat in Michigan, Wisconsin, and Georgia. Overall, it appears that the magnitude of ideological differences between competing candidates has been higher in Michigan and Wisconsin than in the other two states. In part, this is because the parties in the two states are quite distinct ideologically in the current era; in part, it is because of the partisan element in Michigan's formal system for supreme court elections and the frequency of ideological contention in Wisconsin's supreme court contests in recent decades (Kritzer 2015, 17–21).

For this reason, all else being equal, we expect election outcomes to have a greater impact on justices' voting and thus on court policy in those two states than in Arkansas and Georgia. But all else is not necessarily equal, because so many factors can shape the relationship between election outcomes and supreme court policy and a sample of four states is too small to control for those factors. Thus our expectations about differences among states are not as strong as our expectations about differences between policy areas.

## Analytic Approach

If it is important to determine the impact of election outcomes on supreme court policy, as we think it is, the question is how to estimate that impact. As we have noted, our strategy focuses on the votes cast by holders of individual seats on a court. Thus, we need to reach meaningful judgments about what difference it made that one candidate rather than another won in any particular election. Making such judgments is more complicated than it may seem at first. Before turning to our data and analyses of the consequences of elections in criminal and torts cases, we describe the challenge and our solution to it.

Consider the situation in which challenger Y defeats incumbent Justice X in an election. We want to know what difference it made that Justice Y replaced Justice X on a court. It is tempting simply to compare X's and Y's voting records. Say we were to find that Y votes for criminal defendants 10 percentage points more often than X did; this would give us reason to conclude that he is more liberal in matters of criminal law.

Unfortunately, the reasons would not be terribly strong, and this conclusion would be too hasty. The problem is that the cases Justice Y has been deciding are not the same as Justice X decided when she was on the court. The more recent cases may, for whatever reason, involve circumstances or law more favorable to defendants than the cases Justice X decided. If so, then Y's more "liberal" voting record would be a function of the cases the court heard during Y's tenure. In reality, he might be no more liberal than Justice X was—perhaps even less so.

To put this another way, "How does Y's voting compare to X's?" is not the right question to ask when comparing a former judge and her successor. The right question is the counterfactual one of how X would have voted in the cases Y has participated in if X had stayed on the bench and decided them in Y's place.

Like any counterfactual question, this cannot be answered with certainty; after all, the whole point of the enterprise is that we never get to observe Justice X voting on the same cases as Justice Y. What we can observe is how the justices vote in *similar* cases. There are a great many ways in which cases can resemble or differ from each other. Assuming a pair of cases from the same area of law involving the same types of litigants, the most important single variable in the counterfactual comparison is the degree to which the circumstances and law in a case favor one side or the other.

Imagine, for instance, that in an analysis of criminal cases, we did not have to content ourselves with comparing the proportion of Y's cases in which he voted for the defendant with the proportion of X's cases in which she did. Instead, imagine that we could identify cases where the prosecution and defense held positions of roughly equal strength and that, in such cases, X voted for the defendant 45 percent of the time and Y voted for the defendant 52 percent of the time. And we could identify cases that strongly favored the defense and found that X voted for the defendant 85 percent of the time and Y voted for the defendant 98 percent of the time. Now we would be justified in concluding that Y really was more pro-defendant than X was.

The first premise of our approach, then, is that it is necessary to compare cases in terms of the relative strength of the parties' positions. In an ideal world, the relative strength would be assessed through a wide array of case characteristics; however, in reality, coding these characteristics would require far too much time and independent judgment.[10] Fortunately, there is a source of information that is both more reliable and more readily available: the justices' votes—or, more precisely, the votes of all the other justices aside from the one in whom we are interested. Other things being equal, the number of votes for each side in the case should reflect the relative strength of the case each side presented. If the other six justices on a seven-member court all vote for the prosecution, that vote indicates that the prosecution has a considerably stronger case than if there were a 5–1 split for the defense. The second key premise of our approach is that, because the votes of the other justices reflect the relative strength of the parties' cases, a measure based on those votes can serve as a proxy for case strength.

We will explain the precise form this measure takes after completing our description of the general approach and introducing our data. For now, suffice it to say that the measure incorporates information about both the number and the identity of the justices voting for each party in a case, leaving aside the justice occupying the seat about which we wish to draw inferences.

Our strategy for using this measure to estimate how Justice X would have voted in Justice Y's place proceeds in two main stages. We illustrate with a pair of Michigan justices from our dataset: Diane Hathaway and the justice she ousted from office in a 2008 election, Cliff Taylor. The question is how Taylor would have voted in Hathaway's place had she not defeated him. First we model Taylor's actual votes as a function of two variables: litigant case strength, as measured by the behavior of the justices on the court other than Taylor himself, and the winning party in the court below.[11] In a logit model of all Taylor's votes in criminal cases, where a vote for the prosecution is coded 1 and a vote for the defendant is coded 0, the coefficients are:

| | |
|---|---|
| Prosecution case strength | 4.95 (standard error = 0.86) |
| Lower Court for Prosecution | -1.42 (0.60) |
| Constant | 1.27 (0.48) |

Next, we turn to the cases that were decided by Hathaway after she defeated Taylor. For each case, we calculate the case strength measure from the votes of the six justices other than Hathaway. We then plug that score and the score for the party winning below into Taylor's model to generate a logit score that can be transformed into a probability of a pro-prosecution vote. This tells us the estimated probability that Taylor would have voted for the prosecution in a given case that Hathaway heard if he had sat on the case in her stead. For example, in *People v. McGraw* (2009), Hathaway was part of a four-member majority (with Justices Kelly, Cavanagh, and Markman) to overturn a conviction. Justices Corrigan, Young, and Weaver dissented. This produced a weighted score of -0.038 in the case. When we plug that score into Taylor's model (along with a score indicating that the defendant was the appellant in this case), the model yields an estimated probability of a pro-prosecution vote of 0.42. In other words, our best guess is that there is a 0.42 probability that Taylor would have voted for the prosecution here. In this manner, the counterfactual Taylor probabilities from all of Hathaway's cases can be compared with Hathaway's actual votes to assess the consequences of her having occupied the seat instead of Taylor.

## Data and Methods

With the essentials of our approach in mind, we now turn to the specific data examined here. As already explained, our cases come from four states. All of the cases are found in a dataset created by Matthew Hall and Jason Windett (2013). The dataset, which contains all cases decided by state courts of last resort from 1995 to 2010, identifies parties, procedural backgrounds, justices' votes, and case topic areas through automated textual analysis of published case decisions, using state-specific protocols. For criminal cases, we selected all cases in the target state that were classified as "Criminal Law and Procedure Cases."[12] For tort cases, we ran a text search for key words over the procedural history of each case, taking all cases that included at least one key word. We then read every tort case (or, in Arkansas, every other case)[13] to ascertain whether it involved an issue related to tort and of a sort that typically pits an individual plaintiff against a large institutional defendant. We excluded cases that did not meet these criteria, for instance those involving financial torts between businesses, legal malpractice, or defamation.

For each case, we determined the original status (plaintiff or defendant) of the party that ended up winning at the supreme court. In cases where each side was partially successful and reasonable people might disagree about which party emerged better off from the supreme court, we coded victory on the basis of the emphases in the court opinion: if the court devoted considerably more space to explaining why a particular party should prevail in one aspect of the case, the case was coded as a victory for that party; if not, it was excluded from the analysis. Through the Hall-Windett codes supplemented by our own reading where there were separate opinions, we then determined whether each justice joined the majority or dissented. Where a justice concurred and dissented in part, the judgment was much the same as at the court level: include the vote if the justice clearly favored one side or the other, exclude it otherwise.

The dependent variable in all models is the individual justice's vote for one party or the other. For consistency in coding positions usually understood to be liberal or conservative, in criminal cases a vote for the defendant is coded as 0, a vote for the prosecution as 1; in tort cases, a vote for the plaintiff is coded as 0, a vote for the defendant as 1.

The key independent variable is our vote-based measure of litigant case strength. We explain how the variable is constructed, using tort cases as an example. Recall that the object is to gauge the strength of the tort defendant's case as reflected in the votes of the justices (excluding the vote of the justice whose decisions are being modeled, to avoid circularity). The simplest measure of case strength would be the number of other justices voting for each side. This measure would be informative but would suffer from an important limitation.

Consider, for instance, what we could make of a 3–3 split among the other justices. Our initial thought might be that the justices split evenly because the litigants' positions were equally strong; however a moment's reflection shows that this inference is questionable. It might be that the plaintiff had the stronger case but the justices were predisposed to favor defendants or that the defendant had the better case but also the bad luck to face a court that leaned toward plaintiffs. A sound measure of the plaintiff's case strength must take into account both the number of justices voting for the plaintiff and each justice's tendency to vote for or against plaintiffs.

Our specific solution is to weight each justice's contribution to the case-strength score, with less typical votes weighted more heavily and more predictable votes being discounted. Consider a pro-plaintiff vote cast by a justice who typically supports the defense; the unwonted vote for the plaintiff gives us reason to believe the plaintiff's case is particularly strong. In contrast, a pro-plaintiff vote by a justice who usually votes for the plaintiff does not provide much information about the strength of the plaintiff's case; it might range anywhere from very strong to fairly weak. Accordingly, in construction of the case-strength score, the former vote would count as more than a single vote whereas the latter vote would count as less than one.

The precise discount for each judge is a function of that justice's voting tendency relative to the other justices on the court and is allowed to vary over time. The decision to make the discounts relative was unavoidable—because justices' votes are a function of case stimuli as well as their own predilections and we cannot measure case stimuli very accurately or precisely, it is impossible to describe justices' positions in absolute terms. Instead, we ask how much more or less likely a justice is to vote for the tort defendant than the other justices on the court. Counting a vote for the defendant as +1 and a vote for the plaintiff as -1 (so that a perfectly balanced set of votes yields a score of 0), we calculate the mean score across all cases for the other six justices and subtract that from the mean score of the justice whose discount we are calculating.

Say the mean score of the other six justices on the court is +0.18, indicating that they support defendants slightly more often than plaintiffs. If the justice whose discount we are calculating also had a mean vote of +0.18, her contributions to the case-strength score would not need to be weighted at all. A vote from her for the defendant would count as a full 1.0 and a vote for the plaintiff as a full -1.0. But say she voted for plaintiffs more often than defendants, resulting in an average vote of -0.12. We would then adjust her weighted contribution by 0.3 in either direction; so a vote from her for a defendant would contribute 1.3 to that case's defendant-strength score, whereas a vote from her for a plaintiff would contribute -0.7. When it comes time to model an individual justice's tort votes as a function of defendant case strength, the case-strength score is simply the mean weighted score for each of the other justices who participated in deciding that case.

Although it would be simplest to assign each justice a single discount to be used in all cases, this would ignore the possibility that justices move to the left or right over time. Instead, we calculate a new discount for each justice for each year.

We have no strong theoretical reason for preferring to calculate discounts annually rather than, say, every two or four years. However, experimentation with alternatives did not yield any approach that generated notably more accurate predictions, and the annual computation has the advantage of requiring weaker assumptions about stability in justices' positions.

The final thing we must explain before turning to results is how we chose our counterfactual comparisons. For each race, we asked whether either of the following conditions was satisfied: (1) the winning candidate and a losing candidate both served on the court between 1995 and 2010; or (2) both the winning candidate and a losing candidate have a known association with rival political parties. If either was satisfied, then the winning candidate was included in a comparison, with the counterfactual determined as follows. For contests meeting the first criterion, the counterfactual is obvious: we compare the actual votes of the justice who won with the predicted probabilities of votes of the justice who lost but sat on the court at another time. For example, Justice Louis Butler was defeated by Michael Gableman in 2008 in Wisconsin. Both the winner (Gableman) and loser (Butler) have a record of votes in the dataset. We use Butler's votes on the court, from his appointment by the governor in 2004 to his replacement by Gableman in 2008, to estimate how he would have voted in the cases Justice Gableman heard had Justice Butler retained the seat instead.

Although this is the more intuitively obvious and common counterfactual involving two people who sat on the court, it is also possible to reverse the temporal order. For example, incumbent Justice Diane Sykes fended off a challenge from the same Louis Butler in a 2000 election, raising the question of how Butler would have voted in Sykes' place had he won. For this comparison, we can take advantage of the fact that Butler did make it onto the court, using his later votes to generate counterfactual estimates of how he would have voted had he, rather than Sykes, been on the court between 2000 and his actual accession to the court in 2004.

The pairs selected by this criterion are our ideal comparisons, but they are few in number. The incumbency advantages that sitting justices enjoy mean they usually keep their seats until they are ready (or required by law) to retire. Situations like Butler's, where a candidate loses but eventually makes it onto the court are, of course, fairly rare. Most justices who gain their seat through election do so by winning a contest for an open seat. Where, as is almost always the case, the losing candidate in an open-seat race did not sit on the court either before or in the future, we cannot model the losing candidate's votes and hence have no way to predict how he or she would have voted once on the court. In those situations, we adopt the next-best solution of assuming that the losing candidate would have voted in the same way as the typical justice on that court from his or her political party.

This is possible where we can determine the losing candidate's party affiliation, either whether the candidate ran with a party label in a partisan election, or participated in a partisan primary, or through some other clear indicator. We supplement this information with several assumptions. First, we assume that in Wisconsin, with its highly polarized judicial elections, the final electoral rival is of the opposite party. Second, we assume that in Michigan, with its multi-candidate lists, voters had the option to choose a candidate from the other party.[14] We then use all members of the court from the opposite party during our study period to estimate a composite model and resulting counterfactual vote probabilities.

For example, Justice Young, a Republican appointee, was re-elected in Michigan in 2000. Because we have no specific information about the likely voting behavior of his unsuccessful challenger, aside from his Democratic party affiliation, we compare Young's voting behavior to that which would have been expected from an average Michigan Democrat in his place, using all votes taken by Democrats from 1995 to 2010 to generate a prediction model of their votes. We choose to use all Democratic votes between 1995 and 2010 rather than specifically during the years of analysis to reduce noise and to get a sample of Democratic and Republican justices that is as broad as possible, to better approximate the average.

Making comparisons under the second condition was more difficult in Arkansas after the switch to nonpartisan ballots, and in Georgia, which saw little competition from candidates with political experience. We do not assume partisanship for people with no political background, such as practicing attorneys challenging a sitting supreme court justice. In some cases, outside evidence indicated a partisan connection. For example, Bonneau (2007, 60) describes the clearly partisan campaign pattern in Justice Sears's 2004 re-election in Georgia, which we analyze. However, only a few contests in the two states—three in Arkansas and the 2004 election in Georgia—met our criteria for inclusion.

To clarify how this sort of comparison works, let us use another example from Michigan. In this instance, Republican Justice Robert Young defeated Democratic challengers Maggie Drake and Martin Brennan to retain his seat. Because neither Drake nor Brennan served on the court, we cannot model their voting directly. Instead we can assume that they would have voted like a typical Democratic justice in Michigan. Hence, the predictive model is derived from all criminal-case votes of Democratic Michigan justices in the dataset. The logit results are:

| | |
|---|---|
| Prosecution Case Strength | 1.33 (0.17) |
| Lower Court for Prosecution | 0.528 (0.19) |
| Constant | -1.03 (0.15) |

In *People v. Plunkett* (2010), Young wrote the opinion in favor of the prosecution for a 4–3 majority. The specific alignment of justices in the case produced a prosecution case-strength score of 0.095. In the model of typical Democratic votes, this results in a predicted probability of 0.287 (i.e., a 28.7 percent chance that a Democratic justice in Young's seat would have voted for the prosecution).

This example shows how we can move from the level of individual votes to collective decisions. In every case in which the justice of interest was part of a bare majority on the court, the probability that the outcome would have been different with a different justice on the court can be estimated. In *Plunkett*, for instance, there was a 71.3 percent chance that the defendant would have won if a Democratic justice had been elected rather than Justice Young. These estimates can be aggregated across cases to measure the likely number of decisions that would have turned out differently had a different justice sat in the seat in question. To continue our example, the estimate for criminal cases for Young's seat would be the additional number of criminal defendants who would have won their cases.[15]

## Results

Before turning to results, it makes sense to ask how much reason there is to take those results seriously. We tested our method through several analyses of subsamples, asking how well a model based on one subsample could predict votes in the other. The toughest test, because it included the fewest cases, involved Justice Butler's votes in tort cases. Twenty-eight votes were randomly chosen to generate his voting model. The model results were then applied to the remaining thirty votes. The model predicted that Justice Butler would vote for the defendant 25.3 percent of the time in those cases; in fact, he voted for the defendant 30 percent of the time.

There is some error here, but the results are still reassuring. The model works even better where there are more cases for it to rely on. For instance, Justice Taylor participated in over 150 criminal cases. When we split those and compare the model's predictions with actual votes in the other subsample, the figures are 72.5 percent predicted pro-prosecution, 70.3 percent actual pro-prosecution. When the comparison group is average Republican or average Democrat, there are more cases to draw on, of course. For average Democrats in Wisconsin criminal cases (with over 500 cases in the sample), the predicted and actual pro-prosecution percentages in the subsample are 53 and 51.3 percent respectively. For average Republicans in Wisconsin criminal cases (with over 1,000 cases in the sample), the figures are 69.7 and 70.2 percent respectively. In short, while our model's predictions are necessarily imperfect, they are easily accurate enough to justify drawing broad conclusions from them.

Table 10.1 displays, for every comparison satisfying one of the conditions explained above, the difference between the proportion of votes cast for the defendant (tort) or prosecution (criminal) by the actual justice and the proportion estimated for the counterfactual justice or justices. For each comparison, the set of actual votes analyzed begins at the start of the winning candidate's term and ends either at the end of that term or in 2010 (when the dataset's coverage ends), whichever comes first. To clarify and provide some context for them, we begin

**TABLE 10.1** Difference between Actual Proportion of Votes for Prosecution or Civil Defendant by Justice in "Winner" Column and Estimated Proportion by Justice or Group of Justices in "Comparison" Column

| *State* | *Year* | *Winner* | *Comparison* | *Torts Dif. (SE)* | *Criminal Dif. (SE)* |
|---|---|---|---|---|---|
| WI | 2009 | Abrahamson | Avg. Rep. | -0.206 (0.153) | -0.340 (0.094)* |
| WI | 2008 | Gableman | Butler | 0.334 (0.079)* | 0.235 (0.049)* |
| WI | 2007 | Ziegler | Avg. Dem. | 0.270 (0.077)* | 0.234 (0.044)* |
| WI | 2000 | Sykes | Butler | 0.212 (0.047)* | 0.195 (0.036)* |
| WI | 1999 | Abrahamson | Avg. Rep. | -0.263 (0.032)* | -0.294 (0.034)* |
| WI | 1997 | Wilcox | Avg. Dem. | 0.256 (0.027)* | 0.267 (0.022)* |
| WI | 1996 | Crooks | Avg. Dem. | 0.197 (0.026)* | 0.211 (0.024)* |
| WI | 1995 | Bradley | Crooks | -0.072 (0.055) | -0.005 (0.025) |
| WI | 1995 | Geske | Avg. Dem | 0.095 (0.034)* | 0.020 (0.032) |
| MI | 2008 | Hathaway | Taylor | -0.636 (0.102)* | -0.239 (0.100)* |
| MI | 2006 | Corrigan | Avg. Dem. | 0.445 (0.065)* | 0.319 (0.058)* |
| MI | 2006 | Cavanagh | Avg. Rep. | -0.305 (0.073)* | -0.308 (0.080)* |
| MI | 2004 | Markman | Avg. Dem. | 0.396 (0.048)* | 0.183 (0.050)* |
| MI | 2004 | Kelly | Avg. Rep. | -0.428 (0.059)* | -0.423 (0.060)* |
| MI | 2002 | Weaver | Avg. Dem. | 0.133 (0.039)* | 0.343 (0.037)* |
| MI | 2002 | Young | Avg. Dem. | 0.443 (0.034)* | 0.333 (0.035)* |
| MI | 2000 | Taylor | Avg. Dem. | 0.356 (0.032)* | 0.272 (0.034)* |
| MI | 2000 | Markman | Avg. Dem. | 0.337 (0.039)* | 0.303 (0.043)* |
| MI | 2000 | Young | Avg. Dem. | 0.348 (0.052)* | 0.310 (0.062)* |
| MI | 1998 | Taylor | Avg. Dem. | 0.384 (0.051)* | 0.310 (0.064)* |
| MI | 1998 | Corrigan | Avg. Dem. | 0.369 (0.029)* | 0.366 (0.030)* |
| MI | 1998 | Cavanagh | Avg. Rep. | -0.387 (0.044)* | -0.372 (0.046)* |
| MI | 1996 | Kelly | Avg. Rep. | -0.409 (0.041)* | -0.356 (0.050)* |
| MI | 1996 | Brickley | Avg. Dem. | 0.210 (0.048)* | 0.036 (0.077) |
| MI | 1992 | Mallett | Kelly | 0.185 (0.068)* | 0.393 (0.081)* |
| AR | 2004 (P) | Gunter | Danielson | 0.059 (0.059) | 0.028 (0.011)* |
| AR | 2000 | Hannah | Avg. Rep. | -0.113 (0.022)* | -0.045 (0.008)* |
| AR | 1998 | Corbin | Avg. Rep. | -0.103 (0.024)* | -0.028 (0.007)* |
| GA | 2004 | Sears | Avg. Rep. | -0.018 (0.034) | -0.048 (0.008)* |

*Notes*: P = primary election; * = statistically significant at 0.05 level (two-tailed test).

with a detailed look at Wisconsin, before turning to a more bird's-eye view of the other three states.

Wisconsin's judicial elections have been officially nonpartisan since 1913; until the late 1990s, they were largely nonpartisan in practice.[16] With occasional exceptions, they were also relatively quiet. But contention on the court between conservative and liberal blocs of justices and controversy over the court's economic decisions have led to more heated campaigns, driven in part by increased contributions to campaigns and independent expenditures by economic interest groups—primarily from the business community.

As campaigns became more visible between 1995 and 2010, candidates and their messages also became more partisan and ideological. As a result, voters increasingly voted along partisan lines—in several contests, at levels usually found when candidates' party affiliations are listed on the ballot (Kritzer 2015, 13). Our study period culminated with a series of three contests between 2007 and 2009 that were well-funded and nasty, with ideological and issue-oriented appeals by the candidates. As measured by county-level correlations with gubernatorial contests, the levels of partisan voting in those three contests were the highest of the 20th century up to that point.

The nastiest campaign and the one that featured the most spending by interest groups was between appointed incumbent Louis Butler and trial judge Michael Gableman in 2008. Although the campaigns by and for the two candidates came largely from labor unions and trial lawyers (Butler) and business groups (Gableman), the most visible part of the campaign was heavily aired television commercials that portrayed Butler as pro-criminal (see Sample et al. 2010). Gableman ended up winning by a small margin.

As already explained, the relevant comparison between Gableman and Butler is between Gableman's actual votes and our counterfactual predicted probabilities of given votes by Butler had he stayed on the court in Gableman's place. Gableman promised to be tougher on crime than Butler, and the second line in Table 10.1 provides strong evidence that he fulfilled this promise: our best estimate is that he voted for the prosecution in about 24 percent more of the cases (i.e., eight or nine out of the thirty-five) than Butler would have in his position. Interestingly, in light of the fact that criminal issues dominated the campaign, the difference between Gableman and Butler is even larger in tort cases, where we estimate that Butler would have voted for the plaintiff in about 33 percent more of the cases (or about eight out of twenty-five) than Gableman did. It seems clear that both voters and interest groups were right in thinking something important was at stake in the contest between these two.

As Figure 10.1 shows, fairly similar results obtain across our Wisconsin comparisons. Only in one, between Bradley and Crooks, is neither difference significant, and that comparison covers only a single year, as Crooks wound up winning an election to the court the following year. In the comparison between Geske and the average Wisconsin Democrat, both differences are fairly small; only the tort difference is statistically significant. For all other Wisconsin comparisons, there are substantial differences between actual and counterfactual voting in both areas of law.

Consider the career of Jon Wilcox, who was appointed to the court by a Republican governor in 1992, won the 1997 election to retain his seat, and served until his term expired in 2007. Between 1997 and 2007, Wilcox was a pivotal vote on twenty criminal cases; had he changed sides, the case would have been decided the other way. Wilcox—and therefore the Court—voted for the prosecution in nineteen of the twenty. Our model estimates that a typical Wisconsin Democrat

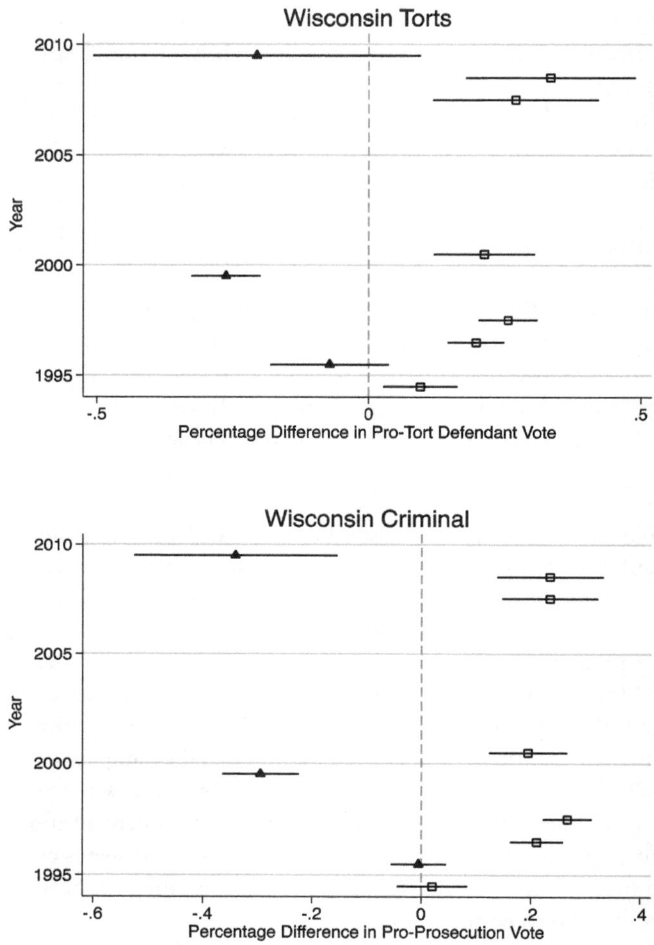


**FIGURE 10.1** Estimated Effects of Election Outcomes on Votes in Wisconsin Tort and Criminal Cases

would have voted for the prosecution in about 29 percent of these cases—that is, in about six of the twenty. That makes thirteen criminal cases across the ten years that would likely have gone for the defendant if Wilcox had been defeated in 1997.

Turning to Michigan, there is something of a tendency for differences in torts to be a bit larger than in criminal law. However, the chief lesson of the Michigan results is that judicial elections there have consequences for judicial decision making.

This is not so clearly the case in Arkansas or Georgia. In most comparisons the differences between actual and counterfactual votes are statistically significant and in the right direction; however, they are generally small. The contrast between these results and those for Michigan and Wisconsin is consistent with our tentative expectations, but the small number of contests that we could analyze in Arkansas and Georgia precludes any meaningful conclusions.

## Discussion

Our empirical inquiry has been a limited one, aimed primarily at demonstrating a method with which to estimate the impact of election outcomes on the votes cast by the holders of particular seats on a supreme court. Thus, we need to be quite cautious about generalizing from our findings. But with that caution, we can consider some implications of those findings for the functions of supreme court elections.

What we found in Wisconsin and Michigan makes it clear that the choice between Republican and Democratic candidates is frequently a choice between conservative and liberal policy positions. In light of the large body of scholarship on the correlation between judges' party affiliations and their decisional behavior, that finding is hardly surprising. But the analytic method that we employed allowed us to specify the impact of election outcomes more directly and with greater precision than in past studies. The magnitude of the impact that we found in many contests is striking.

Our findings also tell us that the impact of voters' collective choices between Republican and Democratic candidates extends beyond formally partisan elections. Wisconsin has a fully nonpartisan formal system, but the choice between candidates affiliated with the two parties frequently has had a powerful effect. Certainly, as both Wisconsin and Michigan indicate, a partisan general election ballot is not a prerequisite for this effect. In this respect, our findings reinforce the conclusions reached by Philip Dubois's (1980, chs. 6–7) study of several states.

However, a party-based relationship between the policy positions of elections and justices is not universal. In some states with nonpartisan elections, opposing candidates do not regularly come from different parties. Even when they do, Democratic and Republican candidates for a seat may not differ substantially in their policy positions. This study's findings for Georgia and Arkansas are relatively sparse, but they suggest the possibility that supreme court elections in those states have more limited stakes than those in Wisconsin and Michigan. To the extent that this is true, attributes of states such as the roles of the political parties in recruiting judicial candidates and the extent of policy differences among Republican and Democratic political elites may account for interstate differences.

The similarity of our findings for torts and criminal law is noteworthy. As criminal justice is both a valence issue for the general public and one that is easily communicated to voters, we might expect that justices from the two parties would converge on relatively pro-prosecution policies. At least in Wisconsin and Michigan, we did not find such convergence.

This does not mean that fear of negative reactions from voters has no impact on Democratic justices. The gap between justices from the two parties in voting in criminal cases might be even greater if it were not for caution on the part of Democratic justices. Moreover, liberal justices might curb their support for defendants quite selectively, focusing on cases in which pro-defendant positions would be easiest to turn into a basis for negative campaigns against them. Still, we are struck by the similarity to party effects in torts, where the desire to reinforce support from interest groups on the pro-plaintiff or pro-defendant side might be expected to accentuate differences between Democratic and Republican justices. In this respect, our findings suggest that justices' policy preferences outweigh electoral considerations in shaping their choices on the bench.

Do supreme court elections matter for legal policy? What we found indicates that, at least in some states, they can matter a good deal. Of course, our study focused on the votes of individual justices rather than on collective outcomes. The selection of a conservative Republican over a liberal Democrat might make little difference for a court that has a strong pre-existing conservative or liberal majority. As it happens, however, the Michigan and Wisconsin supreme courts have often had a close balance between liberal and conservative justices during and since our study period. The balance accounts for the heavy involvement of parties and interest groups in campaigns in many states; party and group leaders have perceived correctly that the outcomes of supreme court elections will have considerable impact on policies they care about.

The question of whether voters collectively are making deliberate choices to favor liberal or conservative policies is far beyond the scope of this chapter. It is, however, an important question, so it merits some exploration. When competing candidates differ in their actual and prospective policy positions, voters are not necessarily aware of those differences. However, knowledge of candidates' party affiliations is universal when it is listed on the ballot. Moreover, that knowledge is sometimes widespread in nonpartisan elections because of candidates' prior political activity or if there is a strong partisan tinge to the campaigns.

In turn, voters' party affiliations have a strong impact on their choices in formally partisan elections and often in nonpartisan elections as well (Bonneau and Cann 2015, ch. 2; Kritzer 2015, ch. 6). Indeed, the tendency to vote on a partisan basis has increased over the past several decades in many states, and partisan voting in supreme court elections (as measured by county-level correlations with the gubernatorial vote) has reached high levels in many Wisconsin and Michigan contests in the past two decades (Kritzer 2015, 185–86).

In that respect, then, voters' choices can be considered deliberate. Most voters can be expected to understand that party-line voting is also voting for liberal or conservative candidates. Moreover, because of partisan sorting, voters in the current era are likely to share broad policy preferences with their party's candidates.

This does not necessarily mean that election outcomes reflect the balance of voters' sentiment. Even when partisan voting is at a high level, partisan and ideological preferences are not the only determinants of voters' choices. Perhaps the leading competitor is name recognition. Judicial candidates can gain an advantage from incumbency, from service in other offices, from campaigns that are more visible than those of their opponents, or simply from having a name that sounds familiar or which has a favorable connotation.[17] Thus victory for a Democratic supreme court candidate who then takes mostly liberal positions in tort and criminal law does not necessarily mean that a majority of the voters favored that candidate's positions.

All this is even more true of states in which levels of partisan voting are lower. In Arkansas, county-level partisan correlations in supreme court voting declined to relatively low levels after the state formally adopted nonpartisan elections (Kritzer 2015, 184). In states in which Republican and Democratic justices differ little in their voting behavior (which might include states with partisan elections) and in nonpartisan states in which competing candidates do not regularly come from opposing parties, voters have even less opportunity to shape policy deliberately with their collective choices. Like the impact of election outcomes on supreme court policy, the extent to which those outcomes reflect voters' collective preferences undoubtedly varies considerably by time and place.

## Conclusions

Even casual observers of the U.S. Supreme Court recognize that the Court's membership has a fundamental impact on the legal policies it makes. The same is true of state supreme courts. It is especially true of those supreme courts whose jurisdiction is primarily discretionary, so that they hear primarily "hard" cases in which a decision on either side can be justified on legal grounds.

When states use partisan or nonpartisan elections to select supreme court justices, the impact of membership on court decisions has a sharp focus: in contested elections, the choice is between alternative candidates, typically two in general elections. Thus, the question arises as to how the victorious candidate's choices as a justice differed from those that the opposing candidate would have made.

In this chapter we have presented an analytic method that can be used to estimate what that difference looks like. The most distinctive feature of this method is that it uses information about other justices' responses to cases during a particular time period to gain a sense of how a justice who served in a different period, or even a losing candidate who never served, would have responded to the same cases. The results that we obtained with this method make intuitive sense, and we think these estimates are substantially better than those that could be based on simple percentages of liberal and conservative votes cast by individual justices or party cohorts on a court.

With appropriate data this method could be applied to a larger set of supreme courts, a longer time period, and a broader range of policy issues. As we have shown, it can be extended from the individual to the collective level in order to estimate how many court decisions in a field would have been different with a different membership and the probability that a given case would have been decided differently.[18]

Finally, analyses that this method facilitates can contribute to the continuing debate over the benefits and drawbacks of electing judges. As we suggested in discussing this study's findings, a particular set of findings about the functioning of judicial elections can often be interpreted in quite different ways. Similarly, people can reach different normative conclusions about the implications of such findings. Even so, judgments about the desirability of judicial elections can gain a firmer foundation as our understanding of the impact of those elections grows. We think that the method we used in this study provides one tool to advance that understanding.

## Notes

1 In this chapter we focus on electoral contests between candidates, leaving aside retention elections. Issues concerning the impact of elections on judicial policy are relevant to retention elections (see Shepherd 2009b), but the analytic method that we describe and use is directly applicable only to contests between candidates.

2 Kritzer (2015, 59–76) presents and analyzes the body of scholarship on the impact of elections on state judges' decisions.

3 The domain of tort law ranges widely and includes such matters as assault and libel. But the preponderance of tort cases (including cases in state supreme courts) concern injuries, deaths, and property damage that result from accidents.

4 This effect is reflected in the studies that have found statistical relationships between state supreme court justices' party affiliations and their voting behavior, studies that are summarized in Pinello (1999, 227–28).

5 The involvement of economic groups and tort issues in supreme court elections is discussed in Cheek and Champagne (Texas) (2005, ch. 3) and Ware (Alabama) (1999).

6 Perhaps the most noteworthy example is the campaign to defeat three California justices in retention elections in 1986, campaigns that focused on the death penalty. The financial support for that campaign came largely from groups whose real interest was in economic issues that the California Supreme Court addressed (Wold and Culver 1987, 350; Reidinger 1987, 58).

7 Information on the states' formal selection systems can be found at "Judicial Selection in the States" (www.judicialselection.us), a website maintained by the National Center for State Courts.

8 Incumbent justices are exempt from that requirement; they automatically go on the ballot if they seek a new term.

9 The discussion in this paragraph is based in part on the biennial reports on "The New Politics of Judicial Elections," published since 2000 by the Brennan Center for Justice, the National Institute on Money in State Politics, and other groups. Available at: www.justiceatstake.org/resources/the-new-politics-of-judicial-elections/. Much of the information in these reports is summarized in Sample et al. (2010); there is considerable information on Michigan and Wisconsin in Rutledge (2008).

10 In certain narrowly defined policy areas, those in which cases are largely parallel with each other, it is possible to take this approach; the classic example is search and seizure (Segal 1985). But in more broadly defined fields such as tort law and criminal law and procedure, this approach is impractical.

11 To the extent the winning party below tends generally to do better or worse at the supreme court, its effect should be captured by case-strength measure. We include it in case justices differ idiosyncratically in their tendencies to favor appellants or defer to lower courts.

12 Note that this is not exhaustive of all criminal cases. Because of the dataset's restriction of each case to a single category, a small number of cases find their way into alternative

topic categories. We have no reason to believe that this process introduces any bias into our analyses.

13 This was because of the large number of Arkansas cases that were initially identified as torts.

14 As very few losing candidates in Michigan ever served on the Court, we did not need to adjust our procedures to accommodate the multi-seat contests that occur in that state.

15 This method of aggregation treats justices as acting independently of each other. Of course, members of an appellate court are not fully independent. However, the assumption of independence is most valid in the closely divided cases in which a single member can determine the outcome, because collective pressures toward consensus are weak or non-existent in those cases.

16 This discussion of the Wisconsin Supreme Court is based primarily on Kritzer (2015, 8–21). Material on the contests in 2007–2009 was drawn from news reports.

17 That favorable connotation may stem from ethnicity or gender (see Klumpp 2011).

18 It could also be applied to the task of estimating the effects of new appointments to the U.S. Supreme Court, an extension that seems promising because the method provides one way of taking into account changes in the Court's agenda that create roadblocks for efforts to compare decisional patterns over time (see Bailey 2013).

## References


Bailey, Michael A. 2013. "Is Today's Court the Most Conservative in Sixty Years? Challenges and Opportunities in Measuring Judicial Preferences." *Journal of Politics* 75: 821–834.

Baum, Lawrence and Bradley C. Canon. 1982. "State Supreme Court as Activists: New Doctrines in the Law of Torts." In *State Supreme Courts: Policymakers in the Federal System*, edited by Mary Cornelia Porter and G. Alan Tarr. Westport: Greenwood Press.

Berry, Kate. 2015. *How Judicial Elections Impact Criminal Cases*. New York: Brennan Center for Justice.

Bonneau, Chris W. 2007. "The Dynamics of Campaign Spending in State Supreme Court Elections." In *Running for Judge: The Rising Political, Financial, and Legal Stakes of Judicial Elections*, edited by Matthew J. Streb. New York: NYU Press.

Bonneau, Chris W. and Damon M. Cann. 2015. *Voters' Verdicts: Citizens, Campaigns, and Institutions in State Supreme Court Elections*. Charlottesville: University of Virginia Press.

Caldarone, Richard P., Brandice Canes-Wrone, and Tom S. Clark. 2009. "Partisan Labels and Democratic Accountability: An Analysis of State Supreme Court Abortion Decisions." *Journal of Politics* 71: 560–573.

Canes-Wrone, Brandice, Tom S. Clark, and Jason P. Kelly 2014. "Judicial Selection and Death Penalty Decisions." *American Political Science Review* 108: 23–39.

Cann, Damon M. 2002. "Campaign Contributions and Judicial Behavior." *American Review of Politics* 23: 261–274.

Cann, Damon M. 2007. "Justice for Sale? Campaign Contributions and Judicial Decisionmaking." *State Politics and Policy Quarterly* 7: 281–297.

Cann, Damon M., Chris W. Bonneau, and Brent D. Boyea. 2012. "Campaign Contributions and Judicial Decisions in Partisan and Nonpartisan Elections." In *New Directions in Judicial Politics*, edited by Kevin T. McGuire. New York: Routledge.

Canon, Bradley C. and Lawrence Baum. 1981. "Patterns of Adoption of Tort Law Innovations: An Application of Diffusion Theory to Judicial Doctrines." *American Political Science Review* 75: 975–987.

*Caperton v. A. T. Massey Coal Co*. 2009. 556 U.S. 868.

Champagne, Anthony. 2005. "Can Business Co-Exist with the Civil Justice System? Tort Reform and Judicial Selection." *Loyola of Los Angeles Law Review* 38: 1483–1515.

Cheek, Kyle and Anthony Champagne. 2005. *Judicial Politics in Texas: Partisanship, Money, and Politics in State Courts*. New York: Peter Lang.

Dubois, Philip L. 1980. *From Ballot to Bench: Judicial Elections and the Quest for Judicial Accountability*. Austin: University of Texas Press.

Gordon, Sanford C. and Gregory A. Huber. 2007. "The Effect of Electoral Competitiveness on Incumbent Behavior." *Quarterly Journal of Political Science* 2: 107–138.

Hall, Matthew E.K. and Jason Harold Windett. 2013. "New Data on State Supreme Court Cases." *State Politics and Policy Quarterly* 13: 427–445.

Hall, Melinda Gann. 1992. "Electoral Politics and Strategic Voting in State Supreme Courts." *Journal of Politics* 54: 427–446.

Hall, Melinda Gann. 1995. "Justices as Representatives: Elections and Judicial Politics in the American States." *American Politics Quarterly* 23: 485–503.

Hall, Melinda Gann. 2015. *Attacking Judges: How Campaign Advertising Influences State Supreme Court Elections*. Stanford: Stanford University Press.

Huber, Gregory A. and Sanford C. Gordon. 2004. "Accountability and Coercion: Is Justice Blind When it Runs for Office?" *American Journal of Political Science* 48: 247–263.

Klumpp, Albert J. 2011. "Judicial Primary Elections in Cook County, Illinois: Fear the Irish Women!" *DePaul Law Review* 60: 821–847.

Kritzer, Herbert M. 2015. *Justices on the Ballot: Continuity and Change in State Supreme Court Elections*. New York: Cambridge.

*People v. McGraw*. 2009. 484 Mich. 120.

*People v. Plunkett*. 2010. 485 Mich. 50.

Pinello, Daniel R. 1999. "Linking Party to Judicial Ideology in American Courts: A Meta-Analysis." *Justice System Journal* 20: 219–254.

Reidinger, Paul. 1987, "The Politics of Judging." *ABA Journal* 73: 52–58.

Rutledge, Jesse, ed. 2008. *The New Politics of Judicial Elections in the Great Lakes States*. Washington, DC: Justice at Stake Campaign.

Sample, James, Adam Skaggs, Jonathan Blitzer, Linda Casey, and Charles Hall. 2010. *The New Politics of Judicial Elections 2000–2009*. Washington, DC: Justice at Stake Campaign.

Segal, Jeffrey A. 1985. "Measuring Change on the Supreme Court: Examining Alternative Models." *American Journal of Political Science* 29: 461–479.

Segal, Jeffrey A. and Harold J. Spaeth. 2002. *The Supreme Court and the Attitudinal Model Revisited*. New York: Cambridge.

Shepherd, Joanna M. 2009a. "Are Appointed Judges Strategic Too?" *Duke Law Journal* 58: 1589–1626.

Shepherd, Joanna M. 2009b. "The Influence of Retention Politics on Judges' Voting." *Journal of Legal Studies* 38: 169–208.

Theriault, Sean M. 2008. *Party Polarization in Congress*. New York: Cambridge University Press.

Ware, Stephen J. 1999. "Money, Politics and Judicial Decisions: A Case Study of Arbitration Law in Alabama." *Journal of Law and Politics* 15: 645–686.

Wold, John T. and John H. Culver. 1987. "The Defeat of the California Justices: The Campaign, the Electorate, and the Issue of Judicial Accountability." *Judicature* 70: 348–355.

Wolf, Richard. 2016. "Samuel Alito Makes His Mark on Supreme Court: After 10 Years, Conservative Justice Earns Respect." *USA Today*, February 12, 2016.

# 11

# JUDICIAL ELECTIONS AND SUPPORT FOR STATE COURTS

*Michael J. Nelson*

We are regularly warned that judicial elections put the legitimacy of state courts in peril. Judicial reform groups claim that exposure to vigorous campaigns will subtract from citizens' support for these institutions and "threaten … the promise of equal justice for all" (Greytak et al. 2015, 1).[1] For example, the Defense Research Institute warned in 2008 that "no one can dispute that the rise of attack advertising of judicial elections and the growth of special interest spending from all sides of the political spectrum is threatening to seriously erode the public's confidence in the judiciary" (Trimble 2008). Legal analyst and Brennan Center fellow Andrew Cohen warned in 2013 that "the very existence of [judicial elections] undermine[s] confidence in the impartiality of the judiciary." U.S. Supreme Court justices have joined the chorus, with Sandra Day O'Connor regularly speaking out about judicial elections (Liptak 2010), and Sonia Sotomayor writing that partisan elections have "cast … a cloud of illegitimacy over the criminal justice system" in Alabama (*Woodward v. Alabama*). The claim is simple: judicial elections pose a grave threat to the legitimacy of state courts.[2]

Obviously, the presence of a strong negative relationship between the use of judicial elections and public support for state supreme courts would constitute a serious reason to reconsider states' widespread use of these institutions to select and retain their jurists. Legitimacy is a fundamental component of any political institution, but it is particularly important to courts because they lack both the power of the purse and the ability to implement their own decisions. Without a store of legitimacy, courts risk non-implementation of their decisions and threats to their membership and structure. In short, they risk impotence (Gibson and Nelson 2015).

Yet this bleak position is not unchallenged. Because they allow voters to select directly their representatives, elections are also legitimacy enhancing (Gibson

2012).[3] As such, judicial elections may actually increase the esteem in which state supreme courts are held because they move the process of judicial selection into the public eye and tie the public directly to the institution through the electoral connection. Similarly, although the tone of some judicial campaigns may be negative, scholarly research on judicial campaigns has demonstrated that the same negative advertising that worries reformers may actually inform voters and improve their support for democracy (Brooks and Geer 2007). Thus, other research suggests that judicial elections may actually benefit state courts.

Fortunately, scholars have developed reliable and valid measures of judicial legitimacy that they draw upon to assess the extent to which (and when) either of these theoretical positions has merit. Scholars have taken up this challenge, producing an impressive body of scholarship over the past decade aimed at understanding the causes and consequences of public support for state supreme courts. The purpose of this chapter is to compare the evidence for these two positions, relying on a variety of observational and experimental evidence. The conclusion is clear: while some components of vigorous campaigning may reduce the esteem in which state supreme courts are held, judicial elections are, on balance, legitimacy-enhancing institutions.

## What is Legitimacy?

Scholars generally agree on the contours of legitimacy theory.[4] Legitimacy is a fundamental property of political institutions that enables them to make decisions that will be respected with neither fear of reprisal nor noncompliance. More formally, it is:

> [A] psychological property of an authority, institution, or social arrangement that leads those connected to it to believe that it is appropriate, proper and just. Because of legitimacy, people feel that they out to defer to decisions and rules, following them voluntarily out of obligation rather than out of fear of punishment or anticipation of reward (Tyler 2006, 375).

Scholars refer to legitimacy with a number of synonyms, including institutional loyalty and diffuse support (Gibson and Caldeira 1992). Legitimacy leads individuals to acquiesce to decisions made by an individual or an institution—even those with which that individual may disagree—because they believe they ought to, rather than because they believe that they will suffer adverse consequences for noncompliance. Put differently, legitimacy is a "reservoir of goodwill" that enables institutions to issue displeasing decisions without adverse consequences.

Legitimacy is different than performance satisfaction (often referred to as *specific support*). Whereas performance satisfaction often fluctuates and reflects short-term support, legitimacy represents a long-term commitment to an institution. Indeed, legitimacy theory suggests that performance satisfaction and legitimacy should not be correlated too strongly (Gibson and Nelson 2015). Whereas repeated displeasing decisions over a long period of time may detract from legitimacy, scholars generally agree that, even in the face of a short-term decrease in support, legitimacy gradually regenerates in the face of a momentary dip in support and typically remains stable over time (Caldeira and Gibson 1992). As such, an institution's legitimacy is generally robust to a handful of displeasing decisions (c.f. Bartels and Johnston 2013; Gibson and Nelson 2015).

Repeated studies have found that the U.S. Supreme Court's reservoir of goodwill is a deep one. Gibson (2007) compared the legitimacy of national high courts across the world and found that "in comparison to other national high courts, the U.S. Supreme Court enjoys an extraordinarily wide and deep 'reservoir of goodwill'—only a handful of institutions has support percentages approaching those of the American court" (522). Research indicates that state supreme courts have similarly high levels of public support. Kelleher and Wolak (2007), relying on data from the 1998 General Social Survey, find that support for the leaders of "state and community courts" is higher than support for state legislatures but was basically the same as support for the leadership of the U.S. Supreme Court; and while 73 percent of respondents had at least some confidence in the leadership of state and community courts, 76 percent of respondents had at least that level of confidence in the leadership of the U.S. Supreme Court. Thus, the American judiciary is held in high regard, both in comparison with other American political institutions and when compared to other courts worldwide.

## The Determinants of Support for State Courts

Whereas comparisons between institutions are instructive, the real question is whether citizens in states with elected judges judge their courts to be less legitimate than do citizens in states that do not use elections. Evidence on this point is mixed. Nownes and Glennon's (2016) experimental data reveal that judicial appointment systems are associated with lower levels of legitimacy. At the same time, Cann and Yates (2016) find a strong, statistically significant, and negative relationship between the use of judicial elections and the legitimacy of state supreme courts, although they (2008) find that the use of partisan and nonpartisan elections only has consequences on the legitimacy judgments of individuals with low levels of political information. Finally, although they study confidence in the state judiciary rather than legitimacy, Kelleher and Wolak (2007) find no relationship between the use of judicial elections and citizens' confidence in their state courts. Thus, prior research presents a mixed portrait of the overall relationship between support for state courts and judicial elections.

I assess the differences in citizens' perceptions of the legitimacy of their state supreme courts by relying on a survey commissioned by National Center for State Courts (NCSC) in February and March 2009 to examine Americans' attitudes toward interbranch relations.[5] The survey of 1,200 Americans includes data about the perceived legitimacy of state supreme courts.[6]

The most common way to measure legitimacy is to ask survey respondents whether they agree or disagree with a series of statements about an institution and then combine the answers into a composite measure of legitimacy (Caldeira and Gibson 1992). For example, respondents might be queried about their agreement with statements like "If the Supreme Court started making a lot of rulings that most Americans disagreed with, it might be better to do away with the Court altogether" or "The U.S. Supreme Court gets too mixed up in politics." Individuals who believe that the Court should not be eliminated and is not too mixed up in politics are those who ascribe high levels of legitimacy to the institution; at the other end of the spectrum, those who believe the Court should be eliminated under certain conditions and is too mixed up in politics are rated as having low levels of legitimacy (Caldeira and Gibson 1992).

When asking about the legitimacy of judicial institutions, most surveys ask respondents to rate their level of agreement with a series of statements, but the NCSC survey asks respondents to select between two opposing statements (or, implicitly, to select neither) rather than asking respondents to rate their level of agreement. The statements (and the percentage of respondents selecting them) were:[7]

- "The decisions of the state courts are too often mixed up in politics" (59%) vs. "The state courts generally put politics aside in making their decisions" (34%).
- "The state supreme court should not be able to decide as many controversial issues as it does now" (23%) vs. "It's important for the state supreme court to maintain its ability to decide such issues" (71%).
- "It's important for judges on the state supreme court to be independent and not too influenced by what others think" (45%) vs. "It's better for judges to be less independent and pay more attention to what the people think" (51%).

I use the number of replies supportive of the institution as the measure of legitimacy. The responses are fairly well distributed, with about one-third of respondents selecting one supportive reply, one-third of respondents selecting two supportive replies, and the final one-third of respondents selecting either all three supportive replies or no supportive reply. Because the dependent variable is ordinal, I use ordered logistic regression to estimate the model.

The key independent variable in the model is whether the respondent is from a state that elects its judges. Interestingly, only half of respondents (51%) were aware of how their state supreme court judges were retained.[8] This suggests that, even when judicial elections are used in a state, a surprisingly large segment of the public is unaware of their use. I use the actual measure of judicial retention rather than the respondent's perceived method of judicial selection because the goal of the analysis is to compare the views of who live in states that elect their judges with those who do not.

Of course, many other factors might affect perceptions of legitimacy. First, scholars have long argued that increased political sophistication—especially political knowledge—is associated with more support for courts (Gibson and Caldeira 2009; McKenzie and Unger 2011). The measure of political knowledge is the count of correct answers to three questions: whether respondents know the judiciary is a branch of state government, whether respondents know that states have state constitutions, and whether respondents know that state courts can invalidate a law passed by the state legislature. I also include four-point measures of education and attention to state politics, where higher values indicate more sophistication for both measures.

Second, scholars routinely include a variety of respondent-level demographic and political characteristics in models of support for courts (e.g., Gibson and Nelson 2015). Thus, I include variables to indicate whether the respondent is female, black, or Hispanic, the respondent's age (measured in six categories), and her partisanship.

Third, models of public support generally include some measure of satisfaction with the performance of the institution and measures of support for democracy writ large. Unfortunately, the NCSC survey does not contain questions regarding these concepts. I include the closest surrogate included in the survey, approval of the performance of the governor. The measure is dichotomous and indicates whether or not the respondent approves of the governor's performance.

Finally, I include measures of experience with courts, on the theory that such first-hand experience provides strong exposure to the symbols of judicial authority, which activate preexisting support for courts (Gibson, Lodge, and Woodson 2014). Estimates of the effects of first-hand experience with courts on support for these institutions have been mixed. Wenzel et al. (2003) find that experience as a defendant in a trial is associated with decreased confidence in the court, whereas they find some evidence that experience as a juror or a witness is associated with increased confidence in local courts. Benesh and Howell (2001) find that Louisianans who were litigants in a case had lower support for the Louisiana state court system than those who had been witnesses or jurors. To this end, respondents were asked about their past experience with courts, and I include a categorical variable that indicates whether the respondent has been selected to be on a jury, has been called (but not selected) for jury duty, or has been a party to a case. No first-hand experience with courts is the baseline category.

The results of the model are shown in Table 11.1. The most obvious conclusion is that citizens living in states that elect their judges tend to report that their courts have *more* legitimacy than those who do not. Indeed, a modal respondent in an elective state is about 10 percent more likely agree with all of the legitimacy-enhancing statements than one who does not live in an elective state.

Other findings from past studies hold. The strong relationship between political sophistication and support is present in Table 11.1, with more political knowledge translating into more legitimacy for state courts; education and political

**TABLE 11.1** The Determinants of the Legitimacy of State Courts

| | |
|---|---|
| State Uses Judicial Elections | 0.43* |
| | (0.18) |
| *Experience* | |
| Called (but not selected) for Jury Duty | –0.34 |
| | (0.19) |
| Selected for Jury Duty | –0.23 |
| | (0.23) |
| Party to a Case | –0.65* |
| | (0.21) |
| Attention to State Politics | –0.13 |
| | (0.11) |
| Gubernatorial Approval | 0.47* |
| | (0.16) |
| Political Knowledge | 0.28* |
| | (0.08) |
| Education | 0.13 |
| | (0.09) |
| Female | –0.14 |
| | (0.16) |
| Age | 0.03 |
| | (0.05) |
| Black | –0.20 |
| | (0.24) |
| Hispanic | 0.11 |
| | (0.28) |
| Income | 0.21* |
| | (0.07) |
| Democrat | 0.14 |
| | (0.18) |
| Republican | –0.26 |
| | (0.20) |
| Log pseudolikelihood | –2835.79 |
| N | 824 |

*Notes*: Coefficients are from an ordinal logistic regression model; higher values of the outcome variable indicate more support for state courts. Standard errors are in parentheses, and * indicates significance at $p<0.05$. Cutpoints are omitted.

attentiveness have a positive relationship with legitimacy. Demographic variables, as is typical (Gibson and Nelson 2015), tend not to affect legitimacy. Finally, there is some evidence that direct experiences affect legitimacy, with individuals who have been parties to a court case ascribing less legitimacy to their state courts. A modal individual who has been a party to a case is about 14 percent less likely to agree with all four legitimacy statements than one who has no experience with his state courts.

## Campaigns and Legitimacy

The discussion to this point has treated judicial elections as homogeneous. Yet, the experience with judicial elections in the United States is a diverse one, with electoral institutions and the vigor of campaigns varying across states and over time (Bonneau and Hall 2009; Bonneau and Cann 2015; Kritzer 2015). Indeed, a significant body of work based on aggregate data analysis demonstrates that voter participation in judicial elections responds to variation in campaigns, with intense competition and large amounts of spending both relating positively to voter participation in these contests (Bonneau and Hall 2009). Perhaps it is the case that the benefits of elections on the legitimacy of courts vary based upon citizens' experiences with these elections and the intensity of the campaigns that surround these electoral contests, just as they do in the context of voter participation.

Gibson (2008) pioneered a growing literature on the effects of judicial campaigns on the legitimacy of state courts, using survey-based vignettes to investigate the effects of judicial campaigns on the perceived legitimacy of state supreme courts. In these studies, survey respondents were read a brief story about a candidate for judicial office and then asked questions about their perceptions of the legitimacy of the court for which that candidate seeks office. Here is an example of one version of the vignette used in Gibson's (2008) original study of voters in Kentucky:

> Now we would like to tell you a story about a judge whom we will call Judge Anderson. We would like you to imagine that Judge Anderson is running for reelection to his position on the Kentucky Supreme Court. This is the court that sits in Frankfort. Judge Anderson receives campaign contributions – that is, money – from corporations and public interest groups that regularly try cases before his court, the Kentucky Supreme Court. Judge Anderson's campaign broadcasts some ads on television which focus mainly on his views and positions on important legal issues like abortion, lawsuit abuse, and the use of the death penalty in Kentucky. He promises that, if re-elected, he will decide these kinds of cases in the way that most people in Kentucky want them decided. Judge Anderson's campaign ads vigorously attack his opponent, claiming that his opponent is biased in favor of insurance companies and other such businesses, and would therefore not be able to make fair and impartial decisions if elected to the Supreme Court.

Respondents were randomly assigned to hear one of these vignettes. Gibson then compared the perceived legitimacy of the court for respondents based upon the version of the vignette they heard in order to discover whether these features actually harm the legitimacy of state supreme courts. In addition to surveying Kentucky voters, Gibson (2009) replicated the experiment with a nationally representative sample, enabling us to determine the extent to which the opinions of Kentuckians can be generalized to the American public. Below, I discuss the effects of each of the campaign components Gibson analyzed on the legitimacy of state judicial institutions.

## *Policy Positions*

Public pronouncements of policy positions are the first campaign attribute analyzed by Gibson (2008, 2009). Candidates for legislative and executive office have long been expected to state publicly their views on the important public policy issues of the day; basic democratic theory assumes that candidates will work to fulfill their promises once elected. The logic differs, however, when one considers judicial candidates, as ethical obligations for judges historically demanded that they did not state their views publicly. However, in 2002, the U.S. Supreme Court ruled in *Republican Party of Minnesota v. White* that codes of judicial conduct which prohibit judicial candidates from stating their policy positions publicly violate the U.S. Constitution's promise of freedom of speech and are, therefore, unconstitutional. To this end, reform groups fear that public statements of policy positions could harm the legitimacy of state supreme courts by giving the impression that judges are prejudging cases (American Bar Association Commission on the 21st Century Judiciary 2003). As Cohen (2013) makes the argument, "[a]ny judge who has to beg future litigants for votes, or who has to promise her constituents that she will employ a particular doctrine or ideology, is tainted."

However, Gibson's evidence suggests that this fear is overblown: in neither the survey of Kentuckians nor in a national survey of the American people is there any evidence that respondents who learn that the judicial candidate is stating his policy positions are more likely to ascribe lower levels of legitimacy to a state supreme court (Gibson 2008, 2012). These results suggest that fears about the potentially deleterious consequences of the *White* decision are exaggerated. Just as voters expect other candidates for office to state their positions publicly, they do not penalize courts when their judicial candidates do the same.

## *Attack Advertisements*

Attack advertising represents a second feature of campaigns that might be injurious to state supreme courts. Since 2000, the tone of judicial campaigns has changed markedly (Caufield 2007), with negative advertisements increasing over the past two decades. Some fear that exposure to these advertisements hurts support for state courts because they equate judges with ordinary politicians (Trimble 2008). Still, in a strong contrast to claims that state supreme court elections are dominated by highly negative campaigning, Hall (2015) shows that between 2002 and 2008, only about one in five contested elections featured even a single negative advertisement. Hall and Zalewski report similar findings through the 2013 election cycle in Chapter 4 of this volume.

Studies indicate that the effects of television advertising on electoral outcomes are nuanced (Hall 2014, 2015; Hall and Bonneau 2013). In the aggregate, attack advertisements have no effect on the electoral performance of incumbents in partisan elections but have a negative effect on incumbents' electoral success in nonpartisan elections. Hall (2015) reconciles these ballot-type differences by arguing that the removal of party labels from ballots has negative consequences on voter knowledge. Alternatively, attack advertisements have no effect in partisan elections on citizen participation in these races but increase participation in nonpartisan elections (Hall 2015). These results strongly contradict the idea that attacks—and campaign negativity more generally—demobilize voters and delegitimize courts.

Gibson addresses the effects of negative advertisements on legitimacy in his experiment, with some respondents learning that Judge Anderson aired negative advertisements to "vigorously attack his opponent" whereas others heard a version of the vignette in which Judge Anderson did not air negative advertisements. In the Kentucky sample, respondents who learned that Judge Anderson had aired attack advertisements were less likely to ascribe high levels of legitimacy to the Kentucky Supreme Court than those who heard that Judge Anderson did not use attack advertisements (Gibson 2008). However, in the national sample, that effect dissipates, with the legitimacy judgments of those who learned that attack advertisements were used in the campaign no different than those who heard that Judge Anderson had not used attack advertising (Gibson 2009).

At the same time, merely reading about the use of negative advertisements is a weak substitute for exposure to the sensory experience that comes from viewing an advertisement; perhaps if respondents were actually *exposed* to advertisements, these results might change. To this end, Gibson (2012) asked Kentuckians to rate the appropriateness of three actual negative advertisements used in Kentucky judicial elections. Respondents indicated that the majority of campaign advertisements—even those that state policy disagreement between candidates in stark and memorable language—are not inappropriate for use in a judicial election. However, respondents did conclude that some negative advertisements are inappropriate. Gibson concludes that such advertisements are likely those that stray from policy disagreement and instead link judicial candidates to ordinary politicians.

Similarly, Gibson et al. (2011) exposed a sample of Pennsylvanians to an experiment embedded in a three-wave panel survey in the midst of the 2007 Pennsylvania Supreme Court elections. In the second wave of the survey, respondents were randomly assigned to view a set of campaign advertisements. Gibson et al. then assessed whether respondents' change in support for the Pennsylvania Supreme Court over the election cycle was related to the set of advertisements they viewed.[9] They concluded that exposure to negative advertisements was associated with less support for the institution, again drawing a connection between politicization and negative advertisements: "We suspect that the message of most ads is that 'courts are the same as other political institutions,' a message that tarnishes support based on the presumption that the judiciary should be a nonpolitical branch of government" (553). In other words, *viewing* attack advertisements may harm perceptions of judicial legitimacy.

Thus, the effects of negative advertisements on legitimacy are nuanced. First, merely hearing that negative advertisements have been employed in a judicial campaign is not necessarily associated with a decrease in support for the institution. Second, citizens broadly accept the use of negative advertisements in judicial elections, with citizens only judging advertisements that compare judges to "normal" politicians as unfit for use in a judicial campaign. Third, actual exposure to negative advertisements is associated with a dip in support for courts, although that decrease in support is likely not outweighed by the positive benefits of elections overall.

### Campaign Contributions

Campaign contributions are the final feature of judicial campaigns assessed by Gibson. The concerns about campaign contributions again stem from the normative ideal that judges should assess each case individually and on its merits. If campaign contributors appear before judges, they may feel beholden to those contributors and therefore become more likely to rule in favor of their donors.[10] Hence, the fear is that campaign contributions harm the legitimacy of state supreme courts by making judges beholden to lawyers and/or litigants that appear before them. The Florida Supreme Court made this claim implicitly, upholding that a ban on direct solicitations of donors by judicial candidates was justified because there is "a compelling state interest in preserving the integrity of [its] judiciary and maintaining the public's confidence in an impartial judiciary" (*Williams-Yulee v. The Florida Bar* 384; see Bonneau and Redman 2015).

This concern is borne out in Gibson's data. In both the Kentucky and the national samples, hearing that Judge Anderson had accepted campaign contributions is associated with a decrease in support for the Kentucky Supreme Court (Gibson 2008, 2009). Moreover, in their national survey of the American people, Cann and Yates (2008) find that citizens who report being concerned about campaign contributions have lower levels of diffuse support for their state supreme court. Thus, the evidence that campaign contributions detract from the legitimacy of state supreme courts is both present and robust.

## Assessing the Consequences

Gibson's work on the legitimacy of state supreme courts indicates that policy pronouncements do not harm judicial institutions, actual exposure to television advertisements may have some negative effect on the legitimacy of state supreme courts, and campaign contributions are associated with a decrease in support for state supreme courts. Exactly how harmful are the consequences of these campaign attributes on overall support for state supreme courts? Assessing the consequences of judicial elections requires us to consider four factors that contextualize the extent of these effects.

## Judicial Recusal

If campaign contributions detract from legitimacy because of an implied quid-pro-quo relationship between a donor and a judge, a reasonable policy solution might be to require judges to recuse themselves from cases in which a donor is involved. Indeed, the potential legitimacy-rejuvenating effects of judicial recusal came before the U.S. Supreme Court in a 2009 case, *Caperton v. Massey*. The case concerned the failure of a state supreme court justice to recuse himself in a case involving a donor who spent several million dollars independently of the candidates. The Court ruled that the Fourteenth Amendment's Due Process Clause requires judicial recusal when there is an unconstitutional probability of bias, not just when actual bias has been demonstrated. The assumption, of course, is that the legitimacy of the court is saved when a justice recuses himself.

This is a testable proposition. Gibson and Caldeira (2012; 2013) investigated the extent to which judicial recusal can resolve the link between campaign contributions and decreased judicial legitimacy. Again relying on a survey experiment in which respondents were given a short vignette, Gibson and Caldeira (2013) asked respondents about the legitimacy of their state supreme court in a situation modeled after the *Caperton* case, experimentally varying whether the justice recused himself. The results of the study indicate that recusal is preferable to no recusal from the standpoint of maintaining the court's legitimacy, though recusal is not a panacea. The broader consequences of these studies are stark: recusal is not a cure-all for these deleterious consequences of judicial elections, and citizens' perceptions of judicial legitimacy are difficult to change.

## Cross-Institutional Comparisons

These campaign features discussed so far are common features of *any* type of election; they are not unique to judicial elections in particular. Thus, an obvious question to ask is the extent to which the deleterious consequences of judicial elections are unique to *judicial* elections rather than a consequence of elections more generally. If the effects of judicial elections are similar to those for legislative and executive elections—the sorts of contests that face much less normative scrutiny—then many of the concerns about the effects of judicial elections might be mitigated.

Luckily, Gibson's research does just this, comparing the extent to which these same three features—policy pronouncements, attack advertisements, and campaign contributions—also impugn the legitimacy of state legislators. Gibson's (2009) analysis reveals that interesting differences emerge across institutions in a nationally representative sample, with campaign contributions harming both the legitimacy of courts and the state legislatures. However, attack advertisements subtract from legislative legitimacy (while having no effect on judicial legitimacy), and there is some evidence that campaign promises actually *increase* legislative legitimacy. In short, the fact that campaign activity may detract from institutional legitimacy is not a quirk of judicial elections; rather, campaigns affect public support for institutions more generally.

## *Citizens' Expectations*

Finally, objections to judicial elections are often based on an implicit assumption that all individuals believe that judges decide cases on the basis of the law rather than on any preexisting ideological view. This assumption is at odds with a bevy of social scientific research on judging, which has demonstrated that, whereas law can constrain judges in some circumstances, appellate judges often decide cases in ways that accord with their own ideological views (Segal and Spaeth 2002).

Yet, this assumption is not borne out by empirical evidence. Gibson's (2012) survey of Kentucky citizens revealed that 44 percent of Kentuckians believed that a "good" supreme court justice should give their ideology a voice in their decisions, and nearly 20 percent said that a good justice should base their decisions on their party affiliations. As Gibson puts it, "some citizens expect the judiciary to make ideologically based decisions, [and] those citizens are unlikely to be put off when judges express ideological views during the selection process" (95). Indeed, Gibson goes on to show that citizens who hold politicized expectations of courts are less affected by negative campaign advertisements than those who hold more legalistic expectations of judges. In short, public preferences about the bases of judicial decisions are not as monolithic as many assume; these expectations color individuals' evaluations of judicial decisions. Where campaigns may have deleterious effects, those are likely seen only among part of the population: those who hold legalistic views of courts (Gibson 2012).

## *Net Effects*

Whereas some aspects of judicial campaigns, particularly those relating to campaign finance, may decrease public support for judicial institutions, Gibson et al. (2011) implore us to remember that, on balance, elections in general—and judicial elections in particular—have legitimacy *enhancing* effects. As a result, the deleterious effects of some aspects of campaigns may be canceled out (or surpassed) by the legitimacy bump that comes by binding voters to an institution through the electoral connection. Thus, a fair comparison to make is whether the benefits of judicial elections and the electoral process on the legitimacy of state supreme courts outweigh the negative aspects of judicial campaigns.

Gibson et al. (2011) make this comparison, assessing the overall effects of the Pennsylvania election against the deleterious effects of the negative advertisements to which respondents were exposed. They conclude that "[r]espondents... expressed more support for the Pennsylvania Supreme Court after the election than before, but those not exposed to politicized content via the experiment increased their court support the most" (552). In other words, whereas exposure to the negative advertisements did detract from support for the Court, the overall election increased support. Gibson (2012) reaches the same conclusion. In short, the net effects of judicial elections appear to be positive.

## Conclusion

Thus, the empirical evidence is fairly clear: the use of judicial elections is not causing a legitimacy crisis for state supreme courts. Whereas the legitimacy of state judicial institutions may be harmed by specific aspects of judicial campaigns, the good that comes by involving the public in the process of judicial selection and retention appears to outweigh the negative aspects of campaigning. This is the same conclusion suggested by the empirical analysis that opened this chapter, which revealed that, on balance, citizens in states that use judicial elections have more support for their state courts than those who live in states that do not use judicial elections. Taken together, this evidence suggests that, on the whole, judicial elections are actually legitimacy-enhancing institutions.

This conclusion is further bolstered by the immense amount of scholarship which has examined voter behavior and candidate success in judicial elections. If judicial elections were truly harmful to the legitimacy of judicial institutions, we should expect to see more vigorous electoral campaigns associated with voter disengagement. Yet, this is not the case. Indeed, voter participation in judicial elections is actually *enhanced* by electoral competition and increased campaign spending (Bonneau and Hall 2009), whereas attack advertising does not lead to less voter participation; on the contrary, it *increases* it in some circumstances (Hall 2015).

This is not to say that judicial elections have no negative consequences for public perceptions. Indeed, the research is clear that some aspects of judicial campaigns negatively affect public support, just as it is clear that these effects are more likely to be felt among some citizens more than others. Whereas the aggregate effects of judicial elections do appear to be positive, the research on this point is not unanimous (Cann and Yates 2016; Benesh 2006), and it is likely that, even where judicial elections have positive consequences, those consequences are not the same for all elections and on all citizens. More research is needed on this front.

The most glaring omission in our understanding of the effects of judicial elections on support for state courts concerns the longer-term consequences of these elections on support for the institutions. As vigorous campaigning becomes more and more common, it might be the case that voters will become acclimatized to campaign practices, and some of the negative consequences of judicial elections will become so commonplace as to not be consequential. At the same time, repeated campaigning may inspire more vigorous campaigning, of the sort that Gibson (2012) warns "crosses the line" and therefore leads to deleterious effects on legitimacy. Only time will tell whether repeated exposure to the trappings of these intense campaigns continues to have the same positive net effects that the research currently indicates.

## Notes

1 These concerns are not limited to the United States. When Bolivia became the first country in the modern era to employ judicial elections to staff its federal high courts, it banned judicial candidates from campaigning entirely, relying instead on a state-run media campaign to inform voters (Driscoll and Nelson 2012).

2 As discussed below, political scientists have pushed back forcefully against this claim (Bonneau and Hall 2009; Gibson 2012).
3 Indeed, the Bolivians adopted judicial elections in an attempt to *enhance* the legitimacy of their courts, though that effort was not entirely successful (Driscoll and Nelson 2015).
4 For reviews of legitimacy theory, see Gibson and Nelson (2014) and Tyler (2006).
5 The survey of a nationally representative sample of Americans in the continental U.S. was conducted by Princeton Survey Research Associates International from February 17 to March 8, 2009. The sample included both landlines and cell phones. The response rate for landlines was 18.7 percent; for cell phones it was 16.2 percent.
6 The survey also included a measure of confidence in state courts (rather than confidence in the "courts in your community" used in Benesh's (2006) well-known study). Only 22 percent of respondents reported having either "not too much" or "no" confidence in their state courts, while 22 percent of respondents reported having "a lot of confidence" in the state courts. Research indicates that a person's level of confidence in an institution is related to the level of legitimacy she ascribes to the institution, but the two are not the same: judgments about institutional confidence reflect a blend of long-term and short-term support for an institution, whereas legitimacy is a long-term commitment to an institution (Gibson, Caldeira, and Spence 2003a). Empirically, the survey supports the notion that legitimacy and confidence are separate concepts; their correlation is only $r = 0.29$. Additionally, replicating the model in Table 11.1 with confidence as the dependent variable reveals no evidence that citizens in states that elect their judges, on average, have a different level of confidence than those in states that use appointment systems. Moreover, additional analysis reveals that the Benesh (2006) finding that partisan elections are associated with decreased confidence does not hold in this survey.
7 The NCSC survey contains another statement, of the kind criticized by Gibson and Nelson (2015): "The state courts can usually be trusted to make decisions that are right for the state as a whole" (42%) vs. "The state courts often don't give enough consideration to what's right for the state as a whole" (49%). Gibson et al. (2011) note that "trust" questions may induce measurement error in measures of legitimacy by contaminating the measure with some specific support variance, so this item is not included in the measure of legitimacy. Including this additional measure does not change the substantive results presented here.
8 Question wording may explain part of this low percentage. Respondents were asked "As far as you know, are the judges on your state supreme court elected by the voters, or not?" I code states as electing judges if they use judicial elections for either selection *or* retention; some respondents may have read this question as asking about only judicial *selection* and therefore gave a wrong answer.
9 The advertisements from this study can be viewed online at http://mjnelson.org/campaignads.html.
10 Individuals may donate to campaigns for various reasons, and an implied quid-pro-quo relationship is only one of those reasons. For example, individuals may donate to candidates who are ideological allies, meaning that an observed vote in favor of the donor is caused by their shared ideological or policy stance rather than by a quid-pro-quo relationship created by the donation (Bonica 2013).

## References

American Bar Association Commission on the 21st Century Judiciary. 2003. *Justice in Jeopardy*. Chicago, IL: American Bar Association.

Bartels, Brandon L. and Christopher D. Johnston. 2013. "On the Ideological Foundations of Supreme Court Legitimacy in the American Public." *American Journal of Political Science* 57: 184–199.

Benesh, Sara C. 2006. "Understanding Public Confidence in American Courts." *Journal of Politics* 68: 697–707.

Benesh, Sara C. and Susan E. Howell. 2001. "Confidence in the Courts: A Comparison of Users and Non-Users." *Behavioral Sciences and the Law* 19: 199–214.

Bonica, Adam. 2013. "Ideology and Interests in the Political Marketplace." *American Journal of Political Science* 57: 294–311.

Bonneau, Chris W. and Damon M. Cann. 2015. *Voters' Verdicts: Citizens, Campaigns, and Institutions in State Supreme Court Elections*. Charlottesville: University of Virginia Press.

Bonneau, Chris W. and Melinda Gann Hall. 2009. *In Defense of Judicial Elections*. New York: Routledge.

Bonneau, Chris W. and Shane M. Redman. 2015. "Much Ado About Nothing: The Irrelevance of *Williams-Yulee v. The Florida Bar* on the Conduct of Judicial Elections." *Vanderbilt Law Review En Banc* 68: 31–41.

Brooks, Deborah and John G. Geer. 2007. "Beyond Negativity: The Effects of Incivility on the Electorate." *American Journal of Political Science* 51: 1–16.

Caldeira, Gregory A. and James L. Gibson. 1992. "The Etiology of Public Support for the Supreme Court." *American Journal of Political Science* 36: 635–664.

Cann, Damon M. and Jeff Yates. 2008. "Homegrown Institutional Legitimacy: Assessing Citizens' Diffuse Support for State Courts." *American Politics Research* 36: 297–329.

Cann, Damon M. and Jeff Yates. 2016. *These Estimable Courts: Understanding Public Perceptions of State Judicial Institutions and Legal Policy-Making*. New York, NY: Oxford University Press.

*Caperton v. A.T. Massey Coal Co.* 2009. 566 U.S. 868.

Caufield, Rachel P. 2007. "Campaigning for Judge: How the Tone and Tenor of Judicial Election Campaigns is Changing." In *Running for Judge: The Rising Political, Financial, and Legal Stakes of Judicial Elections*, edited by Matthew J. Streb. New York: NYU Press.

Cohen, Andrew. 2013. "Politics, not Justice, in Alabama Death Penalty Cases." *Los Angeles Times*, December 4, 2013.

Driscoll, Amanda and Michael J. Nelson. 2012. "The 2011 Judicial Elections in Bolivia." *Electoral Studies* 31: 628–639.

Driscoll, Amanda and Michael J. Nelson. 2015. "Judicial Selection and the Democratization of Justice: Lessons from the Bolivian Judicial Elections." *Journal of Law and Courts* 3: 115–148.

Gibson, James L. 2007. "The Legitimacy of the U.S. Supreme Court in a Polarized Polity." *Journal of Empirical Legal Studies* 4: 507–538.

Gibson, James L. 2008. "Challenges to the Impartiality of State Supreme Courts: Legitimacy Theory and 'New-Style' Judicial Campaigns." *American Political Science Review* 102: 59–75.

Gibson, James L. 2009. "'New-Style' Judicial Campaigns and the Legitimacy of State High Courts." *Journal of Politics* 71: 1285–1304.

Gibson, James L. 2012. *Electing Judges: The Surprising Effects of Campaigning on Judicial Legitimacy*. Chicago: University of Chicago Press.

Gibson, James L. and Gregory A. Caldeira. 1992. "Blacks and the United States Supreme Court: Models of Diffuse Support." *Journal of Politics* 54: 1120–1145.

Gibson, James L. and Gregory A. Caldeira. 2009. *Citizens, Courts, and Confirmations: Positivity Theory and the Judgments of the American People*. Princeton: Princeton University Press.

Gibson, James L. and Gregory A. Caldeira. 2012. "Campaign Support, Conflicts of Interest, and Judicial Impartiality: Can the Legitimacy of Courts Be Rescued by Recusals?" *Journal of Politics* 74: 18–34.

Gibson, James L. and Gregory A. Caldeira. 2013. "Judicial Impartiality, Campaign Contributions, and Recusals: Results from a National Survey." *Journal of Empirical Legal Studies* 10: 76–103.

Gibson, James L. and Michael J. Nelson. 2014. "The Legitimacy of the U.S. Supreme Court: Conventional Wisdoms, and Recent Challenges Thereto." *Annual Review of Law and Social Science* 10: 201–219.

Gibson, James L. and Michael J. Nelson. 2015. "Is the U.S. Supreme Court's Legitimacy Grounded in Performance Satisfaction and Ideology?" *American Journal of Political Science* 59: 162–174.

Gibson, James L., Gregory A. Caldeira, and Lester Kenyatta Spence. 2003a. "Measuring Attitudes toward the United States Supreme Court." *American Journal of Political Science* 47: 354–367.

Gibson, James L., Jeffrey A. Gottfried, Michael X. Delli Carpini, and Kathleen Hall Jamieson. 2011. "The Effects of Judicial Campaign Activity on the Legitimacy of Courts: A Survey-based Experiment." *Political Research Quarterly* 64: 545–558.

Gibson, James L., Milton Lodge, and Benjamin Woodson. 2014. "Losing, but Accepting: Legitimacy, Positivity Theory, and the Symbols of Judicial Authority." *Law and Society Review* 48: 837–866.

Greytak, Scott, Alicia Bannon, Allyse Falce, and Linda Casey. 2015. *Bankrolling the Bench: The New Politics of Judicial Elections, 2013–14.* Washington, DC: Justice at Stake Campaign.

Hall, Melinda Gann. 2014. "Televised Attacks and the Incumbency Advantage in State Supreme Courts." *Journal of Law, Economics, and Organization* 30: 138–164.

Hall, Melinda Gann. 2015. *Attacking Judges: How Campaign Advertising Influences State Supreme Court Elections*. Stanford: Stanford University Press.

Hall, Melinda Gann and Chris W. Bonneau. 2013. "Attack Advertising, the *White* Decision, and Voter Participation in State Supreme Court Elections." *Political Research Quarterly* 66: 115–126.

Kelleher, Christine A. and Jennifer Wolak. 2007. "Explaining Public Confidence in the Branches of State Government." *Political Research Quarterly* 60: 707–721.

Kritzer, Herbert M. 2015. *Justices on the Ballot: Continuity and Change in State Supreme Court Elections*. New York: Cambridge University Press.

Liptak, Adam. 2010. "Former Justice O'Connor Sees Ill in Election Finance Ruling." *New York Times* January 27, 2010.

McKenzie, Mark Jonathan and Michael A. Unger. 2011. "'New Style' Campaigning, Citizen Knowledge, and Sources of Legitimacy for State Courts: A Case Study in Texas." *Politics and Policy* 39: 813–834.

Nownes, Anthony J. and Colin Glennon. 2016. "An Experimental Investigation of How Judicial Elections Affect Public Faith in the Judicial System." *Law and Social Inquiry* 41: 37–60.

*Republican Party of Minnesota v. White*. 2002. 536 U.S. 765.

Segal, Jeffrey A. and Harold J. Spaeth 2002. *The Supreme Court and the Attitudinal Model Revisited*. New York: Cambridge University Press.

Trimble, John C. 2008. "Judicial Election Season: The Public is Losing Confidence." *DRIToday* Oct. 6. Available at: www.forthedefense.org/post/Judicial-Election-Season-The-Public-is-Losing-Confidence.aspx [Accessed 15 Dec. 2015].

Tyler, Tom R. 2006. "Psychological Perspectives on Legitimacy and Legitimation." *Annual Review of Psychology* 57: 375–400.

Wenzel, James P., Shaun Bowler, and David J. Lanoue. 2003. "The Sources of Public Confidence in State Courts: Experience and Institutions." *American Politics Research* 31: 191–211.

*Williams-Yulee v. The Florida Bar*. 2014. 138 So. 3d 379.

*Woodward v. Alabama*, cert. denied. 2013. No. 13–5380.

# 12

# ELECTIONS AND JUDICIAL DIVERSITY

*Drew Noble Lanier and Mark S. Hurwitz*

"Take a look at the appointments I have made … I have appointed as many African Americans to the circuit court as any president ever, more African-American women on federal courts than any other president, more Hispanics, more Asian Americans, more LGBT judges than any president in history. We actually now have a majority of women and/or minorities on the circuit courts, something that has never happened before. So, my record of appointing a judiciary that reflects the country is unmatched."

**President Barack Obama**, defending his appointment of Judge Merrick Garland, a white male, to replace Justice Scalia on the U. S. Supreme Court (Totenberg 2016).

"I believe that diversity of experience matters. It matters that someone has represented someone other than corporate clients. That they've had real experience with people who can't afford lawyers, that they've had real experience trying to fight for the public interest, that they've had real experience doing something other than representing corporate clients."

**Senator Elizabeth Warren** (D-MA), criticizing President Obama's nominations to the federal courts, even though his appointments have been the most diverse in history from racial and gender perspectives (Ruger 2014).

"Justice O' Connor has often been cited as saying that a wise old man and wise old woman will reach the same conclusion in deciding cases … I am also not so sure that I agree with the statement. First … there can never be a universal definition of wise. Second, I would hope that a wise Latina woman with the richness of her experiences would more often than not reach a better conclusion than a white male who hasn't lived that life."

**Justice Sonia Sotomayor**, speaking at the 2001 Judge Mario G. Olmos Memorial Lecture, University of California, Berkeley, School of Law, comments she later repudiated during her Supreme Court confirmation hearings (Sotomayor 2002).

As the comments above regarding the U.S. Supreme Court suggest, the presence in the judiciary of racial, ethnic, and other minorities, who collectively comprise a majority of the United States population, provides enormous symbolic—and no doubt political—import to a vital branch of government. Indeed, in the wake of the sudden death of Justice Antonin Scalia, beyond the issues of whether President Obama should have nominated anyone or whether the Senate should take up the nomination, several persons called on the President to nominate someone who is "diverse" (e.g., McGregor 2016). In fact, Justice Scalia was the Court's first justice of Italian-American descent. Nonetheless, President Obama has nominated Merrick Garland, who does not enhance the diversity of the nation's highest court.

Representative diversity is critical in American politics but may be especially so for the federal courts given that the judiciary is constitutionally designed to be the least popularly accountable branch of the federal government. In fact, when analyzing questions of diversity within courts, analysts typically have focused on the U.S. Supreme Court as it is the ultimate arbiter of constitutionality within the American judiciary. Much of the established literature on the federal bench also has focused on questions of race, gender, and to some extent religious diversity, as those are perennial cleavages within American politics (e.g., Fridkin and Kenney 2014; Hero 2007). Nevertheless, diversity as a concept is broader than issues of race, ethnicity, gender, and religion, as Senator Warren's comments disclose.

What about the state courts, which are not nearly as isolated as the federal bench given that many state judges must face competitive elections or reappointment by governors or legislatures? State courts have the potential to be much more representative due to their institutional design, which is very different from the federal court model. Thus, we ask in this chapter, as in our previous work, whether selection and retention mechanisms in the states influence diversity. Specifically, do judicial elections produce less diverse benches than other systems of selection and retention, such as elite appointments or the Missouri Plan? Are the resultant outcomes of diversity different based on race, ethnicity, or gender?

To address these questions, we examine the composition of state appellate courts and also compare courts of last resort and intermediate appellate courts, which have very different functions. These courts also represent widely varying selection systems, thereby providing a unique window into diversity across contexts. By comparing the relative proportion of women and minorities who have become appellate judges between types of appellate courts and across selection systems, we seek to identify the incidence of political minorities (i.e., all racial and ethnic minorities and women of any race or ethnicity) who have reached appellate benches in the states, their relative success in attaining those posts via differing selection methods, and the changes in both phenomena from the final stages of the twentieth century to the early years of the twenty-first century.

## Expectations on Diversity and Judicial Elections

The presence in the judiciary of political minorities, who collectively comprise a majority of the larger population, provides enormous symbolic and political import to a vital branch of government. Over the final quarter of the twentieth century, numerous efforts were made to increase the number and proportion of women and minority judges on both the state and federal courts (e.g., Goldman 1997; Graham 2004; Haire and Moyer 2015; Hurwitz and Lanier 2001; Slotnick 1988). Contemporaneously, there was a reform movement in the states toward greater use of the Missouri Plan, termed "merit selection" by its advocates (Glick and Emmert 1987; Hurwitz and Lanier 2008). Currently, the Missouri Plan ranks at the top with nonpartisan elections as the single most popular method of selection and retention in the states.

The need for research on the issue of representation remains compelling, in part because some scholars have argued that the goals of judicial diversity and reform may conflict. As Glick and Emmert (1997), Ifill (2000), and others have declared, the Missouri Plan may be problematic for non-traditional judges because these potential jurists are not part of the status quo and may not have the same experiences or opportunities as other judicial candidates, which decreases their chances being of selected. Consequently, these scholars argue that the Missouri Plan may diminish diversity on the appellate bench. Yet, others contend that elections do not produce diverse outcomes in either the judicial or legislative branches.

This issue of representation on the bench is important because judicial diversity may have substantial consequences for state judiciaries and the political system. There may be systematic, empirically discernible differences in decision making between judges of non-traditional backgrounds and their traditional counterparts (Boyd, Epstein, and Martin 2010; Haire and Moyer 2015). Whether or not diversity influences decision making on the bench, the issue of judicial legitimacy is critical (Gibson 2012). In fact, it is argued that legitimacy may be enhanced by non-traditional judges, as their decisions are more infused with "traditionally excluded perspectives," and their presence enhances the appearance of impartiality for litigants who appear before the court and for the public at large (Ifill 2000; Johnson and Fuentes-Rohwer 2004, 9). Others contend that diversity increases the efficacy of the decision-making process in several contexts (Page 2007). Again, diversity on courts matters.

The number of states employing a sundry of selection systems and their potential effect on the advancement of women and minorities to judicial positions at the appellate level also justifies an analysis of the relationship between selection and retention methods, including competitive judicial elections and consequent levels of diversity in state courts. This is especially true today, given the greater attention to diversity and affirmative action in general, with states such as Michigan and California, among others, adopting policies limiting the use of racial and gender preferences in government (and the U.S. Supreme Court's decision permitting these states to move away from preferences based on representative diversity (*Schuette v. BAMN* (2014)).

## State Appellate Diversity and Judicial Elections

In order to understand how judicial elections may or may not affect diversity, we must compare and contrast attendant diversity among the various selection and retention systems. Consequently, we collected data on the racial, ethnic, and gender composition of all courts of last resort and intermediate appeals courts for each of the fifty states for three annual cross-sections: 1985, 1999, and 2005. Our protocol for collecting data for judicial characteristics (Hurwitz and Lanier 2001, 2003, 2008) involved reviewing state and federal court websites and telephoning clerks of court to complete and verify information.[1]

We begin by looking three decades ago, during a time when rates of non-traditional judges were just beginning to increase in both state and federal courts (Haire and Moyer 2015; Hurwitz and Lanier 2008). Consequently, in 1985 there were few women and minorities on state appellate courts, which is reflected in the data presented in Table 12.1. We refer to women and minorities collectively as "non-traditional judges" so as to distinguish them from white male judges, who made up the vast majority of state court judges at the time. As Table 12.1 shows, about 13 percent of all state court appellate judges were non-traditional judges, whereas about 87 percent were white males.

When the data for non-traditional judges are disaggregated by race, ethnicity, and gender, it is clear that few of these judges served on any state appellate bench in 1985. Racial and ethnic minorities made up fewer than seven percent of appellate judges in 1985, a rate similar for females of any race. Of the 1,060 appellate judges at the time, only five were minority females. About 4 percent of judges were African-American males, whereas less than 1 percent were African-American females. Hispanic and Asian/Pacific Islander males made up about 1 percent of state judges at the time. There were no Hispanic or Asian/Pacific Islander females on state appellate courts during this time period.

Table 12.1 also provides information about diversity and judicial selection systems. In 1985, 10 percent of non-traditional judges had reached the bench via competitive elections, a figure statistically significantly lower than the mean but nearly identical to judges who reached the bench via the Missouri Plan. The reason that these results for elections and the Missouri Plan are statistically significant is because of the rate at which governors and legislatures appointed non-traditional judges, as 20 percent of those who reached the bench via elite nomination

**TABLE 12.1** Representation of Female and Minority Judges in State Appellate Courts by Selection and Retention Mechanism and Level of Court, 1985

| | *Total* | *Judicial Election* | *Missouri Plan* | *Elite Nomination* | *Court of Last Resort* | *Intermediate Appellate Court* |
|---|---|---|---|---|---|---|
| Females and Minorities | 13.2% | 10.0%* | 10.7%* | 20.1%* | 12.4% | 13.7% |
| (Non-traditional Judges) | (140) | (55) | (28) | (31) | (43) | (97) |
| Minorities | 6.5% | 4.9% | 4.2%* | 8.4%* | 5.8% | 6.9% |
| (Males and Females) | (69) | (27) | (11) | (13) | (20) | (49) |
| Females | 6.8% | 5.3% | 6.5% | 10.4%* | 7.2% | 6.6% |
| (Any Race) | (72) | (29) | (17) | (16) | (25) | (47) |
| Minority | 0.5% | 0.2% | 0%* | 1.3%* | 0.6% | 0.4% |
| Females | (5) | (1) | (0) | (2) | (2) | (3) |
| African-American | 4.1% | 3.1% | 3.5% | 4.6% | 3.2% | 4.5% |
| Males | (43) | (17) | (9) | (7) | (11) | (32) |
| African-American | 0.5% | 0.2% | 0%* | 1.3%* | 0.6% | 0.4% |
| Females | (5) | (1) | (0) | (2) | (2) | (3) |
| Hispanic | 1.2% | 1.6% | 0.8% | 1.3% | 0.9% | 1.4% |
| Males | (13) | (9) | (2) | (2) | (3) | (10) |
| Hispanic | 0% | 0% | 0% | 0% | 0% | 0% |
| Females | (0) | (0) | (0) | (0) | (0) | (0) |
| Asian/Pacific Island | 0.8% | 0%* | 0% | 1.3%* | 1.2% | 0.6 |
| Males | (8) | (0) | (0) | (2) | (4) | (4) |
| Asian/Pacific Island | 0% | 0% | 0% | 0% | 0% | 0% |
| Females | (0) | (0) | (0) | (0) | (0) | (0) |
| Total Judges | 1060 | 550 | 262 | 154 | 347 | 708 |

***Explanatory Notes:*** An * represents a significant difference from the overall mean at the 0.05 level or better ($p < 0.05$, two-tailed test).

Reading vertically, the first number in each cell represents the percentage within that category as compared to the appropriate total, while the number in parentheses is the actual number of non-traditional judges.

Elite Nomination includes both gubernatorial appointment and legislative selection.

were women or minorities. Thus, the data show that judicial elections were a negative influence on judicial diversity in 1985.

Competitive elections proved to be similar to other methods of selection and retention when it came to representation on the bench for specific non-traditional judges in 1985. For example, the roughly 5 percent of female judges who reached the bench via competitive elections was not significantly different from the overall rate of 7 percent females in 1985. For the most part, this pattern continued for other groups, particularly with respect to rates of diversity being similar for both elections and the Missouri Plan, whereas elite nomination proved to be the most successful path for judges other than white males. Finally, rates of diversity were about the same for state supreme courts and intermediate appellate courts.

As Table 12.2 provides, what a difference a bit over a decade makes. By 1999, the rate of non-traditional judges had climbed to 27 percent, which is double the analogous rate for 1985. Rates of increase were seen mostly across the board for all types of non-traditional judges, particularly female judges. This is likely because women cover a larger part of the political spectrum than racial and ethnic minorities, providing women with broader opportunities to reach the bench (Bratton and Spill 2002; Hurwitz and Lanier 2003). Women also constitute a larger proportion of the population than racial and ethnic minorities. Nevertheless, while the increase of women on the bench was clear, the rate at which females constituted the state appellate bench in 1999 was only 21 percent, certainly well under the 50 percent aspirational figure preferred by many based on the proportion of women in the population. To reiterate, representation on the bench by non-traditional judges was much higher in 1999 than in 1985. Moreover, increases were seen in every sub-category of non-traditional judges, including women, African-Americans, Hispanics, and Asian/Pacific Islanders. Interestingly, the rates of diversity were significantly higher in state supreme courts compared to intermediate appellate courts, a result driven largely by female representation on state courts of last resort.

What about diversity and competitive elections? Recall that, in 1985, diversity stemming from elections fell significantly below the rate at which judges reached the bench through elite nomination, although it was about the same as that for the Missouri Plan. By the end of the twentieth century, times had changed and so had the rate of diversity as a result of elections. As Table 12.2 illustrates, the overall rate of non-traditional judges who reached the bench via competitive elections in 1999 was about 27 percent, which was nearly identical to the overall mean diversity rate and only a percentage point below that for elite nomination. That is, the data show that representation on the bench stemming from competitive elections was no different than for other mechanisms of judicial selection. When the rate of diversity from judicial elections was statistically different from the overall rate for sub-categories of non-traditional judges, it was because judicial elections produced a higher rate of diversity, as evidenced by the results for minority females and African-American female judges specifically. However, there were no judges of

**TABLE 12.2** Representation of Female and Minority Judges in State Appellate Courts by Selection and Retention Mechanism and Level of Court, 1999

| | *Total* | *Judicial Election* | *Missouri Plan* | *Elite Nomination* | *Court of Last Resort* | *Intermediate Appellate Court* |
|---|---|---|---|---|---|---|
| Females and Minorities | 27.1% | 26.8% | 24.9% | 28.2% | 30.8%* | 25.7% |
| (Non-traditional Judges) | (341) | (187) | (92) | (51) | (108) | (233) |
| Minorities | 7.3% | 7.2% | 5.7%* | 8.3% | 7.1% | 7.4% |
| (Males and Females) | (92) | (50) | (21) | (15) | (25) | (67) |
| Females | 21.1% | 5.3% | 19.5% | 20.44% | 24.8%* | 17.74% |
| (Any Race) | (266) | (29) | (72) | (37) | (87) | (179) |
| Minority | 1.35% | 2.0%* | 0.3%* | 0.6%* | 1.1% | 1.4% |
| Females | (17) | (14) | (1) | (1) | (4) | (13) |
| African-American | 3.7% | 3.9% | 2.4%* | 2.8% | 4.0% | 3.5% |
| Males | (46) | (27) | (9) | (5) | (14) | (32) |
| African-American | 0.8% | 1.4%* | 0%* | 0%* | 0.6% | 0.9% |
| Females | (10) | (10) | (0) | (0) | (2) | (8) |
| Hispanic | 1.7% | 1.3% | 2.4%* | 3.9%* | 0.9%* | 2.0% |
| Males | (21) | (9) | (9) | (7) | (3) | (18) |
| Hispanic | 0.4% | 0.6% | 0%* | 0%* | 0%* | 0.6% |
| Females | (5) | (4) | (0) | (0) | (0) | (5) |
| Asian/Pacific Island | 0.6% | 0%* | 0.5% | 1.1%* | 1.1%* | 0.4 |
| Males | (8) | (0) | (2) | (2) | (4) | (4) |
| Asian/Pacific Island | 0.2% | 0% | 0.3% | 0.6%* | 0.6%* | 0% |
| Females | (2) | (0) | (1) | (1) | (2) | (0) |
| Total Judges | 1258 | 698 | 369 | 181 | 351 | 907 |

***Explanatory Notes:*** An * represents a significant difference from the overall mean at the 0.05 level or better ($p < 0.05$, two-tailed test).
Reading vertically, the first number in each cell represents the percentage within that category as compared to the appropriate total, while the number in parentheses is the actual number of non-traditional judges.
Elite Nomination includes both gubernatorial appointment and legislative selection.

Asian/Pacific Island descent who reached the bench in competitive elections. Also, Hispanic male judges were more likely to be found in a state with the Missouri Plan or elite nomination. Nevertheless, this table shows that by 1999 there was little difference in representation on the bench across the several selection systems.

For our cross-section of data in 2005, Table 12.3 indicates that rates of diversity continued to increase across all of the selection and retention methods. Overall, in 2005 non-traditional judges made up over one-third of state appellate court judges, a figure that was not significantly different among selection systems or between courts of last resort and intermediate appellate courts. Increases also are observed in all sub-categories of non-traditional judges. As for judicial elections, rates of diversity were no different for elected judges than for judges who reached the bench via other methods, save for African-American female judges who were more likely to reach the bench via election, and Hispanic male judges who were somewhat less likely to be elected than otherwise. Still, Table 12.3 demonstrates that by the beginning of the current century, rates of diversity were increasing across the board; however, reaching the bench was neither facilitated nor hindered by any particular selection and retention system, including judicial elections.

## Rates of Change and Judicial Elections

Up to this point, we have described the rates of diversity for several cross-sections of data, both overall and as a function of judicial elections and other selection methods. At this point we illustrate the dynamics involved in the change in rates of diversity over the twenty-year period from 1985 to 2005. In particular, Table 12.4 presents the changes in representation of non-traditional judges from one cross-section to another and overall by selection system.

To begin, when looking at all non-traditional judges, the change from 1985 through 2005 was over 21 percentage points, a change that is both substantively and statistically significant. Moreover, the intermittent changes from 1985 to 1999, and then again from 1999 to 2005, were also significant for non-traditional judges. When we disaggregate this category into women and minority judges, we observe increases in diversity for both categories but at very different rates. For instance, the change for women from 1985 to 2005 was about 20 percentage points, whereas the change for minorities on the bench was five percentage points. Clearly, women were the beneficiaries of additional seats on state appellate benches at much higher rates than minorities.

When we discern diversity of non-traditional judges as a function of judicial elections and other selection and retention mechanisms, we note additional and significant increases in diversity over time. For all non-traditional judges selected by elections, Table 12.4 shows that diversity rates increased 25 percentage points from 1985 to 2005, a statistically significant difference, which was higher than the increase observed for the Missouri Plan or elite nomination. That said, the 22 percentage point increase over time for the Missouri Plan was significant,

**TABLE 12.3** Representation of Female and Minority Judges in State Appellate Courts by Selection and Retention Mechanism and Level of Court, 2005

| | *Total* | *Judicial Election* | *Missouri Plan* | *Elite Nomination* | *Court of Last Resort* | *Intermediate Appellate Court* |
|---|---|---|---|---|---|---|
| Females and Minorities | 34.4% | 35.3% | 33.1% | 35.6% | 36.4% | 33.6% |
| (Non-traditional Judges) | (450) | (212) | (166) | (47) | (130) | (320) |
| Minorities | 11.7% | 11.5% | 13.0% | 9.1% | 12.3% | 11.4% |
| (Males and Females) | (153) | (69) | (65) | (12) | (44) | (109) |
| Females | 26.2% | 28.1% | 23.4%* | 29.6%* | 26.6% | 26.0% |
| (Any Race) | (343) | (169) | (117) | (39) | (95) | (248) |
| Minority | 3.5% | 4.3% | 3.2% | 3.0% | 2.5% | 3.9% |
| Females | (46) | (26) | (16) | (4) | (9) | (37) |
| African-American | 5.1% | 5.3% | 5.4% | 2.3%* | 6.7%* | 4.5% |
| Males | (67) | (32) | (27) | (3) | (24) | (43) |
| African-American | 2.0% | 3.0%* | 1.4% | 0.8%* | 1.4% | 2.2% |
| Females | (26) | (18) | (7) | (1) | (5) | (21) |
| Hispanic | 2.4% | 1.5%* | 3.4%* | 2.3% | 2.2% | 2.4% |
| Males | (31) | (9) | (17) | (3) | (8) | (23) |
| Hispanic | 1.0% | 1.3% | 0.8% | 0.8% | 0.8% | 1.1% |
| Females | (13) | (8) | (4) | (1) | (3) | (10) |
| Asian/Pacific Island | 0.7% | 0.3% | 1.0% | 1.5%* | 0.8% | 0.6% |
| Males | (9) | (2) | (5) | (2) | (3) | (6) |
| Asian/Pacific Island | 0.5% | 0% | 1.0% | 1.5%* | 0.3% | 0.6% |
| Females | (7) | (0) | (5) | (2) | (1) | (6) |
| Total Judges | 1310 | 601 | 501 | 132 | 357 | 953 |

***Explanatory Notes:*** An * represents a significant difference from the overall mean at the 0.05 level or better ($p < 0.05$, two-tailed test).
Reading vertically, the first number in each cell represents the percentage within that category as compared to the appropriate total, while the number in parentheses is the actual number of non-traditional judges.
Elite Nomination includes both gubernatorial appointment and legislative selection.

**TABLE 12.4** Change in Percentages of Female and Minority Judges in State Appellate Courts, 1985–2005

| *Series* | *Change in% from 1985 to 1999* | *Change in% from 1999 to 2005* | *Change in% from 1985 to 2005* |
|---|---|---|---|
| ***All States:*** | | | |
| Non-traditional Judges | 13.9★ | 7.2★ | 21.1★ |
| Female Judges | 14.3★ | 5.0★ | 19.4★ |
| Minority Judges | 0.8 | 4.4★ | 5.2★ |
| ***All Non-traditional Judges:*** | | | |
| Missouri Plan | 14.1★ | 8.3★ | 22.4★ |
| Elite Nomination | 8.1 | 7.4 | 15.5 |
| Judicial Election | 16.8★ | 8.4 | 25.2★ |
| ***Female Judges:*** | | | |
| Missouri Plan | 13.0★ | 3.9★ | 16.8★ |
| Elite Nomination | 10.1 | 9.1 | 19.2★ |
| Judicial Election | 16.4 | 6.5 | 22.8★ |
| ***Minority Judges:*** | | | |
| Missouri Plan | 1.5 | 7.3★ | 8.8★ |
| Elite Nomination | (-0.2) | 0.8 | 0.7 |
| Judicial Election | 2.2 | 4.3★ | 6.6★ |

***Explanatory Notes:*** An ★ represents a significant difference from the overall mean at the 0.05 level or better ($p < 0.05$, two-tailed test).
The number in each cell represents the change in the mean percentage for each series across the relevant time period.

whereas the nearly 16 percentage point increase in elite nomination was not significant. Of course, this is a result in part of the fact that diversity rates were higher in the first place in the elite nomination category than for elections or the Missouri Plan, which serves as a continuing reminder that starting and end points of data matter in analyses of political events such as the ones we examine in this chapter.

Disaggregating non-traditional judges into the sub-categories of women and minorities enables us to see similar increases among selection systems, but again with differences in the percentage change between these groups of non-traditional judges. For instance, female judges saw their diversity rates increase in judicial elections by nearly 23 percentage points over twenty years, a figure higher than that for either the Missouri Plan or elite nomination. However, the rate of increase for minority judges was much lower relative to female judges. In particular, minorities recorded a percentage change from 1985 to 2005 of about seven percentage points, a statistically significant change but less than the rate we observed for the Missouri Plan. The rate of change for minority judges who reached the bench via elite nomination was trivial, barely moving over the twenty-year period observed.

## Conclusion

Our findings suggest a number of important inferences about diversity in state appellate courts. First, and most obviously, judicial diversity is not static. Instead, diversity has been ever increasing through the years, at least since women and minorities first started to reach the bench in more than token numbers (Haire and Moyer 2015; Hurwitz and Lanier 2008). The tables clearly show that judicial diversity has grown over the years for all the sub-categories of political minorities examined in this chapter.

Nevertheless, these upturns have not been uniformly distributed. Diversity has changed at different rates over time, depending upon the specific types of non-traditional judges involved. In particular, women have been the biggest beneficiaries of additional opportunities on state appellate benches. Moreover, white women rather than minority female judges have seen the greatest improvements. As an example, in 1985 there were seventy-two women on state appellate benches, five of whom were minorities. However, by 2005 there were 343 women, forty-six of them minorities. In other words, the rate of increase was much higher for white female judges than for minority women.

Whereas the rates of judicial diversity have increased over the twenty-year period examined, they still remain below the numbers of these political minorities in the overall population and the bar. The fact remains that the highest levels of the legal profession do not yet appear to be fully open to women and minorities who aspire to become state court judges and justices, or at least this was the case as of 2005. Additional work is needed to assess current levels of diversity and whether courts reflect the broader populations they serve. What might explain these disparities? Was there a sense among selectors (including voters) that there had been sufficient gains in diversity such that selecting non-traditional judges is no longer necessary, as has happened in the past (Bratton and Spill 2002; Slotnick 1998)? Or, is it that other factors—demographic, political, or social—continue to hinder the advancement of women and minorities?

Although diversity has been dynamic in state appellate courts, increasing ever-upward from 1985 to 2005 as we would expect, we also need systematic analyses of the factors influencing judicial diversity. Interestingly, while much has been written about how diversity influences judicial decision making (e.g., Boyd, Epstein, and Martin 2010; Haire and Moyer 2015), very little scholarship exists on the influences on judicial diversity (but see our earlier work (Hurwitz and Lanier 2001, 2003, 2008)). These, and other related topics, offer exciting opportunities for future research.

Finally, we return to the question of whether judicial elections inhibit diversity. As we demonstrated, in 1985 non-traditional judges benefited most from elite nomination. This result fits with the theory that elections and the Missouri Plan weaken opportunities for non-traditional judges by prolonging the *status quo*. However, as we showed, this pattern and the conclusions that follow are no longer accurate. By 2005, women and minorities were just as likely to reach the bench via election or the Missouri Plan as they were from elite nomination. Overall, judicial elections produce levels of diversity at similar rates to the other institutions of selection and retention, for both female and minority judges. In sum, concerns about judicial selection systems inhibiting diversity on the state appellate bench are now not necessary. We can affirm from the results just reported that judicial elections do not influence levels of diversity in any direction.

## Note

1 The data and results presented in this chapter were previously reported in Hurwitz and Lanier (2008) and are reproduced here with permission.

## References

Boyd, Christina L., Lee Epstein, and Andrew D. Martin. 2010. "Untangling the Causal Effects of Sex on Judging." *American Journal of Political Science* 54: 389–411.

Bratton, Kathleen A. and Rorie L. Spill. 2002. "Moving Beyond Tokenism: The Effect of Existing Gender Diversity on the Selection of Women in State Supreme Courts." *Social Science Quarterly* 83: 504–518.

Fridkin, Kim L. and Patrick J. Kenney. 2014. *The Changing Face of Representation: The Gender of U.S. Senators and Constituent Communications*. Ann Arbor: University of Michigan Press.

Gibson, James L. 2012. *Electing Judges: The Surprising Effects of Campaigning on Judicial Legitimacy*. Chicago: University of Chicago Press.

Glick, Henry R. and Craig F. Emmert. 1987. "Selection Systems and Judicial Characteristics: The Recruitment of State Supreme Court Judges." *Judicature* 70: 229–235.

Goldman, Sheldon. 1997. *Picking Federal Judges: Lower Court Selection from Roosevelt to Reagan*. New Haven: Yale University Press.

Graham, Barbara Luck. 2004. "Toward an Understanding of Judicial Diversity in State Courts." *Michigan Journal of Race and Law* 10: 153–192.

Haire, Susan B. and Laura P. Moyer. 2015. *Diversity Matters: Judicial Policy Making in the U.S. Courts of Appeals*. Charlottesville: University of Virginia Press.

Hero, Rodney E. 2007. *Racial Diversity and Social Capital: Equality and Community in America*. New York: Cambridge University Press.

Hurwitz, Mark S. and Drew Noble Lanier. 2001. "Women and Minorities on State and Federal Appellate Benches, 1985 and 1999." *Judicature* 85: 84–92.

Hurwitz, Mark S. and Drew Noble Lanier. 2003. "Explaining Judicial Diversity: The Differential Ability of Women and Minorities to Attain Seats on State Supreme and Appellate Courts." *State Politics and Policy Quarterly* 3: 329–352.

Hurwitz, Mark S. and Drew Noble Lanier. 2008. "Diversity in the State and Federal Appellate Courts: Change and Continuity Across 20 Years." *Justice System Journal* 29: 47–70.

Ifill, S.A. 2000. "Racial Diversity on the Bench: Beyond Role Models and Public Confidence." *Washington and Lee Law Review* 57: 405–495.

Johnson, Kevin R. and Luis Fuentes-Rohwer. 2004. "A Principled Approach to the Quest for Racial Diversity on the Judiciary." *Michigan Journal of Race and Law* 10: 5–53.

McGregor, Ruth. 2016. "Diversity in President's SCOTUS Pick." Available at: www.azcentral.com/story/opinion/op-ed/2016/02/26/supreme-court-nomination-diversity/80859310/ (last accessed 03/07/2016).

Page, Scott E. 2007. *The Difference: How the Power of Diversity Creates Better Groups, Firms, Schools, and Societies*. Princeton: Princeton University Press.

Ruger, Todd. 2014. "Obama Criticized for Nominating Mostly Corporate Lawyers." *The National Law Journal*, February 10.

*Schuette v. BAMN*. 2014. 572 U.S. ___.

Slotnick, Elliot E. 1988. "Review Essay on Judicial Recruitment and Selection." *Justice System Journal* 13: 109–124.

Sotomayor, Sonia. 2002. "A Latina Judge's Voice." *Berkeley La Raza Law Journal* 13: 87–93.

Totenberg, Nina. 2016. "President Obama's Interview with NPR's Nina Totenberg." Available at: www.npr.org/2016/03/18/470869897/transcript-and-video-president-obamas-interview-with-nprs-nina-totenberg.

# SECTION 5

# Reforming the Judicial Selection Process

# 13

# PROPOSALS FOR REFORMS

## Successes and Failures

*Chris W. Bonneau and Jenna Becker Kane*

The only constant in state judicial selection is change. This applies to the institution of elections themselves as well as to aspects of the conduct of these elections. Indeed, according to the National Center for State Courts Gavel to Gavel website (www.ncsc.org/gaveltogavel), from 2008–2014, there were almost 1,300 bills introduced in state legislatures that would affect judicial selection in the states and an additional 550 bills introduced that would modify the qualifications of judges and their terms of office. In this chapter, we analyze two states that have successfully revised their method of judicial selection (West Virginia and North Carolina) and two states that attempted to change their selection method but failed (Minnesota and Nevada). Finally, we discuss other proposed reforms percolating in the states.

### Successful Reforms

#### *West Virginia*

West Virginians have been electing their judges in partisan contests since 1862 without attracting any major efforts to reform the state's method of judicial selection. That all changed following a 2004 race for a seat on West Virginia's highest court, which saw an influx of special interest spending in one of the nastiest judicial contests where more than $2 million was spent on television attack advertising alone (Goldberg et al. 2005). The rancorous campaign involved sitting West Virginia Justice Warren McGraw, a Democrat, and Republican challenger Brent Benjamin, a corporate attorney backed by mining and business interests and physicians' groups. In an all-time record for individual contributions in a judicial race, Don Blankenship, chief executive of Massey Energy Co., one of the largest employers in West Virginia, donated more than $2.2 million to the political action committee called "And For the Sake of the Kids" in a successful effort to place Benjamin on the court (Nyden 2004). Justice Benjamin later served as the deciding vote in a 3–2 majority that overturned a $50 million ruling against Blankenship's Massey Energy Co. The U.S. Supreme Court's decision in *Caperton v. Massey* (2009) renewed nationwide scrutiny of West Virginia's judicial elections when the Court ruled that Justice Benjamin violated constitutionally protected due process rights of litigants by failing to recuse himself from the case.[1] Interestingly, another justice on the case (Spike Maynard) vacationed with Blankenship in advance of the court's decision on the case. After photos surfaced showing Maynard and Blankenship together, Maynard recused himself when the case was reheard (Dickerson 2014). These high-profile events prompted two major reforms to West Virginia's courts—a public financing program adopted in 2010 and a switch to nonpartisan elections in 2015.

On March 23, 2010, Governor Joe Manchin III signed House Bill 4130 into law, establishing a public campaign financing program for candidates running for West Virginia's highest court. The law created a pilot program to provide public financing for certified judicial candidates for the West Virginia Supreme Court of Appeals (the state's court of last resort) race in 2012, provided candidates agreed to limitations on private campaign fundraising. Funded primarily through a series of filing fees levied on different types of court filings and attorney fees collected through the state's bar association, the public financing program sought to eliminate the types of conflicts of interest highlighted in the *Caperton* case, attract more qualified candidates, protect the impartiality and integrity of the judiciary, and strengthen public confidence in the courts (West Virginia Legislature 2010). By giving candidates the option of public financing, they are thought to be able to run competitive campaigns without relying on wealthy donors who often have cases coming before the court. Candidates opting into the public financing program are guaranteed $200,000 for contested primary elections, and $350,000 for contested elections, with matching funds based on the amount spent by privately financed candidates (West Virginia Legislature 2010). The law also required candidates to adhere to strict financial disclosure and financial accounting of all expenditures on a monthly basis.

The 2012 election in West Virginia, the first in which public financing was available to high court candidates, included two races for seats on the Supreme Court of Appeals—one vacancy created by the retirement of Justice Thomas McHugh and the other by the expiration of Justice Robin Davis's term. Of the four candidates running for the state's high court, one candidate, Allen H. Loughry II, chose to participate in the public financing program and was able to use it to secure a seat on the West Virginia Supreme Court of Appeals. Despite the limited success of the pilot program in the 2012 race, a key provision was quickly subjected to judicial scrutiny by the West Virginia Supreme Court of Appeals. The pilot program guaranteed publically financed candidates an initial disbursement of $350,000 for the general election with additional government funding up to $700,000 based on the campaign spending of privately financed candidates. In light of the U.S. Supreme Court's ruling in *Arizona Free Enterprise Club's Freedom Club PAC v. Bennett* (2011), the state's highest court ruled that the matching funds provision of West Virginia's pilot program placed a substantial burden on the political speech of privately financed candidates by essentially forcing privately funded candidates to choose between curbing their own campaign spending or exceeding a set spending limit and thereby generating matching government funds for their publically financed opponent.[2]

Despite legal setbacks for West Virginia's public financing pilot program, the program was made a permanent fixture of West Virginia's judicial system with the passage of House Bill 2805, which was signed into law by Governor Earl Tomblin on May 1, 2013. In addition to solidifying the public funding arrangement initiated by the Pilot Program, the new law increased the amounts guaranteed to publicly funded candidates in contested primaries and general elections to $300,000 and $525,000 respectively. The law also injected $400,000 from the state's Purchasing Card Administration Fund to the Supreme Court of Appeals Public Campaign Financing Fund in order to keep the fund solvent for the following election cycle (West Virginia State Legislature 2013).

The second major aspect of West Virginia's recent judicial reform came in March 2015 when the state decided to abandon the partisan election of state judges in lieu of nonpartisan elections. This reform came shortly after Republicans gained control of the West Virginia legislature for the first time since the 1930s and made reforming the judicial system part of their legislative agenda. Despite being part of a larger Republican-led effort to revise tort liability laws in the state, House Bill 2010 was passed with overwhelming bipartisan support. Effective June 8, 2015, HB2010 moved all judicial races in the state to nonpartisan contests, removing party labels from the ballot. In addition to changing the partisan nature of state high court races, HB2010 also established judicial elections by divisions when more than one seat for the same court is involved in a single election and fixed the date of judicial elections to the day of primary elections in the state (West Virginia State Legislature 2015). Proponents of the bill believe the move to nonpartisan elections will help to eliminate the appearance or influence of partisan politics on judicial elections and, in conjunction with the state's public financing program (which has yet to be extended to lower state courts), will help to lessen the influence of money in judicial elections (Dickerson 2015). However, detractors of HB 2010 like the West Virginia Association for Justice believe that nonpartisan elections fail to give voters the information they need to make choices at the voting booth and will serve to attract independent expenditures from special interests in judicial campaigns (Burdette 2015), arguments that have empirical support in the scholarly literature (Bonneau and Cann 2015; Bonneau and Hall 2009).

Recent attempts to reform judicial elections in West Virginia were passed with relative ease. Both public financing and the adoption of nonpartisan rather than partisan judicial elections passed with bipartisan support in the state's legislature. This is most likely a result of the long-running public attention brought to judicial elections as a result of the scandal surrounding Justice Benjamin and multi-million dollar expenditures by Don Blankenship, chief executive of Massey Energy Co. in support of Benjamin's 2004 bid for a seat on West Virginia's highest court and Benjamin's refusal to recuse himself in the *Massey Energy* case.[3] This highly publicized series of events and the U.S. Supreme Court's ruling in *Caperton* (2009) raised serious and widespread political and public scrutiny regarding how judicial elections are conducted in West Virginia, thus providing significant impetus for reform.

## *North Carolina*

North Carolina has been successfully experimenting with various judicial reforms since 2002. After decades of failed attempts to replace partisan elections with a merit-based selection system, North Carolina finally passed the Democratic-sponsored Judicial Campaign Reform Act in 2002. Passage of the reform act altered the method of judicial selection used to elect North Carolina's appellate courts from partisan to nonpartisan elections and created a voluntary public financing system for all judicial elections effective in 2004 (National Center for State Courts 2015). However, in recent years, North Carolina's newly instituted judicial reforms found themselves entangled in partisan politics. The election of Republican Governor Pat McCrory in 2012 ushered in the first era of unified Republican control of North Carolina's government in more than a century; this placed the judicial reforms of the early 2000s squarely in the cross-hairs of a Republican agenda that included repealing the newly instituted system of public financing for judicial candidates and the eventual adoption of uncontested retention elections for state high court judges.

As part of a larger bill enacting voter-identification laws and reforming elections, North Carolina repealed its system of public financing for judicial campaigns on August 12, 2013 (General Assembly of North Carolina 2013). Although only in effect for five election cycles (2004–2012), North Carolina's system of public financing for judicial elections was quite successful. During the years it was in effect, two-thirds of all candidates running for the North Carolina Supreme Court participated in the public financing program for primary and general elections (Greytak et al. 2015). The system also appeared to achieve its goal of limiting the need for judicial candidates to raise outside funds. A recent study by the National Institute on Money in State Politics shows that prior to public financing in North Carolina, private donations accounted for 77 percent of all campaign contributions raised by judicial candidates running for North Carolina's Supreme Court in 2000 and 2002. After public financing was available, that percentage dropped to 40 percent in judicial contests held between 2004 and 2012 (Voss 2014). Many proponents of public financing fear that North Carolina's recent repeal of public financing will re-open the floodgates of special interest spending in an attempt to influence judicial campaigns, a concern that may be warranted based on the recent 2014 contests for North Carolina's Supreme Court.

Although there has been only a single judicial election cycle since the repeal of North Carolina's public financing system, the 2014 race for four seats on the seven-member North Carolina Supreme Court saw record campaign spending. In the 2014 race, candidates raised nearly $4 million, an average of $440,000 per candidate, which is substantially more than was raised the last time four seats were up for election in 2006 (Greytak et al. 2015). Without the public financing system, outside groups flooded the 2014 race for North Carolina's Supreme Court with substantial amounts of money in hopes of altering the ideological balance of the state's highest court. Although judicial contests in North Carolina are nonpartisan, at the time of the 2014 contest, the state high court consisted of five justices with ties to the Republican Party and two with Democratic Party ties. With both of the liberal-leaning justices up for re-election in the 2014 contest, the supreme court contests quickly attracted attention from outside interest groups on both sides of the aisle. In total, these groups spent over $2 million through various political action committees created for the race. The Republican State Leadership Committee was the single largest donor giving $1.3 million to a local group called Justice for All NC, whereas the North Carolina Chamber of Commerce and the North Carolina Judicial Council received contributions from many business and corporate interests to support conservative candidates for the high court races. Democratic candidates received support from outside groups like Progressive Kick IE North Carolina and the North Carolina Chapter of the Sierra Club, which spent thousands on mailers supporting candidates with Democratic ties (Greytak et al. 2015). Ultimately, three of four incumbents won reelection, leaving the North Carolina Supreme Court with a narrow 4–3 conservative majority.

The most recent alteration to North Carolina's judicial system came on June 11, 2015, when Governor McCrory signed House Bill 222 entitled "An Act Allowing Voters to Elect, and then Retain, Justices of the North Carolina Supreme Court for Election." The Act, which passed through the North Carolina General Assembly on a party-line vote, introduced the option of retention elections for Supreme Court justices who have been previously elected by the North Carolina electorate (General Assembly of North Carolina 2015). Under this new selection arrangement, any justice on the North Carolina Supreme Court who has been selected through a single contested election can opt to run in uncontested retention elections in order to secure subsequent terms. Unlike a contested race for reelection, retention elections give voters a yes/no choice regarding whether or not to retain the sitting judge. Like most states that use retention elections to retain judges, candidates seeking retention in North Carolina are required to obtain a majority of affirmative votes in order to remain on the bench. Just eleven days after the Act was signed into law, Justice Robert H. Edmunds, Jr.

filed the necessary paperwork to participate in North Carolina's first retention election, which will occur in November 2016. Republican sponsors of the bill argue that the switch to retention elections will stem the rising tide of money in judicial elections, whereas opponents of the legislation call the new law a transparent attempt to help Justice Edmunds keep his seat in 2016, thereby ensuring a conservative-controlled supreme court in North Carolina well into the future (Legal Monitor Worldwide 2015).

All of North Carolina's recent reforms (post-2002) appear to have been possible because of unified Republican control of the state government. Whereas the state's constitution calls for the use of elections to select judges for the state's trial and appellate courts, the actual design and nature of these elections is set by statute. Recent reforms to eliminate the public financing system for judicial elections and create retention elections for state supreme court justices are all structural alterations to the judicial system that are possible through statute (as was the move from partisan to nonpartisan elections in 2002) without meeting the more stringent institutional requirements of amending the state constitution. With Republicans holding a majority of the state's legislative seats and controlling the governor's mansion, statutory judicial reform is a relatively easy endeavor.

## Failed Reforms

### *Minnesota*

Minnesota is no stranger to judicial elections. The state has been using elections to select its judges since 1857 and there have been nonpartisan contests since 1912 (National Center for State Courts 2015). Unlike West Virginia and North Carolina, Minnesota's judicial elections are relatively inexpensive (Bonneau 2007), attract little outside interest group spending (Goldberg et al.2005), have yet to attract televised campaign advertising (including attack ads and other negative messages) (Hall 2015), and produce little partisan activity (Birk 2011). Despite the rather unremarkable nature of judicial campaigns in Minnesota, the state began flirting with altering its system of judicial selection after the Supreme Court's 2002 decision in *Republican Party of Minnesota v. White* (2002), which struck down state judicial conduct codes prohibiting judicial candidates from announcing views on disputed legal or political issues as unconstitutional restraints on free speech.

The *White* decision and the increasingly rancorous campaign activity in judicial elections in neighboring Wisconsin and Illinois prompted concerns from those in Minnesota's legal community that a vigorous re-examination of the state's nonpartisan judicial selection system was needed (Birk 2011). In response, an independent citizen group called the Citizens Commission for the Preservation of an Impartial Judiciary was formed in 2006 with former Governor Al Quie chairing what would come to be called the Quie Commission (Soule 2008). After a yearlong investigation, the Commission proposed a series of changes to Minnesota's judiciary, which included the elimination of nonpartisan elections for the initial selection of Minnesota judges, calling rather for gubernatorial appointment from candidates nominated by an independent merit selection commission and adoption of retention elections as the means of retaining judges for subsequent terms.

The Quie Commission's proposal to move Minnesota to a merit selection system of judicial selection was met initially with great support from the legal community. A group called Minnesotans for Impartial Courts quickly formed to lobby in support of the Quie Commission's report and the plan drew public support from former Governor Quie, former Chief Justices Blatz, Anderson, and Magnuson, as well as the Minnesota State Bar Association. In 2009, legislation largely modeled after the Quie Commission's report and calling for retention elections was introduced in the Minnesota legislature but failed to reach a full vote by the House or Senate. The Minnesota legislature revisited the Quie Commission's report in 2010 when Representative Steve Simon proposed legislation attempting again to move Minnesota's method of judicial selection from nonpartisan elections to a merit selection system with retention elections. HF224 failed to make it out of committee, whereas its companion bill in the Minnesota Senate, SF70, was voted out of several committees but was never considered by the full Senate before the end of the legislative session (Birk 2011).

Despite legislative defeats, attempts to change the way Minnesotans choose their judges continued, with the most recent public campaign attempt launched in early 2014 by a bipartisan group called the Coalition for Impartial Justice. The group lobbied the state legislature for a constitutional amendment to institute a merit selection system as the state's method of judicial selection but failed to get a public commitment from Democratic-Farmer-Labor Party leaders in the Minnesota legislature (Helgeson 2014). It appears that concern over the need for judicial selection reform exists among many of those in the Minnesota legal community, but that concern has not translated into similar levels of concern among the Minnesota public. According to a statewide public opinion survey, 80 percent of Minnesotans report having a "great deal" or "some" confidence in Minnesota's court system and 77 percent reported having "high confidence" in the Minnesota Supreme Court. In addition, the survey also reveals that 81 percent of Minnesotans believe their judges to be fair and impartial (Minnesota Judicial Branch 2007). Based on these statistics, there appears to be little public perception that the current judicial system in Minnesota is in need of serious reform, a necessary hurdle that any public campaign must mount to secure passage of a constitutional amendment to alter the state's method of judicial selection.

## Nevada

Nevada elects its judges in nonpartisan contests. The state constitution dictates that state judges be selected by popular election, but the nonpartisan nature of judicial contests is designated by statute (National Center for State Courts 2015).

Attempts to reform Nevada's judicial selection system have been ongoing since the 1970s, but much like Minnesota, have failed to gain enough widespread public support to overcome the institutional barriers of public approval needed to ratify a constitutional amendment. Nevada voters turned down constitutional amendments calling for merit selection and retention election of judges in 1972, 1988, and most recently in 2010 (National Center for State Courts 2015).

On November 2, 2010, nearly 58 percent of Nevadan voters rejected the Nevada Judicial Appointment Amendment, also known as Question 1, which would have adopted a so-called merit-based system (also referred to as a commission-based system) of judicial selection rather than the state's nonpartisan elections. The proposed amendment called for the creation of a judicial selection panel charged with the responsibility of vetting candidates for judicial vacancies and making recommendations to the governor. From the panel's recommendations, the governor would appoint a candidate to a judicial position for no more than two years after which voters would decide the judge's fate in a retention election. Under this arrangement, judges would have to achieve at least 55 percent of the affirmative vote to remain in office.

Concern over the cost and contentiousness of judicial campaigns does not appear to be the primary catalyst for Nevada's most recent reform movement. Candidates for the state's high court raised approximately $3.1 million in the 2008 alone, but judicial elections in Nevada have seen comparatively little outside spending on attack advertising orchestrated by outside groups (Sample et al. 2010). Instead, the impetus to abandon the popular election of judges appears to have been prompted by a string of judicial embarrassments in the local courts uncovered and reported by more than two years of investigative journalism. A 2006 *Los Angeles Times* investigation revealed that district court judges in Nevada were raising hundreds of thousands of dollars in campaign contributions for contests in which they were running unopposed (Goodman and Rempel 2006). The investigation showed that some of these contributions were solicited from lawyers and litigants just days before they appeared before the judges in court. With additional articles chronicling instances of improper and downright bizarre behavior by other district judges under investigation by Nevada's Commission on Judicial Discipline, many in the legal community worried that the reputation of Nevada's judiciary was in peril (Powers 2008).

This concern within the legal community was enough to spur bipartisan support in the Nevada legislature to pass a proposed constitutional amendment to move Nevada's system of judicial selection to a commission-based appointment system rather than popular elections. The 2010 campaign to alter Nevada's system of judicial selection was backed by a statewide group called the Nevadans for Qualified Judges, which worked in coordination with the American Judicature Society, retired U.S. Supreme Court Justice Sandra Day O'Connor, and numerous state officials and retired judges to educate and urge voters to adopt the proposed appointment system. However, despite widespread concern in the legal community over the rising costs of judicial elections and the appearance of judicial impropriety created by campaign donations uncovered in the *Los Angeles Times* article, the quest for judicial reform in Nevada failed to generate enough public concern to convince the voting public to relinquish complete electoral control over its judges.

## Assessing Successful Reforms

Every state's path to judicial reform is unique; the cases examined here provide some insight into why some judicial election reforms are successful while others fail. First, transitions from partisan to nonpartisan elective systems appear to face fewer institutional barriers than states seeking to transition from elective systems to commission-based appointment systems. This is most likely a result of how methods of judicial selection are instituted in a given state. Judicial selection methods are usually established in state constitutions, by statute, or a combination of both. Many state constitutions, including all of the states examined here (West Virginia, North Carolina, Minnesota, and Nevada) require constitutional amendments to alter the method of judicial selection if that alteration includes an absolute departure from elections. However, because most constitutions that call for judicial elections fail to specify the partisan nature of these elections, reform efforts to move state selection systems from partisan elections to nonpartisan elections can be accomplished through the legislative process, thereby lessening the institutional barriers to achieve state level judicial reforms. Reform efforts like those in Minnesota and Nevada, which seek to move the state to commission-based appointment systems with retention elections, must be accomplished through amending state constitutions and require some level of statewide voter approval, an increasingly difficult hurdle to surmount.

Moreover, the evidence is clear that voters *like* electing judges. Indeed, surveys of voters routinely demonstrate widespread support for the election of judges. Moving from partisan to nonpartisan elections does not involve the disenfranchisement of voters; they still have the ability to choose from multiple candidates. Moving to retention elections, however, relegates the electorate to a role of ratifying the choices made by others. This is a fundamental change. Given the large number of voters who prefer to elect their judges, it is not surprising that it is easier to change the type of election than to move away from elections altogether.

The difference between success and failure for judicial reform movements also appears to hinge on the presence of political factors that serve to heighten public and political concern over the impact of judicial elections on the independence of the judiciary. These factors, of course, are unique to each state. In West Virginia, concern over the impact of campaign financing and partisan elections on judicial independence came from the political scandal surrounding the *Caperton* (2009) case. In stark contrast, the failed attempts at reform in Minnesota and Nevada highlight that widespread concern over judicial elections must exist among both the public and politicians. Despite the heightened concern that the decision in *Republican Party of Minnesota v. White* (2002) brought nationally to judicial elections, the nonpartisan judicial contests in Minnesota were historically mundane affairs that left the majority of Minnesotans with positive impressions of the judiciary (Minnesota Judicial Branch 2007). While some in the legal community feared that contentious judicial elections flooded by outside spending and attack advertising would diffuse from nearby Wisconsin and Illinois, the typical pattern of relatively restrained judicial contests in Minnesota has continued in the post-*White* era leaving both the public and politicians alike with little sense of urgency regarding alterations to their chosen method of judicial selection. Even a series of investigative reports in Nevada that tarnished the reputation of the judiciary and spurred renewed interest in abandoning nonpartisan elections in favor of a merit selection system failed to raise enough public concern to overcome its penchant for electing judges.

## The Future: More Reforms

Even though most bills introduced to reform the judicial system (and judicial selection specifically) are not successful, there is no indication that the pace of bill introduction is slowing. Indeed, a quick look at legislation introduced at the end of 2015 and beginning of 2016 demonstrates the variety of measures states are currently considering. Note that the list below is limited to issues of judicial selection; many more bills are being considered that address jurisdiction, budgeting, administration, etc.[4]

- New Mexico: a reform to the public funding system that would eliminate the need for seed money and permit certain private campaign contributions.
- South Carolina: a bill to compel the Judicial Nominating Commission (JNC) to release the names of all qualified applicants for a judgeship and not just limit the list to three names. As judges in South Carolina are appointed by the legislature, this change would allow the legislature more latitude in selecting judges because they would not be limited to choosing among three candidates. This bill would also change the selection process for members of the JNC.
- Virginia: the state legislature is considering creating a JNC to help fill vacancies. The members of the JNC would be appointed by the state legislature, although no member of the state legislature would be eligible to serve on it.
- Washington: there are currently competing versions in the state legislature of a forced recusal bill. In the House, the proposed limit is $1,000; however, in the Senate, there is a bill to force recusal if a judge received $50 from a party to a case in the previous three years.[5] Additionally, the state legislature is considering reducing the size of the state supreme court from nine to five, and electing those judges in districts, as opposed to statewide.

- Wisconsin: a bill to require recusal of a judge when a reasonable person could question the judge's impartiality. A separate bill would require a judge to explain in writing why he/she declined to recuse himself/herself within 60 days of the disposition of the case. A third bill would mandate recusal if a judge received $1,000 or more in the past four years from a party to the case. This $1,000 would include more than just direct contributions to the judge; it would also encompass contributions to independent groups who supported the judge or who opposed the judge's opponent.

The above list of reforms is illustrative, not exhaustive. Indeed, given the pace at which reforms to judicial selection are introduced, any comprehensive list would soon be outdated and underinclusive. However, the above examples demonstrate that judicial selection remains an important topic in state legislatures, and the pace of proposals to reform does not appear to be slowing any time soon. That said, it is important to note that extant research has shown that there is very little difference in the types of judges one gets based on method of selection. There are no meaningful differences between judges elected in partisan states, nonpartisan states, or appointed states on such factors as diversity (Hurwitz and Lanier 2008), quality (Choi, Gulati, and Posner 2010), or legitimacy (Gibson 2012). So those advocates of reform may find themselves disappointed when formal institutional changes do not have many observable effects on the nature of judicial selection in their state.

## Notes

1 The facts of the case are more complicated than they first appear. Benjamin voted against Massey's interests in several other cases (over 80 percent of the time in fact), and when the case was reheard in Benjamin's absence, Caperton still lost his appeal.
2 The case was *Allen H. Loughry II v. Natalie E. Tennant, et al.* No. 12–0899 (2012).
3 Justice Benjamin declined to recuse himself in the case because he did not feel that receiving campaign support from a litigant would bias his judicial opinion. The fact that Benjamin voted against Massey over 80 percent of the time indicates that he was willing to vote against the company, even when the financial stakes were high.
4 See http://ncsc.org/sitecore/content/microsites/gavel-to-gavel/home for a comprehensive list.
5 Given the relatively low contribution amount that would trigger recusal, if this bill were passed one would expect to see a lot of recusals. This could have an adverse effect on the efficiency of the court system. Moreover, for a corporation with a large financial stake in an outcome, a $1,000 contribution (not to mention a $50 contribution) to a potentially hostile judge would seem to be money well spent to force that judge off the case.

## References

*Arizona Free Enterprise Club v. Bennett*. 2011. 131 S.Ct. 2806.
Birk, Douglas D. 2011. "Stuck Inside of Minnesota Without Judicial Election Reform Again." *Hamline Journal of Public Law and Policy* 32: 507–561.

Bonneau, Chris W. 2007. "The Dynamics of Campaign Spending in State Supreme Court Elections." In *Running for Judge: The Rising Political, Financial, and Legal Stakes of Judicial Elections*, edited by Matthew J. Streb. New York: New York University Press.

Bonneau, Chris W. and Damon M. Cann. 2015. *Voters' Verdicts: Citizens, Campaigns, and Institutions in State Supreme Court Elections*. Charlottesville: University of Virginia Press.

Bonneau, Chris W. and Melinda Gann Hall. 2009. *In Defense of Judicial Elections*. New York: Routledge.

Burdette, Whitney. 2015. "Judicial Elections Bill Incites Disputes: Measures Aims to Remove Partisan Politics from State's Court Races." *Charleston Daily Mail*, April 8, 2015.

*Caperton v. A. T. Massey, Co.*. 2009. 556 U.S. 868.

Choi, Stephen J., G. Mitu Gulati, and Eric A. Posner. 2010. "Professionals or Politicians: The Uncertain Empirical Case for an Elected Rather than Appointed Judiciary." *Journal of Law, Economics, and Organization* 26: 290–336.

Dickerson, Chris. 2014. "Former Justice Spike Maynard Dies." *West Virginia Record*, May 2, 2014.

Dickerson, Chris. 2015. "Groups Debate Non-Partisan Judicial Elections." *West Virginia Record*, April 14, 2015.

General Assembly of North Carolina. 2013. "Session Law 2013–381 House Bill 589."

General Assembly of North Carolina. 2015. "Session Law 2015–66 House Bill 222."

Gibson, James L. 2012. *Electing Judges: The Surprising Effects of Campaigning on Judicial Legitimacy*. Chicago: University of Chicago Press.

Goldberg, Deborah, Sarah Samis, Edwin Bender, and Rachel Weiss. 2005. *The New Politics of Judicial Elections*. Washington, DC: Justice at Stake.

Goodman, Michael J. and William C. Rempel. 2006. "In Las Vegas, They're Playing with a Stacked Judicial Deck." *Los Angeles Times*, June 8, 2006.

Greytak, Scott, Alicia Bannon, Allyse Falce, and Linda Casey. 2015. *Bankrolling the Bench: The New Politics of Judicial Elections 2013–2014*. Washington, DC: Justice at Stake.

Hall, Melinda Gann. 2015. *Attacking Judges: How Campaign Advertising Influences State Supreme Court Elections*. Stanford: Stanford University Press.

Helgeson, Baird. 2014. "Group Pushes Constitutional Amendment to Change Minnesota Judicial Elections." *Star Tribune*, February 26, 2014.

Hurwitz, Mark S. and Drew Noble Lanier. 2008. "Diversity in States and Federal Appellate Courts: Change and Continuity Across 20 Years." *Justice System Journal* 29: 47–70.

Legal Monitor Worldwide. 2015. "North Carolina Judge Edmunds to Run in Up-or-Down Vote for Re-election." *Legal Monitor Worldwide*, July 2, 2015.

Minnesota Judicial Branch. 2007. *The Minnesota Difference: The Minnesota Court System and the Public*. Available at: www.mncourts.gov/mncourtsgov/media/assets/documents/reports/Minnesota_Courts_Final_Report_FINAL.pdf ; www.mncourts.gov/documents/0/Public/Court_Information_Office/Minnesota_Courts_Final_Report-FINAL.doc.

National Center for State Courts. 2015. *Judicial Selection in the States*. Available at: www.judicialselection.us/.

Nyden, Paul J. 2004. "Massey CEO's Political Donations Questioned." *Charleston Gazette*, October 21, 2004.

Powers, Ashley. 2008. "Las Vegas Judge Courts Trouble with her Actions." *Los Angeles Times*, March 31, 2008.

*Republican Party of Minnesota v. White*. 2002. 536 U.S. 765.

Sample, James, Adam Skaggs, Jonathan Blitzer, and Linda Casey, 2010. *The New Politics of Judicial Elections 2000–2009: Decade of Change*. Washington, DC: Justice at Stake Campaign.

Soule, George W. 2008. "The Threats of Partisanship to Minnesota's Judicial Elections." *William Mitchell Law Review* 34: 701–728.

Voss, Gus. 2014. *Stark Contrasts: The Effects of Public Campaign Funds on North Carolina Supreme Court Races*. Helena: National Institute on Money in State Politics.

West Virginia State Legislature. 2010. "House Bill 4130, Creating the West Virginia Supreme Court of Appeals Public Campaign Financing Pilot Program."

West Virginia State Legislature. 2013. "House Bill 2805, Making the West Virginia Supreme Court of Appeals Public Campaign Financing Pilot Program a Permanent Program."

West Virginia State Legislature. 2015. "House Bill 2010, Requiring the Elections of Justice of the West Virginia Supreme Court of Appeals, Circuit Court Judges, Family Court Judges, and Magistrates be Nonpartisan and by Division."

# 14

# TOWARD A MORE SOPHISTICATED UNDERSTANDING OF CONTEMPORARY JUDICIAL ELECTIONS

*Melinda Gann Hall and Chris W. Bonneau*

We began this volume with observations about the intense controversy currently raging in the American states over the practice of electing judges, as well as sharp disagreements about the benefits and disadvantages of any alternatives. Rancorous campaigns that include issue discourse and televised attack advertising designed to disparage judges and their choices, vigorous electoral competition, and issues endemic to campaign fundraising and spending are among the most pressing concerns promoting the fundamental proposition among many in the legal community that the time has come to jettison judicial elections. In the words of the American Bar Association Commission on the 21st Century Judiciary (2003, viii):

> Whatever its historic rationale there can no longer be justification for contested judicial elections accompanied by "attack" media advertising that require infusions of substantial sums of money. These contested elections threaten to poison public trust and confidence in the courts by fostering the perception that judges are less than independent and impartial, that justice is for sale, and that justice is available only to the wealthy, the powerful, or those with partisan influence.

In most ways, the war has already been won against partisan elections, the primary target of judicial reform advocacy since at least the 1960s. As Chapter 1 indicated, only six states presently use partisan elections to select state supreme court justices, and three of these six states conduct retention elections for subsequent terms.

Despite these and other trepidations, thirty-eight states continue to maintain a direct electoral connection between the state court bench and state citizenry, albeit mostly in the form of nonpartisan and retention elections. Perhaps equally remarkable is the fact that only three states utilize appointment plans similar to the federal model of executive nomination, legislative confirmation, and lifetime tenure for judges. Likewise, there has been negligible advocacy to replace any of the state selection schemes, including appointment with fixed terms requiring executive or legislative reappointment, with the federal model. In fact, no state has adopted an appointment plan since 1977 when New York switched from partisan elections to a gubernatorial appointment plan for the high court. In 1960, eleven states utilized judicial appointment plans, and twelve states do so now (M. Hall 2015).

Concomitantly, empirical scholarship on judicial elections has become one of the most exciting and theoretically significant areas of inquiry in political science. Studies of judicial elections are intrinsically valuable in their own right for providing information about how these vital institutions operate in practice. However, theoretically driven empirical research on judicial elections using comparative state research designs also has begun to push theoretical boundaries and bridge subfield divides, resulting in a march toward general theories of politics. Such analyses allow for the testing of hypotheses about the impact of context and other forces operating on the electoral environment and thus inform theories of judicial politics, state politics, and electoral politics while also providing systematic evaluations of the real-world consequences of various institutional reforms by the states. In this regard, there now are rigorous accounts of many of the most important aspects of judicial elections, perhaps best evidenced by the range of topics in this volume.

Relatedly, an extensive body of research has assessed the impact of electoral politics on state supreme court decision making. In the tradition of previous research (e.g., Brace and M. Hall 1993, 1995, 1997; M. Hall 1985, 1987a, 1987b, 1992, 1995; M. Hall and Brace 1989, 1992, 1994, 1996), recent studies have provided accounts of the influence of elections on the justices' decisions on controversial issues such as the death penalty, abortion, and gay rights (e.g., Caldarone, Canes-Wrone, and Clark 2009; Canes-Wrone, Clark, and Kelly 2014; M. Hall 2014a; Lewis, Wood, and Jacobsmeier 2014), criminal cases (e.g., Bonneau and Rice 2009; Savchak and Barghothi 2007), civil litigation between "haves" and "have-nots" (e.g., Brace and M. Hall 2001), docket composition (e.g., Brace and M. Hall 2001; Brace, M. Hall, and Langer 2001; Langer 2002), dissent (e.g., Boyea 2007), judicial review (e.g., Brace, Hall, and Langer 1999, 2001; Langer 2002), the length of judicial tenure (e.g., Boyea 2011; Curry and Hurwitz 2016), the tendency to write separate opinions (e.g., Leonard and Ross 2014), adherence to precedent (e.g., Comparato and McClurg 2007; Hoekstra 2005), and decisions to retire preemptively to avoid electoral defeat (e.g., M. Hall 2001).

This volume reflects these exciting intellectual trends. By focusing on a number of the most significant facets of judicial elections, we have presented the latest empirical evidence about how judicial elections work in practice, for all levels of state judiciaries and all types of judicial elections. In many ways, these results challenge the conventional wisdom about the nature of contemporary judicial elections while raising new issues about the future.

As the preceding chapters reveal in many different ways, the politics of state supreme court elections is complex and dynamic. There is little doubt that some aspects of the electoral environment have changed in recent decades. Among other things, candidate spending in state supreme court elections began to rise in the early 1990s. Fundamental rules shaping the substantive content of the campaign dialogue have changed in some states as the result of the United States Supreme Court's decision in *Republican Party of Minnesota v. White* (2002). Spending independent of judicial candidates by interest groups and other moneyed players has increased, especially in connection with the sponsorship of blistering attack advertising in nonpartisan elections. Political activists are paying greater attention to these races. The U. S. Supreme Court has reshaped campaign finance laws with their controversial decision in *Citizens United v. Federal Election Commission* (2010). Retention elections are now on the political radar as evidenced by the defeats in 2010 of three justices on the Iowa Supreme Court. Television advertising has become the norm in many but not all types of contested races.

With regard to advertising, caution is essential when drawing inferences about attack campaigns in races prior to 2000 (M. Hall 2015). During the 2000 elections, the Campaign Media Analysis Group first started collecting televised advertising in state supreme court races, which may have created the inaccurate impression that derisive attacks are a recent invention (M. Hall 2015). However, intense competition and mudslinging campaigns have been identified as early as the 1890s (K. Hall 1984, 2005), and the Campaign Media Analysis Group missed all of the televised ads from the 1970s (and perhaps earlier) up to 2000. Even so, the trends just mentioned and other transformations in recent decades have understandably raised questions about whether electoral schemes of all sorts have reached their expiration date.

Amid these concerns and the growing body of empirical evidence about contemporary judicial elections, the contributors to this volume have provided the latest evidence about the state of the states on this divisive subject. In many ways, the news in this volume is reassuring, strongly contradicting expectations of a degenerating electoral climate for incumbents, sharp increases in contestation and competition, escalating televised attacks in recent races, and other similar predictions.

Rather than trying to speak on behalf of our contributors by offering general conclusions about how bright or scary the future is, we simply observe that the hyberbolic rhetoric in the judicial selection debate, frequently motivated by professional self-interest,[1] is often inaccurate and counterproductive. Less stridency and greater attention to measured arguments should be the order of the day. In this vein, the results in this volume show that several of the worst fears, especially from the legal community, have not been realized. By some indicators, judicial elections in the most recent election cycles have become *less* noisy, nasty, and costly, which is not a claim that apprehensions about contemporary judicial elections are unwarranted or have been effectively dismissed by the evidence in this volume.

Instead, we highlight several fascinating subjects particularly in need of further investigation, all of which are inspired by these various chapters. First, one of the most intriguing sets of findings in this volume concerns the use of judicial performance evaluations in state retention elections and their impact on the percentage of the affirmative vote received by judges seeking reelection. Both Chapter 6 and Chapter 9 show that negative comments, nonunanimous votes to retain, and the extreme "Do Not Retain" recommendations in judicial performance evaluations all have adverse consequences for the electoral performance of judges. Although these recommendations provide valuable information to voters from experts on the state judiciary, we cannot assume that these reports are objective, especially given compelling research uncovering gender bias in the evaluations (Gill 2014; Gill, Lazos, and Waters 2011).

Thus, it is essential to know more about who constitutes these commissions, their evaluative criteria, and other such information relevant for assessing the objectivity and accuracy of the reports. Whereas it seems unlikely at this point that performance evaluations are the equivalent of attack advertising in contested elections, the possibility nonetheless remains for gendered targeting and other forms of bias from legal elites to shape the election returns.

Another area of inquiry likely to be invaluable substantively and theoretically centers on the nature and consequences of advertising and other campaign rhetoric at all levels of the state judiciary. McKenzie and Rebe take on this intriguing and complex topic in Chapter 8 by evaluating messaging on candidate webpages in contested trial court races. In Chapter 4, Hall and Zalewski describe the tone of all televised messages in state supreme court elections from all sponsors, including candidates, political parties, and interest groups.

These chapters offer significant insights into campaign politics in the judicial context, but these studies represent only the beginning of a scholarly focus on, and systematic analysis of, political communication in judicial elections. To date, we lack knowledge of what happens online other than on candidates' webpages, on radio, in the wide range of print media, by telephone, through mailings, and by direct canvassing efforts, as well as any specific differential impacts (if any) of the various messaging strategies on voters, candidates, and courts. Moving this work beyond its nascent stages holds tremendous potential for understanding linkages between state citizenries and the bench and for informing theories of United States elections, especially in races lacking the partisan cue in which the impact of information is likely to be substantial (M. Hall 2014b; 2015).

Finally, we encourage scholars and judicial reform advocates to move beyond the almost singular focus on judicial elections as a form of selection toward investigations of the operations and consequences of state appointment plans, especially those with renewable terms.[2] Presently, nine states appoint supreme court justices for specific terms of office, which exceeds the number of states using partisan elections. Importantly, preliminary evidence suggests that reappointment practices have profound effects on the fundamental functions of courts. Reappointment requirements impair the exercise of judicial review (Brace, M. Hall, and Langer 1999; Langer 2002), promote judicial deference to executive authority (Johnson 2015), and facilitate strategic voting to avoid reappointment denials (in these scenarios, by deferring to the executive and legislative reappointment authorities) (Shepherd 2009).

Studies of the politics of appointment systems would be valuable and influential in their own right as scientists continue to build a knowledge base about judicial selection in all of its forms and evaluate hypotheses about how alternative institutional arrangements influence the decisions of judges and the operations of courts. From the perspective of judicial reform, pointing out the purported ills of any election system is insufficient for reaching robust conclusions about how best to select judges. The advantages and pitfalls of each system should be taken into account, including strategic voting by appointed justices to forward their own careers, as identified in various research (Brace, M. Hall, and Langer 1999; Johnson 2015; Langer 2002; Shepherd 2009).

As a related matter, integrating studies of judicial decision making across selection systems is essential for making sound inferences about reform. Baum, Gray, and Klein have illustrated in Chapter 10 the pronounced consequences of electoral wins and losses on the subsequent decisions and policy direction of state supreme courts. Although we would all surmise that court membership matters, Baum, Gray, and Klein have devised a method for measuring the effects of alternative officeholders more precisely. Who sits very much matters for the types of decisions ultimately rendered by courts (regardless of the method of selection), and membership change even in a single seat can have transformative effects on state law and politics.

A sizable body of work also has shown that seeking reelection affects the decisions of individual state supreme court justices. For example, state supreme court justices vote strategically to minimize electoral opposition by not voting to reverse death sentences, other things considered (e.g., M. Hall 1987a, 1987b, 1992, 1995, 2014a). These findings are well known in the scholarly and reform literatures and are often used by the legal community as a principal part of the case against judicial elections.

As just mentioned, Shepherd (2009, 1589) found that "in many cases, [supreme court justices] seeking reappointment vote more strategically than judges seeking reelection." Similarly, numerous forms of strategic voting by federal judges have been identified in the scholarly literature, despite the obvious lack of an electoral connection. For instance, United States Courts of Appeals judges vote strategically to enhance their chances of appointment to the Supreme Court during vacancies (Black and Owens 2016). Among other things, judges with the potential to be nominated tend to vote more consistently with the president's preferences and rule in favor of the United States as a party relative to their colleagues unlikely to be considered.

In sum, appellate court judges in the United States, including federal judges, behave strategically in a variety of interesting ways. Both election and appointment systems fail to preempt this fundamental feature of judicial choice. All of this information should be considered in any careful discussion of which selection system should be preferred. From the perspective of science, evaluating judicial behavior within alternative contexts allows us to understand better the incentive structures and internal and external pressures on judges and courts.

## On Normative Inferences from Empirical Data

Although the results and commentary in this volume have significant implications for normative evaluations in the judicial selection debate, we reiterate that this project in no way seeks to constitute an argument for or against the practice of electing judges in the American states.[3] In fact, we know there is little agreement among the authors of this volume on that topic (or on some specific issues between the co-editors, for that matter), and the authors have used their own voices in characterizing their results.

We do caution that discrete empirical findings should not be construed as implicit normative statements for or against a particular selection scheme.[4] For example, the fact that hotly contested races and well-financed campaigns increase voter participation in state supreme court elections is not a tacit or thinly veiled argument about the desirability of intense competition, big spending, or judicial elections. These findings are nothing more than facts to be added to the body of evidence about how judicial selection and retention systems function.[5] Indeed, empirical political science does not typically engage normative questions other than using such propositions to generate testable hypotheses about political phenomena (see, e.g., M. Hall 2015).

Additionally, empirical tests are, by design, quite focused, as with the chapters in this collection. These works typically start with a question, design a means to answer the question by generating relevant information meeting exacting standards for valid inference, and then offer conclusions about the question initially asked. In the case of the judicial selection debate, there simply is no single empirical test for assessing which system is better. Moreover, single studies do not attempt to engage every relevant aspect of a subject. Studies evaluating the impact of campaign advertising on the fundamental features of elections are unlikely to engage in hypothesis testing about judicial decision making.

Finally, we would be remiss not to point out that discrete empirical findings may be subject to multiple alternative normative interpretations. Returning to strategic voting on the death penalty, studies showing that justices in unsafe seats are less likely to reverse death sentences, *ceteris paribus*, could be interpreted as an affront to the rule of law and evidence of the dangers of elections. Indeed, this argument about judges "pandering" to state electorates is prevalent and is viewed by many in the legal community as sufficient for condemning elections. Alternatively, and equally reasonably, this same result could be interpreted as confirming the effectiveness of judicial elections for promoting the rule of law. Fear of electoral reprisal may force liberal justices who oppose the death penalty to comply with state law rather than overturn the proper findings of judges and juries in the absence of legitimate reversible error. After all, the death penalty *is* law in these states, and judges are not empowered to decide controversial cases as their personal preferences dictate.[6]

More broadly, if strategic voting is enough to denounce judicial selection practices associated with such behavior, we are left without any viable options among systems currently operating today. Indeed, research indicates that even the United States Supreme Court, in which reselection concerns and progressive ambition are notably absent, responds to public opinion and the public mood (e.g., Casillas, Enns, and Wohlfarth). In other words, democratic politics also penetrates the nation's most independent court by formal design. Overall, we need to know a great deal more about the intricate relationships between public pressures, judges' preferences, and the rule of law.

## Conclusion

In the end, each system for recruiting and retaining the state court bench has advantages and disadvantages and, in large measure, reflects fundamental beliefs about who should control access to the bench and supervise judicial performance. Even so, knowing more about how all of the various selection systems work and their comparative advantages and disadvantages will facilitate more reasoned decisions about judicial selection, thereby improving the policy decisions of states and elevating the debate currently raging from a crisis-centered frame wracked with stridency to a more measured and rational dialogue.

Of course, ultimately normative preferences at their core are value judgments, and no amount of evidence will alter deep-seated beliefs or preferences. Furthermore, as M. Hall (2011, 2014c) describes, politics and science are quite distinct in their aims and methods. In the battle over staffing state courts, empirical findings that contradict political strategies, goals, and livelihoods are not likely to be acknowledged by many or incorporated into the public dialogue no matter how relevant or compelling. Given the instrumental nature of political action, academic work contradicting other actors' goals is often ignored, dismissed, summarized inaccurately, or even caricatured outside the profession. In short, good lawyering to advocate for a fixed position is sharply incompatible with the principles of science and the search for truth.

In the discipline of political science, studies of state judicial elections have already achieved a great deal in advancing theories of electoral politics and other related concerns. The analytical leverage of comparative state analysis also has helped to bridge disciplinary divides and constitutes the basis for a very bright future for researchers interested in the host of questions endemic to studies of elections and judicial politics. At this point, we simply need to know more. With this volume, we have endeavored to begin to meet this need and sincerely hope our efforts encourage and inspire other scholars to engage in similar pursuits. At a minimum, the chapters in this collection illustrate the myriad questions, interesting methodologies, and theoretical frameworks that can be engaged when evaluating judicial elections or striving to bridge the very wide gap between science and practical politics.

## Notes

1 It is not surprising that the American Bar Association and other organizations in the legal community would prefer selection systems that place lawyers squarely at the center of the process. Commission-retention systems do just that. See M. Hall (2014c) for detailed commentary on this issue.

2 For excellent discussions of the limits of the Missouri Plan, which also has received very little empirical scrutiny, see Dimino (2004, 2005) and Fitzpatrick (2009).

3 Unlike much of mainstream political science, legal advocacy is primarily focused on normative arguments. For a discussion of the persistent gap between empirical political science and the judicial reform community, see M. Hall (2011, 2014c, 2015).

4 Bartels and Bonneau (2014) is an outstanding collection of essays about drawing normative conclusions from empirical research.

5 M. Hall (2016) is an example of how a political scientist might use empirical findings to construct a normative argument. This piece assembles extant evidence to argue that nonpartisan elections are ineffective and should be abandoned. In this essay, the normative stance is both explicit and well defined.

6 To illustrate these concerns, we offer an example. On their webpage *Skewed Justice* (available at: http://skewedjustice.org), Joanna Shepherd and Michael S. Kang, two legal academicians vehemently opposed to judicial elections and funded by the American Constitution Society, claim to show that televised campaign advertising and other forms of spending bias state supreme courts against criminal defendants. Essentially they assert that "[a] large body of empirical evidence now demonstrates that money often manages to buy what it wants in judicial elections," citing their previous research on this issue. Overall, they tout this as the smoking gun for ending judicial elections. However, the same Joanna Shepherd (2009) identified similar behavior in appointment systems with renewable terms, which are exempt from attack advertising, exorbitant campaign spending, and other electioneering. Political science scholarship also has detected strategic behavior of various sorts in the federal courts, including career strategies (e.g., Black and Owens 2016). Moreover, evidence of strategic voting in criminal cases was generated long before the advent of televised advertising or steep campaign spending. The earliest studies (mostly conducted by Melinda Gann Hall) analyzed cases from the early 1980s, and even a sizable portion of the most recent work uses 1990s data. Thus, attributing strategic voting to new trends in modern campaign politics is erroneous, other statistical and inferential problems aside. Importantly, the various Kang and Shepherd statistical analyses, supported by interest group dollars, have not been scrutinized by the peer-review process essential for lending credibility to scientific claims. For a discussion of inferential problems in these types of studies as well as those claiming to show quid-pro-quo relationships between campaign donors and judges, see M. Hall (2016).

## References


American Bar Association Commission on the 21st Century Judiciary. 2003. *Justice in Jeopardy*. Chicago: American Bar Association.

Bartels, Brandon L. and Chris W. Bonneau, editors. 2014. *Making Law and Courts Research Relevant: Normative Implications of Empirical Research*. New York: Routledge.

Black, Ryan C. and Ryan J. Owens. 2016. "Courting the President: How Circuit Court Judges Alter Their Behavior for Promotion to the Supreme Court." *American Journal of Political Science* 60: 30–43.

Bonneau, Chris W. and Heather Marie Rice. 2009. "Impartial Judges? Race, Institutional Context, and U.S. State Supreme Courts." *State Politics and Policy Quarterly* 9: 381–403.

Boyea, Brent D. 2007. "Linking Judicial Selection to Consensus: An Analysis of Ideological Diversity." *American Politics Research* 35: 643–670.

Boyea, Brent D. 2011. "Time Served in State Supreme Courts: Mapping the Determinants of Judicial Seniority." *Justice System Journal* 32: 44–61.

Brace, Paul and Melinda Gann Hall. 1990. "Neo-Institutionalism and Dissent in State Supreme Courts." *Journal of Politics* 52: 54–70.

Brace, Paul and Melinda Gann Hall. 1993. "Integrated Models of Judicial Dissent." *Journal of Politics* 55: 914–935.

Brace, Paul and Melinda Gann Hall. 1995. "Studying Courts Comparatively: The View from the American States." *Political Research Quarterly* 48: 5–29.

Brace, Paul and Melinda Gann Hall. 1997. "The Interplay of Preferences, Case Facts, Context, and Structure in the Politics of Judicial Choice." *Journal of Politics* 59: 1206–1231.

Brace, Paul and Melinda Gann Hall. 2001. " 'Haves' Versus 'Have Nots' in State Supreme Courts: Allocating Docket Space and Wins in Power Asymmetric Cases." *Law and Society Review* 35: 393–413.

Brace, Paul, Melinda Gann Hall, and Laura Langer. 1999. "Judicial Choice and the Politics of Abortion: Institutions, Context, and the Autonomy of Courts." *Albany Law Review* 62: 1265–1303.

Brace, Paul, Melinda Gann Hall, and Laura Langer. 2001. "Placing Courts in State Politics." *State Politics and Policy Quarterly* 1: 81–108.

Caldarone, Richard P., Brandice Canes-Wrone, and Tom S. Clark. 2009. "Partisan Labels and Democratic Accountability: An Analysis of State Supreme Court Abortion Decisions." *Journal of Politics* 71: 560–573.

Canes-Wrone, Brandice, Tom S. Clark, and Jason P. Kelly. 2014. "Judicial Selection and Death Penalty Decisions." *American Political Science Review* 108: 23–39.

Cann, Damon M. and Teena Wilhelm. 2011. "Case Visibility and the Electoral Connection in State Supreme Courts." *American Politics Research* 39: 557–581.

Casillas, Christopher J., Peter K. Enns, and Patrick C. Wohlfarth. 2010. "How Public Opinion Constrains the U.S. Supreme Court." *American Journal of Political Science* 55: 74–88.

*Citizens United v. Federal Election Commission*. 2010. 558 U.S. 310.

Comparato, Scott A. and Scott D. McClurg. 2007. "A Neo-Institutional Explanation of State Supreme Court Responses in Search and Seizure Cases." *American Politics Research* 35: 726–754.

Curry, Todd A. Hurwitz, Mark S. Hurwitz. 2016. "Strategic Retirements of Elected and Appointed Justices: A Hazard Model Approach." *Journal of Politics*: Forthcoming.

Dimino, Michael R. 2004. "Judicial Elections versus Merit Selection: The Futile Quest for a System of 'Merit' Selection." *Albany Law Review* 67: 803–819.

Dimino, Michael R. 2005. "The Worst Way of Selecting Judges – Except All the Others That Have Been Tried." *Northern Kentucky Law Review* 32: 267–304.

Fitzpatrick, Brian T. 2009. "The Politics of Merit Selection." *Missouri Law Review* 74: 675–709.

Gill, Rebecca D. 2014. "Implicit Bias in Judicial Performance Evaluations: We Must Do Better than This." *Justice System Journal* 35: 271–294.

Gill, Rebecca D., Sylvia R. Lazos, and Mallory M. Waters. 2011. "Are Judicial Performance Evaluations Fair to Women and Minorities? A Cautionary Tale from Clark County, Nevada." *Law and Society Review* 45: 731–759.

Hall, Kermit L. 1984. "Progressive Reform and the Decline of Democratic Accountability: The Popular Election of State Supreme Court Judges, 1850–1920." *American Bar Foundation Research Journal* 1984: 345–369.

Hall, Kermit L. 2005. "Judicial Independence and the Majoritarian Difficulty." *Institutions of American Democracy: The Judicial Branch*, edited by Kermit L. Hall and Kevin T. McGuire. New York: Oxford University Press.

Hall, Melinda Gann. 1985. "Docket Control as an Influence on Judicial Voting." *Justice System Journal* 10: 243–255.

Hall, Melinda Gann. 1987a. "Constituent Influence in State Supreme Courts: Conceptual Notes and a Case Study." *Journal of Politics* 49: 1117–1124.

Hall, Melinda Gann. 1987b. "An Examination of Voting Behavior in the Louisiana Supreme Court." *Judicature* 71: 40–46.

Hall, Melinda Gann. 1992. "Electoral Politics and Strategic Voting in State Supreme Courts." *Journal of Politics* 54: 427–446.

Hall, Melinda Gann. 1995. "Justices as Representatives: Elections and Judicial Politics in the American States." *American Politics Quarterly* 23: 485–503.

Hall, Melinda Gann. 2001. "Voluntary Retirements from State Supreme Courts: Assessing Democratic Pressures to Relinquish the Bench." *Journal of Politics* 63: 1112–1140.

Hall, Melinda Gann. 2011. "On the Cataclysm of Judicial Elections and Other Popular Antidemocratic Myths." In *What's Law Got to Do with It? What Judges Do, Why They Do It, and What's at Stake*, edited by Charles Gardner Geyh. Stanford: Stanford University Press.

Hall, Melinda Gann. 2014a. "Representation in State Supreme Courts: Evidence from the Terminal Term." *Political Research Quarterly* 67: 335–346.

Hall, Melinda Gann. 2014b. "Televised Attacks and the Incumbency Advantage in State Supreme Courts." *Journal of Law, Economics, and Organization* 30: 138–164.

Hall, Melinda Gann. 2014c. "Bridging the Gap between Science and Politics: Lessons from the Judicial Elections Controversy." In *Making Law and Courts Research Relevant: Normative Implications of Empirical Research*, edited by Brandon L. Bartels and Chris W. Bonneau. New York: Routledge.

Hall, Melinda Gann. 2015. *Attacking Judges: How Campaign Advertising Influences State Supreme Court Elections*. Stanford: Stanford University Press.

Hall, Melinda Gann. 2016. "Partisanship, Interest Groups, and Attack Advertising in the Post-*White* Era, Or Why Nonpartisan Judicial Elections Really Do Stink." *Journal of Law and Politics* 31: 429–456.

Hall, Melinda Gann and Paul Brace. 1989. "Order in the Courts: A Neo-Institutional Approach to Judicial Consensus." *Western Political Quarterly* 42: 391–407.

Hall, Melinda Gann and Paul Brace. 1992. "Toward an Integrated Model of Judicial Voting Behavior." *American Politics Quarterly* 20: 147–168.

Hall, Melinda Gann and Paul Brace. 1994. "The Vicissitudes of Death by Decree: Forces Influencing Capital Punishment Decision Making in State Supreme Courts." *Social Science Quarterly* 75: 136–151.

Hall, Melinda Gann and Paul Brace. 1996. "Justices' Responses to Case Facts: An Interactive Model." *American Politics Quarterly* 24: 237–261.

Hoekstra, Valerie. 2005. "Competing Constraints: State Supreme Court Responses to Supreme Court Decisions and Legislation on Wages and Hours." *Political Research Quarterly* 58: 317–328.

Johnson, Gbemende. 2015. "Executive Power and Judicial Deference: Judicial Decision Making on Executive Power Challenges in the American States." *Political Research Quarterly* 68: 128–141.

Langer, Laura. 2002. *Judicial Review in State Supreme Courts: A Comparative Study*. Albany: SUNY Press.

Leonard, Meghan E. and Joseph V. Ross. 2014. "Consensus and Cooperation on State Supreme Courts." *State Politics and Policy Quarterly* 14: 3–28.

Lewis, Daniel C., Frederick S. Wood, and Matthew L. Jacobsmeier. 2014. "Public Opinion and Judicial Behavior in Direct Democracy Systems: Gay Rights in the American States." *State Politics and Policy Quarterly* 14: 367–388.

*Republican Party v. White*. 2002. 536 U.S. 765.

Savchak, Elisha Carol and A.J. Barghothi. 2007. "The Influence of Appointment and Retention Constituencies: Testing Strategies of Judicial Decisionmaking." *State Politics and Policy Quarterly* 7: 394–415.

Shepherd, Joanna M. 2009. "Are Appointed Judges Strategic Too?" *Duke Law Journal* 58: 1589–1626.

# INDEX